NIETZSCHE

SUNY Series in Contemporary Continental Philosophy
Dennis J. Schmidt, editor

NIETZSCHE
A NOVEL

David Farrell Krell

State University of New York Press

Published by
State University of New York Press, Albany

For information, address State University of New York Press,
State University Plaza, Albany, NY 12246

Production by Dana Foote
Marketing by Dana E. Yanulavich

Library of Congress Cataloging-in-Publication Data

Krell, David Farrell.
    Nietzsche : a novel / David Farrell Krell.
        p.   cm. — (SUNY series in contemporary continental philosophy)
        ISBN 0–7914–2999–7 (hc : alk. paper). — ISBN 0–7914–3000–6 (pbk.)
        1. Nietzsche, Friedrich Wilhelm, 1844–1900—Fiction.
    2. Philosophers—Germany—Fiction. I. Title. II. Series.
    PS3561.423N54 1996
    813'.54—dc20   96-12165
                                                                            CIP

10 9 8 7 6 5 4 3 2 1

para
Marta Salomé Cosenza

CONTENTS

Preface   ix

General Chronology   xi

Part One   Transfiguration   1

Part Two   Restorations   53

Part Three   The Ways of the Mother   147

                Interlude   247

Part Four   The Ways of the Father   267

PREFACE

Nietzsche—the name could stand for the things he thought about, for a certain literary and philosophical corpus, or for a human being once living but now dead. We would never remember the man if it were not for the œuvre, though we are usually not up to the energies of his thought. To dither about the human being may seem a declaration of bankruptcy on our part, a concession to our mania for biography and our lust for gossip. However, there are things about the man that elude us as much as the writing and the thinking do. This novel—if that is what it is—chases after the elusions of the dead man.

In a dialogue called *Statesman,* Plato has the Stranger tell of the two great eras that make up human history. We now live under the reign of Zeus, a reign that spins out like a top on a string, except that the top is really a yo-yo: when the world spins out to the end of its tether it does not fly off into space but whirls back again to its point of origin, and the second era, the era of regress, is called the reign of Kronos. On the backspin to the origins—to the archaic time of Chaos and the body that precedes both the divine and the titanic reigns—everything seems to be topsy-turvy. People are born as cadavers out of the earth, they grow younger instead of older, their hoary heads take on color, their skin gets softer every day, and like truly rational creatures they learn to talk with the animals. The two reigns or eras enact a kind of eternal recurrence of the same, albeit with reversals of direction. Perhaps that is what madness is like: the backspin gives us all of life once again, all the way back beyond our beginnings in infancy, everything the same, only upside-down and inside-out, as fusions and confusions of a primeval body.

What follows is a story about Nietzsche's ten years of madness, years that allow us to catch crazy glimpses of the forty-five productive years that preceded them. Only one who is as mad as Nietzsche was would believe that the *work* of those productive years could be reproduced by the backspin, that a book such as this one could recapitulate or clarify in any way Nietzsche's own books. It cannot. It can only allude to the elusions of the dead man—and to our delusions touching him.

A general chronology of Nietzsche's life precedes Part One. Each of the four remaining parts has its specific chronology. I have translated Nietzsche's letters as accurately as I was able, but have felt free to take excerpts from them, so that for the most part only bits and snatches of any given letter appear. (By contrast, my translations of the medical reports from the Basel and Jena asylums appear complete, though scattered throughout the text.) Many of Nietzsche's letters, whether they were actually mailed or held back, have survived only as drafts, and they are marked as such in my text. Where oddities of syntax, misspellings, or misinformation appear in these documents, I have let them stand. For the letters and drafts I have used the *Sämtliche Briefe: Kritische Studienausgabe,* ed. Giorgio Colli and Mazzino Montinari, 8 vols. (Berlin and Munich: Walter de Gruyter and Deutscher Taschenbuch Verlag, 1986). For the chronologies I have used Karl Schlechta, ed., *Nietzsche Chronik: Daten zu Leben und Werk* (Munich: Carl Hanser, 1975). My largest debt is to Curt Paul Janz, *Friedrich Nietzsche Biographie,* 3 vols. (Munich: Carl Hanser, 1978; Deutscher Taschenbuch Verlag, 1981). The photographs on the cover and at the end of the "Interlude" are prints made by Neil McGreevy of an original taken by Hans Olde in 1899. The original appeared in a Swiss magazine, *Du,* in the 1950s, which is where I first saw it and rephotographed it. Permission to use the photograph was generously extended by the Goethe-Schiller Archiv—warm thanks to Dr. Roswitha Wollkopf.

The bulk of this book, which began and ended in Greece in 1988 and 1992, was written in Cuernavaca in 1988-1989. My thanks to Helmbrecht Breinig, Jacques Derrida, Teresa y Abel Mejía, Michael Naas, Graham Parkes, Gabriel Pearson, Carola Sautter, Charles Scott, Sophia, Evangelia, and Antonio Tsiboulis, and Anna Vaughn.

Horefto, Pelion   D. F. K.

GENERAL CHRONOLOGY

1844 October 15: Friedrich Wilhelm Nietzsche is born to Franziska Oehler and Carl Ludwig Nietzsche, Lutheran pastor in the village of Röcken, Saxony. Born on the King's birthday, Friedrich Wilhelm inherits the royal name.

1845 Baby Fritz sits on his father's lap, helping him to improvise on the pianoforte. He also assists his father with his Sunday sermons, which are somewhat less improvised.

1846 Nietzsche's sister Elisabeth is born.

1848 Revolution throughout the great urban centers of Europe. Nietzsche's royalist father is dismayed. In March a baby brother is born. Ludwig Joseph will die soon after the father's death, which is imminent. Nietzsche will dream repeatedly of these conjoined deaths.

1849 July 30: Pastor Nietzsche dies after a year of illness, apparently of tuberculosis of the brain. Nietzsche is not yet five years old.

1850 Soon after his second birthday, Ludwig Joseph dies as a result of cramps induced by teething. Widow Nietzsche moves to nearby Naumburg with young Fritz and Elisabeth, along with her husband's mother, Erdmuthe, his sister, Rosalie, and his stepsister Auguste. At Easter time, Fritz starts school; his playmates are Gustav Krug and Wilhelm Pinder; his constant companion is music.

1856 Nietzsche makes excellent progress at school, studies assiduously, practices his piano, composes music and poems. In May, his mother moves with the two children to a new apartment—without Aunt Rosalie. By this time Aunt Auguste and Grossmama Erdmuthe have gone to their rewards. Franziska now goes to hers—a household without Erdmuthe, Auguste, and Rosalie.

1858 During the summer Franziska moves with her children to Haus 18 am Weingarten in Naumburg; here she will remain until her death thirty-nine years later. October 5: shortly before his fourteenth birthday, Nietzsche enters Schulpforta, one of the most renowned secondary schools in Germany. During these years come musical compositions, poems, and a first autobiographical effort, "Sketches from My Life." Myopia, head colds, and migraines plague the boy.

1860 Summer: Nietzsche founds a literary and musical society, "Germania," together with his childhood friends, Pinder and Krug.

1862 Nietzsche writes an essay for "Germania" called "Fate and History." Neither his mother nor his sister would have enjoyed it. The *Edda* preoccupies him, especially the saga of *Ermanarich;* he composes a fragment of adolescent black humor entitled "Euphorion."

1864 Nietzsche's university career begins at Bonn with theology; after his first year he transfers to Leipzig; well before the year's end he drops theology for art history and classical philology. His mother is unhappy.

1865 Sightseeing in Cologne. Somewhat later, in Leipzig, Nietzsche is treated for syphilis, although the evidence for this is uncertain.

1866 Nietzsche studies Greek literature and philosophy at Leipzig; he reads Emerson and Schopenhauer for relaxation; evenings he attends the theater and falls in love with actresses. In Leipzig he befriends Erwin Rohde, the future author of *Psyche,* a pioneering work in the study of early Greek religion and cult. They travel together, talk together, find that they are very much like one another. Later Nietzsche will quarrel with Rohde, as with almost all his friends, and lose him.

1868 February: Nietzsche is a recruit in the cavalry. Although he is the best rider among thirty recruits, his career is cut short by a failed leap into the saddle—he shatters his breastbone on the pommel. October 28: he hears the overtures to *Die Meistersinger* and *Tristan und Isolde* and is immediately converted to Wagner and his "music of the future." November 8: he meets Richard Wagner (though not yet Cosima) at the home of Hermann Brockhaus. During these months, Cosima, the daughter of Franz Liszt, is separating from her husband, Hans von Bülow. She will now be living with Richard.

1869 Nietzsche is appointed professor of classical philology at the University of Basel. The University of Leipzig grants him the doctorate, waiving examinations and dissertation. At Basel Nietzsche meets Professor Carl Burckhardt, the famous historian of classical antiquity and Renaissance Italy.

1870 April: Nietzsche befriends a new colleague in the theology faculty, Franz Overbeck. Overbeck becomes a well-known theologian after the publication in 1873 of his controversial book, *On the Christian Character of Our Theology Today.* During the summer term Nietzsche teaches Euripides' *The Bacchae,* the story of the god Dionysos's revenge on King Pentheus of Thebes. He also sketches some plans for a drama on the early Greek philosopher, Empedocles. August-September: he serves as a paramedic in the Franco-Prussian war, is immediately infected with diphtheria and dysentery, and sent home.

1871 Completes his manuscript of *The Birth of Tragedy from the Spirit of Music.* As though anticipating what the critics will say of his book, he tries to transfer from philology to philosophy—without success. The effects of the dysentery hang on; indeed, Nietzsche is never really well again, certainly not from 1873 onward: migraines, severe myopia, eyestrain, nausea. Often he cannot read or write; he dictates his work to friends.

1872–1876 Nietzsche continues to teach philology at Basel, writes and publishes his four *Untimely Meditations.* Waxing disaffection with Wagner and Bayreuth. He meets Frau Louise Ott, from Paris, in August of 1876. From October 27, 1876, to May 8, 1877, Nietzsche is on leave from the university; he stays at the Villa Rubinacci in Sorrento, Italy, with Malwida von Meysenbug (idealist), Paul Rée (moralist), and Albert Brenner (consumptive). Some say he entertains a visitor.

1878 Nietzsche publishes *Human, All-too-Human: A Book for Free-Spirits.* It is not to the taste of Cosima and Richard Wagner.

1879 Nietzsche writes "The Wanderer and His Shadow," which will become the final part of *Human, All-too-Human.* The ms. is written in the hand of Heinrich Köselitz (alias Peter Gast), who prepares many of Nietzsche's texts from this year onward. Nietzsche is terribly ill throughout the year: migraines, nausea, vomiting, near-blindness, fainting spells. In May he applies for early retirement from the university; on June 14 the request is granted. June 23: he travels to St. Moritz in the Oberengadin for the first time. December: in Naumburg, Nietzsche's health is at its nadir. His mother reads fiction aloud to him, for example, the works of Twain and Poe in translation. Nietzsche often thinks of his father, for he is approaching the age his father had reached when he died.

1881 Nietzsche publishes *Daybreak: Thoughts on Moral Prejudice.* Mid-July: Nietzsche's maternal uncle, Pastor Theobald Oehler, dies, a probable suicide. August 14: the thought of eternal return of the same, as a formula for the unstinting affirmation of a tragic existence, comes to Nietzsche in Sils-Maria, Oberengadin. November 27: he hears Bizet's *Carmen* for the first time.

1882 Nietzsche publishes *The Gay Science (la gaya scienza).* He hears Rossini's *The Barber of Seville* for the first time; he dislikes it. Summer: he and his friend Paul Rée fall in love with a gifted twenty-year-old Russian woman, Lou von Salomé. Lou resists Nietzsche's advances, asserts her independence; Elisabeth intervenes on behalf of "Naumburg morality"; Lou disappears with Rée.

1883 Parts I and II of *Thus Spoke Zarathustra: A Book for Everyone and No One.* February 13: Wagner dies. July: Nietzsche quarrels with his publisher, Schmeitzner, because of the latter's anti-semitic publications. September: Elisabeth is engaged to a leading Wagnerite and anti-semite, Dr. Bernhard Förster. She later writes letters in praise of her husband, backdates them, and signs them "Friedrich Nietzsche."

1884 *Thus Spoke Zarathustra,* Part III. April: Nietzsche promotes a comic opera by his helpmate Köselitz (Peter Gast), *Il matrimonio segreto,* retitled *The Lion of Venice.* April: another in a series of breaks with his sister Elisabeth, who is living now with her mother. Nietzsche's letters to his mother no longer reach her hands. June: break with Franziska Nietzsche. September: reconciliations with both mother and sister, inevitable, half-hearted. December: deathly ill from Christmas to New Year's, as he is almost every year during the season of joy.

1885 *Thus Spoke Zarathustra,* Part IV, privately printed. May 22: marriage of Elisabeth to Dr. Bernhard Förster. Nietzsche is not in attendance. Summer: in Sils-Maria, Nietzsche enjoys the company of Mrs. Fynn, her daughter, and others, including Fräulein von Mansuroff. Mid-October: he wins a lawsuit against Ernst Schmeitzner, and with the proceeds buys a marble slab for his father's grave. He avoids his mother's house.

1886 *Beyond Good and Evil: Prelude to a Philosophy of the Future.* Early February: Elisabeth and Dr. Förster set out to colonize "Nueva Germania" in La Plata, Paraguay. By October the Aryan bastion faces insolvency and rebellion.

1887 *Hymn to Life, for Mixed Choir and Orchestra,* lyrics by Lou von Salomé, music by Nietzsche, orchestrated by Heinrich Köselitz (Peter Gast). (Text from 1882, music from 1873-74.) *On the Genealogy of Morals: A Polemic.* February: Nietzsche reads Dostoevsky's *Notes from Underground.* February 23: during Nietzsche's stay in Nice a severe earthquake strikes the Riviera; over one thousand people are killed. June: Erwin Rohde criticizes the historian Hippolyte Taine, who has recently praised Nietzsche; Nietzsche breaks with Rohde. September: Nietzsche is visited in Sils by his old Pforta chum, Paul Deussen, who brings a copy of his translation of the Sutras of the Vedanta. Deussen notes Nietzsche's altered posture and mode of speech. November 26: first letter from Morris Cohen (Georg Brandes), a university lecturer and critic in Copenhagen who has expressed his enthusiasm for Nietzsche's work. December: for the first time, Nietzsche has a small stove to warm his otherwise frigid winter lodgings in Nice. The following year he orders another such stove for his room in Turin, but there are rumors that the stove is unsafe.

1888 *The Wagner Case: A Problem of Musicians; The Antichrist: A Curse on Christendom,* in ms.; *Dionysos-Dithyrambs,* in ms.; *Twilight of the Idols,* in ms.; *Ecce Homo: How One Becomes What One Is,* in ms.; *Nietzsche contra Wagner,* in ms. Nietzsche's fame begins to spread: reviews and translations of his books become increasingly common; contact with the playwright August Strindberg and the editors of the *Journale des Débats* and *Revue des Deux Mondes.* February 3: final break with Erwin Rohde. April 2: Nietzsche departs Nice for Turin, gets lost while changing trains in Savona because he is almost totally blind. Delighted with Turin when he finally gets there. Summer: Nietzsche's last sojourn in Sils-Maria. "Eternal headache, eternal vomiting." September 21: leaves Sils for Turin, where he remains until January 9, 1889. October: onset of a remarkable euphoria; Nietzsche is writing night and day. He orders his library to be shipped from Nice to Turin. October 28: breaks with Malwida von Meysenbug, a long-suffering friend and supporter. November: Strindberg sends Nietzsche a copy of his drama, "The Father." December 7: Nietzsche expresses to Strindberg his intense interest in Prado, on trial in Paris for the murder of a prostitute, as well as in Henri Chambige, on trial for the murder of his lover. December 21: final letter to Franziska Nietzsche. Christmas: the German colonists of "Nueva Germania" are up in arms, demanding their money back, but the Försters are bankrupt. December 27: Nietzsche plans to call a European summit conference at the Palazzo Quirinale in Rome. His agenda: the destruction of the House of Hohenzollern and the banishment of all anti-semites.

1889 Thursday, January 3: Nietzsche collapses in the Piazza Carlo Alberto in Turin. Not many details about this day are known. There has been some speculation about a horse.

1900 August 25: after ten years of insanity and "progressive paralysis," Nietzsche dies in Weimar. August 28: he is buried in the family plot at Röcken.

PART ONE

TRANSFIGURATION
From Torino to Basel
3–10 January 1889

Chronology

1889 Thursday, January 3, to Monday, January 7: Nietzsche writes post-cards and scraps of paper addressed to many of his (former) friends and to sundry European heads of state; the Turin post office confiscates most of them, but some get through. They announce a Pan-European summit conference in Rome and discuss various features of the Prado and Chambige murder trials.

Saturday, January 5: Nietzsche mails a letter to Professor Jacob Burckhardt in Basel, from "every name in history."

Sunday, January 6: Burckhardt takes the letter to his young colleague in the theology faculty, Franz Overbeck.

Monday, January 7: Overbeck receives a letter of his own from Nietzsche; he consults the Basel psychiatrist, Professor Wille; upon Wille's and Burckhardt's urging, Overbeck departs that evening for Turin.

Tuesday, January 8: Overbeck finds Nietzsche in rooms rented from Davide Fino, who owns a newspaper kiosk on the Piazza Carlo Alberto. Fino's lodger has made the past few weeks difficult for the Fino family. Overbeck spends an eventful twenty-four hours with Nietzsche and Davide Fino.

Wednesday, January 9: Overbeck brings Nietzsche back to Basel with the help of a mysterious German Jewish dentist, Dr. Bettmann (Baumann?). To Nietzsche he is a Stranger.

Thursday, January 10: Nietzsche is admitted to Professor Wille's sanitarium in Basel. The diagnosis is *paralysis progressiva* brought on by syphilitic infection.

8 April of the Year One, A.N.
Torino, Via Carlo Alberto 6, IIIe étage
1600 Hours

What does Overbeck see when he bursts through the door of Davide Fino's salon? The theologian's lantern jaw lights the way to his god. Yet what does Overbeck actually find there? A madman in the church, perhaps? The basilica floor of cracked marble tile, walls of tatty satin yellowed by the jaundiced century, wan afternoon light piercing oblique from high windows overhead. Far off in a corner of the sanctuary, cowering on sagging crimson cushions, a blind spider reading pageproofs. Squatting and squinting. Is this what Overbeck sees? A spider? Or does he see his god?

Oh, the tears they weep! Oh, the embrace! Neither can stand erect, each falls upon the other, the man of god and the man of divinity. Overbeck still smells of train, of chill and engine oil, eighteen eternal hours distant from Basel. The god knows that Overbeck will take him back in tow. Basel was the scene of his first ascension, his elevation to a university professorship; it will be the perfect port of embarcation for the longest journey ever undertaken by man or god.

They collapse onto the sofa, try to speak, seek the words that will make it all seem less terrible, less awful.

—Professor Burckhardt sent me. He got your letter.

—But didn't *you* get my letters, Franz?

—Yes. Yes, of course. But it was Burckhardt who finally understood.

Overbeck is too embarrassed, too awestruck to go on. Altogether too overwrought. And the god is too touched to reply. After all, Overbeck is his friend, the only faithful one, after all these years of failed friendships.

The god remembers the letter in question word-for-word, as though Professor Burckhardt were reading it back to him here and now, declaiming it from his lectern in the Aula of the University. As Burckhardt he reads it while as Overbeck he roots for words to say to himself

To Jacob Burckhardt in Basel

Turin, January 6, 1889

My dear Professor,

In the end I'd far rather be a Basel professor than God; but I didn't dare push my personal egoism so far as to neglect the creation of the world. As you know, one has to make sacrifices, wherever and however one lives.—Nevertheless, I've reserved a small furnished room for myself here, a student's room, across the street from the Palazzo Carignano (where, as Vittorio Emanuele, I was born); in addition, from my writing table I can hear the splendid music they are making below in the Galleria Subalpina. I pay 25 francs, including service, I buy my tea and all my own provisions myself, I suffer the misfortune of bootsoles the worse for wear, and I thank heaven every minute for this *old* world, for whose sake human beings have never been simple and silent enough.—Because I've been condemned to entertain the eternity to come with bad jokes, I've set up a writer's shop here that leaves really nothing to be desired, quite pretty it is, and not at all taxing. The post office is five paces from here; I myself drop off my despatches to the *nonpareil* literary journalists of the *grand monde*. I am of course in most intimate contact with *Figaro*, and just so you get an inkling of how harmless I am, listen now to the first of my two bad jokes:

Don't let the Prado case unnerve you. I am Prado; I am also Father Prado; I daresay I am also Lesseps. . . . I wanted to grant my Parisians, whom I love, a new concept—that of a decent criminal. I am Chambige as well—he, too, a decent criminal.

Second joke. I greet the Immortal Monsieur Daudet who belongs to the forty.

Astu.

Astu? As-tu compris? He can explain everything, really, even if at first it all seems mystifying gobbledegibberish. One thing he knows for certain: Burckhardt's sage gray head, eyes and beak of hawk, comprehends every word of it. Burckhardt sent Overbeck here, Overbeck the theologian, to prepare the way for the god's second coming and sole transfiguration. However, the letter doesn't end with these weak witticisms of Astu. There is now a novel part to the god's epistle, including complimentary close and signatures.

Many signatures. Hoary hawkhead raised, eyes scanning the ceiling, in no need of notes or lectern, he continues the letter:

> What is unpleasant and offends my modesty is the fact that at bottom every name in history I am; so it is with the children I have brought into the world—I have to wonder, with some misgivings, whether all those who enter into the Kingdom of Heaven didn't also proceed *out of* God. This past autumn, outfitted as modestly as possible, I twice attended my own interment: first as Count Robilant (—no, Robilant is my son, inasmuch as I am Carlo Alberto, for that is my nature down below), but then Antonelli I was myself. My dear Professor, you should see that tower of his; because I know nothing about the things I create, you have every right to be as critical as you can be, I'm grateful for every criticism, though I can't promise to take advantage of any of them. We artists are incorrigible.— Today I viewed my operetta—a work of Moorish genius—and took the opportunity to establish to my pleasure that both Moscow and Rome are grandiose affairs. You see, no one can deny my talent for landscapes, either.—Think it over, we'll have lovely lovely chats, Torino isn't far, the most serious demands upon your profession lie not too far afield, a glass of Veltliner we shall be able to locate for you. Strictly casual attire is the only decency permitted.

He signed with heartfelt love, thinking Burckhardt would come, certain he would come. After all, how often does the Great Year turn and Greece revive? Burckhardt, chronicler of the greatest civilization and its renaissances, surely he will come yet! For the kairotic moment he sends a representative of the early Christian community, theology's conscience with a lantern jaw. Yet gods mustn't grumble, it is beneath their station. But O Father Burckhardt how your daimon needs you now! O make haste to help him!

He remembers how they used to frequent that Austrian guesthouse, the only one in Basel, just for Burckhardt's beloved Veltliner red, and how when they left at closing time the professor would take a false step in the direction of the ladies in waiting at the Alley of the Defunct, the only place in Basel that was alive, and the rest of them would take him by the arm—actually touching him, grasping his meager flesh!—in order to preserve his chastity.

—My chastity is as rigid as can be, Burckhardt said, and they were panting with laughter, doubled over, tears and hoots abounding, the night they poured a libation to the daimons in the street. No,

7

not even the Meister, for all his genius and jollity and highly compromised ideality, ever matched dear dear Burckhardt, may the narrator make so bold?

So why has he not come to Turin, Burckhardt himself? *I am old,* he says. *My heart,* he says. *Leave me alone,* he says. *Don't tempt me with your writings, they are beyond me,* he says. Read on, grayhead, glean that letter. It says:

Tomorrow my son Umberto is coming, accompanied by the lovely Lady Margherita, whom I shall receive in my shirtsleeves in this my modest home.

(Malwida told the god to marry money, a nice girl, but rich, then to live in Rome. Lady Margherita of Rome is very rich, as befits a queen. The god's Mama would adjudge her a nice girl, and the god would concur. As always.)

The rest for Frau Cosima... Ariadne... From time to time all is enchantment... I walk about everywhere in my student frock, here and there I slap folks on the shoulder and say, *siamo contenti? son dio, ho fatto questa caricatura...*

I've had Caiphas put in chains; last year I too was crucified by German doctors in the most agonizing way. Wilhelm, Bismarck, and all anti-semites eliminated.

You may make whatever use of this letter you like, just as long as it doesn't diminish the respect in which the people of Basel hold me.—

Silence of the grave.
An eternity passes.
Another commences.
The same.

What have dear dear Overbeck and the god to say to one another when all is said and done? Luckily at this juncture the landlord marches in, His Liegelord Davide, along with daughters Irene and Giulia, son Ernesto, and even the Signora, Donna Candidly Snowhite, whom they haven't seen for days, she's been hiding out back shirking her work, naughty girl. Ah, Davide, Davide, how you hang your hairless head! You've been to the police, no? Don't blame yourself, Fino, the mill of god grinds exceeding Fino. No one in all Thebes understood what came sweeping down from those smoking hills. Least of all the police. Chief Alfazio put all the questions, didn't he, while the fat sergeant took notes? Is not the narrator right in saying that Alfazio shook his head and clucked his tongue while the sergeant picked his nose and snorted and recorded:

—How long you been putting up with this loco, Signor Fino?

—It's been three or four days now, you replied, accurately, fairly, who can blame you, certainly not the god.

—And the piano playing, nights?

—Oh, much much longer. Weeks and weeks it's been going on, every night, in the middle of the night. And it isn't real music, no, it isn't beautiful, he's slamming the keyboard with his elbows and shrieking his head off all the while

To Erwin Rohde in Hamburg

Leipzig, October 27, 1868

My dear Friend,

I simply can't bring myself to preserve a cool, critical distance between me and this music. Every fiber of every nerve in me quivers, and I've long not felt such perdurant transport as I feel with the Overture to *Meistersinger*.

Your faithful friend,
F. N.

—Serenades, you say? Lullabies?

—No jokes, please, Chief Alfazio. It's a nightmare. Nobody can sleep, my family, the neighbors, the whole building. The signora hiding out back in the garden shed . . .

—You'll be home this evening at what time? about ten o'clock, eleven?

—Si, Signor Commandante.

—We'll be there. With reinforcements. He won't escape.

—Of course he won't escape, sir, he's a professor. Be gentle with him.

Calling Card to Franziska and Elisabeth Nietzsche in Naumburg

Leipzig, February 12, 1869

Spread the word!

FRIEDRICH NIETZSCHE
Adjunct Professor of Classical Philology
(with a salary of 800 Thaler)
in the University of Basel.

—Ah, yes, a schoolboy gone sour. That's the worst kind, take it from me. Tell your Signora she won't have to hide no more. He won't get away. We are here to help you, at your service, Signor.

O caro Signor Fino! Ah, Davide, Davide! Molto Fino! You think the god does not know what you've been through today, but he does, he knows everything. Omniscience is part of the package. Tell Overbeck. Go ahead, he is a trusted friend, tell him everything. All morning long you tried to get in to see the German Consul. You forgot the god's totem, he's a Pole, a Swiss Pole. Only later did you go to the police. You cooled your heels until the Consul was ready to grant you an audience. He finally deigned to see you, and when you asked him what you should do with a German national who was slipping rapidly not to say careening round the bend he said:

—Das entzieht sich meiner Kenntnis. What you ask recedes and withdraws utterly beyond the frontiers of my knowledge and competence.

Whereupon you gave indignant and energetic rejoinder, and right you were to do so:

—I have a madman in my house yelling his head off all night kissing animals out in the street all day scaring my little girls, a crazy man, one of your own, and what I want to know is what are you going to do about it?

At which juncture the Consul pledged a solemn oath that he would in due course make the appropriate inquiries and see to the necessary et ceteras. Whereupon you interjected:

—Listen, if you don't help me I am at the police in five minutes. And you know what they will do? On the outskirts of town we've got a manicomio, maybe a dozen of them, and your countryman could disappear for a millennium or two, you understand me, he is not my crazy! I rent him a room. Up to now he pays regular. But he's not my crazy! Giulia and Ernesto are terrified to come home from school, Irene's the only one not frightened out of her wits, she's too much like him, God help her. Her mother, my Candida, hiding out in the garden shed, pretending she's potting plants—in January! she's as potty as he is!—I tell you it's enough, we've had enough, now it's your turn. He tells everybody he's a Pole but his papers are Swiss and I know he's a German!

To Heinrich Köselitz in Venice

Marienbad, August 20, 1880

I'm living here incognito, the most inconspicuous of patients: in the sanatorium's registry I am listed as "Mr. Nietzsche, teacher." There are many Poles here and they all—it is astonishing—take me to be a Pole, hail me with Polish greetings, and when I reveal that I am a Swiss, well, they don't believe me. One of them took his leave of me, quite forlorn, with the remark: "He *is clearly* of the Polish race, but his heart has wandered God knows where."

Faithfully yours,
FN.

The Consul swore he'd do his level best with all deliberate speed—tell us, Davide, was he tall, blond, blue-eyed, and abysmally stupid? Yes, you were in the right building. What a day you've had! Were the god still mortal he'd be mortified. But you came home to find friend Overbeck already there, having come all the way from Basel, and now all will go smoothly, rest assured. Overbeck will tell everyone what is to be done. It is hard for you, of course, you've never had divinity in your home. Fino you may be, Sophocles you are not.

To Cosima von Bülow in Tribschen

Basel, Sunday, *July 19, 1870*

Most esteemed Baroness,

I understand what it means that the Athenians felt able to erect altars to their Aeschylus and their Sophocles and to bestow on the latter the heroic name Δεξιόν, as one who received and entertained the gods in his home. The fact that the gods *were there* in the house of the genius arouses that religious feeling I was telling you about.

Faithfully and devotedly yours,
F. N.

Yet it is harder for the daimon, who has never been a god before. He doesn't know what to expect from moment to moment, doesn't know which way to wend. Overbeck on the sofa beside him, himself on the other side of himself. He can't get over it, is beside himself with joy, all the heavens jubilate. Yet Overbeck will know exactly what they are to do. Retrieve your candid signora from the shed, Davide, it must be freezing out there. The god will not frighten her. Look at him: cool as a cucumber, mild as a mortal. Sh! Mum's the word. What's that you say? Another bromide? Yes, thanks. Nothing better, bromide, elixir of Bromios the Thunderer. Fetch the glass from the table. Better than Barbera. Settles the nerves. The god's had a rough one himself. There now, he feels fit as a fiddle.

—Overbeck, shall I play for you?

Caught by surprise, not knowing what to expect, Overbeck smiles uneasily. He misses Fino's desperate signal, for Fino would dissuade Overbeck.

—Yes, of course. I'm glad you're still playing. Music hath charms . . .

They rise and walk slowly in procession down the hall to the ancient instrument in the sanctum sanctorum. The god loves the sound of his booted heels on the vestibule floor, he gives a little shuffle and click-clack. Evil whisperings behind him, he can hear them. *Maledizzione, gran Madre di Dio, che facciamo?* O my people, put away your troubles and your tremblings, your god is as sedate as a sedan, he shall scarcely touch the keys, he shall dance— Zarathustra is a dancer—and soar ever so leggato. He settles onto the ruined leather of the ancient tripod, as his Father did before him, beneath him. In the bosom of the Father. Something comes over him. He feels the thunderstorm rolling down the sky. He plays. Rather, *it* plays *in* him.

And I beg the storm to come. Doesn't the pealing of bells attract lightning? Now, so close, O storm: purify me, cleanse me, let fragrant rain drench my dull nature. Welcome! Welcome at last! Behold! first blast of lightning, you make my inmost heart quiver, and from it streams a long hazy wisp of fog heavenward. Do you know it, so gloomy, so guileful? Already my eye blazes brighter, and my hand rises against the fog in order to curse it. Thunder growls. A voice resounds: Be purified!

One reverberant chord on the very edge of dissonance, then another over the edge. Infinite pause. The resonance ebbs as infinity passes. Another ringing chord, farther beyond the verge, well over the edge, far down the precipice. Another infinite interruption, trailing off to silence. The god used to insist on melodic line and counterpoint all the way, the very essence of music. Yet now he dotes on the chord, the instantaneous vertical synthesis, the full harmonic spectrum in one sharp blast of thunderous sound dashing all linear essences!

Dull, humid air: my heart swells. Nothing stirs. Then a gentle breeze, the grass in the meadow trembles—I bid you welcome, alleviative, redemptive rain. Here is wilderness, void, death; disseminate afresh!

Behold! a second bolt! Glaring, two-edged, into my heart! And a voice resounds: Hope!

Yet another chord. Yet another eternity passes.

Then a mild musk wafts over the earth, a wind flutters toward us, a storm on its heels, howling, hunting its prey. Leaves plucked from branches it chases ahead of itself. Rain swims after the storm, drunk with joy.

Right through the heart! Windstorm and rain! Lightning and thunder! Right through the heart! And a voice resounds: Renew yourself!!

Would one dare look up to see the rapt gaze and the astonishment on Overbeck's face? He is expecting Wagner. Brahms. Schumann, "The Broken Windowpane." Liszt, O liszt! But he shall hear something out of the ordinary. Come, fingers. Come, Father, let the god feel your breath in his ear, stir the hair on the nape of his neck. Guide those fingers, O Father!

Overbeck and the god, alone in the basilica. The god hopes that Overbeck doesn't see the disheveled bed. Pandemonium of all toiletries, medicines, hairbrush, and bootjack—all will soon be dancing off

To Franziska Nietzsche in Naumburg

Pforta, October 6, 1858

Dear Mother!

Straightway today, the very first day of my life at Pforta, I'm writing you, and I'd have lots to tell, but for lack of time I'll save it until we meet in Almrich on Sunday. Up to now I'm feeling quite well, but what does "quite well" mean when you're in a strange place?! I've met a few fellows here. . . . Generally speaking, I'll feel more at home after a while, but it'll take a long time.—

Won't Lisbeth write sometime, since she's got more time than I do. You must all be very busy with the move, and therefore you have no time to think much about me. Well, then, when we're all settled in, we'll want to visit one another often.—Lots of greeting to Lisbeth, Aunt Rosalie, Auntie Rieke, Aunt Lina, and to Wilhelm and Gustav and everyone else who remembers me. More next time.

Your,
Fr. W. Nietzsche.
Alumnus portensis etc.

1. N.B.
My bootjack:
I need it desperately.
2. N.B.
Why don't you send me
a little box of
wafers.

It finally looks like a proper temple now that Ernesto's prints have been stripped from the walls. Concentrate, keep those thighs still, close that mouth, seal it on both sides, fight the grimace that is coming to stretch it at the corners until the lips split and salt tears flow into the cuts with briny burning saline sting.

Overbeck and the god, alone in the temple. *Pubblico sceltissimo.* The last living Christian, the first since Christ, and the jester of eternities to come, together at last! The god hears his followers approach, his women slim of ankle, high-breasted, dancers all, chanting the dithyramb ululate:

—Euhoi, euhoi! Evohe, Bromios! Iakhe! Iakhe Bakhe! Ika-Ika-Bäh-Bäh! Brekkekekex-koax-koax!

—Come, Zagreus, Lord Dionysos, come!

—Lord of ivy, come!

—Thyrsos-bearer, Σωτήρ, savior of the world, come!

—Come! For you are near!

Thighs of god, keep still. Not yet. No poise and leap, not just yet. Fingers shall dance all alone. All together altogether alone. Skill. Technique. Science of operetta transposed to pure music, refined in the extreme, the most intelligent enthusiasm, splendor without a hint of sentimentality, everything in filigrane, psychologically pseductive, Pied Pipers piping, *piramidale successo,* pardon the Egypticism. Now! Again! Eternity! *Da capo, da capo!* Dance!

To Heinrich Köselitz in Venice

Nizza, November 24, 1887

Dear Friend,

This morning I am enjoying an *enormous* benefit: for the first time a "fire idol" stands in my room—a tiny stove—and I confess that I have already performed a few heathenish hops around it. Up to now it's been frosty blue fingers, and even my philosophy failed to be on its best footing.

Your friend, N.

Overbeck cannot believe his eyes and ears. He wants to approach the daimon but does not dare. It is the aura that enwraps divine flesh, the precipitate nudity of daimonic meat, the elevation of the god's simple slender cat's eye and delicate slit of mouth reaching up to heaven. Overbeck has always dreamed of seeing these things, but he never truly believed he would. It is the thump of naked heels and soles on the chilly marble floor, as long ago on Cithaeron, the cold does not affect him, Sanctus Januarius dances with him, it is the distended toes that repel poor Overbeck, one can see that. Probably he has never seen unshod feet before, the tiny black hairs sprouting across the knuckles of immortal toes revolt him. He can see those hairs each time the god pauses to pirouette. On the highstep all is ablur and he can make out only the sacred processional part, modeled and scarified down its sacred sides. With niches. Each niche concealing a figure of the god. A daimonic figure concealed in each nook and cranny of the rod of god. Overbeck cannot see the figures in the niches of the shaft, he can see nothing at all with his hands over his eyes like that. Pipes timbrels bells tambouras flutes kettledrums and oboes deafen him, he thinks it is Fasnet, he is afraid for his wife, and well he might be! It is death to look on the dancer with cold eye and fishy feet. Will the women tolerate his presence? Even the god will not be able to soothe and assuage them once all are caught in the dance.

Again the god invites Overbeck. Don't be afraid. It will be enough if you touch him. Take his hand. Don't be afraid of the thyrsos, the ivy-wound fennel stalk will not strike you. See how it waves and bobs in the air, plunging and rising with each spring and leap of these prancing feet! See the luxuriant ivy! How it curls and adorns the belly of god! Do not be afraid. No one is more modest than the rigid godhead, the very figure of shame. Come dance with the god. Come. Take you and eat. Don't just chew, swallow. Don't just swallow, listen and learn.

—I am the child of Zeus. Borne back to Theban ground, come home to the land of my nativity. Dionysos, son of Cadmus's daughter Semele, the maid midwifed by fire and lightning. Be renewed! I here, this one, whose form is that of a mortal, godhead disguised, I am come home, behold the man,"Εχω home, present here and now on this ground of smoldering smoking maidenhead. Semele! O my Mother! Great Mother Kybele! Kypris! Smoke betrays fire. Remember her. She will recur. With horns upon her head. Io!

Premier among all the cities of the Hellenes, Torino now resounds with the ecstatic cries of the women *ololuoloujah! ololuoloujah!* He clasps the fawnskin about their tremulous shoulders

15

and places the ivied javelin in their hands. They are come to refute the calumny against his Mother, the slur spread by his Father's sisters . . .

—You mean your *mother's* sisters: Ino, Autonoë, and, most terrible of all, spiked Agave.

—No, my mother's sisters were harmless, they were loyal to the crown. I mean Aunt Rosalie, Aunt Auguste, Aunt Lina, and Auntie Rieke. Not to mention Grossmama Erdmuthe, salt of the earth.

To Erdmuthe Nietzsche in Naumburg

Pobles, June 1, 1850

My good Grossmama!

Just a few words today, since my dear Mother has little time. We are all well and every day I go to school where Grosspapa gives us lessens. I hope you al stay well too and that you think of me who sends lots of

Love,
Fritz Nitzsche

The women had no right to slander her. It was sheer jealousy. They said that Dionysos was not the son of god, that Semele had been nymphomanicized by a mortal maleman, reamed in mortal rut, that she then proclaimed Zeus the proud father of her little oversight. For their offense I have driven the rachitic sisters mad, tickled their fancies, addled their brains, routed them out of their homes, harried and herded them like Argive cows to the mountains. There they wander like lunatics, dressed in the rags of my rites. All the seed of Cadmus, all the womanseed, loosed from their hearths, lost to their looms, expelled from all memory of who they are or what they used to be, out of sight out of mind, ἐξιστεμένα. They will never know the gadfly that stung them, but I shall vindicate my Mother.

—Taint not thy mind, nor let thy soul contrive . . .

To Franziska Nietzsche in Merseburg

Pforta, Monday, 25 August 1862

Dear Mama!

For the love of God these fatal headaches are killing me again: I've been in the infirmary for a week now. The doctor has advised me and given me official permission to go back to

Naumburg and undertake my walking and hiking cures. So I'll be leaving for Naumburg on Monday at noon; I'll stay in our lodgings there, leading the quietest of lives, without a trace of music or any other stimulus. . . . Don't worry, dear Mama, because if I manage to avoid everything that can excite me, the headaches will diminish; but I think I'll stay away a bit longer, so that I can eradicate them root and stem.

Loving you with all my heart,
Your FWNietzsche

—They will apologize in their own brutish way, dearest Mother, for all they have ever said or thought against you. And to all mortals I shall appear undisguised, I shall radiate in full presence as I truly am: a daimon sired engendered spawned procreated and partured by the great god Zeus alone.

—Alone? Then Semele did not bear you?

—Onward, my women! On and on! I, the twice-born god led you out of Asian Naumburg through Basel in Lydia over Tmolus and Gotthard to Thebes. Come and beat your tympanum, pummel the Phrygian kettledrum, sear Rhea's sacred skins and mine. Let it pound at the palace doors of King Pentheus! Give him to know why he bears the name of Mourning and of Grief!

Two knocks at the front entrance of Fino's flat. Two knocks, four. Who could that be? At this hour, who in the world could it be? Friends of Fino's, friends or fiends of Fino's, no doubt. Well, fine!

Never mind! Nobody home! On, my women, while I rejoin the Bacchae in the mountain meadows of Cithaeron! How they whirl and twirl, every girl a whorl of the world in my universe of joy! How they chatter and batter the headsplitting drums! Fondle reverently the verge of god, for it knows no bounds! Gurgle with milk, O earth, bubble with wine, flow with the nectar of honeybees! Sing Dionysos with a barabarabum of drums. To the mountain! To the mountain! Prance like a colt crowding the mare at pasture, lightly leap and frisk and fly! Evohe!

Three knocks at the front door of Fino's flat. Two, three, four knocks. Down the hall scurry all ears, to hover about the threshold. It isn't the god's Father. Strange voices. Gruff voices of gruff men. Interlopers. Overbeck rushes from the god's side, hastens down the hall. Must be friends of his. Friends or fiends of Overbeck's.

One can hear Overbeck's voice now, hushed, urgent; yet not even the narrator can make out what he's saying. Overbeck's Italian is even worse than god's. Wait. Wait. He hears. Now he knows.

They are negotiating his fate while he plays in the garden. Caiphas. Bismarck. The Kaiser in a cast iron straightjacket. Fino takes up the burden now, one can plainly hear the villains of state, with Fino mollifying:

—I know what I told you this afternoon, it's all my fault, this gentleman has come from Switzerland to take him in his charge, it's all arranged . . . yes . . . I'm terribly sorry to have put you . . . no, Sergeant, that was me playing just now . . . here, please, from my cousin, wonderful vintage, you can try it back at the station, of course not, on duty, at home then. . . . Terribly grateful for all your trouble. . . . *Buona notte.*

And so once again the god is saved, to be savior himself elsewhere some other time. It is all too trying. All too exhausting. To bed, to bed!

Thump of heavy boots on the stairway descending. He shall await their return, for everything recurs, but he shall wait in bed. Nothing will budge him he swears it!

To bed! To sleep, to sleep, perchance to awaken!

2359 Hours

Call him Henri. But only if you improve your French. Chambige. Henri Chambige of Colonial Algiers, *à votre service.* Henri feil in love with Mrs Cricket though Mr Cricket demurred. Chirp for Henri, lovely lady of Engellande, O Louise, that he may hear the raspy whisper of your voice as you rub your bare legs together, that he may see the whiteness of your flesh and the roses of your breasts. Your green eyes dart nervously from side to side, you are a cornered animal, magnificent in your terror. You whine at him *If you touch me if I even think you are going to touch me I'm naked before you defenseless* grazing him with those darting eyes on that fatal evening, their last together. Her last altogether. *It has to stop* she said. *You can give me nothing, nothing of this* she said, indicating with one sweeping gesture of one bare alabaster arm the sitting room of the villa, the chandeliers, the curving staircase, the tapestries. All he could think of was how much he had given Mrs Cricket, the gallons of groaning manseed, everywhere upon her without her and within her, and all the waves of seawater she had once lavished on him, and he felt he was drying up desiccating the terrible moment she said those things she shouldn't have said those things her voice suddenly harsh he'd never heard it that way before and it was to stop her from ruining her voice that he fired, first her, then himself. For her he was always the better shot. How unlucky Chambige survived. And now must play the Parisian part of the decent criminal. The pale criminal, upstanding felon, assassin of a goddess. For the tabloids all over Europe, all the way down to Torino and beyond, a divertissement for the morning coffee, a topic for the afternoon tea. He should have used a knife, should have whispered *te amo* as he introduced it, watching his hand turn carmen crimson, it would have made better theater, gayer music, richer monstrosity.

As it is, people confuse Chambige with his comrade in arms, the Spaniard Prado, who paid her with hard metal instead of true coin. They never would have pinched him if he hadn't burgled. That was mean of him. All the world hates a burglar but loves a ladykiller, if she's a lady of loving trying to earn a decent living. Wrath of God, they call him then. Scourge. Comeuppance. Vengeance is mine, saith El Prado. Monster! And with what style! What theater! Prado was tried and convicted right there in the god's modest domicile, Carlo Alberto 6 IIIe, the former Palace of Justice, so that the daimon had a ringside seat.

To August Strindberg in Holte

Torino, via Carlo Alberto 6, III,
December 8, 1888

My dear and distinguished Sir,

Prado excelled beyond his judges, even his advocates, in self-control, esprit, and audacity; nevertheless, the *pressure* of the indictment had brought him so low, physiologically speaking, that some of the witnesses recognized him only by portraits from an earlier time.

In esteem and friendship
Nietzsche, monster.

Yet how could they be certain it was he? Answer: they were not certain. They took the word of that witch. Frogeyes, no chin, lipless mouth, five agglomerated bumps for a nose. That witch cooing morality laid Prado low. Because she could never lay him high. Cooing justice and the rights of woe is man, reveling in her incomparable ugliness. Salivating over Prado's bowed head. Prado was far superior, Father Prado you may call him, Père Strindberg. How happy the god was he was he. And Chambige as well, Henri galant, who loved a lady laved a lady leveled a lady wife; rattled a lady riddled a lady reveled a lady rife. Monster!

P.S.: At that very moment the anointed servant of Christ approached on sable satinslippered feet. Father Prado glided across the wooden platform that supported the machine of the shining blade, drew near the pale criminal in order to bestow the final blessing and to wish him godspeed on his journey to hell. The murderous ingrate repulsed him with a sneer:

—I don't need your God. I can find my own way to the slaughterhouse!

Never had the preacher of death seen such a hardened case, such obduracy, such inveterate criminal depravity; never had the plunging guillotine granted the preacher such titillation such divine delectation such sacerdotal satisfaction.

—Sinnnngggggggkerchunkhh!

To Franziska Nietzsche in Naumburg

Pforta, February 16, 1861

Dear Mama!

I really am fed up with these headaches; they keep coming back and I never get better. The least bit of mental effort causes me pain. And I miss a lot of my lessons, without being able to make up the work. Again today they applied a Spanish flea behind each ear. I don't think it will help.

Your FWN.

9 April of the Year One, A.N.
Torino, Stazione Porta Nuova
1420 Hours

At long last with a pant a heave and a lurch the train pulls out: Salvation Express bound for the Isles of the Blessed.

—Addio, Torino! Bell'Italia, farewell! Oh, the divine broccoli, the ambrosial ossobuchi, the tenderest beef in all the world, oxen of the sun transposed from a lambent Lorrain landscape, and the celestial gelati, oh, mi cioccolato Torinese, addio!

The god is dying of hunger. Both kinds.

—Good-bye, fairest of all the cities that ever harbored god. Ciao, Parco Valentino, with your sylvan paths of secreted lovers!

No more will the god quit his house at break of day, exit onto the Via Carlo Alberto, swing round the corner to the right jauntily down the loggia-lined Via Po all the way to the Piazza Vittorio Veneto, across the buzzing piazza to the Lungo Po, swerving right again down to the Ponte Umberto, O my King and Consort! pardon the shirtsleeves! Nevermore will he cross the Ponte Vittorio held spellbound by that great bronze teat bared to the brazen sky, the vast rotunda of La Gran Madre di Dio. *Great Mother of God!* he shouted the first time he saw it, lurching left beyond good and evil, the river now too on his left spotted with tiny green dots of islands, not a soul on them, not a fleck, the god walking on his Po, no mean feat, until he arrived at the Parco Michelotti. Avenues of plane trees, oaks, limes, and yews, sprinkled with umbrella pines. And one towering fir. His bench beneath it. Where Pentheus met his Mum, where Zagreus gave of himself unstintingly. At the far end of the avenue, in full view beyond the trees, the snowladen Alps of Aosta. The mountains await their god—but they shall behold him no more! Ah, the bittersweet paradoxes of theology!

—Good-bye to you, San Lorenzo, you alone clasp to your stony bosom the veridical veronical veil of the Crucified. You alone—along with thirty-seven of your brethren on this pious and avid italianate soil.

Shall the god go and claim that bloody rag for himself? Shall he condescend to be comforted in his travail before he quits the city forever? No. No crown of thorns, no Lumpenproletariat, no proud woman's face behind the savior's. On this most festive of all occasions let the bells peal and crack, let the organs swell, belch, and fart. Let San Lorenzo turn over a new leaf, medium-rare, sing us a rare new song.

—Torino, you metaphysical city! How splendid you look from atop that tower—the motley member of the Mole Antonelliana, synagogue temple and tower in one, the perfect erectile projectile ejectile—your corsi, your loggie, your piazze, your sinuous rivers converging beneath supernal Superga, your hills frosted green in the distance. Torino, good-bye!

The god hasn't had a single headache since he arrived in Turin this past September, if it was September. By what reckoning? Whose era? He has not vomited. He is not yet entirely blind. The sidewalks are smooth. He has not stumbled. He must be *causa sui* . . .

And as Bromios departs from the city in a first-class ferrocarrilious cabin, lo, a massive earthquake strikes in two successive rapid-fire seismic convulsions of the grandest proportions.

To Reinhardt von Seydlitz in Munich

Nice, Thursday, February 24, 1887
rue des Ponchettes 29, au premier

Nice has just had its long international Carneval (with Spanish ladies at the forefront, incidentally), and hard on its heels, six hours after its final Girandola, even rarer and more novel existential excitements. For we are now living in the interesting expectation of *perishing*—thanks to a well-meaning earthquake which has everyone here baying at the moon, and not just the dogs. What a pleasure it is when these ancient houses rattle over our heads like coffee grinders! when the inkwell suddenly becomes independent! when the streets fill with horrified half-clothed figures and shattered nervous systems! That very night, between 2 and 3 A.M., like the *gaillard* I am, I made my inspection tour throughout the various quarters of the city, in order to see where the consternation was greatest—for the population was camping out-of-doors day and night: there was something refreshingly military about it. And then the hotels! where a great deal had simply collapsed and full-scale panic prevailed as a consequence. I located all my acquaintances, male and female, found them huddled miserably under green trees; they were wearing their flannels, for it was bitter cold, and with even the slightest tremor they were brooding on The End. I don't doubt that this will bring the season to a precipitate close! Everyone is thinking of *departure* (provided one can get away, and the railroad lines are not all "torn up.") Yesterday evening the guests at the hotel where I eat could not be coaxed to take their *table d'hôte* inside the building—they ate and drank outside; and apart from an elderly and very pious woman who was convinced that Our Dear Lord *dare* not do her any harm, mine was the only *cheerful* countenance among the tragic masks and "heaving bosoms."

Truly,
Your Nietzsche

The Richter Scale capitulates and is no judge before them. Meanwhile, the resplendent sun of the languid Pacific isles suffers total eclipse. Countless mortals, bedazzled and benumbed by these meteorological wonders, fearful of what might next come creeping

To Emily Fynn in St. Moritz

Nice (France), rue des Ponchettes 29
circa March 4, 1887

The entire event was extremely interesting—and even more

absurd: it was neither more nor less dangerous than, say, a trip on a *train rapide* at night.

Your obedient servant,
Prof. Dr. Nietzsche.

out of the desert or sweeping down from the Lydian mountains, take their very lives into their own hands, bringing them to an abrupt and tragic close: an epidemic of suicides, ringing out the old, ringing in the new. Such are the ways of god. And what everyone has expected has not come to pass.

—Torino, addio! I came unto my own and my own received me with utmost delicacy of feeling and respect. How is it that now, at parting, they know me not? Am I that changed? Under the pressure of my trial?

The new stature and status, the unaccustomed dignity, has transformed the god's figure and affected his footfall: a moment ago he sauntered down the quai of the station with a divine bearing, with a godly carriage, only lightly listing to starboard, δεξιός. And the crowds! He yearned to embrace each and every creature, women, men, girls and boys, bushes, dogs, and dray horses, but the Stranger prevented him. Twice he and Overbeck held the god back, pinned his arms in order to preserve his incognito and guarantee their own safety in the throng of onlookers. When gods arrive in the flesh, dangers abound.

Overbeck is now prostrate in the seat across from god, the Stranger on the daimon's left. How fortunate they have the cabin to themselves! Less luck than stratagem, however. Whenever someone threatens to enter and interrupt their intimacy the Stranger slips a prosthesis over the teeth of his upper jaw: gigantic enamel choppers jut from his gaping mouth, his lips stretch taut around these horrid canines and cyclopic cuspids, with a grinding grunting noise he greets the would-be interlopers:

—Buon giorno! Buona sera! Veni 'qua, dolcetta di me vita! Buona notte!

Never have you seen people turn tail and disappear with such alacrity, it is all the narrator can do to suppress veritable howls of laughter! The Stranger! He's such a panic! and *so* effective! All through the journey they will have the cabin to themselves. No one will even notice the god's hairnet, no one will be rude about his snood.

The Stranger dispenses Energy Tablets to keep up the daimon's strength for the journey: Torino Vercelli Novara a layover thank God not Savona everyone gets lost there Milano Como Chiavenna Chiasso Chur Lugano Bellinzona Gottardo Luzern Zürich Muttenz bei Basel eighteen hours Overbeck says and he should know. Overbeck. Looks like death on a holiday. He has been unwell all this past summer, couldn't write, not even letters. The long silence frightened the god: his last friend lost to him! Dionysos doubted. For shame!

The Stranger will be their guide, the toothy savior of saviors. Something presses the god's eyelids together, his feet won't obey the dance, and if he sits any deeper in that horsehair (the god quakes no horses) he'll never rise again. When Overbeck and the Stranger talk it is in hushed tones, in order not to break the daimonic concentration. It is as though they were speaking at the bottom of a well. Eighteen hours! And when they arrive they'll be swept away to reception after reception. Fancy dress balls gala concerts dedications inaugurations speeches kissing babes in arms aching feet how will they bear it! The Stranger has seen to it all. That was kind of him. Who is he, anyway?

—He am I who am I. Σωτήρ. Dionysos. Zagreus. Zeus the Father *(le Père, toujours le Père, eheu, Strindberg, divorçons?)* sired him, but not on Semele, for her smoking rooms were blasted by divinity. No, Zeus sired Zagreus on Persephone, the spouse of his brother, Hades the Cockscrow cuckolded. Persephone, Queen of Hell, Deathmother of Dionysos-Zagreus, the god devoured by Titans. Fragmented by Titanic teeth and diluted by Titanic spit, masticated into Titanic chyle, adsorbed by Titanic capillaries, beshat as Titanic shit, washed into the soil by winter rainwater, soaked up by the ivy sucked up by the vine. Ivy. Vine. Scions of Dionysos-Zagreus, creeping along beneath Titanic heel and hoe. Biding time until the languorous spring, hiding in the thigh of Zeus until holy lent and the soursweet smell of yellowgreen leaves and grass bid them both come! Ivy and vine, stir, surge, and thrust!

Who is he? The Stranger?

Then the god remembered that the Stranger was a dentist. The time he lost that enormous filling in St. Moritz. Or when he went to Florence with six hollow teeth for Dr. Martyrdom to fill: good name for a dentist. The Stranger. Another good name. For a sophist, for a man of disguises. He likes pulling teeth, or teasing them out, says he studied orthodontics at Philadelphia University in the Americas. A dentist yanking teeth or a psychiatrist snatching souls, either one, the god cannot remember, Energy Tablets notwithstanding. And then he recalled the Dental Council of Basel, the *concilium subalpinum*. The god told the Stranger what had happened to the women of the Canton, thinking he would be scandalized:

—I happened to be out of the city for a few days. When I got back the reports were flooding in: our women had undergone some sort of pseudoreligious conversion and had quit their homes their looms rooms tombs of neighborhoods and headed for the hills. They called it honoring god but I knew they were humping on the heath and boffing in the bushes, drunk out of their minds and morals, slinking off into hollows and hellholes glens and glades nooks and crannies of all descriptions with anything they could find in pants taking it through the mouth between their breasts and buttocks stroking them hand and foot spreading wide for them the gates of god's heavenly haven: priestesses of Dionysos they called themselves, I call them aphrotitties aphrodoodoos aphrodildos! Acolytes faithful to the finger that fondles them. Obscenity! I swore I'd put a stop to it.

—Presume not the ways of god to scan, murmured the portly Stranger, who reeked of goat.

—They were led by a man, of course. A charlatan preacher. He got them drunk. He sported long blond curls, all perfumed they were. A rosycheeked innocent he looked, the seducer! the sorcerer! Not a bad musician, I must admit, a master of whorish instrumentation. Reeds woodwinds pipes flutes oboes anything for a blow. Percussion. All blows. And in his eyes the charms of aphropeephole. He is with women every moment of every living day and every night all through the night. He lets it dangle before them. He makes them drunk with it, pounding his peapod, wielding his wand! Well, well, we shall see. I'll shorten it a length for him, I swear I will, by the power vested in my royal verge!

—Be not so certain that brute force lends power to the lives of poor humans, said the Stranger. That thought is sick. Do not think it wisdom. Let force and power alike consume themselves in the nuptial ring of recurrence: don't let them consume you!

—These filthy mysteries will be banished with the overman! The discordant twofold will reduce in the fiery retort of wrath to a gentler unifold. A single seamless fugue. We will reconstruct the race!

—That ancient dream . . .

Then the Stranger uttered something that gave the god pause, baffled him. He needed time to think. Was it, as he suspected, the sheerest sophisma? Or was it unworldly wisdom? The Stranger said in his unruffled unmodulated mellifluous voice:

—It is not for Dionysos to compel women to think and feel temperately when it comes to Aphrodite. For purity of heart and singleness of mind dwell within them always, even in their wildest abandon, when they are beside themselves, outside themselves with pleasure: that is the very nature of love, that is its very surging-forth. When it comes to women you have to look within withal without. Even when she is reeling in Bacchic revels a woman who thinks about what she is doing will not be diverted from her proper path. And that path is the way of god.

—You overestimate the gentle sex, snorted divinity.

—Not gentle, cousin: she is mighty among us poor humans.

—If what you say is true . . . I want to see them. *See* them! Will you show me the women? Will you let me feel their power?

—I will, cousin. Come. I shall lead you to their mountain ambush at the edge of the world.

The Stranger's addressing the god so familiarly as his cousin at once reassured and unnerved him. He couldn't help thinking of poor cousin Actaeon, torn apart and devoured by hounds because of what he had dared to see, Artemis splendidly tall, naked at her bath. Did he not yearn to see more than Actaeon had seen? And were not the hounds of Dionysos mountain lions and panthers? In the distance, at an infinite remove, the god could hear the women singing. They were singing for him:

—Life is short. So let us go to Kypris, to Aphrodite's isle, where loves enchant with wonders the mortal heart awhile.

Then some confusion descended on the god. Some family darkness. Who was it that deprived the god of his wand, his sacred verge? Some guessed it was Apollo, confusing Pentheus with that god, mixing up the man of mourning and the god of dream and prophecy. Who was it that sheared the locks of goldigod, those perfumed curls, those fillets of incense unfurling luxuriantly across pillows shared with women? Who sheared the chevelure of god? Who chained the bullroarer? Was he the god, the god who said *You do not know what it means to be alive. You do not know what you are doing. You do not know who you are* or was he the mournful wretch who gave the god cocksure reply *I am Pentheus, son of Agave. Echion was my father.* For then someone said:

—Mournful: your name is apt for misery. Grieving: your name is deeply graven. Grief-stricken: it has a nice ring to it.

The terrible earthquake, the palace hotel in ruins, the guests dispersed, *train rapide,* the two cousins confronting each other in the rubble. Flames licking her grave. Pentheus stabs at the phantom god, then drops his wand. It is his turn now to surrender the sword. His turn, and turn he does, he in turn turns, everything turning, he and the god in a ringdance of confusion. An angel advenes to announce tidings touching the women in the hills: their milk and their menses flowing, suckling fawns, bulls flayed alive, spurting honey and spilling blood, their own and others'; he tells of the serpents who clasped fawnskins or licked cheeks; he tells of the repose and the rampage, the revel and the revenge of the women. Then the angel abandons the two to their quarrel, to the quarrel and confusion of kissing cousins.

—My armor! And you, *halt' die Klappe zu!*

—Stop! Wait! You yourself said it a moment ago. Have you forgotten? Wouldn't you like to *see* the women? Wouldn't you like to make out the maenads mingling in the mountains?

That was when the final twist and turn of enchantment entrancement ecstasy tangled tightened and knotted: the god lost his will and his fury, if it was he, if they were his, if it were not all Ate. Someone said:

—Oh, wonder! I'd give anything to see that sight!

He no longer knew what he was saying or the meaning of his life or who he was. Everything coiled and recoiled, everything veered and swayed in pirouette. There was laughter concerning his curiosity, his craving, if they were his, if he was theirs, Ate eaten, and then the decision already taken that he must go to the mountains. Incognito. Swathed in women's garments, swaying in women's ways, mincing primping and prancing, powdered pampered and painted, his wig bound up in a hairnet, bejewelled and fragrant. Garnished. As if for a feast. Then one of the two said:

—Dionysos taught me all these skills. Let me show you more.

One took the other to his room and was intimate with him. He undressed him and fondled him and dressed him again. He kissed him on his woman's mouth. He placed the thyrsos in his hand, returned to him the rod he had struck from his grasp, if it was he who did it and if it ever was his, the sheathed sword that had slipped from his own hand. And someone O so pretty was led out and O so alluring and he heard them say *He will see the Bacchae, and death will be the price* and he heard their terrible prayer to god:

—Castigate him. But first whittle away at his wits, muddle him with madness.

And would he like to see his Mother? Naked at her revels? O yes, and all her company, three generations of women, O yes! tremulous, terrific, and tottering, O yes!

To Franziska Nietzsche in Naumburg

Pforta, end of February, 1861

Dear Mama!

This morning my schoolwork is at a standstill. The headaches have returned again. I shall have to get used to them. Now, adieu! Dear Mama!

Your FWN

Yet this someone sees all cockeyed now, everything askew, everything double. He discerns two suns two cities fourteen gates, perceives two horns sprouting from the head of a bull, our leader our leaper our Bromios! Or is it Io? She or he? He or she sees even two cousins, duplicitous wretch!

—Tell me, do I remind you of anyone? Aunt Rosalie, perhaps? Or maybe Rosalie Nielsen in Freiburg? Daniel de Ronda? My Mother? Shall we dally in the park on our Po? Oh, be my Valentine!

To Franziska Nietzsche in Naumburg

Pforta, February 14, 1862

Dear Mother.

The infirmary is crowded. I can't write anymore, I'm as limp as a wet rag and someone is pounding my head. Here's to a speedy recovery!

Your Fritz.

—One of your curls has slipped from the snood.

—Oh, do fix me, please. Oh, do. It must have shaken loose while I was dancing. For when I dance I toss my head all wanton— like *this*.

—I shall be your darling and fix it for you. I shall tuck this naughty girl's naughty curl back into place, so that it never slips out again.

—Oh, I am in your hands utterly. Oh, touch me, touch me, do. Oh, I want to kiss you!

—Hold quite still. Don't you see? Your dress is out of kilter: the strap has slipped lubriciously from your slender shoulder.

—Oh, caress me! Yes, my blanched and sloping shoulder! And teach me how to hold my baton. In this hand, or the other? How shall I wave it when I highstep?

—In your right hand. Raise it high as you lift your right foot. No, your *right*. Raise your right shoulder, now. Don't let that strap slip.

—Oh, I can see them already, my Mother my aunts the maenads mating in the bushes like lovebirds, bush to bush, loveclasp and lovetonguethrust!

—Yes, that is your mission, cousin. Go and gawk. Oggle them good. Surprise them if you can.

—My mission, yes, mine alone. Only I am brave enough to go, of all in Thebes. Only I shall go.

—Yes, you alone will bear this burden for the city. Only you, my pretty kid, my precious piglet. An agon awaits you, and you will rise to the occasion, in agony. I myself will lead you there, incognito, in safety. Someone else will bear you back.

—Yes, she who bore me and gave me birth will bear me home, ecco!

—You will be an example to all.

—That's why I'm going.

—You will be borne home . . .

—Oh, but you'll spoil me!

— . . . in your mama's arms.

—Oh, but you'll spoil me rotten!

To Marie Baumgartner in Lörrach

Steinabad, August 2, 1875

You mustn't believe that I was ever in my life spoiled by excess of love. I believe you have noticed this fact about me, too. In this regard I bear about me ever since my earliest childhood some sort of resignation. However, it may be that I never deserved anything better.

Yours,
Dr Friedrich Nietzsche.

—Uncanny you are, O Mourning, altogether uncanny; and you go to suffer something uncanny. To high heaven your fame and glory will rise, curling upward as smoke, descending as ash. *Agave, and all you daughters of Cadmus, reach out and receive him!* I lead this youth to his staggering ordeal. I am the victor, in case anyone should ask. I and the Thunderer who raves behind my mask. But let our play show the rest.

Who is he? The Stranger?

Early that morning the Stranger crept to the god's bed. To his bed this man like a cat he crawled, a black panther this man to his bed, bedman, Bettmann, with a dithyramb on his lips. Purring soothing words. The minute the god laid eyes and ears on him he knew he had a mission. But who was he? Not Silenus. Too young. Too handsome. Too civil. Cleanshaven. Hooknose. Introduced himself as a dentist, a dentist named Leopold, imagine! The god told him he'd have to conjure up a better one than that! King Leopold of Thebes, Emperor Leopold, pulling teeth! No, it wouldn't do, wouldn't do at all, the daimon told him.

He came to the god's bed and asked him to rise and go with him. Jesus to the Crucified. At first divinity balked, fearing the worst. He pulled the rough woolen blankets up over his eyes. The Stranger tried to coax him out, he threatened and cajoled.

—That was the police last night, you know. No telling how long we can hold them off. Professor Overbeck wants to help you. The sooner we can get you to Basel the better. Otherwise, it's the dungeonhole for you, here and now, Bedlam, and no one will ever hear of you or see you again.

The god lowered his blankets, watched the Stranger's lips form and flow with every word, but didn't budge. Gods are not stupid. He said:

—They tried to hold me before, don't you remember? They tried to fetter the bull, tried to slam shut the dungeon door. How could you forget?

The Stranger was very clever. He had studied his lines well. He knew how to improvise.

—I haven't forgotten. Of course they cannot hold you forever. But it would be a terrible scene, one we'd best avoid this time around. Lest we be late for the receptions in Basel.

The Stranger read the god's look of suspicion and distrust. He continued:

—It's all been arranged. When we get to Basel we shall be grandly received. They understand your importance, they have read your Holy Writ, they know who you are.

—The people of Canton Basel have always held me in the utmost esteem. Let us hope that Burckhardt doesn't abuse my letter. I counseled the people, I taught them what learning was all about, I predicted the future of their educational institutes. And now that this has befallen me, they will know to esteem me all the more.

—They love you.

—Yes, of course they do. Shall we go? To the mountain! To the mountain! Gott to Gottardo!

The Stranger retired. The god rose and dressed. He put on his best suit, his only suit, the one his mother—who?! that canaille!—sent from Naumburg. He brushed his hair, saw to his mustache, couldn't for his life pull away from the mirror. The tiniest ears.

—I am the Antidonkey par excellence, he thought.

Broad sweep of brow, furrowed, ravaged and savaged, everywhere scars of wounds inflicted by the Titans' gnashing teeth. Eyes of a stranger upon him within him. In the mirror of himself, the deep-set dim eyes of a stranger. . . .

Of course! That was it! In the mirror! He himself was the Stranger, and he was also his first cousin on his mother's—whose?! that canaille!—side! As though to confirm his discovery the Stranger reentered, approached stealthily from behind, and laid his hand on the god's shoulder. His slender sloping shoulder, the left.

—It's time.

—Do I look delectable? Will we *see* the women? I'm itching to see the women, all of them!

—The women? Of course, all the women, if you like. Yes, you look irresistible. Come now, it's time.

He took a last lingering look about the basilica, the scene of his election and multiple crucifixion: here something had happened that would change history, it wasn't easy for him to leave, he never really left, Turin was not the sort of place one leaves. His nightstand. His pallet. And what's this? A desk. Escritorium. Scattered papers with scattered scribbles. A frenetic hand. Wants calm. Not even a spider could unravel any of it. Gibberish. Gobbledegook. Kauderwelsch.

Postcard to Heinrich Köselitz in Venice

Genua, January 25, 1881

Dear Friend,

Herewith I despatch my Genuese vessel to you! I write so illegibly and see everything so cockeyed. If you cannot guess what I am thinking, then the manuscript is undecipherable.

Truly,
F. N.

Tear the sheets to shreds, don't let them get into the wrong hands, toss the palimpsests the shards into the wastebasket. Along with these last Lire notes, along with the desiccated sacred semen.

—Don't you want to take your papers with you? asked the Stranger, solicitous of the future, pointing to the frailest leaves of him strewn across the writing table.

—With me? Have you ever tried to read or write while perched on the crown of a fir tree? asked his first cousin out of his own mouth.

The Stranger did not reply, the man who came to god's bed, Bettmann, yes, that's it: god's bedmate Bettmann: the Stranger, accompanying the god or mortal whose name means mourning grief fragmentation.

Suddenly and soundlessly, Davide Fino slips into the room. He clutches his nightcap tightly in his hands. He thrusts it at the god. He is crying.

—Here. You wanted this. It is a *ricordo* of me. Take it.

—Ah, Davide, Davide! Caro Signor Fino! My crown of ivy, my hairnet, my snood!

He places Fino's nightcap on his head in solemn ceremony, pulse = 60, coronation of Napoleon I. He turns to the Stranger. What an enigmatic smile he wears! The god too smiles and nods ever so slightly, cryptic to the end:

—We shall go incognito.

Incognito! Incognito! That's the ticket! Don't go to Rome, too many people there, bellelettrists and literate that is rary types sipping café and campari. Don't go to Löscher, too many Germans buying books, pretending to read them. Don't put your glasses on when you go out into the streets, do not seem to see, do not be seen to be seeming to see. Don't mingle with the crowds! Write no letters read no books cast no pearls. Take something to the trattoria to read. Your notebooks, for example. Drink water, never spirits. From time to time purée of rhubarb. Mornings one glass of tepid tea, evenings somewhat warmer. No spectacles out in the street, slake no horses, don't mingle with the crowds. Don't go to Löscher don't go to Rome! Rome? Rome? Don't roam. Don't write any more postcards. Evenings dress warm. Overcoat. Incognito! Rome?

Fino leads them back down the hall to the sitting room. Overbeck is fidgeting on the settee. He should be correcting proofs. Donna Bianca is hiding candidely behind the curtain on the far side of the room, hushing the children. Fino has lined up their satchels at the front door: eagerly they point to the world outside, like hounds straining at the leash. Dogs or panthers or goats.

To Carl von Gersdorff in Berlin

Naumburg, April 11, 1869

My dear Friend,

The zero-hour is upon me: this is the last evening I will spend in my homeland. Tomorrow morning it's out into the wide wide world, to take up a new and unaccustomed profession, to enter into a heavy and oppressive atmosphere of duty and work. Once again I must take my leave: the golden age of free and unconstrained activity, of the sovereign present moment, of the enjoyment of art and of the world as a nonparticipant, or at least as a scarcely involved observer—this period is over, and it will never return again. Now the strict goddess Daily Duty rules. . . . So far I feel no trace of the obligatory professorial hunchback. To become a philistine, ἄνθρωπος ἄμουσος, a man of the herd—Zeus forfend, and all the Muses!

Farewell!
Friedrich Nietzsche Dr.

Poor Donna Candida alias Donna Bianca! She suffers the cry that eviscerates, the moan that tears and twists at her guts: Quit the city, take to the hills, to Aosta and beyond, to the East! Evohe!

—The children are at their lessens? Yes, of course they are! And yes, tell them I shall miss them. Tell Giulia I'm sorry I called her a *brutta bestia* when she crept up to spy on me in the midst of the *brutalitas bestiale* of my dance. And tell Ernesto he can have his bed back now, only slightly used and abused, and that he may tape all his ghastly prints on the walls. As for Irene, tell her . . .

Irene. Peace. Her fawn's eyes, her waves of brown hair, her long white fingers on the keyboard beside his, Rafaela with hands, her mouth slightly smiling, dainty devils crouching in the corners of her eyes, her eyebrows rising toward the center of her brow in one mute question, how the god loves you, Irene, how he wishes you could come with him, O Peace. Shalom. Shalomé. He tried to see her through the keyhole. *Brutta Bestia, te amo,* he tried to say. Never mind. Too late. Peace. Irene.

—Tell Irene not to falter with her practicing. Tell her she plays divinely, more beautifully than god.

Do we hear a suppressed sob a sigh behind the curtain, a shuffle and a hush-hush? Fare you well, Peace. Chocolate almond eyes. Incipient swellings. Ivory ankles. Good-bye!

All those flights of stairs! Three times two is six and always will be. The cab is waiting outside the door of Carlo Alberto 6 III. A different one. He looks back and up at the façade of massive yellow stone, as noble in its own way as the Palazzo Carignano across the street or even the Palazzo Madama please supply your own, up the exterior walls of the Galleria Subalpina, ochreous and austere. How he will miss the superficiality of the *Barbiere di Seviglia*, every evening without respite night after night; the elegant Galleria, too expensive to eat there, have to pay the Barber. Wonderful hall for a congress. *Concilium subalpinum.* From Fino's hallway he could see it open out before and below him. The magnificent glass roof admitting a great shaft of afternoon light plunging to the multicolored marble floor below. At night the roof was black, the lead tracery vanishing into a leaden sky. Yet the most brilliant light flooded the hall from the triplicate globes that hung suspended from graceful iron struts, the lamps sprouting from the wroughtiron railing of the balcony, as though from the railing of a bridge across the Po or that canal in Venice. The entire Galleria in the most exquisite taste. Oh, the brilliant incandescence of those evening concerts during the winter, Torino's finest gathering for the *Barbiere,* the men in their top hats, the women in their delicious gowns! Addio!

To Franziska and Elisabeth Nietzsche in Naumburg

Bonn, November 10-17, 1864

Dear Mama and dear Lisbeth,

An hour ago I was at an extremely noble concert, fabulous luxury, all the womenfolk painted in flaming rouge, constantly englisch gesprochen no speak inglich.

Your Fritz.

They came to swoon over *Tannhäuser* no doubt, while the god pretended to hear not a sound not a single sopping splash and slurp of its Schopenhauerian sea.

Full splendor of sun. The fog has lifted at last. The fog *come in Londra* the vegetable lady said. Yet he never minded. It was like the fog in Röcken when he was a boy. No, it must have been Naumburg, for the sun was always shining in Röcken. The driver adjusts the feedbag. Good man. Good to his horse. That is something. That is a lot. Fino sidles over to the horse and driver as though to intercept the god. Pale criminal.

To Heinrich von Seydlitz in Munich

Address: Torino (Italia), ferma in posta.
(valid until June 5)
Turin, May 13, 1888

Yesterday I dreamt up an image of *moralité larmoyante,* as Diderot calls it. Winter landscape. An ancient drayman, with an expression of the most brutal cynicism, harsher still than the

winter that surrounds him, relieves himself upon his own
horse. The horse—poor berated creature—looks about, grateful,
very grateful—.

Your friend Nietzsche.

They clamber aboard the jouncy cab. Creak creak creak,
Overbeck god and Stranger. Fino's feet are planted firmly on the
curb as they pull away, tears streaming from his heavylidded Chinese sage's eyes, down his cheeks and into his mustache. His bald
pate glistens in the wintry sun.
—Davide! Davide! Carissimo Signor Fino! Addio! Addio?
Ammio! Ammio: he won't understand that. Fino! Finissimo!
His eyes too are moist, everything is ablur as they jigajig past
the newspaper kiosk where Fino first encountered his god and
offered him a furnished room in a house inhabited by a decent family, his own. They joltabolt past Rossetti's Pharmacy on the Piazza
Carignano, the god owes him for Bromios' bromide, don't forget, 9
Lire 90 the ticket said

To Malwida von Meysenbug in Paris

Steinabad, August 11, 1875

Esteemed friend,

Such as we, I mean you and I, *never suffer in body alone*, but
all is profoundly permeated by spiritual crises, so that I cannot
imagine how I could ever regain my health by frequenting
pharmacies and kitchens. . . . The secret of all convalescence
for us is to develop a thick skin, the sole antidote to our massive
inner vulnerability and capacity for suffering.

Yours ever faithfully,
Friedrich Nietzsche.

Now, where is the Piazza Consolata? He's all disoriented!
Shall he stop for one last consultation with Professor Turina? It was
lovelier out at the Villa Turina in San Maurizio Manicomio, no,
Canavese, but too far to travel every day. Professore Carlo Commen-
dator Turina da Torino, Villa Turina Torino Tarantará. Recurrence of
names. The god owed him too for those visits, how many, three or
four, how much? A lot of good they did him. Still, the god was good
for Turina: the place and price of consolation: gave Turina a chance
to see a real psychologist at work, or at leisure.

35

TRANSFIGURATION

Joltabolt and jigajog all the way down Via Carlo Alberto to the Corso, swerve right toward Porta Nuova, the Stazione Termini. Hello! The vegetable lady! She didn't see him, they're fairly flying, how she'll miss him, and what lucky mortal will inherit her sweetest muscats? Ah, the park that fronts the station! Alas, they've shut down the fountain for the winter, subdued the soaring jet. It too will recur. For spring is upon us. The park is lush with vernal bush and velvet grass, vigorous reed and cattail jut from rocks at the center of the pond. Too cold for a dip. Across the oasis of park, mounting like the Gates of Heaven, a vast creamy arch subdivides into slender arcs and squares and circles of glass. Porta Nuova. New Pforta. Old Pforta. Newgate. The Labyrinth: home of the snorting steambeast that will bear divinity in triumph once again to Basel.

The cab brakes to a jerky halt, the door swings open. In stately procession they advance thence don't embrace the cabbie don't embrace his horse either policemen are your friends through the creamy Porta to the quai where the stamping Minotaur awaits. Poor Theseus, done in by the Bullleaper, the Thunderer. They board. Luxury cabin. Hard seats of polished wood. They settle in as best they can, Overbeck in fear of all their lives, distraught, the Stranger matter-of-fact, nonchalant, the god incognito. Later they will change trains, transfer to horsehair. The god quakes no horses. Fewer hemorrhoids. That burning sensation. Chancre.

And at long long last with a pant a heave and a lurch the train pulls out. To pass from one world into the next. From sun to fog *It's just like London* she said, from light to dark, from Ormuzd to Ahriman, from dry soul to psoggy psyche, south to north, spring to winter. To pass over the great Alps, to cross the great divide of his works and days. Gott to Gottardo. Gotthard. Gótthard. Gottárrrdo. His whole life this passage back and forth. His whole life the song of a gondolier. Wait for the tunnel to sing it.

9 April of the Year One, A.N.
Gotthard Pass
Nightfall

On the bridge I stood
not long ago at russet night.
Singing I heard from afar:
Golden drops of it flickered
over the tremulous surface—
Gondolas, lanterns, music—
Swam drunkenly to twilight . . .

My soul, a thrum of strings
plucked unseen, sang itself
a secret gondolier's chant,
trembling all the colors of felicity.
—Was anyone attending?

Was anyone attending? In Torino Sorrento Venezia, was anyone at all attending? In Sienna Rapallo Rome was anyone attending?
In Rome? Roaming? Rome? What day is today? By the old reckoning, what day? No! No, it can't be! *Wednesday?* He can't have
missed it! The paramount political event of the millennium, convoked by his Promemoria to all the courts of Europe, his summons
to a summit of European princes, the instauration of grand politics,
politics now as the organ of universal thought! The train is headed
the wrong way! Pull about! Turn around for Rome! No, not the Café!
To the Palazzo Quirinale! Make it there by yesterday, full steam
backwards!

All the invitations are out, everyone will have been there.
Everyone awaiting the god's arrival, impatient to commence the

grand politics. But grand! For example, their eminences, his King and his Pope.

To Umberto I, King of Italy

> *Turin, circa January 4, 1889*

To my beloved son Umberto:

My peace be with you! Tuesday I shall be in Rome. I should like to see you, along with His Holiness the Pope.

> The Crucified

To the Vatican Secretary of State in Rome

> *Turin, circa January 4, 1889*

My beloved son Mariani:

My peace be with you! Tuesday I shall be in Rome, in order to pay my respects to His Holiness. . . .

> The Crucified

The hated Hohenzollern and his roaming Roman and Romish Minions mollified by promises of collaboration, they too will have been in attendance. He wrote in Gothic letters so that the Prince would be able to read it.

To Otto von Bismarck [Draft]

> *Turin, early December, 1888*

To His Eminence Prince Bismarck:

I hereby, through the presentation of the *very first* copy of *Ecce Homo*, bestow on the premier statesman of our time the honor of declaring him my sworn enemy. Enclosed please find a second copy: the only request I would ever dream of making to Prince Bismarck is that he place this copy in the hands of our young German Kaiser.—

> The Antichrist
> Friedrich Nietzsche.
> Fromentin

In order to forestall the almost certain confiscation of his millennial forgery, his revaluation better transvaluation of all values and his counterfeit autobiography, he duplicitously wrote to his ironclad King as well:

To Kaiser Wilhelm II [Draft]

Turin, early December 1888

I hereby bestow on the Kaiser of the German Nation the highest honor that can ever befall him. It is an honor made all the more significant by the fact that in order to be able to bestow it I have had to overcome my utter repugnance toward all things German. I deliver into his hands the *very first* copy of my book, which announces the onset of something monstrous—a crisis such as Earth has never known, the most profound collision of consciences among humankind, a decision exacted *against* everything that was hitherto believed, required, sanctified.—And withal there is nothing of the fanatic about me: those who know me take me to be an ingenuous man of letters, at most a touch maleficent, a man who can be jolly with everyone. This text of mine, as I hope, portrays something altogether different from a "prophet": and nevertheless—or, rather, *not* nevertheless, inasmuch as all prophets heretofore have been liars—the truth pours from my lips.—Yet my truth is a *terrible* one: for hitherto the *lie* has been proclaimed true. . . . *Transvaluation of All Values:* that is my formula for an act of supreme self-contemplation on humanity's part—for it has fallen to me to gaze more deeply, more courageously, more *equably* into the perennial questions than any prior human being. I do not challenge my contemporaries, I challenge the next several millennia to confront me. I contradict and yet am the very opposite of a *no-saying* spirit. . . . There are new hopes, goals, and tasks of a grandeur for which concepts are still lacking: I am an *evangelist* par excellence, no matter how much I also must be a man of fatality. . . . For when this volcano becomes active we shall have convulsions on Earth unlike any we have experienced before: the concept of politics has been entirely absorbed into that of a war of spirits, all power structures have been blown away—there will be wars of a kind we have never known.—

This text of *his?* What does he mean? If the narrator may make so bold? Transvaluation of All Values? Ecce whom? Ecco home? Ecco! Must be a typo. What sort of wars? One thing remains abysmally certain: if he fails to get to Rome on time ahead of time these typos will regress to their usual bloodbaths crusades programs and pogroms, their burn and run, pillage and plunder, slaughter and enslave. Overbeck, awaken! Stranger, make the train southbound! Where did that emergency brake disappear to? Nowhere to be seen when calamity strikes! He should have known: betrayal of the worst sort, the stab in the back! He never should have let Overbeck in on the secret, never should have mentioned his passport from Canton Basel, never should have communicated the winds of his soul, his doldrums

To Franz Overbeck in Basel

Turin, December 26, 1888. Friday morning.

—I myself am working at the moment on a Promemoria for the courts of Europe, for the purpose of organizing an anti-German league. I shall truss up the "Reich" in an iron straightjacket and provoke it to a war of desperation. I won't have a free hand until the young Kaiser is in my hands, him and all his accoutrements. Just between us! *Very much* between us!—The winds of my soul are utterly calm! I slept ten hours without interruption!

N.

never should have told him that the god would be imposing on him that spring, never should have taken him in any way into his confidence. *Not for a single moment in my life have I sensed any distrust of you or even any pique directed against you: indeed, you are one of the few to whom I am deeply beholden.* No, not Overbeck, not possible. Perhaps he shouldn't have leaked the good news to Miss Zimmern in Geneva *a matter of supreme importance! I believe there is no need for me to request the utmost discretion. My life is now approaching its long-prepared, monstrous* éclat: *what I shall do over the next two years is of such importance that it will upset the entire status quo, the "Reich," the "Triple Alliance," and whatever else these grandiloquent institutions may call themselves. It is a question of the assassination of Christendom, of dynamite planted into absolutely everything that is implicated in the slightest way with it. We shall alter the calendar, I promise you. No man has had more of a right to annihilate than I!* or to Carl Fuchs in Danzig, that Wagnerian fox, that garrulous ogre of Schopenhauerian Danzig, too close to Berlin, he never should have trusted the sly Zorro *the world will be standing on its head in a few years: after we have patted the old God on the shoulder,* after we have given him a silver chalice and a golden handshake, *from then on I shall rule the world*, no, Fuchs a fox without teeth, he couldn't be the whelp who betrayed the god. Nor, certainly not, it is impossible that it should have been Brandes, his firebrand lieutenant in Copenhagen, Morris Cohen, the first to spread his flame and fame (fame! he should have known it: *I fear one must be a bit* canaille *to become famous),* it was Brandes he let in on the specifics of the plot, baring to him detail after detail, down to the legislation banishing Christianity. *Esteemed friend, I find it necessary to communicate to you several matters of prime importance: give me your word of honor that these things will remain between us.*

That was his first mistake: if you have to ask for someone's word of honor then they haven't the honor and all you get is the word. *We have entered the age of grand politics, indeed, the grandest. . . . I'm preparing an event that will in all probability split history into two halves, to the point where we shall have a new calendar initiating a new era, with 1888 as the Year One. Everything that today finds itself at the very pinnacle—the Triple Alliance, the social question—will be toppled, and we shall have a culture of contrasting individualities: we shall have wars the likes of which have never been seen, but* not *among nations and* not *between classes: they've all been blown to smithereens—I'm the most terrific dynamite there is.*

That was his second mistake: if you introduce dynamite the others will reintroduce nations and classes even if you renounce and denounce them till you're blue in the face. These matters are explosive.—*In three months I shall give orders for the production of a* manuscript *edition of* The Antichrist: Transvaluation of All Values. *It will be kept secret: it will serve me as an agitator's edition. I need translations into all the major European tongues: when its time finally arrives I reckon on a million copies in each language for the* first *edition. I've thought of you for the Danish edition, Strindberg for the Swedish.*

That was his third mistake: no doubt a bitter rivalry rages between Strindberg and Brandes, an intrascandinavial scandal or squabble of which he is about to be victim and scapegoat. He and all the rest of the darkening European world.—*Now, it involves an* annihilating strike *against* Christianity, *and it is obvious that the only international power that has an interest in the annihilation of Christianity is Jewry—here the enmity is instinctual, not something "dreamed up" as it is in the case of the "Free Spirits" or the "Socialists." (I have a riproaring time anathematizing the Free Spirits.) Consequently, we have to be assured of the full cooperation of the pow-*

ers-that-be among this race in Europe and America—such a movement as ours will need finance capital to carry out its plans.

That was his fourth mistake: to mention the Jews of America and to forget that his blood sister Elisabeth, his darling sibling the Llama, dwelt there with her husband, one Bernhard Förster, who apart from Adolf Stöcker was the most virulent anti-semite the Reich had yet produced, to colonize in La Plata, Paraguay, a New Germania dedicated to the preservation of Aryan supremacy against contamination by said international Jewry, to purge the only heroes of culture Europe ever had; that he could have forgotten for an instant or a fraction of an instant that the enemy is always at home, always part of one's one big happy family, Lisbeth, his darling darkling sister, how could one forget the scorpion born from one's own maternal womb? *Here we have the only naturally prepared soil for the grandest, most decisive war of history: we can consider whatever other kinds of discipleship there might be only after the* coup. *The new power that will then take shape may well become almost instantaneously the prime* world power: *granted that the ruling classes will at first take sides with Christianity, the axe will already have struck a blow at their roots, inasmuch as precisely all the robust and vital individuals* will indubitably secede *from them. You don't need to be a psychologist to be able to predict that all the spiritually unhealthy races in Christendom will be partial to the faith of their rulers in this instance, and* consequently *will labor on the side of the lie. As a result, dynamite will here have to blast away all armed resistance and every political constitution; the opposition will be unable to assume any other shape: they will go to war as innocents go to the slaughter.*

That was his fifth mistake: to dream that the opposition could do anything with innocence, that thousands of years of ascetic inculcation and hardened degeneracy could be blown away in a single generation. *All in all, the army officers will instinctively side with us: what they will take away with them from a reading of my* Antichrist *will be the judgment that it is supremely* dishonorable, pusillanimous, *even* sordid *to be a Christian.*

That was his sixth mistake: whence in all the world this over-estimation of the military? Nostalgia for the god's cavalry days.— (*My* Ecce Homo *will appear first* there it is again, ecco! that typo, got to correct, *I've told you about it: its last chapter will give a foretaste of* things to come, *and in it I myself emerge as a man of fatality. . . .*) *As far as the German Kaiser is concerned, I know how to handle such dyed-in-the-wool idiots: here a trusty officer will set the pace.*

That was his seventh mistake: to repeat the sixth mistake. *Frederick the Great was a better man: he would have felt in his element here straightaway.—My book is like a volcano. Prior literature doesn't offer so much as a hint of the things said there. How the deepest secrets of human nature suddenly leap out with horrific clarity! It has an altogether superhuman way of rendering the death-sentence. All the while, a grandiose tranquillity and elevation pervade the whole—it is actually a* Last Judgment, *although nothing is too petty and too covert to resist being detected and dragged into the light.*

That was his eighth mistake: to appeal to the Ultimate Tribunal, to invoke the very pride and ignominy of the enemy. To mistake his skin for Michelangelo's—an easy enough mistake to make if the narrator may make so etc. *When you finally have a chance to read the "Proscription of Christianity" appended to* The Antichrist *as its conclusion, who knows, I fear even you may feel all your bones rattling.* Could it have been Brandes, his firebrand, after all? No. No. Morris Cohen would be the last person to betray him. *The government of Earth will be in our hands—and world peace attained. . . . We have overcome the absurd barriers of race, nation, and class: now there is only the order of rank between man and man; indeed, it is an enormously long ladder of rankings.*

Here you have it. The first White Paper of universal history: grand *politics* par excellence.

N.B.: Search out a brilliant translator for me—only a master of tongues will do me.

Can it really be that all the European potentates have misunderstood? Inevitable. Inevitable.

—Emergency brake! My son Umberto and the lovely Lady Margherita will be dragged kicking and screaming into the bloodbath. And it's all my fault! That isn't what I meant, that isn't what I meant at all. Not blood and iron. *Plowshares.* Aristophanic euphoria, Thesmophoria to say, you see, a feast and frenzied festival, annihilation through the grimace and the grin! Kaiser and Pope exposed for what they are, fools, don't you see?

To Wilhelm Pinder in Berlin

Leipzig, Elisenstraße 7, Parterre;
July 5, 1866

Dear Wilhelm,

One can learn a lot in such times. The ground that seemed firm and unshakable now trembles; masks fall from the faces they once concealed; selfish tendencies, now unveiled, reveal their repulsive physiognomy. Above all, however, one notices how slight the power of thought is.

Your faithful friend,
FW. N.

Ridiculed off the stage of world history—that is the god's plan for the *ancien régime*. At least Jean Bourdeau, the editor of the *Journale des Débats,* must have understood it: *I hold it to be quite reasonably possible to restore order to the altogether absurd position Europe has got herself into; restoration through a kind of world-historical laughter, without a single drop of blood having to flow.* But no. This is precisely what for all their qualities they will never have grasped. All assembled in Rome—without him—they would be at one another's throats in five minutes.

—Emergency! Engineer! No time to lose! Divert this train to yesteryear!

That was his ninth mistake.

Unless? Unless?

Unless the postal authorities had long ago seized his letters, had refused to forward his memos promemorias proscriptions and invitations. Infamy of infamies!! Betrayed by the Post Office police!! Law enforcement in the Dead Letter Bureau!! The god would prefer not to!!

Outside his gondola window the mountains deflate to foothills, rolling meadows, and stubblefields, under the earliest suspicion of dawn.

10 April of the Year One, A.N.
Basel Central Railway Station
0820 Hours

Hazy sun filtering through the eternal mist of Basel, pharmaceutical fog now that the silkworms have ceased munching forever. At least it isn't pouring down rain to spoil the reception. Overbeck stirs now in the seat across from the god, yawning, covering his mouth above the jutting jaw. Anxious eyes. The Stranger unearthly down-to-earth, as serene now as he has been all through the night. On the luggage rack above, their satchels and leather cases, like mastiffs, bear on their tags in a dozen different hands every name in history: The Immoralist, Phoenix (that garrulous old fart, how could the Greeks have accounted him wise, might as well have hired Polonius and been done with it) Antonelli Robilant Raskolnikov Prado Chambige Matejko Fromentin Dominique the Dinosaur Hanswurst Jester of the Novel Eternities Σωτήρ Dionysos Marsyas the Crucified. What a court! What a retinue! Basel will never have seen such a triumphal entry! Not since Fasnet last.

The Stranger serves as Adjutant and Master of Protocol. The god turns to him for counsel in all matters of propriety.

—Shall I embrace them all, plant loving lingering kisses on both cheeks? Three kisses, I'm Polish, you know.

—No, my Liege. Beneath your station. A prince kisses no cheeks. Might be misinterpreted.

—Whereabouts then? And what have I to do with princes? You confuse me with Bismarck. Or worse! Luckily, Bismarck is dead. So is the young Kaiser. I've had them thoroughly ventilated. Likewise the anti-semitic army chaplain, Stöcker. My agents are on their way to picturesque Paraguay now to finish the work we are in.

—To be sure, my Liege, not a mere prince. Something higher, something more remote and ethereal. At all events, someone of your stature does not deign, does not condescend to kiss. Remember who you are!

—Yes, of course, I'd well-nigh forgotten. This isn't an easy cross to bear. So many inscriptions notched into it. So many hollows. So many niches.

—Lord of Heaven, no, it is not easy for you. Terribly trying. That is why we must preserve decorum at all costs: no kisses, no embraces, no raucous music, no brass bands, no yodeling. Stealthily we shall make our way through the station. Incognito!

—D'accordo! But whither? We are headed for the countryside, no? To the mountains! To the mountains! Incognito, yes! But where to?

—"Tranquil Meadows" is the name of the place.

—Ah, Elysium! The Blessed Isles! My daughter Joy! Will all the women be there?

—As many as you like.

—But women of my kind, more kind than kith, you understand?

—Any kind you want.

—Will they adore me?

—On their knees.

—Will they offer me their very best love, their profoundest deepest devotion?

—Oh, yes.

The god knows now, piercingly, what he has always suspected, as no one else has suspected it. He knows deep devotion, he knows the very best love. Beyond the orangegrove by the sea. High in the mountains. They bend his fingers back until the knuckles grind the bones crack the sinews do not hold; the skin stretches farthest and is the last to relinquish; they pull his legs apart until the hipball snaps cracklingly out of its pan pushing its lustrous marble through the torn hide of divinity; the god will not even have felt disappear into an eager mouth what once sprouted sported spouted between his thighs so light is its anchorage a slight pulling sensation deep in the groin and gutwall that's all there is to it it's not so bad no yowling please until the hand of his mother at the nape of his neck gathering his hair how could he fail to recognize that withered hand those arthritic fingers reaching to the base of the cranium then yanking the head back with incredible force *à la nuque rompue* until his eyes gaze heavenward

To Franziska Nietzsche in Naumburg

Pforta, presumably October 28, 1861

Dear Mother.

Numb everywhere. In general, just like last year, when the headaches began.

Your Fritz.

the blinding sky more than blue blistering cerulean above the silvery sides of Cithaeron with its patches of sparse scrub at the mouths of what appear to be shallow caves pockmarking its surface. Not a cloud in that sky the eye of god the window of god's house the *Was ist das?* the *Vasistas* searing singeing unseeing his own eyes now bleary with water *hinc meae lacrimae.* All he can make out is the disheveled hair of his mother Agave brushing across his upturned face her chevelure of snakes, spiked Agave, well-named Respect yes he respects her. The fangs mean nothing a mere afterthought a mere pleasantry. It is the arms themselves, yanking his head, godhead, yanking it back with incredible violence a sledgehammer pounding at the base of the cranium pummeling slamming as if to say One more yank and you'll be off One more yank and you'll be off One more yank and you'll be off One more yank and One more yank and One

Tranquil Meadows,
Professor Wille, Director
1000 Hours

The sign sings out in large letters as their cab clatters past the gate.
And the railway station? How did they make it through the crowd at
the tailend of morning rush-hour? How is it that he remembers nothing of their arrival? And the reception? The Stranger wrapped him in
mists of fog and swept through the crowd with him to the waiting
carriage, and off they galloped. Transported as if by magic and
Energy Pills. Such are the ways of a daimon.

Tranquil Meadows. Where are all his daughters? His spouses?
So this is Elysium. Spreading boughs of oak and elm, birch and
beech, no firs in the splendid gardens, the shade will be good for his
eyes. Yes, he will love it here.

Slowly up the gray stairs to the gray door of the graystone edifice. The god's new palace. More imposing than Carlo Alberto 6.
Less so than the Quirinale or Carignano or Madama please supply
your own. Something in between, designed no doubt for the god's
temporary sojourn, a place to hang his weary head. Check is it still
on. Yes, though the tendons are stretched to the ripping point, which
accounts for the lolling from side to side. It's a wonder he can walk
at all. On eggshells all the way. Overbeck and the Stranger prove to
be stronger of arm than anyone would have thought. They must be
as exhausted as he is. Eighteen hours.

Slow and easy, up we go. There now. Ring the bell. Softly!
Hush! Tranquil Meadows.

Gray entrance hall, a grayhaired woman in white. Waiting
Room →. Fine. He can wait, who has spent a lifetime learning to be
slightly less than all-too-human and who will not learn the ways of
divinity in an hour a day a week maybe not even years. He can wait.
His way is arduous tortuous torturous dolorous. And of the long while.

One of the women awaits him in the Awaiting Room. She looks
his way only once, furtively, nervously, in order not to draw attention
to herself. Her gray hair is wound in a single snakelike braid about
her crone's head. Old or young, all must dance. She is one of his own,
he fears. Got separated from the pack. If he can get to his pocketknife
he will have her eyes out before she can turn on him.

Not there. Fumble further, Fritz. Must find. Maybe in the other.
That canaille.

What's this? A key. Two keys. He forgot to return them to Fino
when they left. How will the keys ever find their way back to Torino?
Roaming. Rome?

No knife. Bismarck removed it while the others distracted him. He's up against the cleverest pack of reactionaries, no doubt about it, their agents have infiltrated everywhere. Stakes life and death. Grand politics. If he can make a quick lunge he'll have her by the throat before she. Wait. Wait. Awaiting. Overbeck rises at the beck and call of the sister in white who puts question after question to him and fills in the forms. She leads Overbeck to an office behind closed doors. The Stranger, who has already given the sister his written report, gazes sleepily out the window at the gray sky. Wait. Wait. Awaiting.

Now! Attack! Lunge! Damn, she's fast. Ancient but agile. Slipped from his vicelike grip. Out the door, howling. Go in peace, old mother, a pox upon you! Go in pieces. Easy, Stranger, easy on the god's backbone. It has been weakened by the women. Ah ah ee ee ee. Easy. It will be difficult for god to find his feet with the Stranger on his back. There, that's better. Up we go. All's well that ends well. She's gone. Tranquil Meadows. Hush!

Wait. Wait. Awaiting.

At last Overbeck returns with the sister in white not one of god's thank god. The Stranger takes him by the arm, solicitously, firmly, and with a courtly elegance unmatched in all Europe the entire court quits the antechamber, proceeding thence to the Audience Room. Pale green cracked leather chairs, no horsehair here, that burning sensation, gray carpeting, off-white lace curtains.

A bald man with a fringe of white hair like a sunken pallid halo about his temples steals a glance at the god from behind his mahogany desk, avoids the god's responding gaze, smiles distantly, speaks in a whisper with Overbeck on his left, ignores the Stranger on his right. Leather creaks.

Interruption. The sister in white is at the door again.

—It's Frau Grünegg, Herr Professor. There's been an incident in the Waiting Room. She demands to see you, she's quite upset.

—Gentlemen, you'll excuse me for an instant? I'll be with you in a moment.

"Herr Professor," the sister says. Yet this isn't the University: the ceilings are too low. Now the three of them are alone again. Shall they conspire? Grandly? Overbeck turns to the Stranger:

—Forgive me, Doctor, in all the rush I neglected to introduce you.

"Doctor," he calls the Stranger. Yes, he said he was a dentist, didn't he? Absurd disguise! A Torino dentist touring through Basel. Doubtless here for a Dental Council. Absurd name, Leopold. Still, it wasn't right to ignore him like that. He is after all the god's adjutant his mentor guide and companion. God will defend him:

—Yes, of course, he must be properly introduced. Tell me, who is the balding gentleman who was here a moment ago?

—I don't know, says Overbeck, shifting nervously, thrusting his jaw, playing dumb. I don't know. He didn't say who he was, did he? But I'm sure we'll get a proper introduction when he returns, we must have proper introductions all around.

Again the door opens. Whitefringe baldpate enters quietly and glides swiftly to his desk. Before he can speak and before Overbeck can embarrass them all further with his amateurish feints and dodgings deity assumes command of the situation. The god's gaze leaps over the desk. And his voice:

—I believe you and I have met before, though I very much regret to say that I can't recall your name. Would you mind . . .

—I am Wille.

Wille! Yes, of course, Wille! Who else would wield power here in Basel? Wille! A position the god surpassed so long ago now it seems another lifetime, another fate, an earlier incarnation, he can scarcely remember. Imagine, think, Wille! Where there's a Wille there's a Weh. But the god contains himself. Civility is essential to his disguise. Incognito, the Stranger said, and so he contains himself:

—Wille? Ah, yes, you are a psychiatrist. Some years ago you and I had a consultation concerning religious mania, divine lunacy, don't you remember? The occasion, unless I'm mistaken, was the case of a madman by the name of Vischer, Adolf Vischer. Adolf Vischer of Basel, the religious fanatic. He was insensate, non compos mentis, tetched, poor devil.

Wille is silent, nods in assent. He has a good memory. It has been seven years since they met and spoke. By either reckoning. Surely they have been fertile years for the god, years of most excellent vintage. One wonders where Vischer is now? If the narrator may make.

Another interruption. Not the sister in white but a young, stocky man, he too in a white smock. Must be a priest. An entire sect on the loose here. One will have to keep one's eyes open and one's head down. Low profile.

—Breakfast? Did you say breakfast, my good man? Yes, indeed. We had nothing on the train except for Fino's salami. Molto Fino, si si, but not enough to sate the god's belly, no sir! A bath? A bath? Oh, bliss itself! Have you any idea how grubby those Swiss Italian trains are? You can feel the grease and grit on the saddle beneath you, horsehair, to say nothing of the motes in the sunbeam! That lascivious Louise! If only she were with me now! If only my aim had been untrue! A bubble bath and a breakfast, what do you say, Overbeck? Stranger? What's that, Franz? Ah, yes. Yes, I see.

Overbeck does not need a bath or a breakfast. He has his own domicile in nearby Basel. Gentle Ida waits for him. How misnamed she is, the gentle mouse, with no Zeus to mount her. And the Stranger? Back to Torino? Surely he should overnight in Basel, as god's guest! Nothing but the best! Then it will be back to the daily grind in Torino, after another grueling eighteen hours, who can envy him! Back to drilling al dente? Inevitable. Privileges never last forever.

—Peace of god be with you all your days. Until we meet again! For we shall meet again. Arivederla!

A touching parting, such sweet sorrow. As for Overbeck, he wants to embrace the god, but falters, best not to, might be misunderstood, they'd never let him go. Overbeck gazes on the god. Yet what does he actually find there? The Stranger stands apart, looking away toward Lydia. A solitary flute calls from afar

To Heinrich Köselitz in Annaberg

Turin, January 4, 1889
To my maestro Pietro

Sing me a new song: the world is transfigured and all the heavens rejoice

The Crucified.

Wille, still exercising power behind his unbreachable fortress of mahogany, beckons to the younger, heftier man, who now addresses the god briskly:

—We wouldn't want our bathwater to get cold now would we? We wouldn't want our poached egg to get chilled now would we? We wouldn't want to keep sister waiting now would we?

We? Who is we? Who can we be when every name in history I am?

Curriculum vitae for Georg Brandes

April 10, 1888

My illness must have had entirely *local* causes: no type of fundamental neuropathological disturbance could be found. I've never had any symptoms of mental illness, not even fever, nor loss of consciousness. My pulse at that time was as steady as that of Napoleon I (= 60). . . . People were spreading the rumor that I had been in an insane asylum (and even that I had died there). Nothing could be more erroneous.

PART TWO

RESTORATIONS
From Basel to Jena
10 January 1889 to 11 May 1890

Chronology

1889 Thursday, January 10: first sessions with Professor Wille at the Basel Psychiatric Clinic.

Sunday, January 13: Nietzsche's mother Franziska arrives at the clinic for the first visit with her son.

Thursday, January 17: Franziska insists that the patient be transferred to the University of Jena Psychiatric Clinic, directed by Professor Binswanger. She enlists the aid of two assistants, Messrs. Brand and Mähly, for the trying train journey.

Mid-May: Franziska is permitted her first visit with the patient in Jena. Other visits follow, in summer, autumn, and at Christmas, with sundry effects.

Mid-November: Julius Langbehn, a devotee of Rembrandt and of Aryan culture, author of *Rembrandt as Educator, By a German,* insists that he will "heal" Nietzsche—if granted exclusive custody of the patient for two years. His efforts founder after two weeks.

Early June: Bernhard Förster commits suicide in "Nueva Germania," Paraguay.

1890 March 24: Franziska Nietzsche is granted custody of her son; they occupy an apartment at Ziegelmühlenweg 3, in Jena.

May 11: Nietzsche eludes his mother's watchful eye and goes bathing.

10 April of the Year One, A.N.
Tranquil Meadows
1600 Hours

—Infection, Professor Wille? Ah, yes, I see what you mean. I should be specific. If the truth be told . . .

—By all means, the truth. Otherwise no doctor will be able to help you.

—Yes, I was treated twice for a very specific infection.

—Do you recall the diagnosis? And can you tell me precisely when and where and how the infection occurred?

—Yes, I certainly can: haven't you heard of Pontificating Infallibility? A god of my station, you see, never forgets. I remember it as though it were yesterday. In fact it was just yesterday . . .

—What? When? Where?

—Leipzig, during my student days, it must have been Bonn or Cologne, in 1865 or 1866 or 1867.

To Unknown [Fragmentary Draft, 1866-1867?]

Dear Friend,

On one of those cloudy, gloomy, snowy afternoons, the kind that transport the English to an inspired suicidal mania, the kind that disgruntle us, depending on our mood, just as. . . .

They treated me twice for a dubious discharge before they discharged me myself, said it was a temporary inflammation, an ephemeral fault of fiery youth, defect of a day, iniquity of a night. Then once again in Nice, it was a smiling gap-toothed woman *Je suis un bâtard!* I confessed to her. *Vous êtes quoi, Monsieur?* she replied dubiously. *Ça va? Oui oui, ça va bien.* However, the *specific* specific infection you are referring to, Professor Wille, came much later than Leipzig, and much earlier than Nice or Genua. It invaded from the hills surrounding the beach at Sorrento. It was a dental affection, a buccal debâcle, an infirmity of the oral cavity, a morbidity of the muzzle: I got it through the mouth.

Doctor Wille wears a woeful mask. He is a kindly man. Not terribly bright, but kind. I like him.

—And the diagnosis?

—Syphilis. . . . No, cholera. It was in Ars, near Metz.

—Cholera?

—It could have been dysentery. I mean diphtheria. My throat needed painting.

—But that was when you were in the medical corps, in the war of 1870-71.

—Migraine? Myopia? Chipped breastbone? Sprained ankle? Enlargement of the stomach? Writer's cramp? I put it here *some* place. . . .

Silence. No reply. Wille reads. Wille writes. He looks and listens and reads and then he writes. I like him in spite of myself. What will Wille read and write? What will Wille decide? What will Wille empower?

Status praesens. Healthy-looking, well-proportioned man with rather powerful skeleton and musculature. Thoracic cavity deep.—Percussion of the lungs reveals nothing abnormal, likewise auscultation with stethoscope. Heart murmur not excessive; heartbeat quiet, clear. Pulse 70, regular.—Pupils divergent, the right larger than the left; they react very sluggishly. Convergent strabism, aggravated myopia.—Tongue thickly coated; no deviation, no tremor. Facial innervation not greatly disturbed; nasolabial fold on the right side, one trace effaced.—Patellar reflex intensified, footsole reflex normal.—Urine unclouded, acidic, without sugar or albumin.—

Patient cooperates fully with the examination procedures, speaks uninterruptedly during them.—No proper awareness of his illness; feels uncommonly well, elevated spirits. Relates that he has been sick for the past eight days, though he has often suffered from severe headache in the past. Also that he has had a number of fits. Throughout these too he has felt uncommonly well; elevated spirits; he would love to have embraced and kissed everyone on the street, would love to have climbed the walls in order to attain to the heights.—It is difficult to make the patient concentrate; his answers are all partial and fragmentary; sometimes he fails altogether to answer the questions directed to him and carries on ceaselessly with his confused banter. His senses are significantly benumbed.

Patient remains in bed all day. He has a tremendous appetite, is grateful for everything he is served.—Afternoons the patient talks continuously and confusedly, from time to time he yodels and sings.—The content of his discourse is a wild hodgepodge of former experiences, one thought hard on the heels of another, without any logical connection whatsoever.—Patient reports that he picked up two specific infections.—

Excerpt from family physician's report: Powerful physical constitution, no bodily malformations or constitutional illnesses.—Exceptional intellectual capacity, very fine education, has taught with exceptional success.—Character-type: dreamer. In religious and dietetic questions: extravagant. Earliest traces of illness emerged many years ago perhaps, with certainty from 3rd January 1889.—Preceded by severe headache accompanied by vomiting, conditions that lasted for months at a time. Very modest financial situation. Mentally disturbed for the first time. Occasioning moments: excessive enjoyment or revulsion. Symptoms of the present illness: delusions of grandeur, intellectual debility, diminution of memory and mental activity generally.—Bowel movements regular, urine strongly sedimenting.—Patient is excited as a rule, eats a great deal, demands continuously to be fed; at the same time, he is unable to prepare anything for himself; asserts that he is a famous man; ceaselessly demands women.—Diagnosis: cerebral infirmity. Was seen only once by the physician who hereunto affixes his signature. (signed) Dr. Baumann, Turin.

Dr. Baumann? Or was it Bettman? Wille scribbles in the margins of the text. Marks and remarks. I cannot decipher by the motions of his hand what it is he is writing, but am certain it touches on my earlier illnesses here in Basel. As Adjunct Professor of Philology.

To Erwin Rohde in Hamburg

Leipzig, January 16, 1869

Dear Friend,

The prospects are probable, indeed certain, that in the near future I will be invited to become a professor at Basel University: I must prepare myself to assume the duties of an academic from the coming Easter onward. . . .

We really are the fools of fate. Just last week I was going to write you and propose that we study chemistry together, tossing philology where it belongs—up into the ancestral attic.

Now old devil fate lures me with a philology professorship.

One more thing. Recently, Richard Wagner wrote me a most cordial letter—to my considerable joy. And from now on, Lucerne will not be out of my reach.

Long live art and friendship!
F. N.

Wille remembers how often I had to take sick leave, he tells me so, and I can only confirm it. He completes the form. Under the rubric *Illness* he writes in a neat, decisive hand, for I can see it all clearly now, no obstacles in time or in space can hinder my reading now: *Paralysis progressiva*.

10 April of the Year One, A.N.
2359 Hours

I told her not to jump. I cried out to her, I tried to save her. Lava belching everywhere around us, a fawn crept close, in terror of its life. I begged her:

—Let me plunge alone! Hold onto the ledge! Irene! Louise! Don't do it! Shalom!

—Empedocles!

So saying, Corinna leapt to her fiery death. And now I feel deserving of myriad penitential deaths suffered over and over again into all eternity! I go to purge myself, to cleanse myself for death!

January 11: Patient did not sleep during the entire night (in spite of 1 cc. of Chloral), talked without surcease; he also got out of bed repeatedly in order to brush his teeth, wash himself, etc.—Early this morning he was rather strongly benumbed, although he ate his breakfast with relish.—Lay in bed till noon.—Afternoon spent outdoors in continuous motor excitement; tossed his hat to the ground, occasionally lay on the ground himself.—Talks confusedly. Now and then accuses himself bitterly of having plunged others into misery.—After Senna tea two abundant bowel movements. Pulse strong, slow.—

11 April of the Year One, A.N.
2359 Hours

Raise high the right foot!
Raise high the right hand!
Raise high the wand of god!

May I trouble you to direct me to the tranquil mountain meadows piano?

> January 12: After a dose of Sulfonal (2 cc.) slept 4-5 hours intermittently, with frequent interruptions. More subdued in the early morning hours. When asked about his condition, he replies that he feels so infinitely hale that he could only express his condition in music.

12 April of the Year One, A.N.

2359 Hours

You fondle the kid in your arms, Irene. Waves of thick brown hair impede your stroking hand, you brush them away with a quiet laugh. The strap of your fawnskin slips from your pale shoulder and in one deft movement you pull your arm free of it and expose the chocolate bud of your breast. The kid takes you in his mouth, you wince under his teeth, scold him lightly, lightly laugh. Your milk froths at the corners of his greedy black muzzle. When he pauses to catch a breath I am there on my knees, a cuff from the back of my hand sends him sprawling bleating scampering off

To Carl von Gersdorff in Görlitz

April 7, 1866. Naumburg.

Dear Friend,

Yesterday a mighty storm swept across the sky. I hastened to the top of a neighboring hill called "Leusch" (maybe you can check on the meaning of this word for me?), where I came across a hut, a man who was slaughtering two kids, and his boys. The cloudburst swooped down most violently, all wind and hail, I felt an incomparable euphoria; I realized that we understand nature aright only when we have to flee to it from our own cares and vicissitudes. What was man to me, with all his restless willing? What was the eternal "Thou shalt" "Thou shalt not" to me! How vastly different the lightning, the gusts of wind, the hail—free powers without ethics! How fortunate they are, how forceful they are—pure will, without the intellect's murky admixture!

Your friend,

Friedrich Nietzsche.

You toss your shock of hair and laugh aloud. While your head is still back I cup the dribbling bud in my hand, my mouth applies itself and sucks and sucks. The galactic stream squirts against my uvula, I gag and suck and suck. An old goat, I turn your milk to cheese. Spurts and rivulets of creamy yellowwhite pour into my belly, I am sated, bloated, yet still I suck and suck. Your long white hand soothes my temple, smooths my hair, you giggle into my ear:

—Your mustache tickles me so!

My jaw aches at its hinges below my satyr's ears, not too pointy, I am the Antidonkey par excellence, and through all the ache I suck and suck. With a groan, Irene, I roll over onto my back. Stilled. With a laugh you fumble fiddle find me fasten onto me.

—No, Irene. No, love, you've made a mistake. That isn't a breast. I'm not a. I have no. You are too young, Irene. I do not dare, Irene. Irene? O yes. O yes. Peace.

> January 13: Last night patient slept better, 6-7 hours. He manifests an incredible appetite, demands to eat again and again. Afternoons the patient goes walking in the garden, sings, yodels, cries out to himself. Sometimes he slips off his coat and vest and lies down on the earth. After his walk the patient remains in his room.

14 April of the Year One, A.N.
Tranquil Meadows
1500 Hours

—Ah, my dear dear Mama, my good good mama, my sweet sweet Mama, what a joy it is to see you how have you been when did you get here how wonderful you look. All in black. Fit to kill.

I simper scamper sashay toward her, hands outstretched palms upward, head cocked endearingly to one side, my right. She looks nervously about her at first, then fixes a determined smile on her strained yet benign face. She waits motionless until I reach her, she grasps my hands in hers, chill as death, pecks my cheeks. Her face is wet. She weeps!

To Franziska Nietzsche in Naumburg

Pforta, mid-November, 1858

My dear Mama!

I wait every day now for a letter from the family, yet none turns up. Thus I am writing again. I can't come to Naumburg on Sunday; I've only got two hours and your lodgings are too far away. Come instead to Almrich; we'll meet there. Also, I'm thinking, because no letter from you has come, that you yourselves may be planning to come all the way out to Pforta to visit me. Can Uncle Oscar come out again? I need several things, he could bring them along: my soup slurper, Hahn's *History of Prussia*, cocoa, a mirror, scarves, and above all spectacles. Don't keep me waiting long, okay? I need all these things desperately.——Incidentally, I am almost convinced that homesickness is creeping up on me; every now and then traces of it show themselves.—How is Wilhelm? Is he all better? Give him lots of greetings, Gustav too, and Aunt Rosalie, and Auntie Rieke, and Aunt Lina. Surely Lisbeth too will come to Almrich with you and Uncle!

Your Fritz.

—And how is Uncle Oscar recuperating? Soon he'll be his chipper old self again if he doesn't die, and Elisabeth? How is our delectable daughter and saccharine sister? Things still flourishing famously in romantic old Paraguay? How fare the intrepid colonists? My aren't you just bursting with pride they're becoming so famous a real feather in the cap of Empire O my yes!

So! My old old Mother has come to visit her old old critter well I still can't get over it. All the way down from Naumburg on that big train change at Leipzig change at Frankfurt all by yourself? What's that you say? How am I doing? As you see! Famously! The veal you get in Torino is undescribable, tender and tasty too, and the lamb prepared simplicissime with rosmarino e aglio Mama it is simply paradiso. I'm eating like a horse but I don't drink horses. Maybe I'm a dancing bear: they give me the very best bites and the briefest beatings! No Mother that was a joke. I am treated like God in France we're close enough to Alsace you know that's France in spite of persistent rumors to the contrary. Ask Marie Baumgartner in Lörrach if you don't believe your old Swiss critter! How am I sleeping? Let's pull up a bed and I'll show you. Famously! Apart from the chronic insomnia nights. A divinity in my position can't be too vigilant. Price of freedom. Freedom is one of the most important points, you know. Am I keeping up the music? Later on I shall play for you, when the spirit removes me. Something sublime. Maestoso. Would you like a song, "The Miller's Daughter," or how about a heavenrending sky-splitting yodel? Perhaps a scurrilous dance an energetic shuffle and cakewalk one-two-and-three? You've been worried? Yes yes quite right I should have written so busy writing no time to write.

Postcard to Franziska Nietzsche in Naumburg

Turin, December 11, 1888

My old Mother, don't be chagrined that I never write. I've got so many things I have to write, especially letters, important letters.

Your old Creature.

How elegant you look absolutely smashing in basic black I swear every day you resemble Marie Baumgartner more and more, hair smoothed across the dome of the skull, saucer eyes all innocence faith sacrifice, bloodless lips, and *my* ears on the sides of *your* head, uncanny that, the tiniest ears for the tintinnabulations of tried and tested untruths. Yes, black, always black, as far black as I can remember. Did you get those 30 Marks black from our jolly banker Kürbitz? He isn't holding out on us, then? No Mother that was another joke. I meant return payment for that rascally stove. It finally turned up, I made a present of it to the Fino family, and now it turns out to be unsafe: 68 Marks is nothing to sneeze at, reasonable of course if you get what you paid for otherwise unreasonable in the extreme, do you follow me? Do you follow me? Mother dear I swear sometimes you make a decidedly obtuse impression. What will the good doctors think? Never mind. The family reputation waxes. Lisbeth is becoming notorious, at least in posh anti-semitic circles aren't you just bursting and at long last, after years of hardship penury and utter obscurity, so am I, yes, reputed and renowned, your own little Fritz, the Fritz of your heart!

To Franziska Nietzsche in Naumburg

Torino, via Carlo Alberto 6 III
December 21, 1888

My old Mother,

At bottom, your old critter is a monstrous famous beastie by now: not in Germany, of course, for the Germans are too obtuse and too vulgar for the *height* of my spirit, they've always managed to fall flat on their faces where I'm concerned. I have nothing but *choice* natures for my admirers, nothing but influential people in high positions in St. Petersburg, Paris, Stockholm, Vienna, New York. Ah, if you only knew in what words the *premier* personages express their devotion to me— the most charming women, a certain princess, Madame

Tenischev, by no manner of means to be excluded from this list. I have real geniuses among my admirers—there is no name that is treated so exceptionally well and with so much respect as mine.—I've got the knack, don't you know: without name, rank, or riches I am cosseted here like a petit prince by everybody, down to the woman who sells me my fruits and vegetables, and who will not rest until she has picked out the sweetest of her grapes for me (now 28 Pfennig per pound

up from 24 Pfennig in November I mean February getting scarcer obviously in the dead of winter

).

Fortunately, I am now equal to everything my task demands of me. My health is actually first-rate. The weightiest responsibilities, for which no prior human being has been sufficiently strong, are easy for me. Turin is the perfect place in which to reside; oh, with what *distinction* people treat me here!—

My old Mother, receive my most heartfelt wishes as we ring the old year out, and wish me a year that is equal in every respect to the grand things that are destined to transpire during it.

Your old Creature

But about that oven, really! I received two sacks of feather-weight briquets designed especially for the "Doppelstern Karbo-Teufelshitz" manufactured in Dresden and distributed throughout the world apart from Torino Italia apparently by the Firma Nieske what can you expect from a company with a signature like that? And it would have been better if it had never arrived: it is utterly unsafe carbon monoxide fumes the very devil. Yes yes I know about all those recent testimonials. Maybe they were *last* testimonials? If anything ever happened to little Irene I'd never forgive myself. Penitential deaths. Anyway, our coldest day was in October I mean January and apart from the last week or so—*Nebbia, come in Londra!*—the sun has reigned supreme. Oh Mama I can never decide *anything* important: you've always sent me my teas and salamis, breadrolls and bacon, combs and suspenders, fountainpentips shirts and collars suits and socks and underwear did I really need this stove? In Nizza I needed it. But do I need it now in Torino?
—Torino?

—Torino did I say Torino? *Siamo contenti? Ma dove siamo con questa caricatura? Si si, ma dove?* Mama, my dear dear Mama, open those thickglazed saucer eyes, look on your son and be amazed! IN ME YOU SEE THE TYRANT OF TURIN! IL TIRANNO DA TORINO! IL TIRANNO TORINESE!

Mama dear, my sweet sweet Mother in retreat, where are they taking you? Don't let them lock you away! Prevaricate, Mama, tell them you're Polish! The Swiss can't bear Germans! Mama, don't leave me here alone! Your old critter your monstrous renowned beastie needs you more than ever Mama! Remonstrate with them. There is no one here to rub my hands and feet no one here to warm me spreadeagled I lie awake nights listening to the coils and quoits and springs jangling beneath me awaiting the women with trepidation. Ears cocked for their insane hue and cry. And every night they come. Without fail. To deliver the lessons of deepest love, the profoundest and most devoted love.

She is always at their head like a maddened Penthesilea. So statuesque even in ecstasy. No one has ever come near her for beauty and grace and quiet dignity even when she is shuddering grimacing horrific in orgasm. Now that Theseus is dead and she is finally free Dionysos shall make his move, twenty years too late, but what are twenty years in the lifetime of god? He shall make his move

To Cosima Wagner in Bayreuth

Turin, January 3, 1889

They tell me that in the past few days a certain divine Eulenspiegel has finished the Dionysos-Dithyrambs. . . .

Good news for Ariadne, an evangel of the first order, the Nereiad of Naxos. Higher Minne, lower Minne, take it as it comes and goes. Any Minne, mine no more. Get your Minne by the shore. If she holler, you adore. Any Minne, mine no more. Any Minne

To Cosima Wagner in Bayreuth

Turin, January 3, 1889
To Princess Ariadne, My Beloved.

It is a mere prejudice that I am a human being. Yet I have often enough dwelled among human beings and I know the things human beings experience, from the lowest to the highest. Among the Hindus I was Buddha, in Greece Dionysos—Alexander and Caesar were incarnations of me, as well as the poet of

Shakespeare, Lord Bacon. Most recently I was Voltaire and Napoleon, perhaps also Richard Wagner. . . . However, I now come as Dionysos victorious, who will prepare a great festival on Earth. . . . Not as though I had much time. . . . The heavens rejoice to see me here. . . . I also hung on the cross. . . .

To Cosima Wagner in Bayreuth

Turin, January 3, 1889

From Bayreuth you must let the word go forth, *breve*, to all mankind, under the heading THE GOOD NEWS.

From lowest to highest, from bedrock to topsoil, from vale to crag, from seabed to briny foam. Who will apply the order of rank here Mama? Who will rank the Minne Mama? What old meanie? Many moil outside every height and depth Mama and they are condemned to ignorance unto death Mama. The rare ones mount and plunge and do not bicker about the balance—these are the gods Mother and goddesses. Who will rank the Minnies Mama? I say Calina alone. Corinna. If that was her name. If she ever wore a name. Never wore a stitch of signature, names all ablur, a fog of confusion. Yet I would know her unfailingly by her taste.

And by the sign of the starry diadem.
And by the sign of the orangegrove sun.
And by the sign of the hardwood chair against the wall.
And by the sign of the downward-gazing profile.
And by the sign of wingspread knees.
And by the sign of diamondframe fingers and thumbs.
And by the sign of the smoldering earth.
And by the sign of the purpleveined grotto.
And by the sign of mother-of-pearl.
And by the sign of the savory sea.
And by the sign of the earthshaker.
And by the sign of the ship and the butterfly.
And by the sign of the bride of the wind.
And by the sign of the cross of Marsyas Satyr.
And by the sign of Marsyas flayed.
And by the sign of the fear that knows no name.
And by the sign of the love that knows no shame.

Agave, Mother, do you know it? Of course not, darling Mama dear, it is a Mediterranean succulent, you'll find it at the base of every wall in Nice and in Liguria gracing every rockgarden of every villa: it must be the living being that is closest to stone. Pale silver-green leaves, if one can call them that: great shafts launched from some hidden center, reaching up and out, curving down only at the gnarled brown ends into woody thorn, each fleshy shaft laminated with an impregnable layer of armor that rises periodically in hooks sweeping upward at regular intervals like crests of waves in the sea with the most horrific thorny barbs. No doubt it has a soft center Mama as vulnerable at its heart as anything that lives Mama but with a superficies as steely gray as foreboding as forbidding as any ratcheted machine of war. Mother and sister. Infernal machine. To be tossed then sucked into the center of Agave Mother is to be harpooned hooked gaffed lanced and mauled by jags and spines that will not suffer counting, each spinosity each spiculum exuding injecting insinuating a miniscule amount of nettlesome irritant to the skin, so that each puncture or tear is laced by a pungent acrid searing droplet of poison my old Mama. *There is so much* superfluous *calamity in life; one ought to have enough with pain* Mama. To be catapulted down the shafts of this Titanic crown of thorns is to be rowled raw by each aculeate cusp each ensiform fang Mother dear each cornute dentiform spur, your mangled flesh of critter mollified rendered supple and limp as pulp by the caustic Mother blood of my heart. Agave. To soften your hair Mother. Agave. To palliate your parched and horny skin Mother. Agave is Semele's sister and that makes us first cousins almost interchangeable one with another, of one mangled mawed mashed and kneaded flesh. My old Mother Your old Creature. Your Animal. Your Unanimal. Your Monster. Your Dinosaur. Your Phoenix. Your every name in history.

> January 14: Slept 4–5 hours, otherwise spoke and sang continuously.—Will be visited today by his mother. *Information supplied by patient's mother:* Father [a country pastor who developed a cerebral infirmity after a fall down a stairway] died at age 35 and 1/2 of dissolution of the brain.

To Carl von Gersdorff in Hohenheim

Basel, January 18, 1876

It is laborious for me to write, and so I shall be brief. Dearest friend, I've just put the most terrible, painful, uncanny Christmas of all behind me! On Christmas Eve, after many preliminary attacks, which advened with increasing frequency, I suffered something like a total collapse. I could no longer doubt

that I am plagued by a serious illness of the brain, and that my
stomach and my eyes suffer only because of this illness in the
central system. My Father died at the age of thirty-six of an
inflammation of the brain; it is possible that matters will move
more quickly in my case. . . . My uncanny state has *not* been
alleviated; at every instant I am reminded of him.

Yours faithfully,
FN

Mother alive and healthy [but gives the impression of being
not very bright].—Grandparents died at a ripe old age.—A
sister of the patient lives in Paraguay; she is healthy. One of
the mother's brothers died in a psychiatric clinic. The
father's sisters were hysterical and rather eccentric.—
Pregancy and birth were perfectly normal. As a child, patient
tended to be quiet; learned well at school.—Was a theologian at first, then a philologist; in addition, he pursued studies in philosophy. At age 24 invited to Basel as professor of
philology, where he worked for 9 years.—Excessive
involvement with Wagner and his music.—

To Erwin Rohde in Kiel

Basel, November, 1872

Did you know that a psychiatrist, employing the most
"distinguished language," has proved that Wagner is *insane*,
and that the same diagnosis has been concocted (by a different
psychiatrist) for Schopenhauer? You discern that the "healthy"
know how to help themselves: for any *ingenia* who make them
feel uncomfortable they decree, not the scaffold, but that
conniving and most malicious of insinuations. It serves their
purposes better than a sudden annihilation: it undermines the
confidence of generations to come.

Most heartily,
Your F.

Already during his tenure here at the university the patient
suffered a great deal from headache and ophthalmic compli-
cations. He had to terminate his teaching career on account
of them, retiring in order to seek convalescence.—In letters
written recently to his mother the patient was euphoric, said
that of late he felt infinitely well, his spirits elevated; he

praised Turin, where he'd been residing for the past three months, as the most beautiful and splendid of cities, wrote, furthermore, that he'd never been so productive as during said sojourn in Turin. These letters are dated November and December 1888.

The mother's visit cheered the patient visibly. When she entered the room he went up to her, embraced her endearingly, calling out, "Ah, my dear and good Mama, I'm so pleased to see you."—He discussed various family affairs with her, behaving perfectly correctly, until suddenly he cried out: "You see in me the tyrant of Turin!" After this exclamation he began to speak confusedly once again, so that the visit had to be terminated.—In the evening, a cold shower. Sulfonal, 2 cc.—

January 15: 4-5 hours of sleep last night, during the remaining hours very loud.—Afternoon quieter.—Patient drinks a great quantity of water.—Afternoon spent in the garden, walking about, screaming to himself and gesticulating.— Sulfonal, 2 cc.—

January 17: Last night patient slept very soundly; early this morning more subdued than usual.—Paresis of the left facialis much more noticeable today than in days past. Bowel movements daily during the past several days. No demonstrable speech impediments.—Divergence between pupils, right > left.

To be transferred this evening to the Jena Insane Asylum. Weight: January 10, 143 lbs.; January 17, 144 lbs.

> 17 April of the Year One, A.N.
> Basel Central Railway Station
> 2100 Hours

Blinding lights. All people and things in haloed profile larger than life. Rumbling of iron wheels screeching of steel brakes. Smell of vintage urine and diesel oil. Mother and Professor Mähly's son and Herr Brand from Tranquil Meadows are my constant companions in arms. And who should come to see us off but faithful Overbeck, his lantern jaw still aglow, still thrust forward in search of his god. Again we embrace, as we did an eternity ago. I tell him I love him more than any other person in the universe. Onlookers pause, mildly curious, nothing bizarre about two old friends embracing in the station at a crossroad of their lives. I wonder will I ever see him again?

The pounding at the base of my skull commences. I know it from of old. Hammerblows boarding up my mouth nailed slats depriving me of speech. I can feel the grimace the mask of pain that used to be my face. Keep smiling. Keep smiling. The slogging searing pain slides upward and across my skull toward the front of my head.

Where is the Stranger? Back in Torino by now pulling teeth. Must keep up my dignity for his sake. Erect posture. Aristocratic carriage. Pace and footfall firm, with the grace of god and gazelle.

Back in Torino? Then Torino is not here.

To Meta von Salis at Marschlins

Turin, November 14, 1888

Esteemed Fräulein,

Turin is not the sort of place one leaves.

With exceptional devotion,
Your Nietzsche.

Here is Basel. Here is Overbeck. Forgot to give him those keys to return to Fino carissimo. Fumble for them now no not the pocketknife.

—Friend Overbeck! These keys (hand them over ceremoniously) are to be returned to my landlord. I took them by mistake. In my trousers pocket. Inadvertently. Will you see to it that he gets them back? Fino, Davide. Carlo Alberto, 6 III. You won't forget?

Davide Fino to Franz Overbeck in Basel

Turin le 14 janvier 1889

Monsieur le prof.eur Overbeck,

Je vous prie d'observer dans les habillements de notre affectionné professeur Nietzsche, que peut être vous trouverez deux clefs du logement qu'il oublia de nous laisser; vous serez si aimable de nous les expédier.

D. Fino

—Of course I won't forget. He'll have them before the week is out, I promise you. I promise you.

Davide Fino to Franz Overbeck in Basel

20 janvier 1889

Très honoré prof.eur Overbeck,
nous avons reçu les clefs du logement et nous faisons tant de
remerciments.

D. Fino

—No need for tears, Overbeck. It's only a key or two. Little
things for doors, comings and goings, passings. Nothing at all, no
need to get upset.

—Of course not. Sorry. I feel a bit sheepish.

Brand interrupts us. He's in a flaming hurry.

—Excuse me, sir, we really must board now, have to find our
wagon and cabin. The reservations, Herr Doktor Mähly?

Mähly holds up a fan of tickets to the glaring light. His spectacles glint as he scrutinizes them. The very image of his father.
Always ready to help in times of need.

—Wagon seven, cabin three, seats one-hundred-and-twenty-
eight to thirty-one.

We pass now from the vast, brilliantly lit hall to the pedestrian
tunnel that leads to the platforms and the tracks, Brand grasping my
right arm, marked for life I suppose, Mähly my left, Mama behind
with Overbeck. Good of him to keep her at bay. My neck too stiff
for me to turn around and see them but I am certain they are there.
Together with Father. Closing off the rear.

To Gustav Krug in Naumburg

Basel, November 17, 1869

Dearest Friend!

I must explain why I am such a terrible correspondent: the
demon of my *profession* stands behind my chair. And before the
devil comes to fetch him, the demon fetches *me*.

With heartiest greetings to you and Wilhelm,
in tried and true friendship,
Fr. Nietzsche Prof.

She is still marvelously light on her feet. The fruit of all that
prancing on mountain meadows. Must hurry. Nearly time.
Straighten that back! Square those shoulders! Suck in that belly act
like an officer of the cavalry get those feet to march! They swing free

like pendular marionette limbs with a mind of their own circling back to the rear door of eternity agile as boxing bears and naked boys in gymnasia. A bit unsteady. The gardens at Tranquil Meadows too confining for real exercise. Atrophy setting in. Jena will be different. I shall wander with my Kleist

To Rosalie Nietzsche in Naumburg

Pforta, presumably November 26, 1859

Herewith my Christmas-wish list:

Heinrich von Kleist, Collected Works.
Gluck's *Iphigenia in Tauris.* Piano version, published by Leo in Berlin.
Beethoven's *Symphony in A major.* Piano version for two hands by Markull.
etc.

FWNietzsche

and I shall wander with my Novalis. Nights at Saïs, lifting the veil. Of my Sophie my Dorothea my Caroline. Day trips to Weimar. Schiller and Goethe and Greatgrandmother dallying under the rose trellis with the necromancer.

If only I can get this sledgehammer to stop. The mallet of misery slides forward in my head.

Clouds of steam envelop us. Thus I passed from the field of battle to her splendid bed, fogswathed, fogborne, foglifted *come in Londra* she said. Always selecting her sweetest moscati for me. How I will miss this place! Good-bye Torino! Fare ye well, Davide, molto Fino, here is the key to the gates of heaven. Porta Nuova. Don't let it roam! Rome?

Ladies first. Up we go, Mama. Mähly, you next. Spitting image of your father, you know, chip off the old block. Brand, you Etna, give us the loan of your shoulder, a bit of a boost please. Upward ascendant. Jena bound. Like Prometheus. Mähly locates the cabin, Brand heaves the luggage, Mama sits and holds a handkerchief demurely over her nose aren't we delicate, I go straight to the window and roll it down. Overbeck has descended from the train in the nick of time and rushed down the quai to our window. He is so close I could touch him.

—Friend Overbeck! Who knows when our paths will cross again? Jena is far. Farther than Lydia is to Thebes. An immortal journey. How can I thank you enough for all you've done? You think I don't know you think I'm not aware but I am aware I know. Everything.

Fondly I gaze into the lambent limpid liquid eyes of a friend.

To Erwin Rohde in Kiel

Basel, Mid-March. No! circa March 22, 1873

Overbeck is the most earnest and independent-minded researcher and (in personal terms) the most uncomplicated, lovable human being one could want as a friend. Furthermore, he has that radicality I require of everyone I have anything to do with.

Yours faithfully, and thinking of you always,
Fridericus

Honest eyes. Brimming now. It is a difficult moment for him. So much of our past we have squandered together. Broad expanse of brow, unruly hair. Something boyish about Overbeck, though not mischievous. Something relentless, too. Foursquare but with rounded corners. Wonderfully soft face. If only I could touch it, lay my palms against it, kiss it on the mouth, why don't I, Jesus did

To Franz Overbeck in Basel

Naumburg, October 22, 1879

Dear, dear Friend,

In the midst of life I was "surrounded" by my *good* Overbeck—otherwise that other companion would perhaps have risen to greet me: *Mors.*

Love,
FNietzsche

kiss the rim of the ardent lantern, lick the lip of the flickering flame. With a gesture of supreme and ultimate devotion, as a sign of friendship unstinting in its generosity, Overbeck reaches his right hand into the inside pocket of his furlined winter cape

To Franz Overbeck in Steinach am Brenner

Sils-Maria, Tuesday, August 14, 1883

Do remember, dearest Friend Overbeck, to come up with something absolutely distracting! I believe that the situation now calls for the extreme remedy, the uttermost means.—You can't imagine *how* by day and by night this madness rages in me.

Yours faithfully,
Nietzsche.

and extracts a massive oak-handled black-barreled matt-finished army pistol of the kind I am familiar with from my cavalry days, levels it in one smoothly descending arc on a line with my forehead and ever so gently squeezes off a shot of regrets a single deafening report Chambige a single neat aperture just right-of-center penetrating my brow above the myopic upturned right eye where the hand that holds the mallet is instantly stilled.

—For everything you ever wished for me I thank you from the bottom of my divine heart, I murmur as the train pulls out.

Overbeck waves a limp white handkerchief in ultimate capitulation until fog and night and the infinite distance between us swallow us engulf us engorge themselves on the two of us. Man and god alike.

17 -18 April of the Year One, A.N.
Basel-Jena
2100-0935 Hours

Nights in trains. You sit in obscurity and the world unravels beneath your seat. A rumble clacknclatter so regular so insistent it is more silent than the quiet, more intransigent than motionlessness. Had anyone told me that divine transport was contingent on the efficient operation of night trains hundreds of kilometers of steel rail swerving bumping fairly flying I wouldn't have believed them. Wish that itching would stop. Horsehair.

Train slowing now. Stopping. Station? Freiburg-im-Breisgau. Somewhere over there in the dark looms the Freiburger Münster, steeple of red sandstone, carved lace. Too black to see anything. Starting up again. Young Brand snoring at my side. Mähly across from me next to the window chatting with an old lady in widow's weeds who daintily pinches a handkerchief across her nose. Slowing again. Stopping. Station? Baden-Baden. I could do with a cure. A good long swim to take the stiffness out release all the tension. Not at night though catch a death. Baden-Baden. Must be well past midnight.

Hold on. What's the rumpus out there? A passenger out on the quai quarrels with a porter. No wonder. Porters redcaps draymen the epitome of rudeness boorishness bumptiousness. Must be a foreigner, that gesticulating one. Dressed all in white. In April with snow and ice on the ground everywhere and he all in white! Either an angel or a foreigner. Beautiful shock of white hair and a cowcatcher like mine. So close to me now I can see the fire blazing in their eyes, I can hear the tourist remonstrate and the porter curse:

—Doss isst zoo feel! Doss isst feel zoo feel! Nine! Nine! Noor *eins* Mark!

—Verdammte Amerikaner! Hol' mal dein dreckiges Zeug selber! Herr Gott nochamol!! *Drei* Mark! oder die Polizei!!

Arguing about a couple of Mark. Silly. A pauper's pittance, no need to fuss. Still, a solitary traveler hates to be taken in, bamboozled, trampled abroad. Mysterious stranger in a foreign land. I know how he must feel. I rise and move ever so silently to the window, all my cabin crew fast asleep now. I roll the window squeakily down. An icy wind rises to meet my face. Pervasive stench of oil and urine. There are eternal truths, by the dog!

—May I help you, my friend?

—Who's that? Oh, hello. No, no use. I've paid him his pirate's ransom and he's off to plunder the seas once more.

—Pirate? Ransom? Yes, of course. It's more romantic that way. You must understand: he's a German.

—Not all Germans are like that one!

—Don't be too sure.

—There is yourself, for example, ready to help a poor innocent like me!

—Ah, but my friend, there's nary a trace of German blood in me: I'm a pureblooded Polish nobleman, you see: my ancestors were Polish aristocrats, Niëzky by name. It seems the type is well-preserved in me, despite three German "mothers." When I'm abroad people usually take me to be a Pole; one winter in Nice I'll never forget they registered me as polonais. People tell me they've seen my head in Matejko's portraits.

Torino, circa January 4, 1889

To the Illustrious Pole:

I belong to you, I am more a Pole than I am God, I shall bestow honors on you such as only I am able to bestow. . . . I live among you as Matejko. . . .

The Crucified

—I should have known! Should have known! Polish! Didn't recognize you. My profane apologies, sir. Nostrovya!

He is obviously a cultivated man, even if like all Americans he's a bit rough around the edges. Suddenly a brilliant idea, a veritable brainstorm, overtakes me:

—How would you like to translate my books into American? You would thereby join the ranks of Hippolyte Taine, Georg Brandes, and August Strindberg, all of them geniuses of the first order. Your chance for fame, sir, if not fortune!

Brand is tugging at my arm from behind now, no, not Brandes, not Morris Cohen, alas, but Brand. Who has no interest in the propagation of my work. My work? Ecco!

—Well, now, what sorts of things do you write?

—Write? I? Books. . . . Poems perhaps. . . . And songs, no doubt. Hymns. Drinking songs and processionals. Ditties . . .

I allow Brand to pull me back into the cabin. He quickly rolls up the window. I can't hear the disheveled diabolangel in white any longer. He gesticulates once again, this time with fraternal feeling, his white hair blows wildly in the steam of our departing train, and we are gone.

Karlsruhe. Mannheim. That unforgettable evening. So much began then and there, my life as a cavalier, O cosmic Cosima, smooth your skirts and hasten to your god. No, not him, the other one, don't you recognize me, am I that changed? Prado under indictment? It's the stiffness, the drowsiness, I can scarcely move. Must take another Energy Tablet. Not a dance left in me. Sit this one out, thank you. Not itching, burning. Not horsehair, their thorny caustic.

Darmstadt. Getting on for Frankfurt. Goethe abandoned it soon enough, and so will I. Did the shaman poet actually manipulate Greatgrandmother's buttocks in the garden, did he play his Faust against her Gretchen? That would make a luscious line of poetry or at least a savory sideline for our family tree, wouldn't it! Two masters of the tongue suspended like oozing figs from one branch—granted a bit of grafting, a hybrid slice and splice of bastardy. None of it from her side of the family, however, the oily side. Look at her. That absurd face behind that absurd handkerchief. She jerks into and out of sleep, thrusting a filthy ham sandwich at me every time she starts from oblivion; I've been watching her, spying on her, waiting for her galling machinery to grind into gear and begin to turn. For turn it will. And mere absurdity turn to horror and deicide.

Frankfurt. Wonder if that bright young Doctor Eiser is still here? Best medical I ever had. Blabbed everything to Wagner.

To Dr. Otto Eiser in Frankfurt

Naumburg. Early January, 1880

Dear Doctor,

My existence is a *terrible burden:* I would have cast it off long ago if I hadn't been conducting the most instructive tests and experiments in the intellectual and ethical domains precisely during this period of illness and almost total deprivation—this joyfulness, thirsting after knowledge, brings me to heights where I triumph over all martyrdoms and all hopelessness. As a whole, I'm happier than ever before in my life. And yet! Constant pain, a feeling of being half-paralyzed, a condition closely related to seasickness, during which I find it difficult to speak—this feeling lasts several hours a day. For my diversion I have raging seizures (the most recent one forced me to vomit during three days and three nights—I thirsted after death). Can't read! Only seldom can I write! Can't deal with my fellows! Can't listen to music! My consolations are my thoughts and perspectives. On my walks here and there I scribble something on a sheet of paper; I write nothing at a desk; my friends decipher my scribbles.

Yours faithfully,
F. Nietzsche

Several times already I've had lengthy periods of unconsciousness. Last spring in Basel they gave me up for dead.

Since my last eye examination my vision has deteriorated significantly.

The train rocks me gentle. Itch. Burn. And then a grinding sound rends the night. Her tiny head of straw suddenly sprouts spokes armed with hooked spikes. Cogs complain then mesh as the gears engage and the whole horrific contraption begins to turn. Agave, Mother, do you know it? It is a mangle, a complex and diabolically organized mangle designed for flesh and blood, destined for one's own kith and kin, imported from Devil's Island. It smiles and kisses my hand, which I have extended in fear, sucks up my fingers palm wrist forearm to the elbow, pulls with unbelievable force, I feel the arm separate from the shoulder hear the grinding snap of sinew the ka-pok of bone, see through the blinding pulsing pain my limb disappearing into the maw of this unspeakable machine, first one arm then the other. I am left with my vulnerable torso, a magnificent reclining statue of Apollo awaiting the head of Dionysos due from Sweden by post, sublime, yet of softer marble. And bloodier. The machine whines into a higher gear. My head pounds in time to its infernal rhythm. My head! The machine will be satisfied with nothing less. That is why she traveled all the way down to Torino or where was I not to rock me on her bosom but to mangle and maul me. Maul me in the maw. Ma. Ma. Me. Me. Calm down now. Easy. Easy. Keep control. Check carefully, check exceedingly carefully. Stealth above all things. Mähly's head is back, he's sound asleep. Brand too is finally succumbing. Be rational now. If you can rise ever so softly without letting Brand feel it through the seat of his pants and if you can reach across ever so gracefully with these arms miraculously restored to you more muscular now in fact than they have ever been before and in one deft and gallant motion get a good grip and squitch the wind out of her windpipe before her knees grow rigid in reflex reaction kicking young Brand to furious wakefulness her eyes dangling from their sockets her black tongue lalling down to my thumbs pressed so immovably so implacably against her trachea until she soils herself. Losing control. A cry rises in my gorge:

—You filthy bitch! Your offal will stink up the entire train! Conductor engineer gondolier stop this instant! Swing about for Lydia! And toss this baggage overboard! Écrasez la femme! Puah Puah Pfui! Ika-Ika-Bäh-Bäh!

Brand is marvelously muscular, wonderfully virile, altogether agile, really. Mähly is what one would expect of a professor's son. Get down off the seat, you fool, your shoes have been in shit!

And she with astonishing alacrity truly light on her feet for her age the ogre already slipping out through the sliding door of the compartment running for cover she'll bide her time till the next strike the next grinding attack of her infernal machine. Yes yes my sweet mawmaw maumau maman go ahead and fly! Flee! What have you to do with *my* women? Turn in your sex, you're through, barren crone! Brand is truly impressive, remarkably robust, arms like iron grips. Mähly you oaf get your feet off the horsehair if the conductor catches you up there we'll all get a tonguelashing you don't know these Germans as I do.

Frankfurt. She's gone now. Under the trellis with Goethe. Things are quieting down at long last. The handkerchief lies crumpled on the floor, a ruined white carnation. Were I human again I could weep. Human again, all too. Or one of Achilles' horses weeping for poor Patroklos dismantled like me by Apollo not a torso but a part of the machine, he knocked the thyrsos from my hand, I swear, I saw the ivy unraveling from my javelin, the cluster of grapes 28 Pfennig up from 24 undone smashed on the ground beside the white carnation. Soiled in the ordure. Were I once again human instead of beast and god = philosopher. Not my turn. Not yet. All things turn: the machine, my fate, but in their own time: all things recur, but in their own eternity. Something else awaits me now. Come Jena, come Weimar. We have not finished. Not just yet. There is more to this election than even I can dream of, and I can dream as no mortal has ever dreamed.

18 April of the Year One, A.N.
Jena Institute
Professor Binswanger, Director
1435 Hours

Prince Bismarck and the Kaiser are more impressive than I expected them to be. Balding eagles heraldic. I show the fledgling Prince how he might expect his Kaiser to act, to wit, not as my footman. They direct me to my quarters, no audiences today, we wish to be alone for the coming eons we thank you lugubriously with all our heart, we acknowledge your curtseys fair ladies of the court and your prostrations gentlemen of the press with mere suggestions of bows and slightest inclinations of this our ventilated Dionysoshead otherwise we keep our eyes glued on the ceiling having received our right to rule on a beeline from heaven. His lieutenant here on Earth for the duration of secular time. Right foot ahead, left foot apace; left foot ahead, right foot apace. Back straight shoulders foursquare remember what you learned in the cavalry good training for an imperial Caesar. Right foot ahead, left foot apace; left foot ahead, right foot apace. Takes twice as long to get there but keeps the civil service civil, keeps the mortals in line.

—Le agredesco molto for this très très bel Empfang, grandiosissimo, è vero.

Courtesy above all things. Demonstrations of heartfelt gratitude. Noblesse oblige.

—Your hand, sir. You wish to kiss my ring? Yes, of course, no lip contact please, pathos of distance. Everyone off your knees, I implore you! There's no need come come. Levate! Levate!

The simplest of rooms, utterly unadorned, yes, this is our pleasure. Basic white. That cross above the bed will have to be removed. No reminders. Basin in the corner handy for cooling the champagne. And for washing my socks. Lovely soft white walls yes this touches our hearts and soothes our minds. Ever so salacious I mean solicitous. Not an itch; a burning sensation.

—*That* you will have to take up with our legation's counsellors, it is beneath our station. You will be so good as to instruct our myriad porters redcaps draymen coachmen ladies in waiting attendants beefeaters servants in livery menials domestics aliens retainers chamberlains chamberpots pages fascicles stewards equerries lackeys flunkies orderlies disorderlies ushers major domos valets de chambre

To Franziska and Elisabeth Nietzsche in Naumburg

Leipzig, second half of February, 1869

Dear Mother and Sister,

In the meantime you might do me a favor. Please scout about for a valet I can take with me. My desires, or rather, my requirements, are as follows: he should not be too young, must be inclined to cleanliness and probity. It would be good if he had been a soldier. I hate the local Naumburg dialect. An unparalleled obtuseness would not be desirable. He may exercise a craft, as far as I am concerned, as long as it is clean and pleasant-smelling. . . . All the best, and think often on your

Fr.

scullerymaids bondswomen handmaidens footmen kaisers grooms bellboys hostlers bonnes ayahs waitingmaids wetnurses filles et femmes de chambre scullions villeins sycophants dogsbodies dogrobbers catspaws batmen myrmidons and hirelings to bring up the luggage? We thank you for these your ministrations from the bbottom of this ours. Bburning. Ccaustic. From ear to ear this Ccaesarian smile bbeams for you alone.

Main Listing No. 814   Year 1889 No. 8

JENA INSTITUTE
FOR THE CARE AND CURE OF THE INSANE
(Grand Duchy of Saxony-Weimar)

1. Admitted: January 18, 1889
2. Name: N i e t z s c h e. First name: Friedr.
3. Place of Birth: Röcken

4. Most Recent Home Address or Residence: Basel, Insane Asylum
5. Date of Birth: October 15, 1844
6. Marital Status: Single
7. Religion: Lutheran
8. Occupation or Profession: Professor, retired
9. Duration of Illness Prior to Admission: 10 years
   A. Family History: Mental illness in: I. Father. Talents in: III Siblings
   B. Other Causes: Syphilis
13. Form of Illness: Paralytic psychic dysfunction
16. Was Patient Ever in Insane Asylum Before? Yes

17. Whatever Happened to the Three Questions Normally Designated by the Cardinal Numbers Subsequent to the Novennial and Prior to the Tridecennial Whole Integers as well as the Two Queries Customarily Indicated by the Cardinal Numbers Subsequent to the Tridecennial yet Prior to the Sexidecennial Whole Integers? Apparently lost in the shuffle.
18. Did Patient Take Note of the Discrepancy, Perhaps an Error of the Typographic Sort, Ecco!, for which at least in His Arachnid Prime He Possessed an Abnormally Keen if Myopic Eye? Apparently not.

---

1. Details of Patient's Arrival: Brought here by his mother and a local doctor from the Basel Sanitarium. He had been taken to the Basel Sanitarium, where he resided for several days, after having been picked up in Turin. Given a bath. Bed rest. Central Wing. Medical history from Basel.

2. Family History: Father † dissolution of the brain. Father's sisters to some extent rachitic, unusually gifted. Mother, living, not very gifted.

To Franziska Nietzsche in Naumburg

Basel, September 21, 1873

My dear, good Mother,

Our good Auntie Rieke has passed away, and once again we are lonelier. To grow old and more solitary seem one and the same thing, and in the end one is all by oneself, making the others lonelier through one's own death.

Precisely because I know so little of my Father, and have to imagine him on the basis of occasional stories, his closest relatives were always more to me than I suppose aunties usually are. I'm happy when I think of Auntie Rieke and all the folks at Plauen, who retain their own special character into old age and who are so little dependent on the dubious good will of their fellows: I'm happy about it because I see in it the quality of the race that calls itself *Nietzsche,* the quality that I myself have.

My good aunt was therefore always disposed in the friendliest manner toward me, because she felt that in that single most important respect we were related, namely, that most important *Nietzschean* aspect. And so I honor her memory by desiring with all my heart that if I should grow old I should at least not collapse into a state that is beneath me, which is to say, beneath the spirit of my Fathers.

Expect no more of me than that, my dear Mother, overworked as you are, because you are always so willing to help, and think kindly on

Your Son,
Friedrich Nietzsche

Siblings: 1. Friedrich; 2. Elisabeth, living, married to Bernhard Förster, healthy; 3. Joseph † at two years of age, brainstroke.

3. Curriculum vitae: Always was somewhat unbalanced. Very gifted. Pupil of Ritschl. On the latter's recommendation Professor in Basel already at 23 years of age. 1866: infection with syphilis. 1869: becomes Professor of Classical Philology at Basel.

4. Medical History: 1878: surrenders his professorship because of nervous illness and ophthalmic disorders.

Status praesens: January 19-21, 1889: Tall man (5' 7"), average in musculature and distribution of adipose tissue. Weight: 145 lbs. Brown hair, thinning somewhat. Iris: hazel. Right ear: 5.8 cm. long. Left ear: 5.6 cm. long. Diameter of skull 57 cm., pointed processes on the helices of both ears at the downward-turning edge; glossopharyngial arch extends to the uvula. Face highly flushed. Heartbeat weak, pure. Vasomotor flushing after applied pressure normal. Arteries soft, pliant. Tips of lungs normal. Tongue lightly coated. Extensive chronic eczema of the genitals. Urine acidic, free of albumin. Scar tissue on the right portion of the frenulum; the lymph ganglia swollen in several places, especially in the left inguinal region. Pupils: right, distended; left, rather drawn, narrow, slightly irregular. Left eye: all reactions intact. Right eye: only the convergent reaction, synergic reaction in the left eye only. Opening of the left eye noticeably narrower than that of the right; left eye can be opened as wide as the right at will, however. Movement of the eyeball unhindered, no secondary deviation to the inner corners. Frowning in the brow, blinking of eyelids symmetrical. Gnashing of teeth somewhat more energetic on the left side, right corner of mouth turns downward somewhat lower than the left. Closure of mouth on the right side occurs more promptly. Laugh symmetrical. Tongue tranquil, with deviation to the right when extended. Uvula erect. Handshake somewhat stronger with the right than the left.

Writing: Tremor in the hands (only when excited). (Writing tests: "regiment," "Uhlan," "brigadier.")

No Romberg. When walking the patient compulsively raises his left shoulder high, leaves the right shoulder hanging. Oscillates when he makes an about-face. Idiomuscular excitability is enhanced, reflex action enhanced slightly at elbow. Knee-jerk reaction enhanced. Achilles reaction ditto; on the left side a hint of tremor in the foot, epigastric reflex slightly enhanced. Cremaster reflex on the left side of the scrotum is particularly weak. Plantar reflex rather enhanced. Testing the sensibility of the patient when he is in a state of agitation is not practicable at the moment; apparently a generalized hyperaesthesia. Cranial percussion not sensitive; pressure-points in face and head sensitive to applied pressure. Pressure-points on the rump not testable due to hyperaesthesia. Patient claims to hear the ticking of the craniotympanal clock better on the right side. Hearing spectrum apparently intact on both right and left sides. No reading hindrance. Significant myopia. Speech disturbances scarcely present: at rare moments, patient hesitates before initial consonants. Tactile representations intact.

January 19: "The patient follows us to the ward, bowing all the while in a most courtly fashion. He walks majestically to his room, enters, gazes to the ceiling, then thanks us for the 'splendid reception.' He does not know where he is. At one moment he believes he is in Naumburg, the next he thinks he's in Turin. He provides correct data concerning himself. His mien is self-assured and confident, often smug and affected. He gesticulates excessively and speaks pompously, always in a stilted tone of voice, sometimes in Italian, the next instant in French. Countless times he tries to clasp the doctors' hands. One cannot help noticing that the patient, although long in Italy, often uses the simplest words in his Italian sentences incorrectly; occasionally he does not even know the words to be used. As for content, one notes the rapid flux of ideas in his jabber; occasionally he speaks of his magnificent compositions and sings excerpts from them, invokes his 'delegation's counsellors and servants.' While talking, he grimaces almost incessantly. At night too his diffuse palaver continues almost without interruption." The patient eats ravenously.

19 April of the Year One, A.N.
Jena Institute
2359 Hours

   —I can explain everything, Mother. Don't pull my hair so, please don't, I can hear the roots tearing, the pain is ah ah eeeee excruciating. Remember what happened to Papi.

   —Let me cradle your head in my arms, boy. You were very very naughty on the train, boy.

   —Relent, Mother. Release or at least relax your grip. My brain is melting. It is a case of mistaken identity, I assure you. You have ah ah eeeee confused me with my cousin, your sister's son, no one is ah ah eeeee perfect.

   —A mother knows her own son, boy, flesh of her flesh. Let me cradle your hyperaesthesic head in my not so very bright arms, boy.

   —No, Mother, please. The doctors prescribe sleep. Release me at once, please, Mama.

   Outside my window the diffuse gray light of approaching twilight, the earliest suspicion of dawn. The women disband scatter vanish into rocky clefts among scrub pines and towering firs. Till tonight, my loves and my doves, till tonight! Come barking up my tree, my pretty panthers!

January 20: Despite 3.0 cc. of Amylenhydrate patient did not sleep. Transferred to the W. Z.
January 21: Despite 2.0 cc. of Chloralhydrate continuous screams. Patient finally had to be isolated.—On one occasion he claimed that his father "also suffered from dissolution of the brain."

85

RESTORATIONS

22 April of the Year One, A.N.
1031 Hours

—May I read you something, Professor Nietzsche?

—Yes, of course, Herr Doktor Zieher. It is a book you have there, I see, a slim unprepossessing volume with a sober not to say somber black cover uneven in texture not to say bumpy. Austere as a tombstone, more deathly missile than missal or missive: books are to be read with hinterthoughts, my dear Pullman. Proceed. Backwards.

—"To develop a breed of animal that *can* promise—is that not precisely the paradoxical task that nature assigned herself with respect to humanity? is that not the problem *of* humanity proper? (. . .) That this problem was solved to such a high degree of refinement must seem all the more astonishing to anyone who is capable of acknowledging the force that is pitted against it—the force of *oblivion*. Oblivion is not some mere *vis inertiae*, as superficial folk believe; rather, it is an active power of inhibition, positive in the strictest sense of the word. . . ."

Doctor Zieher pauses and turns the page, stealing a glance at me. I wish I could have afforded heavier, higher quality paper. Another page, too flimsy, and he continues:

—"'How does one concoct a faculty of memory for the animal man? How does one stamp something into this partly dull-witted, partly distracted ephemeral intellect, how does one coin something there in such a way that it can remain present to such incarnate oblivion?' (. . .) This primeval problem, as one might well suppose, was not solved by the very gentlest of means, the very mildest of responses. Indeed, there is perhaps nothing more horrific and uncanny in the entire prehistory of humankind than its *mnemotechnic*."

Horrific silence. The significant look that Zieher now bestows on me, the lingering look. Hinterthoughts indeed. He expects me to say something. And so I shall.

—Let that be. Fell the infernal family tree. Forget it. Tell it

To Carl von Gersdorff in Göttingen

Bonn, August 4, 1865

My dear Friend,

I am a little too critical to be able to deceive myself any longer about my own gifts. Therefore, I shall seek above all to develop my critical faculty. . . . Forgive, dear friend, this uncongenial letter. But the stabbing pains in my head prevent me from holding anything together.

F. W. Nietzsche.

🜉!

Think rather of my compositions, Herr Doktor! My hymns and processionals! My delectable ditties! When will they performed—fireworks for the edification of our enlightened friends and benighted subjects? Let us declaim them

To Erwin Rohde in Kiel

Naumburg, August 6, 1868

My dear Rohde,

The poetic spark in our friend is not strong enough to kill an ox but is sufficient to anesthetize a human being, so that I have pleaded with him to surrender his hazardous fireworks.

Tried and true,
Friedrich Nietzsche

Would you like me to sing snatches of them for you now?

—By all means, smiles the good doctor, waves of revulsion and nausea rising from the pit of the stomach up the gorge and into the head to becloud the eye.

—Unfortunately, I am indisposed at the moment. Tones and texts alike come pouring out the hole every time I try to sing a headtone.

—The hole? Headtone?

Point. Indicate. Show him. Place his pudgy digit in it. Demolish doubt.

—Splitting headache, Herr Doktor. I am indisposed. Paying now for earlier excesses. You will excuse me?

January 22: Wishes to have his compositions performed. Complains about headache over his right temple and behind the forehead over his right eye.—Suggests that this is the cause of his having been somewhat too lively.
January 24: Very loud. Now and then has to be isolated.
January 26: Recognizes the doctor immediately. Calls him *Herr Doktor*.

Mayday of the Year One, A.N.
1058 Hours

—Herr Doktor, if I understand you well, you wish me to tell you once again about the eternal recurrence of the same?

—Yes. Yes, I do, Nietzsche.

—Herr Doktor, do you suppose that a pristine thought, a precious unguent, can be spread abroad by everyone in every direction at every moment?

—I don't know. Never thought about it. But, then, why not?

February 1: Weight 135.3 lbs. (down 10)
February 3: Smears filth. Mode and content of speech unchanged.
February 10: Very loud. Often enraged, renders inarticulate screams, no external motive.

20 May of the Year One, A.N.
1033 Hours

—I know you've written some very fine books, Professor Nietzsche, treatises of some sort?

—Ah, you've been talking to Henri Taine no Hippolyte my Panama Canal my Lesseps to France? Strindberg? Brandes, i.e., Morris Cohen? They all acknowledge me in the most flattering terms, simply because of my books. Not literature, mind you. Books! Boxes cases and crates of dynamite! Nobel Prize a year after my death, just you wait!

—Could you tell me what your most recent book was about? I'm interested in your work, you know.

—Of course. *In psychologicis.* I understand entirely. So was your colleague, Turina da Torino. My most recent book? May I think a moment? It has been a while. I've been traveling. *Wanderjahre.*

My *Ecco* he will not have seen, nor anyone else for that matter. That typo, again, must correct! *Ecco.* Echo. "Εχω *home.*

To Meta von Salis at Marschlins

Torino, November 14, 1888

Esteemed Fräulein,

This homo, namely, I am myself, including the ecce. The

attempt to shed a bit of light *and fright* about me seems to me
to have succeeded almost too well.

With exceptional devotion,
Your
Nietzsche.

Not in any of its versions will he have seen it. No. *Ecce* he cannot
mean. *Ecco!* There we go again!

Contra Wagner? Have I corrected the pageproofs for it yet?
Yes, there on the sofa at Fino's. Has it already appeared? My memory is getting. Oblivion. Active force. *Contra?* No. *Case.* Both will
hurt her egregiously. Nothing to be done about it. She has to learn
the truth about the three of us sometime. She wouldn't have banished me to this hellhole if the terrifying truth hadn't already begun
to dawn on her. Love does that. *Dawn?* No. Too far back in the mat-
utinal mists, earliest suspicions, he cannot mean that one.

Can't be the *Genealogy.* He's already read that one, already
forgotten it actively. Which one, then? I was working on them all all
at the same time.

Twilight? Yes, of course. I recognize the cover. It's just like all
the others.

The Antichrist he can't have seen, either. Nor anyone else. If it
were *The Antichrist* he wouldn't hold it so plumply in his outstretched palms, he'd fear infection, he'd grasp its edges with his fin-
gernails. No, his hands are too clean for that terrible that awful
book. And his ears too long, the right 11.6 cm., the left 11.2 cm.
approx., par excellence.

Ariadne! Of course, the *Dionysos-Dithyrambs,* the very last
hymns to flutter from my hands. All of them old songs. Can Naumann have set them so quickly? And would Herr Doktor Zieher be
reading poetry on the sly? Only a fool! Only a poet! Not on your life,
you're on the wrong track, Pullman. I don't follow you.

—I give up. Which one is it?

—May I read you its opening lines?

—That all depends. Are you certain we are ready for them?

—That is precisely what I'd like to determine.

Herr Doktor Zieher grins a lot. His teeth are very white. They
are not his. Prosthesis. Not nearly as impressive as the Stranger's.
Herr Doktor Zieher is proud of his profession. Driller of souls.
Extractor of ecstatics. Enjoys power. He too is a case. Nothing like
Wille, nothing like Binswanger. Nobility is far from him. Better pla-
cate him. Play dumb. No. Play mad.

—Read on, Herr Doktor. I'll riddle and ravel as you read.

—"Indeed, what occupied me most profoundly was the problem of *décadence*—I had my reasons. 'Good and evil' is only one rendition of that problem. If one has developed an eye for the telltale symptoms of decline, one also understands morality; one understands what lurks beneath its most sacred words and value-formulations: *impoverished* life, the will to an end, the great weariness. . . . My greatest experience was a convalescence."

More significant silence. Another lingering look. Tiresome. Let him come to the point and be done with it. Here it comes.

—Well, is it yours?

—Mine? Mine? Never! Too fine for the likes of me, too noble: look at this wreck! Wreckage, I tell you! Illiterary remains, decapitated cadaverous wasted wretchedness! Mine? How dare you, Sleeper!

February 20: No longer recognizes the beginning of his most recent book.

23 May of the Year One, A.N.
1800 Hours

All my life I have suffered from my table companions: day after day, meal after meal, nausea for dessert. And so I explain my position to him most patiently.

—I know who I am. That is the difference between us, you balding cretin. Eat your supper. Stuff your toothless maw.

—I am the Lord thy God, thou shalt not have graven images before me!

—Nor after you, if we can help it. Your beard isn't curly enough; your omniscience is on the weak side; your aura is a disgrace. Besides, if you are Yahweh I shall have to kick you up the bum for being so naughtily irresponsible.

—Atheist! You'll burn in hell for this!! Kick me, will you? Who do you think you are?!

—I know who I am, you am who am. Most recently I've been Friedrich Wilhelm IV, by the grace of God King of Prussia, Sometime Duke of Cumberland, and my own Father. Happy birthing to me.

Yahweh rises wrathfully from the mess table, his right hand poised to swipe. His nostrils flare, his eyes bulge from their sockets. It's true, he resembles no one so much as Pancreator Synopticon, judge of us all in the popular imagination, Platonism for the rabhole. He turns his back on me, bows low, and with his inverted head planted squarely between his knees screams at me. Supple for his age. I am stiffer than he. Ouch! Right cheek. Turn the other. What's that he howls at me, our inverted Yahweh? Can't make it out through the froth and foam. He is beginning to annoy me, I can feel the choler rising in my throat. Perhaps it is my solemn Christian duty to give a good swift one

To Franziska and Elisabeth Nietzsche in Naumburg

Leipzig, Sunday, November 5, 1865.

My dear Mama and Lisbeth,

"Do your duty!" Very well, honored sirs, I shall do it, or strive to do it, but where does it cease? Whence do I know all that it is my duty to fulfill?

Farewell, my dears!
Fritz.

—Kick me, will you?! Go ahead, I dare you! Kick Jehovah?! I dare you! I turn from thee; my face thou wilt not see; to thee I turn my tail!!

February 23: Suddenly regales a fellow patient with a series of "kicks." "Most recently I've been Friedrich Wilhelm IV." February 26: Patient himself attributes muscle cramp in the glutimus maximus to a pinched sciatic nerve on the right side.

28 May of the Year One, A.N.
1048 Hours

—May I ask you a question, Herr Doktor Zieher?
—Of course.
—Why precisely am I here?
—Here?
—At the Jena Institute for the Care and Cure of the Insane. Why am I here in Jena? Who has put me here?

To Erwin Rohde in Jena

Basel, May 16, 1876

It disquiets me somewhat that I haven't yet seen your "novel" announced—I hope some novel imp hasn't gotten in your way.

I am your FN.

—Very good. Very good. For care and for cure, Herr Professor Nietzsche. There you have it. That is your answer.

—I very much want to get better, to convalesce and recuperate.

—That's what we all want. We are all working together to that end, are we not?

—But I am afraid.

—Don't be afraid. . . . Afraid of what?

—Afraid of what the doctors will do to me. You, for instance.

—Afraid of me? Don't be absurd!

Those white porcelain teeth. That beatific patronizing grin. Perhaps one day I shall relocate it to the rear of his head. Keep calm. Reason with him. Bestow a psychology on the Enlightenment.

—Illness has been my life, doctor. It has given me everything I value. If I get completely well again I'll be exactly like everyone else. Like you, for instance.

—That wouldn't be so bad, now, would it?

He laughs a hearty jocund rotund rolypoly bellylaugh.

—I constructed my philosophy from the unhewn rock of illness.

—It won't stand, Nietzsche. If the stones aren't cut foursquare they won't build walls. You must get well. We will concentrate all our energies on that. We shall restore you to yourself. Once you are well you can plunge into your quarry once again with chisel and hammer!

—And dynamite!

—You must remain calm. You must remain silent. You must sleep nights. You must stay clean. Then you will be allowed to teach at the university again. Or, at the very least, you'll be able to write again.

February 28: Patient smilingly requests of the doctor: "Give me a tiny dose of health."

1 June of the Year One, A.N.
1030 Hours

—You're looking very well, Herr Professor. Putting on weight, I see.

—Wagner gets the credit. He rescued me from vegetarianism. You have an excellent kitchen here, Herr Doktor Zieher. All we need now is a luxuriant grotto where I can conceive an opera. Conceive generate and gestate it, write rehearse and stage it!

—Rosy cheeks as well, eyes sparkling! You look like a school-boy cutting pranks in the pastor's orchard!

—I've been out in the garden enjoying the roses.

—Roses? But the roses won't be out for months yet. . . .

—The thorns. I enjoy the thorns. They remind me of my earthly Mother. And of my Father in Heaven.

—Perhaps you'd like to tell me about that.

—Agave, Doctor, do you know it?

—The desert succulent? Or is it a cactus? Yes, but tell me about your mother and the roses.

—Let's leave Naumburg out of this. Let's change the subject. Have you nothing to read to me today?

—You'd rather read? Fine. I'll read some things, and you tell me what books they are from and what they mean. Some day you'll tell me all about your parents and the rosethorns.

—Agreed. You read and I'll riddle. It sounds like fun. May I light up a cigar while you read? One of Havana's finest?

—Certainly. Here we are. Guess this one!

Zieher chooses a slender volume from the pile of books on his desk, opens it to a page preselected by a bookmark, and in a smooth, mellifluous voice begins to read:

—"Apollo stands before me as the transfiguring genius of the *principle of individuation*, through which alone we truly attain redemption in radiant appearance: whereas under the mystic cries of exaltation that rise from Dionysos the spell of individuation is exploded and the paths lie open to the Mothers of Being, to the most intimate core of things."

Zieher pauses, the lingering look scrutinizes, he thumbs pudgily through the pages to a second tagged passage:

—"Tragedy resides in the midst of this excess of life, suffering, and pleasure. In sublime rapture it hearkens to a remote, melancholy song—which tells of the Mothers of Being, whose names are Will, Will-o'-the-Wisp, and Woe."

He is not Wille. Nor even Binswanger. I give him no pleasure. No truth. No excess. He is not my Mother. He sends me nothing.

—Let's try another.

Zieher selects a somewhat heftier tome from the stack. His literacy pleases me. I almost like him when he reads. Especially when he reads aloud. Reassuring voice.

—"The Prisoners."

—Sounds captivating! I'm all ears! All yours!

—"One morning the prisoners turned out into the workyard. The warden wasn't there. Some of the prisoners went to work immediately, as they were accustomed to do; others lounged about and glanced sullenly from side to side. Then one of the prisoners stepped forward and announced: 'Work as much as you like, or do nothing, it's all the same. Your secret schemes have come to light, the Prison Warden heard everything you've said, and in the next few days he will summon you to face a merciless tribunal. You know him: he is hard, and he never forgets a grudge. Yet pay heed to what I now say: up to this moment you have failed to recognize me; I am not what I seem, but am so much more. I am the Warden's Son, and I mean everything to him. I can rescue you—I want to rescue you—but (observe the following, if you please) I shall rescue only those of you who *believe* me when I say that I am the Warden's Son. The others will reap the fruits of their disbelief.'

"After a moment's silence one of the older prisoners spoke up: 'Now, what can it possibly matter to you whether we believe you or not? If you really are his son, and if you can do what you say, then put in a good word for us all, there's a good chap: that would be decent of you. But all this talk about belief and disbelief—let that go, will you?'

"A younger man interjected: 'Well, I for one don't believe him: he's got a bee in his bonnet. Bet you in a week's time we'll be the same as we are today, and the Warden knows from *nothing*.'

"'And if he did know something, he surely doesn't know it anymore,' said the last of the prisoners, who only now came down to the workyard. 'The Prison Warden dropped dead a moment ago.'

"'O-ho!' cried the men as a group. 'O-ho! My Lord Son, what did the Old Joker put in his last will and testament? Maybe now we're *your* prisoners?'

"'I've told you,' mildly replied the one they were addressing, 'I will release everyone who believes in me, as surely as my Father still lives.'

"The prisoners did not laugh, but shrugged their shoulders and left him standing there."

Zieher closes the volume slowly, silent as a shadow. I am deeply moved.

—A remarkable parable, Pullman. My patrimony in a nutshell. Inspirational. I liked the one about the Mothers even better, though. Have you got more where that came from? It will lead us to the thorns, I promise you!

March 1: Little understanding or memory of thoughts and passages from his works. Weight: 141 lbs. (up 5 and 1/2 lbs.).

March 10: Ravenous appetite. Designates the doctors always correctly. Calls himself the Duke of Cumberland or the Kaiser, etc.

March 20: Transferred to M2. Daily 1 gr. of mercury, applied as a balm. Recently, upon receiving a cake from his mother, patient remarked: "Really? from Naumburg?"

23 June of the Year One, A.N.
1045 Hours

—I know where I am. And I know who brought me so low. I know where that frown came from, and these gray hairs. We never should have married. I thought she only wanted to play the piano. Like Irene, like Anna, like Marie. I had no idea.

—You never married, Professor. Sit down, Professor.

—Higher Minne, Herr Doktor, a marriage made in heaven with all the voluptuosity of hell. Neither you nor most women can understand it. She understood it once upon a time, I'm certain of that, else she never would have run off with the Meister. Now she chases her Aphrodite through the bushes all alone. A nun with thick ankles. Me she has put away forever. Here I sit, I can do nothing else.

March 23: Augmenting paresis of the right side of the mouth and face while at rest.

March 24: White hairs in the patient's moustache are to be found on the right side only.

March 26: Often demands to go to bed in the middle of the day. Ambles through the ward singing, stomping his feet.

March 27: "My wife, Cosima Wagner, brought me here."

27 June of the Year One, A.N.
2359 Hours

—Let me cradle your head in my arms, boy. Where does it hurt, son? Ah, yes, this .45 caliber aperture above your right eye, it wasn't there when you were born, son. It makes a lovely *Vasistas* to the core of your lurid mind, boy.

—Is it softening, Mama? Is it in dissolution, like his?

—Dissolution of the brain? Yes, of course! And I thought it was pus! Silly Fritzens silly Mutti! Liquefied brain, boy, yes, that must be it. Spitting image of your Father. Slop off the old block.

—No! Stop it up, sop it up, Mama! Don't mock me. Don't let me dribble and leak away! Mockery!!

To Franziska and Elisabeth Nietzsche in Naumburg

Bonn, Saturday, February 18, 1865

My dear Mama and Lisbeth,

Among the students I am taken to be an authority on music and an odd fellow besides, just like all the other Pforta alumni who belong to the Franconia. I am not by any means disliked, although my manner is somewhat *moquant* and I am taken to be a satirical type. This characterization of me in the judgments of other people will not be without interest to you. I may append my own judgment, which is that I will not let the *moquant* part prevail, that I am often unhappy, that I am too often morose, and that I am delighted to harass just a little bit—not only myself but the others too. . . . Hold me in your love,

 !

In spite of this letter.
Friedrich Wilhelm Nietzsche.

—Let me cradle your head in my arms, boy. Where does it hurt, Fritz of my heart? Ah, yes, I shall cauterize the wound for you.

She bends over me. Her chevelure of serpents brushes my face. The forked flashing tongues lick the perimeter of my wound, daubing it with caustic venom. Not an itch. A burning. The hissing sound is not the voice of the serpents, who are silent, but the sizzling ssszzz of raw meat under the searing venom ah ah eeeee.

March 28: Often complains of severe neuralgia above the eye on the right side.

28 June of the Year One, A.N.
2359 Hours

—No, Mama, not there. It doesn't hurt any more, I swear, Mother! Let me be!

—Naughty Fritz, you've been neglecting your rhubarb, haven't you, boy? Bend over!

—Regularly I partake of it, Mama, plus the Naumburger wonderworker pills, I swear! Not there, Mama, please!

—You should have been a pastor like your Father. I told you so but you wouldn't listen. You'd have been on your feet all day long except for Saturday afternoons when you'd retreat to your study in order to prepare your sermon. As it is, you write too much, boy. Diarrhea of the pen.

To Franziska and Elisabeth Nietzsche in Naumburg

29th of May, 1866, written in Leipzig

Dear Mama and Lisbeth,

I cannot reasonably ratiocinate a reason why I should write you any more. I don't have any news, my philological results don't interest you, philosophical discussions you dislike, I've already negotiated with you concerning a letter, money, and laundry, and the only thing that's left to say is hello-goodbye.

All our hopes are pinned on a German parliament. I wish the Paris Congress a blessed bowel movement.

With that, I commend myself to you with a bow and a crook in my spine as

Your Fritz.

—German parliament! Paris Congress! Communist plots, son. He contracted them in the Reading Room of the British Museum and now they're spreading like wildfire. You don't want a spectator to be haunting Europe, do you, boy? I thought not. Let me hold you very very still, my Torso of Apollo in Pain. Here too my Asclepulaic serpents will cleanse and cauterize you, heal and anneal you, seal and suture you. Be not afraid, son.
—Ah ah eeeee.

March 29: External hemorrhoidal swellings.

30 June of the Year One, A.N.
2359 Hours

At night they come, first the horrid crones, saggingbreasted, lolling tongues and rolling eyes of fools. Her coven. Witchfingers and ghoulnails clutch at my divinity, they would suck and pluck it. I do not let them. I employ a ruse: I empty myself, I paint apotropaic unguents gifts from Naumburg in a ring about me on the floor where I sleep. They dare not cross, they have a horror of the balm's occult power. They tug at their bitchdugs and howl at the moon. Then the angels of paradise descend into my protective zone, where no one suffers the misfortune of bootsoles the worse for wear. They alight unscathed and sport by the dozen. Whatever they ask of me I surrender to them, I am their milk and honey. Gaping mouths. Feed me. Take this and eat. Yum. Now slake your thirst. Now help me paint. Slip off your fawnskins, put on my smock. We are all the fools of a midsummer night's mare. Fools all. Fools.

April 1: Smears filth. "I request a nightshirt for the sake of my thoroughgoing Redemption. During the night twenty-four whores were with me." Weight: 147 and 1/2 lbs. (up 6 lbs.).

April 4: Temporal artery on the left side more pliant than on the right.

April 5: Urinates in his boot and drinks the urine.

April 17: "At night they curse me, they say Mother shat all over everything. They bring the most horrific machinery to bear against me."

April 18: Eats filth.

19 July of the Year One, A.N.
1030 Hours

—I wish to report a theft, Herr Doktor Zieher.

—A theft?

—Bismarck has stolen my pencil. He knocked my weapon from my hand. Before I could recover it he snatched it up and was gone in a flash.

—What would the Chancellor want with your pencil?

—Pullman, in matters political you are a blubbering innocent. I suspect he slipped it to *her*. He deciphered my notes on the wall, cracked the code, read and retained the slogans I devised to precipitate his downfall.

—How did Prince Bismarck get into your room, Herr Professor?

—The unguents have no power to deter him. He produces them himself. Besides, he has an accomplice, she is beautiful but ruthless, *la belle dame*. If as I suspect it is the Grand Duchess herself who is aiding and abedding him, and if it is she who is responsible for these abuses and assassinations against me (she never forgave my Father for touching her there under the trellis on that fatal day, though it wasn't his fault, he only wanted to see if they were as firm as they looked, which they weren't, they never are, and she never forgave him for that) then I must have a revolver. Get me a pistol, a .45 caliber Cavalry Special! Get me field artillery, damn it!

—This Duchess of yours: how does she abuse you? What assassinations do you mean?

—Not what you'd expect. Not what you're always insinuating. She is making me ill here (show him, touch the rim of it, don't be afraid!) on the right side of my forehead just over the eye. By the taut temporal. Can't you see? What are you gaping at you inflated fart you bungling bunghole!!

April 19: Writes illegible scrawl on his walls. "I wish to have a revolver, if my suspicion is correct that the Grand Duchess herself is committing these piggeries and atrocities against me." "I am being made ill on the right side of my brow." Refuses vociferously to give a precise account.

April 25: Must always be placed in isolation nights.

April 27: Often explodes in rage. Smears himself with filth.

April 29: Every now and then he reads, and what he reads he retains.

May 1: Weight: 153 lbs. (up 5 and 1/2 lbs.).

5 August of the Year One, A.N.

1056 Hours

—Herr Doktor, my room is no longer impregnable. Can you hold something in security for me? Have you a safe deposit box?

—The Institute has a safe, yes. What is it you want us to hold for you?

—My will and testament.

—Your will?

—Yes. I know you have doubts about my capacity to prepare such a weighty document. But it was not difficult at all. I left out the initial participial phrase and the rest went perfectly smoothly.

—Why do you feel the need to write your last will and testament?

—I didn't say it would be the last.

—But why a testament at all?

—Because I'm running out of ruses. How long will I be able to keep them at bay? Surely it will be a matter of weeks. Months, at most.

—Come come, now. You're as fit as a fiddle, Professor. You'll outlast us all!

—How long can I hold the throne swaying in my crown of fir?

—Throne? Crown? Fur?

99

—Sooner or later they will topple me. By brute force or cunning. And I must leave my work in good hands. Overbeck will get my trunk out of Torino, but what then? Who will protect my papers? If my Mother ever gets hold of them, or my simpering sibling, they will combust and compost them all to fire and phosphates. Unbeknownst to them, I'm leaving everything to my brother.

—I didn't know you had a brother, Nietzsche.

—Look up the "Family History" in my file there in front of you, Zieher, under "Siblings."

Zieher hesitates, then obeys. Good man. He opens the file, his wary eye still upon me. He glances downward, scans, reads aloud:

—"Siblings: 1. Friedrich."

—He's no sibling, I assure you, Pullman.

—"2. Elisabeth, living . . ."

—Yes, after a fashion, in New Germanaguay.

—". . . married to Bernhard Förster, healthy."

—Healthy as a horse is the llama, though I cannot vouch for her hyperaryan spouse. Doctor, are you Jewish?

—I should say not. Why?

His fatuous grin suddenly vanishes. Without it Zieher looks like a mad dentist. Cruel. Remorseless. Pullman.

—Good. Then you have nothing to fear from my brother-in-law, dear Pullman.

—"3. Joseph † at two years of age, brainstroke."

—It wasn't a brainstroke, Zieher.

—Your brother is dead, Nietzsche. You can't leave your earthly possessions to him.

—The only possessions I had in mind for him were the subterranean ones. It wasn't a stroke, at all events, I'm almost certain of that.

—How then did he die?

—Some say it was stomach cramps, brought on by teething.

—Unlikely. Far-fetched in fact.

—Agreed, Pullman. Others take the view that my Father ate him.

May 5: Hands the doctor a soiled, crumpled scrap of paper. Unreadable script. Says it is his testament.

15 August of the Year One, A.N.
2359 Hours

Occasionally I am not sufficiently vigilant and they are over the line before I am alerted. Mama holds my head by the hair, her knuckles press deep into my skull at the temples, I hear the roots like grass when the cows at graze tear it out in clumps. Her dugs dribble watery pus. I clench my teeth in resistance. Another crone pries upward the right corner of my mouth. The stench is overpowering the nausea I am gagging gagglegurgle garglegargoyle galagilagalapagos gallongalactose gallglandulargalore gallimaufry glottisglopglitch glutengrislygruelglut gluggluttongobbleguzzle gulpglopgoo gobgobblehobgoblin gullguilefulgorge gulliblegulletgobbledegookglas.

May 16: "I am being poisoned over and over again."—
Relates that earlier he took Chloral every three weeks, 2 gr.
three times a day.
May 18: Screams inarticulately at regular intervals.

Postcard to Heinrich Köselitz in Venice

Zürich, Wednesday, May 4, 1887

My prescription: long hikes through the mountains; cities are useless now, cold water cures are dangerous, they are mere stimulants. As opposed to these, I recommend **massage**, to you too, my friend, naturally, as self-therapy. (I'll send along a booklet of instructions shortly.)

Your faithful friend, N.

May 25: Knows very well whether or not he has received a massage on the previous evening.

31 August of the Year One, A.N.
2359 Hours

My agents should have infiltrated La Plata by now: Nueva Germania, Paraguay. My operatives the Good Europeans are at this very moment slipping the final dose of a lethal extract distilled from the phloem of the Wauhluahuatl tree, employed for centuries by the indigenousingeniousindios in their hunting and fishing and intertribal warfare. Administered in minute doses, blended lovingly into the evening soup over a period of several months, the fatal concoction will induce a death virtually identical to that resulting from the usual stress and strain of colonial life and the perfectly normal perfectly respectable perfectly agreeable fibriliation coronary thrombosis cardiac arrest and cessation of bloodflow to the brain, such as it is. The last anti-semite surreptitiously discreetly yet nonetheless ever so efficiently eradicated. Wait. No, not the last. One more to go, one more, closer to home, though every bit abroad. A riddle. Who? His faithful consort. Mmama's llittle llama. Move over, Joseph † , make some room, siblings are a wearying business.

June 1: Weight 140 lbs. (down 13 lbs.).

9 September of the Year One, A.N.
2359 Hours

Because I need slivers of glass. Not merely for the pleasure of it, not simply for the music of it, not simply for Schumann. Splinters of glass arranged in mosaic about me, carefully laid out in a tableau depicting their deaths. When they cross it in the night their feet will be punctured and will bleed. A taste of their own medicine. Their screams will awaken everyone in the Institute. As the women fall to the ground and clutch their soles in agony the shoeman will goat-frisk springbuck silenleap and billygoatgruffgambol saltatory over and away to freedom! While Agave groans in grief clutching her prince's severed head no more will she dance I shall cut capers flounce and bounce vault and hoptoad to safety! The prince of prance the king of dance jumping jack and flea. Sorry sorry mother dear you stay away from me.

June 10: Suddenly shatters a pane of glass.
June 14: Takes the Chief Assistant to be Bismarck.
June 16: Often begs for help in the struggle against nocturnal tortures.

17 September of the Year One, A.N.
1042 Hours

—My gymnastics, Herr Doktor Bismarck? I do them only on the right side, to fight the stiffness, to quell my rebelling ischias. Ça me fait chié, mon ischié, oui oui. Limbering up the limbs. Every dancer is out on her limbs, you know. No need to get exercized, Pullman. Are the others complaining? We'll have to break some more knees around here, won't we, ha ha! Kick up a few more bums, hee hee! Cudgel a few more caputs, ho ho! No, no, only joking, feeling a bit mischievous today: mental gymnastics, you know, good for the soul. I'm laughing out of the right side of my mouth. We'll see if I can jack it up into a divine grin. That would suit you, wouldn't it, Pullman? You always wear such a becoming smile! But what is it becoming, can you tell me that?

—Never mind about the gymnastics. Fine. But it doesn't explain the nose.

—The nose? Ah, yes, I sense your sense; I snuffle your gist. Well, all my life I've simply adored mountain air. (My life started when I got to the Alps; before that it was all plain nightmare.) Have you ever noticed the air you are forced to inspirate here in the Institute, Pullman? All those insalubrious exhalations expirations exudations expurgations expectorations excrescences excretions exhumations of the insane, Herr Doktor, are they not carried on the wind? Do you not fear contagion? Do you not suspect that if you spend sufficient time within these four lustrous white walls you too may be driven stark raving lunaticklish?

—You needn't be unduly concerned about me, Herr Professor. I see so much of it every day, it never touches me. Perhaps we should start at the beginning?

He reopens my file. I love it when he reads. He becomes so vulnerable.

—When precisely were you admitted to the Institute?

—On the 23rd of November 1888, by the old reckoning, or the new, I misremember.

—And why did you have to be admitted?

—Conspiracy. Between my publisher E. W. Fritsch and the stove manufacturer Nieske. I demanded all my books back from Fritsch—he was Wagner's publisher, you know, and it was too silly that he should be mine as well. That's why I switched over to Schmeitzner, who was so much more trustworthy.

Postcard to Ernst Schmeitzner

Basel, March 14, 1879

Herr Schmeitzner! Herr Schmeitzner! *To print something* from my *letters* I reckon among the truly egregious derelictions. It hurts me so much, as few other things can hurt me—it is the most vulgar breach of confidence.—

F. N.

We fought through the post, Fritsch and I, pitched battles by letter, card, and telegram. He conspired with Nieske in Dresden when I instructed Kürbitz, our banker, to get our 68 Marks back, the stove was unsafe according to government health authorities. Carbon monoxide poisoning. I blew the whistle on the whole firm. They lost no time: the very next day I was here in chains. And it's all his fault, if you ask me: Fritsch Nieske.

> June 17: Does gymnastics, often pinches his nose tight for hours at a time.—Revels in puns, word-plays. Gives the date 23 November 1888 as the day of his commitment.
> June 18: Speaks in a purring voice, extremely affected, at times bathetic.
> June 21: More subdued.
> June 26: One hour in the garden daily.
> June 28: Slight convergent strabism in the left eye.
> July 1: Weight 138 and 1/2 lbs. (down 1 and 1/2 lbs.).

2 October of the Year One, A.N.
2130 Hours

—To your health, O my Father!

July 2: Urinates in his water glass.

4 October of the Year One, A.N.
2131 Hours

You will help me now to fend them off. You will be my amulet. Or at least my journeyman apprentice. Let me explain, Papi. They hate bloody feet, it hinders their dancing. You begin near the door on that side, close to the threshold, and I'll begin over here.

To Ida Overbeck in Basel

Sils-Maria, mid-July, 1883

And so it overwhelmed me like a fit of madness. The damage is irreparable. For almost a year my fantasy and my compassion have had to wallow in the muck of these experiences. I believe I have already withstood five times the aggravation that would have driven a normal human being to suicide: and it isn't over yet. . . . The *contrast* of all these things to the state of mind I was in last spring was altogether horrific; it was strong enough to shatter a glass that had already withstood really quite a lot.

Your F. N.

Don't let a single fragment go to waste, Father. Each has been consecrated, each has the deterrent power of a fortress, a crystalline barricade. O Papi, I sure hope this works!

> July 4: Shatters a waterglass, "in order to protect his doorway with slivers of glass."

8 October of the Year One, A.N.
2359 Hours

Soon it will be my birthday, dear Overbeck, soon it will be my nativity. Won't you join us in the ringdance, clasp hands in the roundelay? The god does not say who must dance and who may not; he demands his due of all. But let's forget demands! Abjure commandments! Shake off exhaustion! On your feet, man, with this camouflage smoothed over our naked skin unctuous in the extreme they'll never spot us! Highstep over the ring! (Caution is called for at this crossing, extreme caution!) There now! In the ring of deterrence, the ring of recurrence, the kairotic moment is upon us now and now now now and now now now and now now now the thundering three-step! Ankle, knee, and wisdom of hip! Chora! Kore! Chorioditis! Chloral choreography! Kyrie in unison! Shake that wand boy! Hold it high in your left like me! Let it sprout shoots of ivy! Come! Ivory ivy and verdant vine! Evohe!

> July 9: Leaps like a billy goat, grimaces, draws the left shoulder high.
> July 14: Smears filth.
> July 16: Smears filth.
> July 18: Massages himself with urine.
> July 20: Often refuses to get out of bed, says he is too tired.
> July 23: Sciatica now on the left side: "I am stupid in my hip."

29 October of the Year One, A.N.
2359 Hours

How lovely to see Mother today, they don't often let her come, they take my grumbling too seriously. I grumble because my chest hurts. My chest hurts because I quake no horses. Fritz of my heart, she says. A darling, really, she is. So placid. So simple. Artless. Homespun. Overbearing I mean forbearing. Never complains. Nary a grumble. I must try to become even more like her.

105

—And how is our dear daughter and dire sister? Ah, you've brought a portrait, how lovely! All the way from Paraguay, imagine! Do they have cameras over there? Incredible progress, Mama, this will change everything in La Plata.

I study the likeness. My ears again, yet even more elongated, llamalike, 17.4 cm. the right, 16.8 the left approx. par excellence. The ambitious eyes, slightly crossing, must see things askew. Tight-wound curls of closecropped mousebrown hair. Nononsense chin. Something difficult to identify in the look, the look of a devoted dedicated zealous perfervid indefatigable parvenu jewbater. And I her first jew.

—How sweet, Mama, Lis looks famously well, bristling with health. Really, she'll last another forty years, she'll outlast all of us poor old critters, for we are aging, the two of us, don't you know!

To Franziska Nietzsche in Naumburg

In honor of February 2, 1871
Basel, presumably January 27, 1871

How old, most esteemed Birthday Girl, are you today? As well as I can remember, you go back about to the turn of the century, and it gives me great pleasure to be able to congratulate you on your *seventy-first* birthday, an age you can look upon as a real achievement. . . . This rapid aging of mothers should produce the opposite effect in their children—and, of course, we have the example of our daughter, who can't get beyond seventeen, even though she's been working at it for the past eight years. So, I guess you and I will just have to console one another. I'm content, as you are, though in the meantime I'm suffering the infirmity of old age somewhat more than you, seeing as how I'm celebrating my 87th this year. Maybe it's time I retired. With honors, of course, and a jubilee cup of genuine silver, from which you may sip a nip or two if you like.

Hearty greetings from your
Fridericus.

Basel, January 31, 1872

Today, my dear Mother, just the tiniest birthday greeting. . . . At the moment I haven't the time to calculate which birthday it actually is that you are celebrating. Is it a moderate assumption if I should imagine that soon you will be approaching the *middle* of your life?

In heartfelt love,
Your Son.

Basel, the last Sunday of January, 1875

My dear and good Mother...

I assume that, according to my rough-and-ready calculation, you are now concluding the first half of your life; yet nothing refutes a quite different notion, one you may prefer; for instance, that you have served out only the first third of your life. . . . In the latter case you would still have time to lavish time on the earth until 1973, in the former case, only until 1924. Because I myself have undertaken to grow insufferably old, we might as well get used to looking upon one another as approximate contemporaries. Who knows, perhaps in ten years' time you may look younger than I do! I just about believe it, and I shall not be amazed. At some point, people who know no better will take me to be your older brother (and perhaps Lisbeth, if she continues to mummify herself in her youth, they will take to be our grandchild). The result will be a delightfully inverted world! And whence does it arise? From the fact that Madame Maman refuses partout to grow old. For which on this day I send heartiest congratulations.

Keep in your love your
Fritz

The institutionalized hoi polloi assemble with their guests in the waiting-room, obstructing the entry. Sunday rush, entertain a loony uncle, distract a balmy aunt. They lead us into the auditorium, a splendid room, where I give my public lectures. *Pubblico sceltissimo.* The University of Leipzig has issued a call for me, a veritable summons, importunate really, we're negotiating salary and perquisites right now. Rohde has offered me the regal apartments he used to occupy, but I find it hard to leave Basel. And Burckhardt! How could I abandon that dear hoary head? And how could Overbeck survive without me?

Mama and I sit down in the first row close to the lectern. My foot rolls over something at once smooth and bumpy. A pencil! *My* pencil, the one the Chancellor snitched from me. Quick, Mama, paper! Any sort of paper hurry that old envelop will do nicely thank you.

☞   Desperately I need as soon as possible some large and some small blue notebooks, the large ones not more than four fascicles, the small ones not more than two. In addition, a large notebook of about 10 fascicles.

In sum: 6 large with 4 fascicles,
1 large with 10 fascicles;
2 small with 2 fascicles
Send me the camera obscura and my boots

I write. *Regiment.* Chipped breastbone.
I write? *Uhlan?* Who is Daniel de Ronda?
I am writing. *Brigadier.* Until I hurt my ankle.
I am? Writing? This trembling hand? Writing? Now?
We shall have to read about that. It flows too smoothly, like talc on the heel of my hand after my bath. Like unguents of massage, quicksilver, chocolate, liquid gold. Like water on a polished tabletop drawn by the finger in capillary action. Without the jerk and toss of my feathery quill and its savory snowy ink. Too effortlessly it flows, like blood from a decapitated still palpitant bodystump, and stains as indelibly. Uncouth. Something I wouldn't be caught dead. Yet like a thief in the night I steal out of the auditorium with my pencil and my paper and the few mystic runes I have inscribed there. Mama chides me:

—You old Fritz you, you're a little squirrel you are, squirreling away what doesn't belong to you!

I bend over her ear, her left ear, so much like my own, one-fifth of a centimeter less donkeylike than the right, and I whisper me:

—But now King Oak Crescent the First has something to do when he creeps back into his squirrely treehollow!

She is stunned. She doesn't believe I can have remembered. Of course I remember King Oak Crescent the First! I clutch my pencil. Yet I wouldn't be caught dead.

July 29: Visit from mother. Very pleased.
August 1: Weight 135 lbs. (down 3 and1/2 lbs.).

2 November of the Year One, A.N.
2247 Hours

The dwindling year, the first nine months of my reign. My dentists promised me it would get better and it has only gotten worse. Dr.

Stranger, Torino; Dr. Martyrdom, Firenze. Dwindling deteriorating the year. My shaky legs my stiffening joints my singing rump my burning groin my tightening chest my pounding head my unseeing eyes. All that riding when I was in the mounted artillery as a caval-hero caballero chevalier, her cavalier, before I smashed my breastbone against the pommel of the saddle with that heroic leap. I was their best rider until I soiled my seat. They lost me to the medics.

To Carl von Gersdorff in Berlin

Naumburg, June 22, 1868

My dear Friend,

Most recently I'd been riding the fieriest, spookiest horse in the entire Battery. One day I botched a quick leap into the saddle, smashed my chest against the pommel, and felt on my left side a shuddering, rending sensation. I stayed calm, rode on, withstood the pain another 36 hours. On the evening of the second day afterwards, however, I fainted twice, and from the third day on I was nailed to my bed by the most severe pain and high fever. The doctors examined me and found that I had torn two muscles in my chest. Internal bleeding brought on a devastating infection of the whole muscle and tendon system in the pectoral region. About a week after the accident they opened my chest; several cupsful of pus welled forth. Three months later the infection still hadn't subsided, the incision in my chest wouldn't heal. They discovered that I'd damaged the breastbone, and that this was preventing my recuperation. One evening the first irrefutable testimony came—a bone fragment that the pus had flushed out. It happened again, and the doctors tell me to expect more of it. The Staff Surgeon has put me on the sicklist for the time being; and it is possible that my body will retain a chronic debility at that particular spot.

F. N.

Here I am. Here I am. Now. Now. Tic. Time. Flux. Hurry up please. I shall have to lose a few months. Surrender them to the god. I mean gain a few months. By mortal reckoning. Depends which way you look at it. Losegain. Gainlose.

> August 3: Complains of "tension in the chest and general atrophy." Ravenous appetite.
> August 6: Massages one leg with filth.

August 8: Traces his eye affection, chorioditis, back to the
year 1864 or 1866. Gives the current date as early August
1889.
August 10: Wets himself.

13 November of the Year One, A.N.
2359 Hours

—Good morning, Nietzsche. We've been waiting for you.

—Good morning, Herr Doktor Zieher. I see we've brought in
some consultants.

—Yes, indeed. Together we are going to get to the bottom of
what's been troubling you. It's gone on far too long now. A man your
age! May I introduce you to our distinguished panel?

Each of the four doctors steps forward and smiles knowingly in
my face as Zieher calls out her or his name, then steps adroitly to
one side in order to let the next insultant advance.

—Frau Doktor Malwida von Meysenbug!

A nurse's starched cap with flaming red cross perches on her
bushy head of hair. She is perhaps sixty years old, maybe more. Her
eyes sparkle with a volatile mix of motherly solicitude and unbend-
ing unbudging unforgiving idealism.

—Herr Doktor Otto Eiser!

A man my own age, he winks in a friendly, familiar, even intimate way as he steps forward. About his neck hangs a monogram
stethoscope in the form of a G-clef.

—Herr Doktor Rée!

A round, cherubic face smiling shyly, the tenderest eyes, their
gaze scarcely meeting mine. He steps to one side and continues to
leaf through a featherweight pamphlet on the moral sensibility.

—Chief Magus Shaman Richard!

A dashing figure beneath a rakishly perched broadbrimming
beret steps forward briskly, the very picture of creative genius and
virile vitality, cocks his head to one side in order to meet my gaze
foursquare, raises the thumb of his right hand and squints along it,
sizing me up in painterly fashion. He raises his right eyebrow in an
expression of world-weary remonstrance, good-humored exaspera-
tion, slowly shakes his head, clucks his tongue, and steps aside.

They form a circle about me, gradually advancing, tightening
the ring, as Dr. Zieher summons them one-by-one to pronounce
their diagnoses.

MALWIDA VON MEYSENBUG *(looks lovingly on the patient,
then somewhat askance, and finally altogether disapprovingly as*

she addresses spiritedly her freespirited colleagues): I devoted a full
year to his convalescence—it was the winter of 1876-77 in scenic
Sorrento, I remember it well. Corporal and spiritual works of mercy
I lavished on him, I was like a mother to him without the crass ani-
mal-physical bonding.

To Malwida von Meysenbug in Rome

Good Friday, April 14, 1876. Basel.

Most esteemed Fräulein

About a fortnight ago, of a Sunday, I hied off to the shore of
Lake Geneva and spent the entire day, from early dawn to
moonlit dusk, quite close to you: with my senses restored to
health, I read your book to the end, saying to myself over and
over again that I'd never experienced a more consecrated
Sunday; the mood of purity and love did not forsake me, and all
of nature on that day was the the mirror image of this mood.
You passed before me as a higher self, a *much* higher self—but
more encouraging than disheartening: thus you hovered in my
imagination, and I measured my life against your paradigm,
asking myself about the many things in me that were
wanting. . . . For me your book is perhaps a more stringent
judge than you yourself would be in person. What must a man
do in order not to prove unmanly in the face of this image of
your life?—this question I have asked myself many times. He
would have to do all the things you have done, not one whit
more! Yet in all probability he will not be able to do them,
lacking as he does the unfailing guiding instinct and the love
that is always ready to lend a hand. One of the supreme motifs,
one I have come to be aware of only through you, is that of
maternal love without the physical bond of mother and child: it
is one of the most splendid revelations of *caritas.* Bestow on me
a portion of this love, my most esteemed friend, and look upon
me as a son who needs such a mother—and I mean really needs
her!

Fare ye well, I am and remain *yours* in truth,
Friedrich Nietzsche.

I counseled him: *Marry money,* I said, *a nice girl, but rich.* He promised me he would. I offered him my own eldest adopted daughter,
with all my Herzen, but she turned us both down flat. I racked my

brains for likely candidates, scoured Europe for possible victims, came up with no one and nothing. Empty-handed.

SHAMAN RICHARD (*still shaking his massive beberetted head, but smiling broadly now*): Empty-handed? You perhaps, Frau Dr. von Meysenbug, but not our dexterous friend here. (*General laughter.*)

MALWIDA VON MEYSENBUG: I know, I know. Furthermore, I saw Trina, my maid, sneaking into his room at siesta time.

PATIENT: Not true! She was doing my laundry! (*General laughter. Patient turns to Dr. Zieher imploringly*):

To Unknown, 1866-1867 [?]

Honored Herr Doktor!

If I may make reference to an appointment

—

—

Palimpsest

I can explain everything, Honored Herr Doktor! Cherries, my pince-nez, flaring nostrils, my fez, blackbird heading north, my jester's cap n' bells, Freitag's portable triangle of dramatic rise n' fall, all testicle tube I mean all testify too—

DR. PAUL RÉE (*benign, earnest, an angel in white, obviously disappointed in the patient, interrupting suddenly*): No use denying it, dear friend. Do you think I could sleep next door with all those slurping noises saturating the paperthin wall that barely separated us?

PATIENT: She was washing my socks in the sink!

SHAMAN RICHARD (*briskly*): You should have been writing an opera, writing it and staging it. Instead you lulled carols, canticles, and cantatas, you mumbled ditties, you mammered under her breast. Tsk tsk. Tonguetied, eh?

DR. PAUL RÉE (*casting a significant look in the direction of Dr. v. Meysenbug, pseudoconsolingly to patient*): I won't say a word about that girl from the beach at Sorrento; not a word about Calina, or Corinna, never fear, we shall say that she was visiting me, no one will ever know, my lips are sealed. Incognito!

PATIENT: Hush! Yum's the word!

MALWIDA VON MEYSENBUG: I'm afraid it all fits. He wrote me that he was desperate to find a girl, said he would pick one up out of the gutter if he had to.

PATIENT: Dearest motherlike idealistic womanfriend! It was only a manner of speaking. A mere turn of phrase, an idiom. Only the Higher Minne appealed to me, you know that. I was a fundamentally unerotic person. Heavens, woman, read my biographers! Higher Minne alone!

DR. PAUL RÉE: That is correct, I can vouch for it. Minnie was indeed buxom, uxorious in the extremes. Those horrid sounds! They deprived me of my much-needed afternoon rest.

DR. OTTO EISER (winks conspiratorially at patient, smiles knowingly, in-on-the-jokily, addressing his remarks chiefly to the Chief Magus): I knew the patient only briefly. I too had been fooled by his books. He traveled to Frankfurt for an examination.

SHAMAN RICHARD: And what were your findings? The diagnosis?

DR. OTTO EISER: I'm bound to silence, of course. (General laughter.) My colleagues and I were unfortunately unable to determine the cause of the neuralgias, the migraine, the dry heaves three or fours hours on end several times per week, the near blindness, the bone fragments, the sprained ankle, the rash, the melancholia. But we did come up with a theory concerning that coating on the tongue.

MALWIDA VON MEYSENBUG: Discretion is advised, Herr Doktor Eiser!

DR. OTTO EISER: Yes, indeed, Frau Doktor! (General laughter.) Yet may I touch upon that intermittent acne about the neck and face of the culprit?

SHAMAN RICHARD (suddenly assuming the form of a crêpe-paper dragon slithering chinesily across the stage): Certainly you may! Feel free! Now we're penetrating to the core! Now we're striking bedrock! Company: present arms!

DR. OTTO EISER: A distinguished Neapolitan colleague who alas was detained and could not be with us today but who did examine the scoundrel reported to the Chief Magus and myself his diagnosis and his suggested therapy: he distinctly intimated that Nietzsche should marry!

PATIENT: Only out of irony!

SHAMAN RICHARD: Ha!

MALWIDA VON MEYSENBUG: Ha!

DR. PAUL RÉE: I found a marvelous candidate for him, a gentle, well-bred Cossack girl. He rejected her outright, he virtually shoved her back into my arms, there was nothing I could do.

PATIENT: Liar! False brother! Gigolo! Iago!

SHAMAN RICHARD *(turning on the patient furiously, flames leaping from his flaring dragonnostrils):* The truth is, ladies and gentlemen, he never really wanted a woman, though he eyed concupiscently my own faithful consort, who was, I assure you, utterly appalled by his filthy advances. I'm afraid he held to the old adage the dictum the farmer's wisdom of the bird in the hand etc. Ultimate diagnosis: Sexual perversion of the two most ludicrous sorts—he is a cunning linguist and a master debater.

MALWIDA VON MEYSENBUG *(chagrined, crushed, forlorn, wistful):* I can only confirm it, gentlemen. He read the New Testament to us every evening, commenting with originality on each hallowed passage. It was like living in a modern cloister, we were the ideal family, the family of a woman idealist; it was to be a college of education, the ideal colony, *l'université libre.* Yet all the while he was shielding his eyes behind a fan of white linen and sporting a Turkish fez in bed—he called it his sleeping cap! He pretended to be mild-mannered, the very soul of reconciliation, but his mind was an acid bath. Cynicism and solitary lechery were in his heart.

PATIENT *(hastily unfolding two letters which he has extracted from a concealed pocket of his black-and-white-striped uniform):* It is an accident of literature, a mere publisher's peccadillo, an editorial foible, I can assure you. These letters will exonerate me and restore me to your good graces. *(He reads aloud the two letters. Was anyone attending?)*

To Franz Overbeck in Basel

Leipzig, June 20, 1886

Dear Friend,

I found out in the nick of time that my publisher Schmeitzner was thinking of playing a *dirty* trick on me: he was going to sell my entire corpus to one of the filthiest, most prurient figures in the Saxony publishing world (the character in question has repeatedly been found guilty of peddling pornography; he is a Social-Democrat; everyone knows he can be bought, etc.).

To Constantin Georg Naumann in Leipzig

Sils-Maria, August 2, 1886

Free copies of my book, please, to the following editors of journals, etc.:

(...)

L. von Sacher-Masoch
                    Editorial Office of *On the Heights*
                         Leipzig, Arndstraße 40

(...)

MALWIDA VON MEYSENBUG *(ever more wistfully):* You see, it was my plan to found a missionhouse for adults of both sexes dedicated to the free and full development of the most ethereal ideal life. We were all to go out into the world in order to disseminate freespiritry, scatter refined seed, toss logos spermatikos, fecundate a new spiritualized culture. Doctor Rée and Professor Nietzsche declared themselves prepared to sow and reap. I was convinced that I could find many young women to be their pupils, nubile neophyte women who could be molded and shaped into the noblest representatives of emancipated womanhood. They scoured the shoreline at Sorrento seeking grottoes and hollows that would be suitable to our purpose—the spotless Doctor Rée, to be sure, in good faith.

SHAMAN RICHARD: And all the while our Tannhäuser there had his hands in his pockets, pretending to be in a dither about Dido but dallying with Dick and Harry.

MALWIDA VON MEYSENBUG: He couldn't bear to be alone with a woman.

PATIENT: O mortal insult! *Tutte le donne sono furbe!* My head was pounding, my stomach queasy. I was not myself! Let me be! Let this chalice pass!

MALWIDA VON MEYSENBUG: How unmanly! How illiberal!

DR. OTTO EISER: He spurned the tincture of matrimony, scorned the elixir of conjugal life, took matters into his own hands.

DR. PAUL RÉE: I heard him crying out in the throes of hellish voluptuosity and illicit pleasure!

PATIENT: Never! It's a lie! I was only trying to write I was a prisoner the warden's son I lost my head let this chalice pass!

August 14: Once again very loud. Drank his urine again.
Claims that his screams are caused by headache.
August 16: Suddenly shattered some windowpanes. Claims to have seen the barrel of a rifle aiming at him from outside the window.
August 17: Quicksilver massages terminated.

20 November of the Year One, A.N.
2359 Hours

Cara Mmama, Cara Llama, I thought I'd write the two of you a lovily little envelopy loveletter it has been so long since I last, to tell you both precisely how dear you are to, how snuggleclose how wonderwarm how intimate I feel about, howsomever Lisbeth darling you must promise

To Franz Overbeck in Basel

Venice, first week of June, 1884

Dear Friend,

Please do me the favor of addressing and mailing the enclosed letter to my Mother in Naumburg. For about the past two months I have not succeeded in getting a letter into her hands; the post office can shed no light on this repeated disappearance of correctly addressed letters and cards. Finally, I suspect something that I'd rather not say any more about.—

With hearty greetings,
Your Nietzsche.

to let this one get through to Mama, I know you've been protecting her from my missives for months now please don't intercept this one it's for you both don't let it go astray I hate losing things umbrellas notebooks letters

To Elisabeth Förster in Naumburg

Sils-Maria, August 21, 1885

My dear Llama,

And how is our dear Mother doing? I haven't heard from her in a long time. I trust my letter has reached her by now, through your amicable mediation?—

Your F.

I promise I won't mention lou-know-who I promise I won't visit Lanzky or Paneth any more I won't mail my photo to Morris Georg Cohen Brandes and in general in rée Jewish friends I've given them all up for good I swear so please this letter is for the two of you oh all right you can share it with our dear brother-in-law Bernhard (did you know that when you contract with the devil you get to call him brother-in-law coincidence isn't it!) just the three of you then this epistle this missile from beneath the bottom of my heart though I'm feeling a touch shy tonight truly vacuous drained empty and I don't know whether I should slip it slidingly aposteriorily through the imperial post or retain it here for you apriorily poste restante in ferma until you all come to visit Your loving son and brother and brother-in-law Fritz.

> August 20: Folds filth into a sheet of paper, places the paper in a drawer of his table.
> August 27: Loses handkerchiefs etc. often. When he misplaced his notebook today he remarked, "It took matters into its own hands and went into early retirement."
> September 1: Weight 136 lbs. (up 1 lb.).

4 December of the Year One, A.N.
1031 Hours

—I know where I am. I know who I am. I am very ill. Give me a touch of health, Herr Doktor. Health in infinitesimal doses.

> September 4: Apperceives still quite sharply. Now and then conspicuous awareness of his illness.

5 December of the Year One, A.N.
1032 Hours

—I should have mentioned this before, Herr Doktor Zieher. It may prove significant for your investigation.

—Examination, my good fellow, not investigation. I'm a doctor, not a detective. Tell me. What is it?

—Until my seventeenth year I suffered from periodic attacks of epilepsy.

—Epilepsy?

—Epilepsy. I never lost consciousness during these attacks, so it was difficult for people to observe them. Doctor Zimmermann never had an inkling of it when I was at Schulpforta.

—What were the attacks like? Describe them to me.

—I would have them sometimes while riding in a coach, sometimes while reading books or newspapers in my room, usually in the late afternoon or evening. Each time it was the same. Deep down inside me a vague premonition would begin to rise.

—The aura.

—Yes, like ripples radiating from the center of a pool after bubbles have risen from the muddy floor to burst on the surface. The ripples swelled higher and higher and became waves—or rather one single enormous tidal wave gathering force in me. I would close my eyes, inviting it to come, afraid it would sweep me away if it did come, afraid it would make me soil myself.

—A bowel movement?

—An orgasm. If I opened my eyes and clenched my teeth and concentrated on something, anything, some object in the room, my own hands, I could quell it. Suddenly it would pass through me, leaving me untouched. Then I would hear him behind me, hear his voice. The silent swift movement of his weightless body, the rustle of his gauzey garment.

—Who was it?

—My Father, of course.

—What did he want of you?

—Why don't you ask him yourself? He's behind me now. Don't be alarmed if he does not reply at first. He's awkward with children and strangers.

> September 5: Patient requests recently published books or newspapers. Asserts that until his 17th year he suffered from epileptic fits, though without loss of consciousness.
> September 6: Gives the date as December 7.
> September 7: Sleeps almost always on the floor beside his bed.
> September 9: Claims he is in Turin today. Otherwise, he does not know where he is.
> September 10: Drinks urine again.

15 December of the Year One, A.N.
1841 Hours

After supper I cross the path of our illustrious Assistant.

—Good evening, Pullman.

—Good evening, Professor. I understand you had a visitor today.

—Yes, indeed. My dear old Mother. All the way from Romberg I mean Naumburg, no vacillation. She brought a Linzertorte with her. 'Tis the season, you know. My favorite tart.

Postcard to Franziska and Elisabeth Nietzsche in Naumburg

Genua, December 28, 1881

Here too I was able to give a few presents. I sent a lovely Christmas fruitbread (Pane dolce) to my landlady's son, who is in the insane asylum.—

F.

—I'm pleased the visit went well this time. You were able to remain calm?

—As the Pacific in spring.

—Good. Excellent. Calm is the key to it all. We've been saying that all along, haven't we?

—We certainly have. Well, I'm off!

—Good night, Nietzsche. What's the hurry?

—Good night, Pullman. I've got to get upstairs and write my Mama a letter. She enjoyed the last one so much she's begging for more.

—Good. Excellent. Incidentally, Nietzsche: the name is Zieher, Doctor Zieher. Not Pullman.

—Good night, Pullman, good night!

I perform a brisk, faultless aboutface and march down the hall to the stairway.

September 15: Remembers quite well at evening time a visit from his mother that morning.
September 23: Does not know the Assistant's name. No Rombergian oscillation.

24 December of the Year One, A.N.
2359 Hours

Due to unforeseen circumstances Christmas will be canceled this year and every year hence. We apologize for any inconvenience. Have a Merry one anyway. Trim your trees, not your sails.

New Year's Day of the Year Two, A.N.
1035 Hours

—That is excellent news, Doctor. Yes, I've noticed it myself. I've turned over a new leaf: a genuine 24-carat noncounterfeit authentic remission. Ring out the old, ring in the new! The headaches have diminished, my eyes are stronger than ever, even the right, and the women are fewer and farther in between. That's a

119

joke. You can tell by my mischievous smile, rising on the right. Fearful symmetry.

—Perhaps we can increase your mother's visits, she's dying to see you.

—I doubt that very much: she's a survivor. Another joke, never mind. It would be lovely to see my precious Mother more often. Perhaps we can take walks together, if it isn't too blustery.

—Yes, indeed. As long as we keep the excitement down. We have to keep our nerves as steady as possible. No highs, no lows. The even plain for us! Doldrums of the soul!

—That is what I have always wanted for myself, Doctor.

—No rough seas, no maelstroms or tornados, no headwinds or hurricanes, everything smooth as silk.

—I'll make it my New Year's resolution, it is what I yearn for, now and forever, Herr Doktor! Herr Doktor Zieher!

To Franziska and Elisabeth Nietzsche in Naumburg

Bonn, end of December, 1864

Dear Mama and Lisbeth,

I love New Year's Eves and birthdays. For they give us hours which we might often make for ourselves but only rarely do, hours when the soul stands still and can survey a stretch of its own development. Decisive leaps forward are born in such hours. My custom is to take up again the manuscripts and letters of the year flown by, and to jot down a few notes. For several hours one is sublimely beyond time; one almost steps outside of one's own development. One secures and certifies the past and receives encouragement and resolution to set off on one's ways once again.

Your Fritz.

—I think we are doing splendidly well, Nietzsche!
—I think we are too!

October 1: On the whole, a significant remission. Weight 141 lbs. (up 5 lbs.).

First of February of the Year Two, A.N.
1135 Hours

—May I take you to the library, Mama? The Institute has a wonderful collection, though they haven't got all the journals I need in order to keep abreast. I'm finally well enough to use it. Even my eyes. And my kettledrum head. The doctor says I'm doing very well indeed. Every day I come to the library, ransack the stacks, and turn over a new leaf.

Mama tells me not to read so much. She says that too much reading oppresses the mind. Mama is right. Mama is always right. You don't have to be smart to be right.

—No, Mama, no philosophy books. They don't have any. Light verse, mostly. Vapid novels. Classics. I read a good one the other day called *Lucinde*. A bit naughty. Papi wouldn't have liked it. I'm sorry, Mama, may God receive his dear dear soul in Heaven. Maybe he would have liked it. God is love. Charity never faileth. Trust me. Have confidence. By the bye, Mama, you yourself have only one month of life left to live. How do I know? A man in my position knows things, Mama. I'm as sorry about it as you are, Mama, dreadfully dreadfully sorry. Please don't cry, you know I can't bear it. Yes, Mama, I'll remember. No, Mama, I won't forget. My memory is getting. No character in a work of fiction etc. Good-bye, Mama!

> November 1: This evening he remembered quite precisely a conversation he'd had with the doctor the previous evening.—Steals books.—After a visit from his mother, overexcited. Weight 142 lbs. (up 1 lb.).
> November 10: Continuous severe headache on the right side. Gives the date as "March 1897."

12 February of the Year Two, A.N.
1533 Hours

Gainlose. Losegain. Getting used to time again. Herd at pasture knows no time. Children at play. Aion. We wake them up, shake them up, with time. Lanternlight piercing the foggy night. Abandonments, things slipping away, trailing off, one after the other. Counting, calculating your losses, that is time: rushing forward into your not being there at all anymore, begone bygones. It was lovely being god awhile, seeing how the other half dies.

> November 12: Gives the correct date today, after having been given it yesterday.

21 February of the Year Two, A.N.
1033 Hours

—May I tell you about a dream I've had, Herr Doktor?

121

—I don't put much stock in dreams myself. Some psychiatrists do. You can tell me or not, as you like.

—It was a very vivid dream, every scene painted in the most vibrant colors, every detail scintillating, as the dreams of morbid people usually are, with supreme verisimilitude.

—You aren't morbid, Nietzsche.

—I was a boy, about seven, walking with my Father through the village where I was born. That's the first thing that is uncanny: my Father died when I was four. Yet in this dream I was seven, I remember this detail explicitly, and even so I was holding my Father's hand, cool and soft. We were on our way back home— home to the cemetery where my little brother was buried. And my Father as well, if you see what I mean.

—Cemetery? Home?

—My Father was a country pastor, you remember.

—Ah, then, that makes perfectly good sense, doesn't it? You lived near the church, and the cemetery abutted the church?

—Yes. What doesn't make sense is that in my dream my little brother dies when he is a tiny infant, six months of age, whereas in reality he died when he was a bouncing baby boy of two. Odd. Yet that's where we were bound, my dead Father and I, for the grave of our departed son and brother. Our way took us past the village inn. I never liked the inn because there were always motley groups of people there who were drunk. Guffawing and jeering louts with the stench of alcohol about them. I've always hated inebriation. Not that I've ever known it myself, not that I've ever had to confess it

To Franziska Nietzsche in Naumburg

Pforta, Thursday morning, April 16, 1863

Dear Mother.

If I am writing you today it is nonetheless one of the most unpleasant and saddest things I have ever had to do. For I have committed something terrible, and I don't know whether you will or can forgive me. With a heavy heart and against all my own natural inclinations I take up the pen, especially when I call to mind the splendid conviviality we enjoyed during the Easter holidays, a conviviality no discord was able to darken. Well, last Sunday I got drunk, and I have no excuse other than the fact that I don't know how much I can hold, and besides I was rather excited that afternoon. As I was on my way back to school, Professor Kern caught me. He had me called before the Synod on Tuesday and they demoted me to third place in my class and gave me an hour's detention for the following Sunday. You can imagine how depressed and upset I am, one of the worst things about it being the fact that my little adventure will cause you worry, and it is all so unworthy of me, it is worse than anything that's ever happened to me in all my life. I'm so irritated with myself I can't make any progress on my assignments; I can't calm down and get a hold of myself. Write me soon and be strict with me, for I deserve it; no one knows more than I how much I deserve it.

—Incidentally, please don't let the affair get out, if it hasn't already been bruited all over the place. . . .

Farewell for now, write me soon, and don't be too angry with me, dear Mother.

Disconsolately,
Fritz.

A great crowd gathered in front of the inn as my Father and I approached. The farmers and their womenfolk were celebrating some local festival, and they were all disgustingly drunk. They thronged about a large cart that was tied up in front of the inn, one of those draycarts they use for hauling lumber or casks of vodka.

—Vodka?

—However, the surprising thing about the cart was that it was being drawn, not by a proper drayhorse, not one of those beautiful brawny horses with fringes over their massive hooves, withers they call them, I think, but by a scrawny grayish brownish hag I mean nag of a mare. The old mare was all skin and bones. My Father said it was a miracle that the old hag I mean nag had made it to town in the first place. Just then a whole crowd of drunken boors and matrons leapt into the cart.

"Come on, I'll drive you all home!" shouted an obese, flush-faced scoundrel.

He raised his whip and lashed the poor hag across her back and shoulders. The mare strained with all her might but she couldn't budge the cart. Her hipbones poked horribly at the insides of her mangy coat, she snorted and pulled for dear life, but the cart didn't move. The brute on the driver's seat thrashed her. Someone in the crowd tried to put the fear of God into him—not my Father, someone else, an old man. The driver flailed all the more.

"My property!" he shouted over and over again. As if that is what life were all about.

The horse staggered under the blows, kicked frantically at everything and nothing, her eyes rolling, her mouth frothing with foam. The crowd laughed at her futile kicks: it looked as though she were dancing a crazy jig, the old hag, and still the cart didn't budge.

"I'll fix her!" shouted the bully.

He reached down into the bottom of the cart and pulled out a heavy wooden pole. It was difficult for him in his drunken stupor to wield the pole, but finally he managed to raise it high over the horse's head. He let it fall. A dull, sickening thud, blood at the muzzle, crimson foam. The horse never neighed. She stood stockstill. As though concentrating, deliberating on a decision.

"Whip her over the eyes, over the eyes!" shouted someone in the mob.

The peasant clambered down from the cart, extracting from it an iron rod used to support the removable sides. With the whip in one hand and the rod in the other he lashed and bashed the hag's head and eyes. All four legs went out from under her at once. Under the remorseless rain of blows she stretched out all four legs, arched her savaged neck and head, heaved a vast sigh, and died.

I broke from my Father's grasp and ran forward, ignoring his calls. I rushed to the dead horse and threw myself upon her, the beautiful animal, blood flowing freely from her battered muzzle and mouth, steam rising from her twitching flanks, her eye fixed upon me. I clasped her shattered head, kissed her nose and lips of gore, tasted the salt, and laid my hand over her glazed eye.

My Father, buffeted by the crowd, for they all wanted in for a look, finally threaded his way to me. He tried to pry me loose, to pull me away. His voice behind me terrified me. I felt it as an iron rod. Finally he wrenched me free. The last thing I saw, over my shoulder, was the old hag shivering and trembling at her still steaming flanks. Her hooves were once again in wild agitation. At last she was hauling that cart.

I woke up. . . .

Zieher shifts uncomfortably in his chair, the leather creaks, complains. He is scowling. He did not like my dream, I can tell.

—Perhaps we should concentrate on what's been bothering you.

November 21: "I have a headache, so that I can neither walk nor see."

124

First of March of the Year Two, A.N.
1031 Hours

—You've never told me about your friends, Nietzsche. Tell me about them.

—Friends, Herr Doktor?

—Yes. Everyone has friends. Tell me about yours, anyone who comes to mind.

—They all come to mind. What I couldn't get them to do was come to Basel. You see, I'd called the Basel Council in order to proclaim People Fallibility, and they all demonstrated the principle— Gersdorff, Deussen, Rohde, Romundt, Overbeck, Gustav and Wilhelm, Malwida—by not coming because they were too busy. I never really expected the Meister to come, nor his Mistress. We also called it the *concilium subalpinum* because that was the name of my eventual residence in Torino *transalpinum*. We were going to imbibe joy, we were going to suckle at the breasts of nature. But no one showed up. I've offended them all by now. The Council will never convene.

To Carl von Gersdorff in Ostrichen

Naumburg, December 23, 1872

My valued Friend,

When I recall how our lives' paths and goals have intertwined ever more intimately—or, to be more precise, how they approached each other ever more closely until finally they flowed together in one, like two brooks that flow into *one* stream and toward *one* ocean, well-nigh unwittingly—when I hold all this before my mind's eye, Pforta the university period Leipzig the war years Tribschen, then I know that this past year has imprinted seal after seal upon our confederated friendship and that from now on our mutual dedication, which has been signed, sealed, and delivered, will last us for the rest of our lives.

Most faithfully,
Your F. N.

To Paul Deussen in Minden

Basel, Wednesday, February 1870

My dear Friend,

Surely you will want to share your heart and soul with someone: and I am experienced at getting erotic letters (that is

125

to say, from friends who have fallen in love and who need to pour out heart and soul). I confirm the fact that philosophy has nothing to say here: here all that matters is the true sympathy of a friend and one's own *discernment*.

May you fare well, dear friend, and write me all about it. Why do you always choose such fine words and cadences? We understand one another better without that obfuscating and concealing cloak of rhetoric.

Faithfully and in friendship,
Your
FN.

To Paul Deussen in Minden

Basel, July, 1870

Dear Friend,

When we next meet, how will it be? Will we still understand each other? Will we do so perhaps for the first time? Who knows?

My friend Rohde, after residing in Italy for fifteen months, visited me for fourteen days here in Basel: he passed the test that all friends must take, the test of absence (circa three years), passed it with flying colors.

Even a name as magical as that of Schopenhauer does not help in this regard: what matters is that the friends are one, or at least of one mind. Whether each one finds the identical formula for expressing himself is not the most important thing.

We believe that we expand ourselves when we absorb a great genius. In truth, we diminish the genius so that he can be squeezed into us.

In all serious matters, each human being is his own μέτρον. What is friendship? Two human beings and one μέτρον.

Won't you visit me sometime?

Faithfully, your old friend,
Fr. N.

(You've surely read by now that I've been full professor since March?)

To Erwin Rohde in Florence

Naumburg, October 7, 1869

Outside my window lies autumn in repose, so rich in thought, basking in the clear, mild, warming sunlight, the northern autumn which I love as one of my best friends because it is so ripe and so unselfconscious and so content. Without a gust of wind the fruit falls from the trees.

And so it is with the love of friends: it needs no exhortation, no agitation, before it quietly falls to the ground and makes us happy. It craves nothing for itself, but gives itself whole and entire.

Just compare such friendship with the repulsive avidity of sexual love!

F. N.

To Erwin Rohde in Rome

Basel, end of January, 1870

My dear Friend,

I miss you incredibly: grant me the feast of your presence, and see to it that it isn't a short visit. Under such hermit-like conditions, in these difficult years of my youth, my friendship takes on a truly pathological character: I beg you, as a sick man might beg, "Come to Basel!"

Farewell! Farewell!

To Erwin Rohde in Kiel

Basel, January 31, 1873

Friend of my heart!

I really don't complain any more, except when I think of you, my beloved friend. Why do you have to dwell up north like a lonely polar bear?

To Erwin Rohde in Jena

Basel, May 23, 1876

It strikes me that you say very little in your book about relations of pederasty: yet the idealization of Eros and the purer and more languorous sensibility in passionate love among the Greeks grew first of all in this soil. From there, it seems to me, it was only later *transposed* onto love between the sexes, whereas *earlier* it positively hindered the more gentle and more refined development of sexual love. That the Greeks of antiquity founded the *education* of men on that passion, and that as long as they underwent this older education they looked generally askance at love between the sexes, is bizarre enough—yet it seems to me to be true. Eros, as the πάθος of the καλός σχολάζοντες, is during the acme of Greek antiquity pederastic: the *opinion* concerning Eros that you call "somewhat exaggerated," according to which Aphrodite is superfluous to Eros, merely occasional and accidental, while φιλία is the main element, does not seem entirely un-Greek to me.—However, it appears that you have intentionally avoided this entire area. Jacob Burckhardt too never talks about it in his lectures.

Farewell, my faithful friend!

To Erwin Rohde

Rosenlauibad, August 28, 1877

Dear, dear Friend,

How should I even name it? Whenever I think of you I feel profoundly touched. And when someone recently wrote me of "Rohde's young wife, a supremely lovely creature whose noble soul shines forth from her every feature," I shed tears. I can't give any viable reason for it. Sometime we shall ask the psychologists: they will reveal that in the end it is envy, that I begrudge you your happiness, or am upset because someone has abducted my friend and is holding him captive God knows where, on the Rhine or perhaps in Paris, and refuses to release him!

Meanwhile, may my friend's happiness blossom and burgeon. It always does my heart good to dwell on you, my beloved friend. (I see you now by a lake garlanded with roses; a beautiful white swan is swimming toward you.)

In brotherly love,
Your F.

—Tell me about one of your friends, Nietzsche, any one of them. Everyone has friends. Tell me.
—I have no friends, Herr Doktor Zieher. They all got married.

December 1: When we try to move the patient to one of the second-class wards, with someone to watch over him, instead of letting him sleep in his cell, he makes so much racket that we have to isolate him again. Weight 146 and 1/2 lbs. (up 4 and 1/2 lbs.).

2359 Hours

When she pulls at her wasted dugs rivulets of ochreous pus flow over my upturned face. Chunks of breastbone clot the rivulets, sting my cheeks as they rain down on me. It is difficult for me to speak, difficult to overcome the nausea.

—Mother, stop this lugubrious masquerade, release me glandulargalore at once! I won't stand for it! I won't swallow it! I can't stomach it!

> December 2: Claims to have seen during the night old
> women who were stark raving mad.
> December 9: Vomiting. Mistake in diet not demonstrable,
> yet patient often eats far too quickly.

14 March of the Year Two, A.N.
1032 Hours

—Really much better, thank you, Herr Doktor Zieher. The vomiting has subsided. Something I ate. Sour milk. My headaches are old friends to me now, my faithful companions, my domestics and housepets. My eyes have never been better. I borrow books from the library every day.

—So I hear.

—I'm certain it's a remission, Herr Doktor. I'm feeling altogether restored. Not nearly so testy and unsettled as I once was. I'm a new man. I'm almost all-too-human again. Hard to stop a stone that's rolling downhill!

—We've had this conversation before, haven't we, Nietzsche?

—An infinite number of times, each time the same.

Dr. Zieher shifts and swivels in his chair. He is thinking he might say something further but is still unsure. There. He has decided. Good. Doctors should be decisive. And I really am feeling much much better. The misery and squalor of my condition strike me now with full force. I feel cleansed, as of old: I am filthy, I am wretched, at last!

—How would you feel about some conversations with a man of ideas? A man just like yourself?

—Ideas?

—A young art critic who has come to our attention, an expert on Rembrandt, it seems. He's read your books and is dying to meet you.

—Another one.

129

—I believe he was a student of yours. You must know him. A kindred spirit. He'd like to take you for walks around the grounds and share ideas with you.

—Yes. Why not. Who is this man of ideas who knows me yet is dying to meet me?

Dr. Zieher checks his notepad to get the name right. So vulnerable.

—Dr. Julius Langbehn, from Dresden, originally from Kiel, historian of art and freelance critic. Studied in Munich. Has the Ph.D. Is about to be published.

—Dr. Longlegs? Should be good for walking. Which leaves only the ideas. And they'll have to come to us, won't they. Kiel? I wonder if friend Rohde knows him?

—What do you say, Nietzsche?

—I say, bring on Daddy Longlegs! We shall share a libation from the Castalian Font, the well of Mnemosyne. Surely, it won't be lethal?

December 14: Drinks rinsewater.

20 March of the Year Two, A.N.
Gardens, Jena Institute
1503 Hours

—Ah, but you see, despite what you have written, the Greeks had not a trace of Dionysian intoxication about them. Frenzy was purely Asiatic, altogether foreign to Homer. The Greeks were too intelligent for that: they would never have allowed something so powerful to elude the grasp of intellect. Not for nothing did they resist the hegemony of the Persian!

—Rohde made the same objection.

—*Insightful* objection! That is my therapy, you see. It will make you well, I swear it! You take the Dionysian to be a sign of superabundant life; yet it is the epitome of decadence and decline. It is life-force run amok, transgressing the bounds of redemptive intellect. And this is precisely what has happened to you, if I may say so. We must find another route back to redemptive intelligence. Not the antique route: Homer touches us no longer. Fear Dionysos. The Bacchic god is unwholesome, his touch is madness! The tiger and the ape, precisely as you once feared! Which is the proper route, then? That must be our question!

Dusk is beginning to settle in already, but we continue our steady pace along the gravel path. How long will I have to endure this? Two weeks now of being saved by Daddy Longlegs. Soon I'll expire of salvation.

It began well enough, with talk of Venezia, Tiziano, the aristocratic-heroic style, the Piazza San Marco between ten and twelve noon in the shade of the porticoes and colonnades, the very best place for work. Women in lavender and cream strolling past the cafés, children starting the pigeons. The blues and golds of the Duomo at the far end of the square, and inside the dark niches, impenetrably dark, here and there a muttering crone. Venezia. The most wonderful sidewalks in the world, with the possible exception of Torino. And to the west Bergamo Lecco Orta Garda Como, jewels of cities, gems of lakes. The splendid Villa Olmo on the lakefront across from Como, how slowly the evening came down, superb violin concert that night in the rococo sala where I met that effervescent architect what was his name yes Lovechilde, he was Polish, too. Walking the gravel paths through the geometric gardens smelling that pungent hedge what is it called I always forget smell of pepper and genitals wondrous boxwood that's it and the cool fresh water they say it's fabulously fathomless Lago di Como looking across the tremulous surface to the lights of Bellagio. Yes yes it began well enough.

Suddenly out of the blue empyrean now almost black as I am hearing his droning voice again I remember something I had forgotten even to forget about, anamnesis recovering unaccountably from amnesia, amnesia retaining reremembering anamnesis, and it was fully there my idea as if for the first time the very first time once and for all:

—May I tell you a vagrant thought of mine?

—Yes, of course, says Langbehn, surprised at the interruption. Surprised and relieved, for he has been jabbering politely on and on about Titian red and how it was produced and the effects of age with the incumbent problem of restoration of the authentic chromaticity after having tired of the search for the most convenient route to my own redemption and restoration.

We sit down on a stone bench. The cold creeps into the base of my spine and slowly up to the crook. The burning cacoethes is quelled for the moment. My head is lucid, without pain.

—It is an idea I had long ago, I believe, but I've just now had it for the first time as well. It comes to the same, you see?

He did not see.

—It comes to the same, even though the same is the prime fiction, the fiction of all metaphysical suffictions, that any one thing, much less any two things, ever is or are the same.

He smiled politely. I continued. Evidently I had caught the contagion from him.

—I have it now. I have it. Listen. And don't forget.

To Heinrich Köselitz in Venice

Sils-Maria, the 14th of August, 1881

Now, my dear and good friend! The August sun shines over our heads, the year is fugitive, it grows quieter and more peaceful on the mountains and in the woods. Thoughts have been looming on my horizon the like of which I have never seen—I don't want to say a word about them, I want to preserve an unruffled calm in myself. It seems I shall have to live *several* years longer. Oh, my friend, sometimes the realization runs through my head that I am actually living a supremely dangerous life; for I belong among those machines that can *explode!* The intensities of my feeling make me shudder and laugh aloud—already on several occasions I was unable to leave my room for the ridiculous reason that my eyes were inflamed—from what? On each occasion I had been weeping excessively during my hikes the day before; no, not sentimental tears, but tears of exultation; during which I sang and muttered nonsense, filled to the brim with my new vision, which I am the first of all human beings to have.

In heartfelt love and gratitude,
Your F. N.

(I've been ill a lot.)

If we assume truly infinite time, infinite forward and back, to hold onto these imaginary directions for a moment—we will soon have to let them go—and if we also assume that the clusters of forces or constellations of events in the universe are finite in number (and we have to assume that if the amount of matter and energy in the universe is constant and is conserved), well then, you see the consequent, don't you?

He did not see. He no longer smiled. Yet he would smile again later unperturbed, I was certain of that. I continued:

—If what we have assumed is the case, then everything that *can* have happened *will already have* happened, and whatever *has* happened or *is* happening now will recur—indeed, will already have recurred countless times. And it has come and will come again each time as the same.

—The same?

Now it was my turn to smile, my turn to laugh. And my turn would return. Eternally. Would his? The same?

—But you called that a suffiction.

—It is mathematically irrefutable.

—I believe you. But what are the consequences? Are they not monstrous? For how could we be surprised by anything? And where is freedom? And how could you ever have forgotten such an insight?

—Forgotten what?

—What you were just saying! What you have written: "And you and I and this spider in the moonlight. . . ."

—Yes. Go on. What about that squinty spider? What has become of it?

Postcard to Elisabeth Nietzsche in Naumburg

Sils-Maria, August 18, 1881

A human being in the midst of a web, the web of my thoughts, shooting up around me on all sides—that is a frightening thing. And if I cannot guarantee my solitude from now on I shall leave Europe for many years, I swear it! I have no more time to lose, I have already lost much too much time. Whenever I am not *miserly* with my good quarter-hours I have a wretched conscience.

In heartfelt love and sincerity,
Your Brother.

—"Will not we too recur?"

—Yes. Go on. It's the same thing, incidentally. Go on.

—I don't have it all in my head. That's what books are for!

—To enable us to forget?

—No, to remember!

—Doesn't it come to the same?

And so on.

And so on.

Two hours every morning, two hours every afternoon, these two weeks. Seems like an eternity. It is. That was the one thing he could not accept: that there is nothing that happens once and for all, nothing that has its own unique inimitable unrepeatable history, nothing that can fall just once and be hoisted to its feet just once its knees brushed off and its tears wiped just once just once once and for all. Nothing even remotely like that could he accept. That everything hallowed hides a hollow where repetition is always already underway: I can hear his teeth gnashing at the thought.

And yet so much about the two of us is the same, so much brings us together, the smallest gap separating this longlegged enthusiast of art and myself, what I can distinctly remember of me: our love of Italy, our trembling in awe of Greek tragedy. What was it he said he had written in Munich? Something for Wagner's loony Ludwig—winged figures in Greek art? Cupids, no doubt. Late Hellenistic sentimentalities, no doubt. No chapters there on the κῆρες. Kitsch, not κῆρες. This, then, is to be my Savior? My Σωτήρ? Dionysos in flaxen curls, surrounded by chubbycheekcherubs? No. No. He's moved on to another Savior, he's switched allegiances. Parsifal on his knees before the Grail. Not the first one to do so, nor the last.

We rise from the bench and continue our walk. Dark and chill descend on Jena. After a long silence, he begins again.

—It was in Darmstadt that my entire life changed. Five years ago.

He seems both keen to talk about it and reluctant, fearful, as though it were decisive and could drive us apart. He is anxious to talk about it. I try to help him over the hurdle.

—Darmstadt? I had an interesting experience there myself not long ago, passing through by train with my Mother.

—Tell me about it!

—You first.

We round the rear corner of the massive Institute and head for the English gardens in the back. It is always easier there to accept the things he says. I must see to it I don't stumble.

—I saw in Darmstadt for the first time Rembrandt's "Christ's Scourging at the Pillar." It changed my life. I remained in the city for a week. I lived with that painting from the opening till the closing hour every day. It penetrated parts of my soul I never knew I had, opened uncharted territory in me.

Again he pauses. Dwelling on his Master. Rembrandt. *Rembrandt as Educator.* Curious title. Nice ring to it. I call him Le Petit Rembrandt, though not to his face, no need to be cruel. I call him Le Petit Rembrandt for purposes of contrast, remembering the steely glinty glare of the grand old man: the portrait of the artist as a disillusioned disabused no longer hoodwinked not even by himself observer of the species, his own, our own. None of the haughtiness and panache of the earlier portraits, though with all their confidence, all their mastery. Rembrandt young, Rembrandt old. And, with me now, the infantile, petty German Rembrandt, contradictio in adiecto.

—For a long time, years and years, I searched for the mortar that would lime our Hellenism with our Germanity. It wasn't enough that our languages worked in the same way, the almost identical grammar and syntax—but I won't lecture you on that!

Good. Forever grateful. Must say something. Be kind. Calm down. Remember what Zieher says. Doldrums.

—And you found Rembrandt to be the mucilage that would paste antique Athens onto imperial Germany?

—Not as strange as it sounds. Rembrandt *is* German for all practical purposes.

—For all practical purposes—such as pastiche?

—You're in a good humor today! But I'm not joking. This is serious. Everything hangs on it. This is the crux of my entire book.

I apologize to him, though his words sting my memory and the future of all memory. Lethal. I ask him to go on, though I fear what is coming.

—We will never regain Greek cheerfulness, the serenity of the archaic smile on the faces of youths and maidens, they are gone forever. We have learned too much about ourselves, too much about our tortured, fallen selves.

—As Christ in that canvas has fallen under the strokes of the cat-o'-nine-tails?

—Yes, exactly! But only insofar as He is human, only inasmuch as He has freely taken on the debility and shame of our humanity.

—Which is now being scourged out of him.

—Yes! You *know* the painting, I see.

—I admire it more than I can say. The silvery skin of the Savior, the bloody brow and argentine breast: they are painted with the same loving attention to detail as the slaughterhouse sketches and canvases. The magnificent meat, so beautifully hung, no longer even beef, more like . . .

—Wait a moment. Hold on there. How can you compare them?

—By grace of their spirituality. The identical spirituality in both subjects, and in their depiction.

—Oh, you're teasing me again! Playing the immoralist again! You want me to lose my patience, but I shan't, I can't, there are pageproofs waiting for me when I get home, and I really have to be at my best.

—That spider again. Do you know what Emerson says about correcting proofs? He says that proofing proofs is the best proof of human finitude.

Langbehn throws back his head and shakes with silent laughter. It is too dark now to see his blazing blue eyes, his turbulent profile. But I can feel it, can feel the frigid hysteria. It invades me. It upsets me. We are under the oaks. The path of soft loam and moist moldering leaves, muddy in places, is redolent of earth.

—It's about time we started back.

—Yes, I must get back to my work. But I haven't finished telling you about my integration of Hellenism and the Nordic!

I can no longer help it. The mistake is out of my mouth before I can even know what I am going to say:

—And the Hebraic, of course.

—Now, just a minute.

—You yourself introduced the Nazarene, the Galilean, on his knees at Roman Pilate's pillar, you remember.

—I introduced the Christ. Precisely as Rembrandt depicts Him. Eyes heavenward, all His Body heavenbound, nothing Jewish about Him! Cankerous Jewishness is wholly canceled obliterated purged expunged in the new dispensation, whatever was of value in it has been elevated by the Christ, by the silvery skin of the Christ, as you yourself said—and we are left with the scabs!

I knew it was coming. All the way from Paraguay on the ricochet. Or on the fast train in reverse from Vienna and Berlin. I quicken my pace. Langbehn scurries alongside. If only I can get to the entrance in time. They are rising in me now. Not howling yet but rising clambering in me storming me.

—Infiltrating all our institutions, botching the mortar, bitching the synthesis. Look at our universities! As soon as my book is published I'm going to nullify my doctorate, I'll send it back to them shredded. And this very Institute! Look around you: professors and jews! Why do you think they've been ignoring you, keeping you locked up in solitary, condemning you forever to the wretched fallen state you are in? They know an implacable enemy of international Jewry when they see one! Wait! Stop!

I'm on the run. My sciatical legs unsteady my back stiff my head hammering my eyes watering not seeing but on the run. Langbehn is well named. He catches up. I reach the door just ahead of him but he sticks to me like mortar like mucilage like pageproofs.

—I'll liberate you, I'll get you out of here, I swear I will! If it's the last thing I do, I'll save you from them! From the Zionist ignominy!

I am behind the long mahogany table that stands at the rear of the reception area near the stairway. The flowers are artificial, there is no water in the vase when it topples. He pleads with me:

—You are my prince and my king! But you are a schoolboy, too, one who has fled the fold and fumbled and fallen!

I can hear myself screaming. The sound frightens me and so I scream. His arms reach out to me across the table. In one agile motion, showing strength I did not know I possess, I grasp the lip of the monstrous mahogany table and upset it on him with a crash that does not stop reverberating until I am up the stairs down the hall behind my door and braced against it panting.

Safe!

December 20: Recently the patient has taken several walks with one of his former pupils.—Essentially no impact on his illness.

First of April of the Year Two, A.N.

2240

Coldest spring on record, snow and ice everywhere. Where is my ivy? Where is my fennel stalk and vine? Nature refuses to cooperate with the new dispensation. Can't count on her if she can't count. She's playing me for a fool. Getting used to living in time again is harder than I thought it would be. Losegain. Gainlose. Thank goodness for these rags and scraps of paper: a trick I learned from the swallows and packrats and fieldmice. Snug in my nest. But, oh! how cold marble is, oh! how bone hard, harder than the sidewalks of Venezia, harder than the pavements of Torino, harder than the stone benches out back, harder than the altarstone on which I lay as a baby boy near the man sacrificing his kids.

January 1, 1890: Recently the patient has been collecting things, altogether worthless things for the most part, slips of paper, rags, etc. Always bows most courteously to the doctors. Weight 147 lbs.

21 April of the Year Two, A.N.

1135 Hours

Köselitz! Maestro Pietro! Enrico Sassone! Peter the musical cuddlebear comes to visit! My guest! I cosset and kiss him, embrace him and clasp his hands in mine, how long has it been? Two years by any reckoning. No, not a bear, this Köselitz, but a lion: *The Lion of Venice*. Tell me, what has become of your grand opera—and the future of German music? Danzig? Splendid! There will be dancing in Danzig! Schopenhauer's birthplace, you know: his morose spirit hovers

137

there still. Disperse it! There will be Poles in the audience—that bodes well! Poles apart from the Germans! Poles have the most refined ears, absolute antidonkey, the right 5.9 cm., the left 5.7 approx. par excellence. During our strolls through the gardens I cannot take my eyes off him, or my hands: the great mane of frizzy hair, the mustache and beard tinged now with gray. Have I done that to him? I made him read too many proofs, gave too much meaning too much finitude to his existence. How restive he is, how jumpy, how he avoids my gaze! No guilt, no shame, Maestro Pietro! Lift up your heart and sing, Maestro Pietro! Something new! Just don't mention the name Rembrandt to me it makes me howl.

You were right, Simon Peter Sassone, you were the only one who knew how to respond: *Grand things must be happening to you! Your enthusiasm, your health . . . will no doubt rouse even the most vitiated human beings; yours is a contagious health; the epidemic of health you once wished for, the epidemic of your own health, is now inevitable.* My health? Constitutionally sound. Never mind the angles and specialties! The infernal machine is making me ill in my head above the right eye old war wound and here on my left the breastbone that riding accident from my cavalry days. The food? Fit for a prince! Wouldn't feed it to my footman.

—May I have another biscuit, please, Pietro? Thanks ever so!

With little bites and beatings I get on, cuddlebear, I get on. And you? How do you fill your time without my pestilential pageproofs to plague you? Tell me all about you, Maestro Pietro! My guest!

Mayday of the Year Two, A.N.
1055 Hours

—Yes, Herr Doktor Zieher, my hand scarcely trembles. Tranquil as the snowladen meadows of Canton Basel in February.

—Your visitors appear to be doing you good. Apart from that first incident. Regrettable.

Bow again. Agree with him. Bow. Hard to do when you are sitting. Courtesy curtsey above all things. Obsequiousness is health. Show him. Bow.

—Yes, yes, a world of good. Yet I think it is our conversations—yours and mine, together, I mean—that have helped me most of all. The therapy, I mean.

—Perhaps.

He beams. Easy. Don't overdo it. Not too thick he'll think you're balmy. Then you'll never get out. Nor will anyone get in to see you. Easy.

—Granted, I was a hopeless case to start with, and not much could be achieved.

Zieher tosses back his head and roars. Good. Good. Humor soothes the savage.

—Stop, Herr Professor! Before I have to record your full and unequivocal restoration to health!

—'Tis a consternation devoutly to be wished, Herr Doktor Zieher!

—I think we should encourage more visits, don't you, Nietzsche?

—I do, Herr Doktor Zieher.

—And maybe even an afternoon out on the town, what do you say?

Something rises in my throat. I almost recognize it. It is something between hope and animal fear. The world outside!

—Perhaps we shouldn't move too far too fast, Herr Doktor Zieher.

February 1: Speaks somewhat more coherently.—Somatically, no change. Weight 152 lbs.

24 May of the Year Two, A.N.
Konditorei Kraus, Jena
1547 Hours

Overbeck! Overbeck is spending his Fasnet holiday with me, three glorious days! I can hear the shrill pipes and rattling drums of Basel all the while we talk in the Konditorei over cakes (how many have I devoured already? must be careful not to make a pig of myself!) no coffee for me thank you coffee stimulates. I can practically see the whimsical floats the glowing candles the Chinese lanterns of colored paper. Overbeck's jaw like the comic masks of dwarfs freaks grotesques warty chins bulbous proboscises monstrosities prodigies giants and fiends. Fiends and friends, Franz and Fasnet! Easy. Talk to him.

—You remember the year we finally coaxed Burckhardt to the Faculty Fasnet Ball, Franz?

—Yes, of course! He was outrageous! What was his costume? I can't remember.

—Oh, Franz, how could you forget? He came as Borgia, resplendent in Papal white. He spent the entire evening bragging that he'd never made a mistake, don't you recall?

139

—Yes, and he kept pouring a potion into people's drinks: sug-arwater dyed a sickly peagreen.

—A dozen phials of it he had tucked away in his inside pock-ets. He had invaded a pharmacy and picked up their throwaway brown bottles, he filled them with his sugarwater—or so he said!—and brought them along in order to dispatch the entire company!

—He never came to another ball after that one, you know. You were the only one who could drive him to such lengths, Fritz.

—You're right, Franz. Some time after that, a year later I think it was, he invited me to his place for the annual blessing of the dai-mons.

—Blessing of the daimons?

—Yes, you remember, our daimonic devotional. We drank a couple of bottles of Rhône syrrah and carried a bottle with us out into the streets. Luckily, the nightwatch was nowhere to be seen. At the fitting moment . . .

— . . . the καῖρος . . .

— . . . yes, at the kairotic moment, when the spirits of the true faith gripped us by the scruff of the neck, we both shouted χαίρετε δαίμονες! at the top of our lungs. They might have heard us in Kiel or Berlin where our synchronized brothers were doing the same. Then Burckhardt poured out half the bottle into the gutter. Its liquid substance saturated the stones, its essence traveled by air and sur-face to heaven and hell! Two hundred years earlier they would have burned us for warlocks! Fortunately, no one recognized us, the pass-ersby chortled behind their hands *tsk tsk for shame* and we passed on into the glorious gloom of night. Next day I had a kairotic khairetic daimonic headache, simply splitting, I can tell you!

Franz cannot control himself, he laughs freely. How beautiful he is.

—Oh, Franz, how I wish I were back there with all of you! Will it be possible some day, do you think? Without salary, I'd be glad to do it, I owe Basel so much anyway because of the pension. How loyal she has been, more loyal to me than I ever was to her! Some day? Will it ever be possible?

The smile vanishes, the pain returns. He hesitates an instant too long. He believes that I will never be well again. The scabrous burning the stiffness. He speaks slowly now, falteringly.

—But all the intervening years. . . . Your work. . . . What about your writing?

—Of course, I'll go back to it, I promise, once my health is fully restored. My Theognis dissertation has to be updated, so much has been published in the meantime.

—Theognis? Yes. Yes, of course.

Again he pauses too long, toys with his coffee cup. Change the subject. I ask him whether he and Ida are still out of the church. He nods. A faint smile plays across his lips. Good. There. That's better. How proud of him I am! The only living Christians, Franz and Ida, and the two of them driven out of the church! It is too delicious a historical irony; no, it is the strictest historical logic. Always that way. The others never forgave him for his modest tract, and he never forgave them for being what they were.

How proud of him I am! How can I tell him without embarrassing us both to death? Always the same. Always I bubble over and babble on and make a mess and drive them away. Rohde. Overbeck. Always that way. Desperation.

To Franz Overbeck in Basel

Genova, March 22, 1883

My dear friend, I feel as though it has been ages since you wrote. Yet perhaps I deceive myself: the days are so long, I no longer know what I am supposed to do with them. All my "interests" have vanished. In the deepest part of me an immovable, black melancholy. Otherwise, weariness. Mostly in bed. Also it's the most rational thing to do for my health. I've lost a great deal of weight; people are amazed. Now I've found a good trattoria and will fatten myself up once more. However, the worst thing is this: I no longer grasp the reason *why* I should live even for another six months; everything is boring painful *dégoutant*. I am deprived, and I suffer too much. Furthermore, I've begun to grasp the imperfection, the mistakes and the genuine calamities of my entire *intellectual* past, and these are inconceivably vast. It is too late to make up for them; I won't be doing anything good anymore. Why do anything at all!—

Your friend,
FN.

His delicate fingers spin the blue and white porcelain cup in its saucer. I love the sound and the smell of coffee. Stimulant. I love his hands. Caffeine. I love Franz. Excites the central nervous system. He can see what is happening in the corners of my eyes, the impending deluge. He pretends not to notice. He steels his voice, speaks now in a commanding, businesslike way. He wants to protect me from myself. How beautiful he is.

141

—Köselitz and I are having some problems with your last manuscripts . . . I mean your most recent ones. May I ask you about them?

—But of course, Franz!

—*The Antichrist* seems to be complete. I made a copy of it last February. But in your letters you also wrote about *The Transvaluation of All Values,* projected in many volumes. We've found dozens of sketches for it, but no manuscript. Do you remember where it might be? In Nice, perhaps? Is *The Antichrist* part of it? Or *all* of it?

—Whatever you say: I'll follow your advice. What do you think would be best?

He wants decisions. I cannot give them to him. He is disappointed in me, I can see it in his face. His honest face! Frank Franz! I must try to do better lest I lose him too. He continues, slowly, deliberately, infinitely patiently:

—Köselitz and I have been wondering too about *Ecce Homo, Twilight,* and the new Wagner book. We're worried especially about the last one. It doesn't seem an opportune time to offend the Wagnerites—you know the sort of people they are. And the censors may well intervene on behalf of both church and state. What should we do?

Decisions. Decisiveness. Determination. Firmness. Amendment. Resoluteness. Resolve. Verdict. Sentence. Execution.

—It really would be best if we had them all shot.

How bleak he looks. I have miscalculated. He is chagrined. They will never take me back now. I reach across the crumbscattered table and take up both his hands in mine. The wet begins to fill and overflow my eyes. I cannot speak. He speaks.

—Perhaps we should be heading back, Fritz. They'll be expecting us.

—Franz, I'm sorry. I'm so sorry. I'm doing my very best.

—I know you are, you're doing amazingly well. Really, we're all proud of you.

No Franz no, not over the top please.

—Everything will be all right, you'll see, Fritz.

—When, Franz?

—I'll speak with Professor Binswanger and Dr. Zieher when we get back.

—When, Franz?

—This very afternoon, I promise.

When, Franz?

March 1: 147 lbs.

20 June of the Year Two, A.N.
Restaurant "The Star," Jena
1331 Hours

Opus 31 Ludwig van Beethoven piano sonata pianissimo, tutti decrescendo, because Mama wants it that way, because we don't want to disturb the guzzlers and masticators, all these people in the dining room: we don't want to spoil their lunch now do we? We certainly do not. Beethoven as bromide. Bromios as sedative. Avoid all stimulants. My fingertips trip lightly over the keys. Trip and occasionally stumble. Stiffening. Something like arthritis. Agave smiles.

—Do you remember when I gave you your first lessons, darling Fritz?

—That was Papi.

—No, dear, God rest his soul. Your Father had passed away by that time.

To Malwida von Meysenbug in Rome

Naumburg, January 2, 1875

Dear and highly esteemed Friend,

If, according to Schopenhauer, the will is inherited from the Father, the intellect from the Mother, then it seems to me that music, as an expression of the will, is also a legacy of the Father. Examine your own experience: in the circle of my own, the assertion is true. As ever, with hearty wishes to you and yours,

Friedrich Nietzsche

—I'll try to remember better, Mama.

—It doesn't matter, my sweet. Just go on playing. Quietly.

—May we go to the bakery after this, Mama? I didn't get my rolls this morning. One carrowayseed one sesame seed one onion one poppyseed one baconbits one pretzel one salzstange, please?

—But sweet, we've just eaten.

—And then to the Delicatessen? 250 gr. dried dates 200 gr. desiccated figs 150 gr. walnuts 125 gr. hazelnuts forget the Brazilnuts too close for comfort.

—Yes, of course, some lovely nuts.

—And will you read to me again when we get back?

—Yes, we shall read, and I'll stroke your forehead softly upwards to the hairline, just the way you like it.

—Don't brush anything into the orifice if you can help it, Mama. Constant danger of infection.

March 24: Released on probation.

24 June of the Year Two, A.N.
3 Shingle Mill Road
2159 Hours

—Don't forget my sugarwater Mama just in case I waken during the night. Please don't put any dye in it.

—Here it is, darling, on the night table. No dye in it? Of course not, you silly Fritzchen!

She bends over the bed, kisses my forehead. Her bloodless lips are dry and cool.

—Another chapter please Mama! Will Injun Joe hurt the boys Mama?

—We'll find out tomorrow. I'll read to you tomorrow and every day.

—No Mama now! Another chapter!

—Be good, my boy. Professor Binswanger says you are to obey me and if you don't I must return to Naumburg and you must go back to him. And to Dr. Zieher.

—Let us read some more tomorrow Mama. I have to get my rest. Mama can we stay in our new house forever?

—Yes, forever.

—Have you got a night light for me?

—Professor Binswanger says we'll have to do without a night light from now on. And no matches.

—Have you padlocked the doors and windows?

—Yes. All secure. No one can get in.

—But can we get out in a hurry if we have to if there's an emergency?

—There won't be any emergencies, Fritz darling. Rest easy, boy.

—May I kiss your hand good night Mama? Thank you Mama. I adore you my sweet my good my dear Mama. Our dear Lord *dare* not do you any harm!

Main Listing No. 814   Year 1889 No. 8
Name: N i e t z s c h e, Friedr.
Occupation: Professor, retired

Date of Birth: October 15, 1844
Place of Birth: Röcken, near Lützen
Address: Most recent address, Turin
Date of Admittance: January 18, 1889
Date and Type of Release: March 24, 1890 (probation)
Diagnosis: Paralysis progressiva.

13 August of the Year Two, A.N.
Jena Railway Station
0713 Hours

Mama peers out the open window of our train compartment. Keeping an eye out for the police. It is all my fault. I never should have gone swimming. Sometimes it is hard to know what the law will countenance.

—Sit down, Fritz. Be still.

—Yes Mama. Sorry Mama. My fault Mama.

—Be still!

But it was not my fault. It was his fault, the attendant's fault, the engineer's fault. He chose that day of all days to flush out the heating unit, he closed down the pool just because he knew we were coming, he knew that that was our regular day. He closed down the pool. And so I had to wait until yesterday. All through the night I was crying for water to give myself to crying for the water and by morning I was parched desiccated as a fig secco secco and you fussing about which coat I should wear Mama I swear Mama what ever were you thinking of?

And after I slipped away you looked for me in the baths at the Eye Hospital where you did not see me and you looked for me back home on Shingle Mill Road and you searched in Paradise where we eat so delectably ambrosia and nectar we used to eat sunbeams in The Star and you looked in at the barber's then back home again nowhere nowhere to find your forlorn Fritz. To the police you were about to turn (a mistake Mama Fino made it too nearly cost me a lifetime in a manicomio) when sauntering down College Street my favorite street we met at last. You and Me and the Man in Green. He was a very nice man. He showed me the most profound deference and respect. He lent assistance. He helped me with my bootlaces. He asked me for my name and address, and I was ready for him this time:

—I am Professor Nietzsche from Basel a Swiss Pole

145

RESTORATIONS

To Malwida von Meysenbug in Rome

> *Nice, Thursday, March 26, 1885*

Honored Friend,

It is the humor of my situation that people constantly confuse me with—the erstwhile Basel Professor Herr Dr. Friedrich Nietzsche. May the devil fetch him! What do I care about that fellow?!—

> Your
> N.

I was born not far from Lützen in Röcken my Father was the tutor at the court of Altenburg with its marvelous walnut trees until he became pastor in Röcken where I was born as you see me now Professor Nietzsche. Haven't we met somewhere before Officer? Have you ever been to Torino? Do you quake horses?

    in a pond i was

    because the pool was closed

    to give myself up to the water to feel my body whole again restored replenished all the fragments bound annealed embraced coherent in buoyant restitution all the wounds rents lacerations laved by tears soothed by the costliest unguents the most fragrant salves the most oleaginous balms the most alleviative anodynes

    and because i knew youd never forgive me mama if i got my clothes wet.

PART THREE

THE WAYS OF THE MOTHER
From Jena to Naumburg
13 May 1890 to 20 April 1897

Chronology

1890 May 13: Franziska and her son flee Jena for Naumburg—home at last! December 16: Widow Elisabeth Förster-Nietzsche arrives from Paraguay.

1891 Professor Binswanger confirms that the patient is "incurable." January 23: The premier of Heinrich Köselitz's (Peter Gast's) comic opera, *The Lion of Venice,* in Danzig. Moderate success. Otherwise, Köselitz prepares a new edition of Nietzsche's collected works for C. G. Naumann of Leipzig. Spring: Elisabeth prevents the publication of *Thus Spoke Zarathustra* Part IV, which is already in print: she objects to "The Ass Festival."

1892 February 4-6: Köselitz visits Nietzsche. April Fool's: A visit to Professor Binswanger in Jena. The patient says nothing. June 2: Elisabeth departs for Paraguay in a last-ditch effort to salvage "Nueva Germania." Up to now she has had nothing to do with the patient. October: the fits of rage begin again. Köselitz fears for Franziska's safety.

1893 Nietzsche's back begins to stiffen in paralysis; he is able to walk only for an hour; otherwise the housemaid, Alwine, transports him in his wheelchair. Early September: Elisabeth liquidates her assets in Paraguay and returns to Germany in search of a new career. December: Elisabeth plans a "Nietzsche Archive," which she will direct.

1894 Waxing agitation of the patient. Bathing at the public pool is now impossible. Spring: Köselitz, the only human being who can read Nietzsche's handwriting, is fired by Elisabeth. October 15: Paul Deussen, a friend since Pforta days, pays the patient a birthday visit.

1895 Late February: a bout of pneumonia; increasing paralysis, including now the patient's jaw; eating becomes exceedingly difficult. Spring: the first royalties are paid out to Franziska, who is her son's literary executor. Not until December can Elisabeth convince her mother to surrender all the rights to her, Elisabeth. September 24: Overbeck visits Nietzsche for the last time. The patient says nothing. Early December: Professor Binswanger is satisfied.

1896 Elisabeth cannot find editors who produce books fast enough. August: With financial support from Meta von Salis, Elisabeth moves the Archive to new quarters in Weimar.

1897 Waxing paralysis. January 11: Erwin Rohde's death. April 20: Franziska, exhausted by the care she has expended on her son and weakened by influenza, dies in Naumburg.

No one ever understood a little boy better than his Mother. My life isn't easy but from the bottom of my heart I thank our Lord God that my son has been restored to the bosom of his Mother so that I can now care for this child of my heart open your mouth please please open you must eat Herzensfritz. I who never even knew what the word *nerves* meant when Rosalie used it for the first time and I was afraid to ask your Father he would have taken it as a criticism of his sister and hence of himself he was so sensitive. So I asked my mother the next time I was home as soon as the guests were gone what nerves were and she said *I'm not sure myself I think it's a general weakness of some kind, a universal lability.* So sensitive. The time I asked him why his mother always had to have the first and last say even in matters where I knew best no one knows a husband better than a wife and he took his food to his study and didn't come out again till the next noon. Open up nice and wide there now ah ah good. That was the last time I tried to match swords with Erdmuthe and I never ever dared speak up to Rosalie with her nerves and her razor tongue. She was bright no doubt of that she read the newspaper you take after her although there's a lot of Papa in you. Your Grandfather Oehler. How ashamed he would be of the two of us if he could see us now. *Illness is moral decrepitude* he would say and *If there's a will there's a way* and he always found a way. Don't just swallow. Chew Fritz of my heart.

Oh, you *are* an unsightly mess look at you your bib your frock your arms your mustache! Nothing for it but a bath, my darling Fritz. I promise I'll rub you down hard with the bathtowel afterwards, I'll briskly buff and chafe, something you've always simply adored as long as I can remember which is certainly longer than you can remember yourself. No one can remember longer than a Mother. Scrubbing between your toes that day you laughed so hard it tickled you so your head slipped back into the water you came up spluttering what a fright you give your poor Mother! Slipping off with the other boys to swim at the trout pond behind my back you thought I never knew I knew. Everything. Water was always the cause of trouble between us, though thank the Lord Jesus for it we'd never get this gruel out of your hair without it would we my sweet? Always the cause of trouble. Water was the reason we had to leave Frau

Schrönn's place at Jena Shingle Mill Road. How beautiful it was two big rooms facing sunward with the balcony all geraniums the elms in back you wouldn't have thought you were anywhere near a city it was like at home in Pobles where I was a little girl but without the chickens and pigs. I could have stayed in Jena forever and so could you you loved it so. I remember how you laughed the day we slipped away forever if you had only known. Like fugitives we had to slink off at six in the morning. It went like clockwork thanks to Pelzers and their friends what would I have done by the grace of God without them?

You and your bath, O rumpled Fritzchen, that will be the story of our life together you know. First the sea of angels in my belly it's as though you never really ever came out I'm sorry I didn't mean that. Lift your leg, love, up up goes the drawbridge scrubascrub goes the tugboat sponge. That was the day after the policeman brought you back from the duckpond how mortified your poor Mother was but it wasn't your fault I never should have run upstairs to get your overcoat. He was very kind although I'm sure he had to report it he would have gotten into trouble if he hadn't. That's how Ziehen and Binswanger found out my blood boils my teeth rattle my bones quake every time I think of them. They didn't lift a finger to help you for weeks and months to get you back to yourself until that Doctor Langbehn came don't remind me of him either I'll get too upset and told them if they couldn't do anything for you he certainly could and would. That put the fear of almighty God into them I can tell you even if he turned out to be as mad as I'm sorry I didn't mean that.

Ziehen. Binswanger's bossy assistant. More pushy than pully if you ask me. Sitting me down in his office lecturing at me like I was simpleminded or something lording it over me like the peasant I suppose I am well I've had enough of that in my lifetime Fritz of my heart I can tell you I've had enough. Ziehen looking down his bulbous disapproving nose at me saying *You realize Frau Pastor that the Institute cannot allow this sort of thing to happen with a patient under our charge even if he is ambulant on probation we all know you are doing your best but it has become clear he's too much for you to handle* imagine who can handle a boy better than his Mother? I was fuming. If Father were alive he'd have boxed his ears for him preacher and saint though he was. Mother too no one to fool with. Sometimes I think your sister Lisbeth is just like Mama. Ziehen. Papa would have pulled his hairy ears for him. *I'm afraid it has caused the most dreadful uproar a scandal really not his fault of course that's the whole point Frau Pastor nor yours either it takes special training Frau Pastor.* Bah! Papa would have remedied it per-

fectly well with his watercure. Not warm and sudsy like this my
sweet baby up up that other drawbridge leg sweet scrubascrub, no,
coldshock buckets of icewater I swear over your head and oh the
ache! O Papa! *Most unpleasant for the staff doctors I must say Frau
Pastor.* You'd think people had never seen a naked man before of
course they were right we can't have that sort of thing going on in
broad daylight with women and children everywhere, of course the
children wouldn't have minded they would have followed suit. O
Fritz, you and your bath, spread wide now my flower, what shall we
ever do with you?

•

no mama it wasnt because the water embraced me as no one ever
did not you not aunt auguste not auntie rieke and certainly not aunt
rosalie or grandma erdmuthe not even papi it was because in the
water you dont have to see to see theres nothing there to see you
see. no ball or stick to hit you on the head the boys laughing mocking raucous jeering only the slivers of sunlight and splashings in
your stoppedup ears when you blow out through your mouth and
the regular rise and plunge of the arms like a windmill left arm up
face free sucking breath head down right arm up and blow through
your mouth because the water holds nothing against you mama but
your own displaced weight nothing against you but its liquid stroking hands. it negotiates with you as you negotiate it. at pforta it was
my best no my only sport and because of something else mama

To a Friend [Draft]

Naumburg, early July, 1864

I begin my day at 8:30 in the evening. I go swimming, enjoying
the stream's darkness and the good cheer of my thoughts. I
offer my breast to the tide in friendship, I offer my brow to the
wind and my heart to the dusk. I return full of rare images,
which I model and mold in a contented dream. . . .

Satan! Ink, pen—can I not write without soiling, the words'
dreadful moiling, and I, poor wretch, always here toiling?

You know my way, my mania for cleanliness in this
particular point. O God! And precisely in this particular point
everything disperses once again, like my thoughts, which
likewise have no idea what they . . . you . . .

something important which is that in the water you are on your own
no one else no dullness of wit no obtuseness banality envy rancor

meanness of spirit animus chiding chafing for the water dissolves absolutely all ties bonds dependencies up up goes the drawbridge relationships obligations the only thing i could never forgive the water was that it could not transmogrify my lungs altogether into gills it almost did that summer i nearly drowned in the river saale and that eventually i would have to come up for oxygen sputtering gasping my mouth sucking air.

i watch you open your mouth in sympathetic magic the teeth yellow black silver and gold as you raise the giant spoon big as a shovel why dont you use a garden spade while youre at it mama and save time because you think what am i saying *think* if you open yours ill open mine *do ut des* always the same black dress shiny sable adorned with dull black lace black on black hows that for sheer chromatic joy faded washed bleached effaced expunged eradicated by piety good goody gooey gluey grueling gruel. open. shut. open. i slake no horses mama.

•

Your Father Fritz darling your Father and his homecures! He was worse than my own. Your Father and his mailorder "Nature's Apothecary" set and when it arrived COD we never had any peace. Yarrow in the soup mallow in the tea ribwort in the stew. He couldn't wait till someone got sick. With Rosalie in the house he never had long to wait. Belladonna for her nerves I mean Valerian. I never let him prescribe for me, though, however much it irritated him, Papa's watercure was always enough for me. He took offense I remember as though he were jealous of my own Father he was so sensitive how happy we were then. Now there is only Alwine. And Naumburg. Count your blessings. Two.

She's a dear, Alwine is, she danced such a joyful jig around you the day we arrived home you'd think you were *her* son. I hated Naumburg as much as you did you in your shadowy backbedroom for years you would wake up crying in the night. After your Father died. We moved to Naumburg only because your Grandma Erdmuthe had relatives and friends here I did my best to join in I hated it I have always hated Naumburg. And you grew up thinking I loved Naumburg thinking I was Naumburg and Naumburg was a mother to you and to me both. Yet I must say when I saw the house after all those weeks in Jena when I saw Alwine jumping up and down like a lunatic I'm sorry I didn't mean that on the sidewalk by the front door the lantern on the corner of the house still aglow in search of us it seemed like home to me then and it seemed so God be praised to you too Fritz of my heart your only real home ever. Welcome home my boy.

●

phantom lanternlight in the fog that april night it was late it must have been after midnight mama. my pillow still wet because i had been crying id never play with helmbrecht and ulrich again. they had come across the farmyard to play that evening but all we could do was cry we all cried. how old was i? five, five and a half? they were cut from a different cloth, rough homespun, i was oriental silk mama. still they cried and i cried the same and my pillow was soaked through it was cold against my cheek and i awoke after midnight i heard the noise outside and i thought it was father come back again on the prowl. i went to the window again but the fog was too thick i couldnt see if the tomb was still closed or whether he was up and about again. then i heard voices coming from the front of the house. i crept downstairs. in the courtyard men and drayhorses nags hags and carts. they were loading up our furniture: the diningroom table and chairs, the sofa, aunt rosalies upholstered readingchair, grandma erdmuthes rocker, aunt augustes sewingsettee, all bound round with cord, trussed up like a christmas turkey. and hanging from the wagons at front and rear, from the drivers perch and the lowered loading gate, the ghostly lanterns; they gave off something other than light it was an aura a halo of jackolanternlight, ignis fatuus will o' the wisp lighting the way to the mothers of my fate, a glow that disappeared for a second or two then reappeared in another spot who knew where it would lead next? to the gloom of naumburg. good-bye papi. papi good-bye. forever farewell papi until we meet again.

●

Evenings you would sit out on the veranda under the grapevine trellis you loved the sound of the wind rustling in the velvet leaves. You harbored your own thoughts there. *What on earth can he be thinking about?* I would ask myself. And mornings after breakfast we would begin our daily round of walks, the Burghers' Garden with the balloonman and the flowerclock and the geese, the beech wood with all the scolding squirrels remember your favorites the little oak tree crescents, and our dear Mr. Tittle fifty paces behind us in case you acted up you never did except the first day he came with us and you threw your breakfast roll onto the grass and said *if you dont let me go to Leipzig this minute ill kill myself* you thought you had lectures to give there you were muddled a bit lectures in chemistry you said or on your Greeks as knowers of human nature you said you certainly were a little confused but I knew it was because Mr. Tittle had come between us and had broken our little circle Baby and Mutti and so I asked him after that if he couldn't follow us fifty paces behind so you wouldn't see him and upset yourself. He didn't dare complain, dear soul, he had his apartment in our house rentfree plus the dinners Alwine cooked for him he loved walking anyway. Still it was worth it to me and to Professor Overbeck too when I wrote him about it and he said to make sure nothing else untoward happened it would bring on the police again and they would take you away from me again this time for good O child of my heart no need for that. No need at all because you were as good as gold except for the days you insisted you had to return to Turin *i have to get my things mama* you were worried about your papers and books *they arent packed away anybody could get into them and take terrible advantage of me make me a laughingstock make me a saint of their private sect* you said *id rather be a satyr* and I told you Professor Overbeck was such a reliable friend thank God every day of your life you have him I said, Overbeck will surely see to it and you said *no one can see to it besides me* but I knew if I could find some distraction some bauble any queer thing because everything you looked at you saw as though for the first time a brand new world freshbaked each and every day you would forget all about it and praise God so you did.

In the shadows of the oaks and beeches that lined the country road we would walk as the sun rose higher to noon. When we came to that sunny clearing you would laugh gleefully at your stubby shadow it was shrinking away yes to nothing. Then home in the nick of time the barber waiting at the door he would let you slurp the brush around and around in the cup the foam lathering up and let you paint your own face how funny you looked you certainly knew how to make your old Mother laugh! Those birthday letters for example

To Franziska Nietzsche in Naumburg [Draft]

Nice, January 29, 1888

I have given the Germans of our time works of prime importance precisely during the period of their intellectual decline. On account of these works posterity may well forgive that period for its having been. Have I received even a single word of profound thanks? the millionth part of the honor due me?

None of you have any faith in me—my mother as little as
my sister

How beautiful you were then so tanned from the sun putting on
weight every day bursting the seams of all your shirts and trousers I
remember that was when we could dress you no you dressed yourself all by yourself not in these white napped flannel baby snugglies
or frocks or whatever they call them I hate them on you but Lisbeth
says they are cheaper to have laundered she's right she's always
right about saving money so I let it go.

The afternoon siestas were the only thing that saved me
because nights at eleven I would sink into bed to sleep the sleep of
the dead and the just had it not been for those winks and nods after
lunch how could I have made it through the day? Before lunch and
after our nap and sometimes late evenings too after our last walk
together through the neighborhood you would play. As you still do
now my darling and how I bless the Giver of all Gifts that He has
kept your music alive for you. And such music! Always surprises,
not just your basic Beethoven Haydn Mozart, but the endless improvisations

To Franziska and Elisabeth Nietzsche in Gorenzen

Second Sunday of Advent
Pforta, 6 December 1863

Dear Mama and Lisbeth.

Our life is often for stretches at a time a poetic improvisation,
and one only has to have a bit of imagination in order to sense
it as such.

Fritz.

the themes and the infinite variations. Little Sophie Pinder would
leave the house in tears and all the Krugs who knew their music better than anyone they too astounded all of them by your playing so
sensitive so intelligent. We knew you couldn't be sick if you could
play like that. Those were my happiest my proudest moments just
like old times to watch the faces of the people listening to you rapt
to your music I swear it is that that keeps me alive keeps my faith
alive too God forgive me if it can't be more than that.

Our ham on butterbreads and our cocoa and our spins around
the block to watch the red of evening and the purple of night come
down and the little verses you would recite as we walked until a

passerby would upset you *do I have to shake his hand mama?* you would say and I would tell you no ignore him and then you would be your cheerful chipper self again just like a normal person. Evenings at home worried me most because I knew I would have to talk with you, have to make conversation, it would have been so much easier for Lisbeth but she was still in Paraguay poor Dr. Förster had just died of his heart attack I don't care what they say leaving the whole colony in her hands on her weak woman's shoulders poor darling though she'd always been the one in charge anyway. I was afraid of the talk with you just as I was afraid of your Father's talk God rest his soul when the other pastors came to visit not my own Papa he never came and if he had come he'd have made plain talk no frills no fancies no vast profundities that was what tore us apart my darling Fritz your schooling and all those years of study in the university the youngest professor in history how was your poor Mother supposed to cope with all that? I said to you one evening I remember it as clear as a bell *You should have someone around you who is well-educated like yourself, someone with your own interests, not the likes of me* and you replied I remember it like yesterday how could I forget *as we two live together my darling Mother there is simply no one who could ever take your place* you always knew how to make your Mother glow with pride and happiness and if you ever balked all I had to do was turn away from you without speaking a word the silent treatment always worked best

To Franz Overbeck in Munich

Sils-Maria, Oberengadin. Sunday, August 18, 1884

Dear old Friend,

It does me good that no letters from Naumburg have come. Yet you will understand how shattered and sick I am in this regard when I tell you that I was seriously ill for two days after each letter I wrote to my mother this summer.

N.

or quietly close the parlor door without saying a word shutting you out or maybe saying *Very well you may do as you like as far as I'm concerned Fritz* and it wouldn't be two minutes you'd be kissing my hands both the backs and the palms as you did when you were a boy at cathedral school and even later at Schulpforta pleading *what was it you wanted me to do dear Mother i shall do exactly as you say Mother knows best* docile as the lamb you always were at heart O child of my heart my Herzensfritz.

Such a good boy! I remember the day you came ambling home from school through the pouring rain. Primary school it was though I'd already taught you how to read and write and your music your piano was coming along famously you must have been bored to tears it was only a village school but you never complained. Such a good boy! You carried it to extremes. The rain was pouring down in buckets just at the time school let out. Your aunts and your grandmother and I were all crowding the front door looking down the street to see if you'd be dashing through it and catching your death or if you'd have enough sense to wait it out at school. One by one the children came storming sloshing by, Wilhelm, Gustav, all of them on the run, already drenched.

—Where's Fritz? we called, but they didn't stop to answer, they probably didn't even hear us.

At long last we caught sight of you. Walking at not exactly a slow pace but with steady, deliberate footfall, utterly unhurried, with your slateboard over your head and your white handkerchief spread over the slateboard as though to fend off the driving rain.

—Run! Run, you silly boy!

You heard us but marched steadily on through the storm. By the time you reached our door you were soaked to the skin, drenched to the bone, how I scolded you your Aunt Rosalie and your Grandmother chiming in, your Aunt Auguste fussing over you trying to get you out of those sopping clothes. And when we asked you whatever had gotten into your head you issued your proclamation:

—But, Mama, the school ordinances stipulate that boys should not jump and run when leaving school but go home quietly in a manner befitting a young gentleman.

Oh, how we laughed! And we had sent you to the public school so you could be with children from the lower stations, we thought they would bend you a bit and relax your rigor. How we laughed!

•

this is the way we go to school go to school go to school, this is the way we go to school early in the god bless our king and our lord though not necessarily in that order. he has my name my king friedrich wilhelm. the fourth. my birthday is a holiday. the fifteenth. come dear schoolmates let us play together a game that befits our station.

—Hey! Here comes the Pastor Widow's kid! Give us our daily dose of Bible, come on, let's hear it!

—Amen amen I say unto you, how about a game of stick n' ball? Roll-a-hoop? How about hide n' seek? Lazarus Come Fourth? Simon Peter Sez?

—Hey, fellows, Goldilocks here wants to play a game with us. What do you say? Everybody fold your hands! Down on your knees! Let us play!

—Suffer the little children . . .

—Oh, yeah? We'll see who's to suffer! Cross that line, go ahead, I dare you! Knock this chip off my shoulder, I dare you! Step into my circle, said the spider to the fly!

—Unless ye become as little children . . .

—Come on, baby hazel eyes! baby crosseyes! baby cockeyes! Come on, churchmouse, we dare you!

—Yea, though I walk through the valley of death, I fear not. At least no more than befits a young gentleman.

—You're quaking like a leaf!

—I quake no horses, in the name of my Father, his Son, and the Hokey Ghosts.

—You're shitting your pastoral pants! Cross that line, flick that chip, lilyliver!

—O ye of little faith. I have not seen such bullies in all Saxony and Thuringia. And, discretion being the better part of valor . . .

—Ducklingdivine! Graveyardrat! We'll see who's to suffer!

•

Schulpforta. Those heavenly gates. Pforta. How you loved passing through those gates. And yet the day Maestro Köselitz and I took you back to your alma mater such fond memories you had you loved your school no matter how strict they were you began to moan it was eerie as we spun past the poplars and the gateposts. The clean fresh spankingwhite buildings the magnificent spire of the chapel pointing to heaven how you loved it there as a boy! You were to meet the new rector he invited you after all you were one of their most accomplished pupils but you wouldn't have any of it. What a fuss you made, you naughty Fritz, you wouldn't set foot on the place and we had to turn right around and head back home, it was hours before you finally settled down whatever got into you? Whatever it was, home's best, that's for certain, home's best for Fritzchen.

Before we went to bed nights we would read aloud not that you ever paid much attention to what I was reading except for one or two things of your own then you would perk up and follow every word as it crossed my lips. Generally it was the gentle mumble murmur meander the mutter of my voice I could have rattled off a greengrocer's list except for those poems of yours high mountains you liked especially your other dancing song, though I feared the look on your face the grimace of pain or joy no one could have said. Yet the language itself was so beautiful I began to hear it as emptily as you did merely for the nice noises all the words made, the singsong without sense the boom of thunder without enlightening birds brooks seas a lullaby sleep baby sleep your father herds the sheep. Some of them I will never forget, I read them so many times, slips of phrases over and over again, lovely noises: *Golden boat in the seas of night, the girl listening with her toes. When you are near me I am afraid, when you are far I love you.* You who? Always calling. Yoo hoo. Who's you? Oh, yes, Life. *Swirling swooping owls and bats, their tiny teeth. "Are you parched? I could give you something, but you wouldn't want to drink it."* The whip. I never liked that business. You were just teasing I know trying to get some of your own back but I never liked it much, especially not a whip with lilacs and ribbons. *Noise slays thoughts. Ah, this crazy old woman Wisdom!* Why is she always a woman? Either a woman or a snake? Your Father would have explained it but it's beyond me. *There is a massive ancient bell, a monstrous bell tolling in the night. One! Twelve! For I love you O Eternity. Never yet have I seen the woman. Children. For I love you O Eternity. The nuptial ring of rings, ringing the ring of return. To dance the astral dance. For the earth is the table of the gods, a table trembling with new creatorwords and with a noise of dice cast by the gods. The redemptive grain of salt. It is my alpha and omega that all heavy things grow light, all bodies ballerinas, all spirits birds: and surely that is my alpha and omega. Flying with my own wings in my own heaven. Sing! Speak no more! For I love you O Eternity!* It was just like reading the Bible Sundays in front of Papa so stern in his frockcoat when I was girl the same beautiful noises weightless on my lips. Shapes of breath. Nothing at all. I was present to them, so close, it was easy to be close to the words. And how proud I was of your Bible study you'd been working hard all that last summer and autumn countless notes and jottings on your most beloved verses, Professor Overbeck told me you recognized almost every passage, you knew it better than he did and he a theologist and I a pastor's daughter, you really were a pastor's son, bless the Lord God. One day you were showing Little Sophie Pinder the family albums and you pointed to cousin Anton and I told you he had died the year before of pneumonia and you said as quick as a flash

I could scarcely believe my ears *blessed are they who die in the name of the lord* and they call you an atheist well they can't fool your poor old Mother.

•

reading yes reading mama when i was a boy at grandpa oehlers in pobles or at home in röcken except that your voice is all crinkly now and it seemed to me every now and again mama you didnt know what you were reading you didnt think about it much mama the rhetors golden ring around your neck connecting you to heaven. the bland reading of all my joy my suffering your apathy mama maybe it is the only thing that will save us both now.

my legs. cut shorter every day as the scythe swings round. our walks a thing of the past. herr tittlemouse lord jotntittle tiptoing thirty meters behind ducking and dodging if i should glance nonchalant over my left shoulder catch him whistling to the treetops shading his gaze with his hand studying the toes of his shoes spinning in circles *now where did I put that? nobody here but us geese honkhonk peek-abooiseeyou hideandgoseek allaroundmybaseis readyornotherei* as if i had never noticed him. in case i acted up. a lot of good he would have done mama. shall we run maestro pietro? come on lets run be my guest. run you slowpoke come on lets run i never felt better never hippetyhopped better the spring in my step is primavera come on lets run.

my fingers. are they really mine? stiffer every day the pain spilling over from the top of my spine flowing out into my arms my hands my fingers. even the playing is excruciating now. hard to hear the music when the fingers scream so shrilly. out on the veranda under the grapes his grapes my gods grapes i listen to what my fingers whisper when they arent screeching you have to lend an ear mine is the shortest approx.

my eyes. for reading never better if they dont leak out through the aperture. imagine if he hadnt given it to me the hollow boom the hammer it would deafen me it would drive me mad. every time i laugh or nod my head it cracks and booms i am learning to keep very still very still indeed deathly still.

my ears. approx. par excellence. i liked your german title better, maestro pietro, the lion of venice it suited your leonine nature your mane your vast yawn. yes yes i know il matrimonio segreto sounds more like mozart weddings draw crowds like accidents not to mention secrets. at least they didnt boo you out of the theater in danzig you can count on the poles to be upright.

my cheeks. the day you tried to take me back to pfortas dreary dungeons shame on you maestro pietro. pforta. bolted portals. more a prison than a school more a monastery (cistercian) than an upstanding prison. more like the army than anything else. a school-state. poets banned in the classical tradition. excess of fathers there. what did the rector announce the day we all arrived?

—A second paternal home. Spirit of discipline. Obedience to the law and to the will of one's superiors. Rigor and punctual fulfillment of obligations. Self-control. Serious work. Invigorating initiatives in matters of one's own choice, purely out of love for the thing itself. Thoroughness and methodicalness in one's studies. Regularity in the apportioning of one's time. Unfailing tact. Self-assured firmness in all dealings with one's peers. Discipline and rearing.

regular apportioning of time. 4:00 a.m. dormitory unlocked 5:00 a.m. warning bell the dormitory inspector:

—Get up! Get up! See to it you're mustered out on time—otherwise it will be delightful little castigations for all you featherbed-lovers!

off to the washroom cold water only fight for a place among the rude boys. 5:25 a.m. first bell for prayer 5:30 a.m. second bell to the chapel where the inspectors enforce absolute silence. teacher marches in with famulus, inspectors report absences laggards rascals. then the organ sounds. that horrible instant that welling up of fright each day every day. i was afraid it would be he. with outstretched arms flowing white linen cerements of the gaping grave the almost empty church in the fog of early morning *come in Londra* she said. i awaken i come out of it i shake it off with the morning hymn the our father my father the concluding psalm. 5:45 a.m. to our rooms where pitchers of warm milk and plates of rolls await us. 6:00 a.m. bell for classes, lessons and study halls alternating till noon. 12:00 noon books back to my room napkin down to the dining hall where the inspectors enforce absolute silence teachers march in absences laggards rascals reported inspector prays on behalf of all the boys and teachers:

—Lord God, Heavenly Father, bless us all and these Thy gifts

To Franziska Nietzsche in Naumburg

Pforta, October 3, 1859

Dear Mama!

In a human being's life there are moments
When we forget that we dwell

On a solitary point in measureless space!
Be of good cheer! Your Fr WN.
Send me a
teaspoon
Discs of sealing-wax
a knife
The Messias
cocoa
laundry
matches
Rosen's steeltip pens
my ice-skates

which we are about to receive from Thy tender bounty through Jesus
Christ our Lord, Amen.

✝

Gloria tibi trinitas
Aequalis una deitas
Et ante omne saeculum
Et nunc et in perpetuum!

daily menu fixed no variation week after week except for the vegetables in season plentiful cheap boiled spoiled. thanksgiving hymn.
some filched bread and the stained napkin returned to my room,
down to the mailroom hoping against hope for a letter or a package,
out to the schoolyard, fruit from the fruitlady her very best muscats
for me. bowls balls walks. 1:15 p.m. bell for classes, five minutes
grace. lessons till 3:50 p.m., rolls and butter with plum jam lard fruit.
study hall greek latin mathematics, 5:00 p.m. five minutes pause,
study halls till 7:00 p.m. evening meal: repeat midday meal. schoolyard till 8:30 p.m. evensong. stertorous groans of the organ. 9:00
p.m. to bed. anacreon. snuff with deussen. dreams: study hall day,
sunday, chorus, swimming days, mama in naumburg one hour away
by foot the hour of eternity the hour of infinite distance. secrets:
under my mattress away from the probing inspectors eye my poems
my motets my christmas oratorium. sonatas for four hands, *four
hands,* ariadne!
      the day you tried to take me back there. it was a punishment.
mama never forgave me for the larks i pulled on the professors there,
my reports as weekly inspector of buildings and equipment: *In the
main auditorium the lights have grown so dim that pupils are being
tempted to let their own lamps burn bright* and *In one of the class-*

rooms the benches were recently painted; since then the pupils
have exhibited an unprecedented proclivity to stick to their seats
and you wrote me mama about tact and vanity and abominable pre-
sumptuousness and discretion and my inner my better voice and all
i could do was get straight about these things myself i certainly never
breathed a word of it to you *Nothing more topsyturvy than remorse
over things past, take it as it is, draw lessons but live on unperturbed,
regard oneself as a phenomenon whose particular traits constitute a
whole. Be solicitous of others at most be regretful of them, never let
them irritate you, don't become enthusiastic over anyone, they are
all there for us, for ourselves, to serve our ends. Whoever understands best how to dominate will also understand human nature
best. Every deed done under necessity is justified; every deed that is
useful is necessary. Every deed that unnecessarily causes an other
trouble is immoral. We ourselves become excessively dependent on
public opinion the moment we experience remorse and doubt ourselves. When an immoral action is necessary, it is moral for us.* that
was macchiavelli for herr buddensieg. unfortunately i could not
obey my own code mama i was never any good at morality i was
too selfish to become a real egoist.

the day you tried to take me back there. shame on you maestro
you wanted to have me committed be my guest you tried to send me
to the rectors office dont you know what they do to little boys in
there they arrange a matrimonio segreto for your posterior analytica
take it like a man like an alumnus made good made god mad god
he will make me feel shame i wont go dont try to make me im not
going i tell you. ill fail all my examinations aeschylus under platos
pillow aristophanes designing his tragic robes hebrew herbrew ale-
phlisbeth i cant face it cant bear the opprobrium i tell you. so you
and mama finally relented and we drove out the portal past the gateposts past the sentinel poplars the puffclouds jouncing homeward.
ecco! home! safe!

•

Pinder and Krug, dear Wilhelm and dour Gustav: they stayed at
home while you went away, but what wonderful friends they were
to you all the years you were at Pforta. The letters you wrote back
and forth, the poems dramas essays sonatas! The other boys were up
to their silly pranks, smoking cigars in lofts, swilling beer out in the
wood shed, while you three devoted yourselves to spiritual production. *Germania* you called yourselves, just like Lieschen later in Paraguay: each boy promised to send the other two an artwork a

month, twelve works through the year; the other two would be critics and judges for their soulmate, each of you exposed to the keen critical knives of the others.

To Wilhelm Pinder in Naumburg

Pforta, mid-February, 1859

Dear Wilhelm!

—I'm sending you today my "May Song," just as I promised. I wrote it when I was truly saturated with the feeling of the approaching spring. When I went walking at noon and the sun shone down so mildly I was filled by spring's delights, so that I was literally compelled to write this refrain. It may at least serve as a proof that whatever changes I have undergone have nonetheless left intact the same desire for poetic endeavors. Please send me soon one of your recent poems. We'll want to offer one another *very precise* critiques, dispensing blame and praise as merited. I think this would be loads of fun.—

Semper nostra manet amicitia!

Your Fritz.

I'm enclosing a kind of continuation of my biography. More pages will follow. Please keep them in a very secure place!

It was a Tuesday morning as I drove out through the gates of the city of Naumburg. Morning twilight still hovered over the meadows, and on the horizon only a few dimly lit clouds betrayed the approach of daylight. In me too a kind of twilight held sway: in my heart the sunlight of true joy had not yet risen. The terrors of a fraught night besieged me still and the future ahead of me lay wrapped in a gray veil full of portent. For the very first time I was to leave my parental home for a long, long period. I stepped forth to meet unknown dangers. My farewell had left me forlorn, and I trembled at the thought of my future. Add to that the examination that awaited me, which I had portrayed to myself in the grimmest of colors and forms; and the thought that from now on I could never give myself over to my own thoughts, that my schoolmates would drag me away from my most beloved preoccupations;—this thought oppressed me terribly. And, preeminently, the thought that I was to leave my dear friends, that I would have to abandon

congenial relationships in order to step forth into a new, unknown, unrelenting world—this thought crowded my heart. Every minute became more terrifying to me. Indeed, as I saw Pforta shimmering in the distance, it seemed to me more a prisonhouse than an alma mater. I drove through the gate. My heart overflowed with holy sensations, I was lifted up to God in silent prayer, and a profound tranquillity came over my spirit. Yea, Lord, bless my entry and protect me too, in body and in spirit, in this nursery of the Holy Spirit. Send your angel, that he may lead me victorious through the battles I go to fight, and let this place extend true blessings, blessings that will last me through times eternal. This I beseech Thee, O Lord!
    Amen.—

You must have suffered more than Wilhelm and Gustav, though not for anything they said or did: they went on to do exactly what their fathers before them had done while you went off on your own. And it was you who held *Germania* together during those three years, just like Lieschen later in her own Germania, the new one, you who goaded the other two boys never giving them a moment's peace until they fulfilled their pledges. I'm afraid you were a bit of a bugbear, a touch of a tyrant, my testy Fritz

To Wilhelm Pinder in Naumburg

Pforta, March/April, 1859

Dear Wilhelm!

Please send me some sort of theme for a paper in German, preferably a speech or an essay. I think I'll have some free time during the days following the exams and I have to keep in practice, otherwise I'll lose the knack.—Here is a theme for you: *On Divine and Human Freedom.* Maybe you can find an hour or two to reflect on the matter and write about it. Freedom is one of the most important points, you know. Just pose the questions What is freedom? Who is free? What is freedom of will? etc. Farewell for now, my dear Wilhelm, and often think of and write to

Your
Fr. W. Nietzsche

Nostra semper manet amicitia!———

pinder krug prometheus. aeschylus our common grandfather and agonist. a tragedy in five acts: how earthly criticism douses fire stolen from heaven. prometheus my first quashed love. titanic mortal in whom all gods meet their match.

To Wilhelm Pinder in Naumburg

Pforta, April/May, 1859

Dear Wilhelm!

I had some lovely days in Naumburg before we left for Pobles. I wrote several things too. First, an abortive drama called *Prometheus*, stuffed with false conceptions concerning its object. Second, three poems on the same theme, which I carried over into a third work. This third text, incidentally, is a peculiar thing, as yet unfinished: six closely-written quarto sides bearing the title, "Question-Marks and Notes along with a Universal Exclamation-Point concerning Three Poems Entitled 'Prometheus.'" Here a poet is presented as an antipode to his public, and the whole thing is a mixture of nonsense and silliness. Among other things there is one sentence that covers a whole page. Thereupon follow terribly ridiculous distortions, totally stupid subjects etc. etc. I don't know how I could come up with such crazy ideas. Fourth, a very superficial essay on the theme, "All human beings are good, it's just us who are bad," which, incidentally, can really be well done if you keep an eye on causes and consequences. Fifth, a poem I wrote in a tearing hurry, something profound, or at least obscure, where the thoughts that are missing are marked by thoughtful caesurae. By the bye, after long reflection I gave it the title, "Poesy and Destiny." When I wrote it I didn't understand it; only a more exacting confrontation made it clearer. Unfortunately, I'm out of paper. Therefore fare ye well, greetings to all, and often think of and write to

Your
Fr.

Semper nostra amicitia manet.

i never wearied of carrying the torch for prometheus. alle götter müssen sterben: all deities must die. *With all this we do not want to slip into a merely didactic style; rather, we want to write so radiantly, so picturesquely, in as lively and gripping a manner as possible; in short, to be rather brilliant. Naturally, we can weave in a poem here and there. . . . We shall both want to write an introduction and a conclusion, and then we will select the best one and put it into our good copy.* all deities must die: zeuss end: ermanarichs death. ermanarich the overman. how long were you with me, my primeval prometheal friend? five years or more. after you how could the meisters ring mean anything to me? it meant nothing it was not the ring of eternity. no counterpoint. krug and his tristan couldnt compare with my ermanarich. *That twilight of the gods when the sun turns black the earth sinks into the sea tornadoes of fiery ash singe the all-nourishing cosmic tree and the flames lick the sky: it is the most grandiose invention human genius ever contrived, unexcelled by anything in the literatures of all times, infinitely bold and horrific yet dissolving in enchanting euphonia.* an essay a symphonic poem an epic *the death of ermanarich* like hölderlins never finished then a piano fantasia then a drama a treatise for professor koberstein at pforta the scenario for an opera that died of the treatise ermanarichs death empedocles death zarathustras death whatever happened to him? revoke the fourth part it needs reworking needs an injection of irreversible downgoing.

so you think i was too hard on pinder mama? just because i praised his penmanship in lieu of everything else? just because i wrote him about the nine poems he submitted so shamelessly to germania *What adheres to W. Pinder, scarcely allowing him to produce a single pure lyric poem, is a certain aridity of feeling, a certain coagulation in the fancy, and a lack of maturity in formal construction* so you think i was too harsh mama? you never had to read his drivel mama. all i wanted him to be was byron mama not even shakespeare mama not even me:

> Round about me, summer evening's breezes;
> Across the sky, ribbons of gold.
> In the churchyard, roses' breathings;
> Joy of things the children told.

●

Don't run, love, walk. Don't run you may fall and break something you're not as steady on your feet as you used to be. Still you are very beautiful darling Fritz your eyes softer and sweeter more trusting every day full of love like a puppy's. Divine love. Don't run, love, walk. You'll be back one day some day soon when we least expect it; then this nightmare will be over my darling and you'll be restored completely to me whole and entire. Your memory will stop playing tricks on you, you'll write again and get your datives straight not accusatives how many times do I have to tell you—you still were getting it wrong in Gymnasium and now you're slipping back into the same old bad habits. Strange. As though time were running backwards. Yet one day it will all be over and Professor Binswanger will eat his words *incurable incurable incurable* a dagger in my heart that day he read out to me aloud that insult to your Father he fell on the stairs, Lieschen saw it happen, he hurt his head that was all there was to it no need to insult your Father my brothers and sisters *hereditary hereditary hereditary* Papa would have boxed his ears for him. Mama too, it would be as much her fault if it were true which it isn't, not for a minute. If anyone then Rosalie, she was never quite right, anyone could see that, bright as she was with her newspapers and her nerves. What do we need them for anyway? A question to ask our great and good Lord on the Last Day, He'll be putting the questions to us, I suppose, no one will get a word in edgewise I'm sorry I didn't mean that it's my nerves.

Walk, love, don't run. Watch where you're stepping sweet don't soil your shoes. Aren't you looking handsome today? Brown from the sun, all these hours on your feet in God's fresh air no medicine like it not even the watercure, anyone can plainly see you're thriving it's just a question of time as that nice Herr von Hagen said it's only because we nonphilosophers don't know how to judge the case: your peers would see nothing but radiant health in you he said. Binswanger. He's already eaten his words once, the day we met at the Jena railwaystation restaurant first-class.

—How are your eyes? he asked.

—Really much better, you replied.

—Are you still getting those headaches? he queried.

—Never, you responded.

That was a bit naughty of you, I've seen you cradling your head in your hands, I've seen you on the bad days wincing, grimacing, but you wanted to please the Professor and you certainly did. He said a man in your condition couldn't be doing better. So much for incurable! I knew he would have to eat that word. And he'll eat the other one yet before I'm through. Blame the parents that's always the way.

—What are you doing to keep busy? he asked.

—I play the piano and I sing, you replied.

Which was very naughty of you because we've prohibited the singing for some time now haven't we darling for the neighbors' sake? Professor Binswanger worried about that until I got him in a corner after lunch and explained it to him, he was so relieved. No more police.

—I'd be surprised if his condition left anything else to be desired, Professor Binswanger said.

I was beaming. I reported everything, your diet, the swimming twice weekly, four hours of energetic walking every day for your nerves, but not overdoing it.

—He looks splendid, the Professor said.

I was thrilled. Of course that's nothing new, I've always taken such good care of you. Too good, really. That's what that young Dr. Goodyear said, who came to see Rosalie almost once a week when you were a baby and I asked him why you weren't speaking yet. Two years old and not a peep out of you. I was afraid you weren't normal, imagine! but he put my mind at ease:

—Why should he speak, Frau Pastor? You bring him everything he wants before he even knows he wants it. With such an excellent mother, why should he speak?! Too good, really.

Binswanger's visit was a resounding success. I was ecstatic. If only you could have *looked* at Professor Binswanger when he was speaking to you instead of fixing your eyes on me no matter who you were talking or listening to, that's very disconcerting you know, it isn't normal, and I asked the Professor how in God's name and with His grace we could improve your spiritual condition.

—Rest, rest, and more rest, he said.

Which is no doubt true. But we have to keep up the reading and writing, too. What would a professor be if he couldn't read! What would a philologian be if he couldn't write! What would a philosopher be if he couldn't do either! Even if it's only a dedication on a photo portrait or an envelope every now and then *Greetings from yrs—friend Nietzsche* but please don't write *fool* again or *madman* no one thinks it's funny no one's laughing. We must keep on reading, me to you, you to me. But with an open neck, without your collar, otherwise you get read as a beet, the blood rushes to your head the Professor said, as though reading were something else, and that's why you get loud.

•

my turn now mama my turn to read may i read now please mama. yes? the book. green cloth cover good to the touch. how well it fits into my hand my left itself opened like a book thumb verso palm and fingers recto wearing the book like a green glove the right hand to trace the lines and turn the page. read now. collar? open. fine. go ahead. with expression. evohe.

—"'TOM!!'

"'Y-o-u-u, *Tom!!'*

"Tom PRESENTED HIMSELF before AUNT POLLY that was sitting by twenty per cent of Tom's statement. TRUE!! as Tom's MIND!! and the first thing then he said: "'Huck, have you EVER TOLD ANYBODY about THAT?!!' There comes a time in every rightly constructed boy's life when 'RUN!!' said he; 'RUN FOR YOUR LIFE!!' As the EARLIEST SUSPICION of DAWN—"

mama that is the most beautiful line trope turn of phrase set of words i have EVER HEARD in my life i am going to remember it and use it if i haven't already used it: *the earliest suspicion of dawn.* im sorry im sorry ive lost the thread where are we here we are: "appeared on Sunday morning, TUESDAY AFTERNOON came, and waned to twilight. . . . WANED to TWILIGHT!!"

i dont believe this mother i really dont cant believe it *waned to twilight* all right all right dont scold patience mama yes the thread the thread ariadne: "The rest on Tuesday night, SAD AND FORLORN!! Huck said: the reader may rest SATISFIED!! that Tom's and Huck's windfall

CONCLUSION!!

So endeth this chronicle."

that was lovely mama wasnt it those little rascals just like pinder and krug and me when we were young tom and huck and missis fynn would you like another i would i confess i love his silliness more than german cleverness before we turn in. . . .

wait. wait. IVE LEFT SOMETHING OUT!! wait. here we are: "It being strictly a history of a boy, it must stop here; the story could not go much further without becoming the history of a man."

there. finis. snap it shut. beautiful sound. ka-pok. my shoulder. evohe. good night mama ah ah eeeee sleep tight.

•

Ever and ever more my soul is filled with inmost utmost gratitude to our dear Lord and good God: if only I can nurture this child of my heart and, whether it be burdensome or light, act upon this same feeling of intense gratitude; the single prayer I pray to Him is that He preserve in my keeping this dear dear child of mine. It is just as she says in the adventures, in one of the parts he skipped he skips almost everything I wish he could slow down and let one line flow into the next you miss too much his ragtale way she says *I'm thankful to the good God and Father of us all I've got you back, that's long-suffering and merciful to them that believe on Him and keep His word, though goodness knows I'm unworthy of it, but if only the worthy ones got his blessings and had His hand to help them over the rough places, there's few enough would smile here or ever enter into His rest when the long night comes* there is a mighty truth in those words even if they are a little rough around the edges, a rock-of-ages truth, bedrock, so that there's as much hope for him in the end as there is for me. If I didn't believe that how could I go on? Soon I'll be seventy how long can I keep this up? Even with His help?

It is the walking that is most trying this time of year. One day sleet, next day snow, one day rain, next day ice: it's a wonder we don't break our necks or catch a death. Yet I don't dare miss even a single outing, he's become so methodical it upsets his inner clock and the energy has to come out somewhere. That's why I never say anything about the sheets either. No use. Like talking to a waterfall. God put it into him, into them all, till they're bursting with it. Safety valve. Otherwise terrible explosions like that chemical plant in Ludwigshafen. Still how beautiful they are those enormous moist flakes of March so wet and heavy you can feel each one hit the wool of your cloak, see the crystal pattern each one different He makes them that way. That alone would be enough to prove it as if anybody needed proof. He runs forward squealing with delight, his head tossed back, left shoulder held high why is that? his tongue stuck out so far twisting to the right I don't remember it's being so enormous can it have grown? but then when would I have ever seen it before? except when he was a boy at the doctor's colds all the time it seemed. Now he's the very picture of health, all that fresh air, and even when we get soaked to the skin like today pointless to carry an umbrella it just whirls up from underneath on every gust of wind, even the wet feet, how can I keep his galoshes on the way he runs stumbling over his own feet how full of joy he is he needs no proof does he? How it makes me laugh to see him gambol, our frisky Fritz, I wouldn't stop him even if I could, even his wetting, not his fault, it's the cold every boy does it he needs a hot bath anyway once we come in after a day like this. Then a quarter-hour of reading and already his jaw drops, his heavy head sinks forward, and it's all I can do to get him into bed. Exhausting business. How quiet he can be through the night if only we keep all things regular, everything in its assigned place at its prescribed hour, how quiet then he can be, like a true philosopher.

The Professor was probably right. Professor Binswanger. I fear it. Not about hereditary but about incurable. I don't let myself paint a picture of what looms ahead, of what may be coming, the kind of care he'll need then and will I always be here? I shall be. I shall be. As long as it takes. He will not end his days huddled in a corner; he will not end his days in squalor. For that be thankful, Franziska, be thankful I am thankful I am full of gratitude if only I can nurture.

•

my feet. socrates inverted i am am i. his hemlock announced its morbid effects first in the feet and ankles, advancing up the calves knees and thighs to his sterile midwife's loins then on to his belly and chest and finally at long last to his frogeye and his working mouth, that jawing flapping mouth stilled last of all. whereas with me it all began over the right eye in my forehead, shifted to the back of my neck, silenced my mouth early on, stiffened my back and shoulders arms and hands. now my backbone has gone rigid i feel the chill reaching down my spine. but when the last inch of me is unbudgingly rigorous it will not have reached my feet and toes they will be wiggling tapping eager to fly hungry for the dance my cock i will owe to terpsichore turvy topsy terpsichore turning on her heady inverted socratic feet.

•

How afraid I was of your dreams, Fritz, your dreams and your will-fulness or your willpower, your second sight, I don't know what to call it. Your Inspector at Pforta told us how you burned your hand. Some Roman got himself burned that way and one of the boys said how could he stand the pain and you took a packet of matches, lit them, and lay them on your outstretched palm. When the Inspector saw what you were up to he cried out and knocked them out of your motionless scorched hand. You were badly burned but you didn't wince didn't flinch didn't shed a tear. My little hero it wasn't natural and I made you promise never ever again to play with pain.

And those dreams of yours! My dear Ludwig and darling Little Joseph God rest their souls in the first dream I wanted to stop you from telling it but I couldn't to spite myself I needed to hear it; then my own Papa, your Grandfather Oehler, the summer before he died at least you left him some gracetime. The whole manor at Pobles lay in ruins, you said, the bakehouse, the shed, the neighboring farm-house and barn, the pig sty. And the pastor's house, my Father's house, my own home. Beneath the rubble of cracked and fallen beams rooftiles glass and dust my Mother sat alone, her fingers clawing her hair above the temples on either side, her mouth and eyes gaping in one protracted silent scream. You woke. Couldn't fall back asleep no wonder. In the morning you told Lisbeth and me your dream and we begged you to tell no one else not to tempt fate. Papa was so robust and so full of life that summer who would have thought? Even though he was seventy who would have thought? I believed he would endure forever. Dear Papa, he should have. Perhaps he would have but for the dream.

•

grandpapa oehler at pobles. all the books in his library i took them one by one out into the garden. it was he who explained to me about the chickens and the hogs, what they were up to, doing gods holy work. rutting and rearing ashes rubble debris time.

•

It wasn't only your dreams. You always seemed ready to think and believe the worst of your own family even of your own Father God rest his soul. Lisbeth says he fell down those stairs and that is good enough for me why can't you accept it and be done with it? And poor Dr. Förster's heart attack, you wanted to make a sordid drama out of it, what you don't know can't hurt you let sleeping dogs lie leave well enough alone nothing wicked about the dead. Rosalie I'll have to grant you she was on your Father's side; but you had no right casting aspersions on your Uncle Theobald like that everybody in Altendammbach loved him. A pastor doesn't do that sort of thing

To Franziska and Elisabeth Nietzsche in Naumburg

Sils-Maria, circa July 9, 1881

My dear Mother,

I am deeply saddened by your loss, a loss to us all! He was such a gentle and decent man, our Theobald, tough on himself and yet not fanatical; I took him to be the best of all the Oehlers. Who knows whether it wasn't his father-in-law's quackery more than his own theology that caused the greater part of his nervous illness! He preferred death to the madhouse, and it was probably a wise choice. We shall always be touched by the

175

memory of him. With all my heart, and with the request that you not take anything the wrong way,

Your Son and Brother

Certainly not in the bathtub anyway. How could he have known who would find him there? He never would have inflicted himself on anyone that way. You always had to think the worst. If you hadn't had your wise old Mother to set you to rights what grief would you have spread?

Postcard to Franziska Nietzsche in Naumburg

Sils-Maria, July 13, 1881

Yes, what you say sounds more probable: poor Theobald was in a state of overexcitement and wanted to take a bath (in order to calm down) and that's when a brainstroke supervened. It happens all the time, all the time!

Fr.

Though who knows what you told the whole world once my back was turned, you naughty Fritz, you never missed a chance to knock your own family down a peg, especially my side of the family us oilers the side with heart. Who knows what tales about us you sent abroad Fritz this is your punishment I suppose.

To Paul Rée in Rome

Genua, March 21, 1882

Yesterday I was bathing in the sea, exactly at that famous spot where ———. Imagine: last summer one of my closest relatives was so overtaken by a seizure at his bath that—because, as it happened, there was no one close by—he drowned.

Your faithful friend,
FN.

This is all your own fault. He's paying you back in coin. The things you said that Easter when you were sixteen only weeks after your Confirmation. You were supposed to be confirmed in your faith not your suspicions. Trying to get Lisbeth to read that atheist life of Jesus the two of you mere babes in arms, what right did you have to confuse her although you never did. Of course, it wasn't all your fault.

Someone at school was influencing you, you couldn't have come across a book like that on your own. And so you stayed home on Friday and mocked Sunday, which should have been the most joyous day of the year except maybe for Christmas because of the children. Birth gives more joy than death, even if Easter slaughters death. Anyway, you apologized so sweetly afterwards it was almost worth a blasphemy or two what am I saying

To Franziska Nietzsche in Naumburg

Pforta, end of April, 1861

Dear Mama!

A word with you alone, dear Mama, if I may. To me as well that otherwise lovely Easter holiday seems to have been overcast and darkened by those ugly events; it strikes me as a most painful thing each time I think of it, that I could have saddened you so much, I beg your forgiveness with all my heart dear Mama! For it would be sad indeed if this discord were to disturb our beautiful relationship, our reciprocity. But forgive me dear Mama, and, I beg you, never again dwell on these events, regard them rather as never having happened. Furthermore, I shall try as hard as I can through my conduct and my love for you to repair the rift I have opened. Write me about this sometime, dear Mama!

From one who loves you dearly,
Your Fritz.

Farther and farther from me you drifted. That terrible terrible Easter of 1865 you came home from the university with a snarl on your lips and refused to attend the eucharist. Bonn. The University. It wasn't good for you. You were abandoning theology and with it the faith of your Fathers. And the faith of your Mother to boot. Lisbeth stood by you even though she didn't believe in your disbelief not for a minute your poor Mother's whole world came down in ruins. Everyone needs something to hold onto in life because people die and everything slips through your fingers. You have to clutch. You have to cleave. You have to believe. You sneered. If only you had been as stubborn in your faith as you were in your stubbornness. He sees into the heart. He will drag you kicking and screaming just you wait and see back into the fold of His bosom His bounty.

•

bountyhunter. bonn. to the unknown god. highwayman. hangman. be content mother rest easy mother im kicking im screaming.

•

Our darling daughter your sister Elisabeth elected you Lord of Heaven and Earth long before you ever dreamt of nominating yourself, you naughty boy, and she never stopped worshiping at your altar. I know that you have always adored her too no matter what you say

To Elisabeth Nietzsche in Dresden

Pforta, end of April, 1862

Dear Elisabeth!

As I write, I'm standing here at my lectern, the lectern stands at the window, the window looks out over a lovely lime tree in blossom, and in the distance lie the sun-strewn mountains of the Saale: gentle nature, however, reminds me vividly of Dresden and the pleasant days I spent there. And yet for me to remember you, dear, dear Lisbeth, requires the application of no such elaborate leverage to my memory: on the contrary, I often think of you, so often that there is no other relevant example of the phenomenon, I am really almost always thinking of you. Even when I'm asleep, there is no exception to the rule: for I rather often dream of you and of our being together. . . .

By the bye, enjoy your life, may you fare well and think without any further sentimental spurts on one who loves you so dearly:

Your
Fritz.

Even now she loves you, even now as she is doing these things to her own Mother your own poor old Mother, and to you. When you left Bonn after that wasted year all that squandered money the piano rental to study at Leipzig when was it? 1865? she cooked up the scheme that the two of us should follow you there and set up a Naumburg residence in exile for you: you could devote every living moment of every living day to your philology, theology was out for the moment though I knew that by some roundabout route it was in your bloodstream it would return

178

To Franziska Nietzsche in Naumburg

Pforta, May 2, 1863

Dear Mama.

As far as my future is concerned, it is the practical considerations that disquiet me. The decision about what I shall study will not come all by itself. Hence I must think everything over myself, then choose; and it is this choice that is causing me difficulties. To be sure, I shall endeavor to devote myself whole and entire to whatever I study, but that only makes the selection more difficult, for I must choose the discipline in which I may dare hope to achieve something whole and entire. And how deceptive these hopes often are! How easily one lets oneself be carried away by some momentary preference, a venerable family tradition, or someone's particular wishes, so that the choice of one's profession appears to be a lottery in which there are lots of losers but very few winners. Now, I am also in the particularly unenviable position of having interests in really quite a few of the most distinct disciplines; satisfying them in a well-rounded way would make me a learned man but hardly a professional beast of burden. It is clear to me that I must cast off some of these interests. It is likewise clear to me that I shall have to attain some new interests. But which are to be the unlucky ones that I must toss overboard?—Perhaps the very children I love best!

Fritz

and we would shop and cook and clean and darn and tidy up for you and be your sole entertainment.

—A student's life can be so lonely and so subject to distraction, Lisbeth said, and I knew she was thinking of Cologne and of what lured you and the other students there.

We had that in common, Lieschen and I: we sensed the danger and we wanted to spare you and to share you. Yet I had a bit more confidence in you than she did, even though you were never my God. I knew you'd be better off on your own than with the two of us suffocating you, better off wretched than stunted, it was good training for the future, that misery. We stayed in Naumburg.

•

leipzig leipzig leapfrog to leipzig to study chemistry and physics to learn how the world turns. im late for class. years late. now too late now. lange showed me long ago what theognis never knew nor diogenes either. molecules rule the world demokritos sovereign atoms leukippos chief shining horse. last time i was in leipzig i frittered away my time on kant and sophistry, hypotyposis and the two absolutes. two as good as none. hegel with my morning coffee without the coffee no stimulants don't roam to rome, and if he didnt agree with me i grazed on a bouquet of strauss, my diet of the whole and the half. cant and heckle cashed in for that scowling hatchet, that pest in mist, that wizened head spewing its poison chopping logic chopping hour by hour.

To Franziska Nietzsche in Naumburg

Leipzig, January 31, 1866

Dear Mama,

I've set aside one evening a week on which Gersdorff and I read Greek together, and one evening every fortnight when he and Mushacke and I all go a-schopenhauering together. This philosopher has assumed a significant place in my thoughts and in my studies, and my respect for him waxes incomparably great. I also make propaganda for him and lead certain other people (for example, my cousin) to him by the nose. Which hasn't been much use. For all dyed-in-the-wool Saxons follow one command alone: *primum vivere, deinde philosophari!*

Your Fritz.

i was drunk with him mama. and i promised you i would never get drunk again. it was the fog and rain of leipzig it was the moist molecules made me do it mama. it was good you and lieschen stayed home. ecco.

•

Why did my Lieschen have to go back to Paraguay? Fifteen months she was gone to liquefy her assets and by the time she came back— September it was, September of '93—you were long gone, more remote than she had ever been all the way to Paraguay and back. It was as though she paid you no mind.

To Malwida von Meysenbug in Rome

Venezia, San Canciano, Calle Nuove 5256
Early May, 1884

When Fräulein Schirnhofer visited me recently in Nice I thought of you with gratitude, for I guessed that *you* wanted to do me this good deed: and truly it was a well-timed visit, useful to me and quite cheering (especially because no disruptive conceited goose was on hand—oh, pardon me, I meant my sister). . . . For heaven's sake, don't dream of mediating and achieving a reconciliation between us—between me and a vengeful anti-semitic goose there is no reconciliation. For the rest, I spare her in every possible way, for I know *what* can be said by way of excusing my sister and I know what stands behind what I regard as her shameful and unworthy behavior:—love. It is altogether essential that she set sail for Paraguay as soon as possible.

Devotedly yours, and in gratitude
Nietzsche.

Hardly a word escaped your lips but we had days and nights of shouting screaming bawling whooping yodeling bellowing roaring with the most cheerful restrained even demure look on your face, the sounds emanating not from that face, more a mask than a face, but from some deeply hidden hollow behind it, as though at some remove from your own self I know that sounds crazy. How suddenly the change came! The plunge. Week by week I could see you deteriorating could see my hopes diminishing in step with you. O my darling, O Fritzchen of my heart! Professor Binswanger came to see you again and even though you were having a very good day and he was effusive in his praise of your poor old Mother I knew he was only being considerate and he admitted there was no way ahead now it was full steam backwards a retracing of steps but without the sense those steps once had *regression* he said ugly word sounds like aggression transgression *regression* he said it again and it sounded true. The stranger's voice that screamed out of your throat stepped farther and farther back into the hollow the louder and louder it grew. Out of all sight and even beyond normal hearing.

Massages helped to settle you, soothe you, the way you clutched my hand to your breast as I read to you, you always knew how to make your poor old Mother happy. Most of all my hand upon your forehead. You would turn quiet at once, close your eyes,

THE WAYS OF THE MOTHER

smile ever so faintly, as though rapt to some recollection of long ago. If my Father patented the watercure I suppose his daughter should be credited with the hand-on-brow cure maybe it will make me famous. Such concentration it gave you, as though for an instant all your powers had been restored to full strength, I could feel the power of thinking at work in you again though God only knows what sort of muddle it may have been and probably was inside.

That year 1893 more than any other of my life wore me out, my darling. So worried would Lieschen ever come back of course she would with Dr. Förster gone forever to his reward but what about all those indians? Worried about you and your bellowing, the long walks canceled, your legs got so bad, all that pentup energy and no outlet. That was when the jaw cramps started. I thought you would starve outright, thought you would perish utterly like your little brother. Coincidence. Worse than anything was that infernal rubbing: in bed at night all night long you'd be rubbing your left breast with your right hand harder and harder the bawling rising louder and louder till you were bathed in sweat and the house reverberating with the noise. Was that where you hurt yourself when you were in the army? It was better when we could walk, there was less rubbing, less caterwauling, deep in the forest where no one could hear you and take fright. How is it that a pastor's daughter a pastor's wife a pastor's widow has to live day in day out in terror of the police? The police are there to help godfearing citizens, that's what they say, but I fear them more than I ever did my Lord and Redeemer. You were getting so stiff, could scarcely straighten your back, a half-hour turn around the block in the evening couldn't undo the damage of hours in bed on the sofa in your wheelchair on your stool in front of the window playing with the coins from your five leather purses and pretending to read Hasekiel's *War Songs* upside down. The old soldier in you.

To Hermann Mushacke in Berlin

Naumburg, Friday, October 4, 1867

My dear Friend,

We are seldom masters of our fate, though when it has favored us for a long time we think we are. This is not to be the introduction to a tragedy, but only a preliminary remark to a musical intermezzo which I had hoped never again to hear in this life: fife and drum, a warlike clangor! The sword hovers no longer over my head but at my side, the pen in my hand will

soon be a weapon of death, these papers covered with notes and
sketches will probably soon exude a whiff of putrefaction. The
god of war has taken a liking to me, i.e., I've been declared fit
for service in the army, just as I was on my way to a
philologists' conference in Halle, believing that this chalice had
passed me by.

Addio a rivederla
Fritz Nietzsche.

On those final walks of ours the few snatches of phrases that bub-
bled up in you were simply rude you wouldn't let me chant any
more verses you interrupted me constantly you naughty Fritz you
made me cry, and me wasting my breath correcting you trying to get
you to hear the nonsense you were uttering I told you over and over
again *liebe,* not *bebe; liebe,* not *bebe; liebe,* not *bebe,* until I was
blue in the face and you were still shaking and quaking horses
instead of loving them.

To Franziska and Elisabeth Nietzsche in Naumburg

Leipzig, Tuesday. End of June, 1867

Dear Mama and Lisbeth,

Every afternoon between 4 and 5 Rohde and I take our horses
out for a good run, and we feel exhilarated both during and
after the exercise. Agitation works wonders for the abdomen.
Afterwards we are thirstier, hungrier, and sleep much more
soundly than other mortals do.

Your Fritz.

•

more light. more light. there. i can see them now. among the women
on the mountain meadow at midday the stallion and the mare, the
stud the filly and the foal, the dappled and the dun, the sorrel chest-
nut and bay, the sable and blancanieve. weaving easily in and out
of the herd, the gods the panther and the goat. silence broken only
by the sound of hushed hooves on dry grass, the solid sound of thud-
ding earthdepth. i cluck cluck with my tongue and the dappled
moves easily toward me, mortal pedasos, head held high, long
white mane flowing in waves down to his shoulders, forelock swept
high in the wind. pedasos, sired by zephyr on the harpy podarge,
approaches me and kneels at my feet, whinnying

THE WAYS OF THE MOTHER

To Erwin Rohde in Kiel

Naumburg, February 1-3, 1868

My dear Friend,

May one not feel proud when one is declared the best rider among 30 recruits?

F. Nietzsche
in faithful friendship.

i mount smoothly, my heart pounding against my breastbone. ride me. i am tall and beautiful. equestrian statue. take me

To Carl von Gersdorff in Berlin

Naumburg, February 16, 1868

Dear Friend,

I hear from my officers that I sit well in the saddle, and that this gives me a remarkable advantage. Truly, dear friend, I never thought that in this domain too I would have occasion to become vain.

Your friend,
Friedrich Nietzsche

slowly he rises, and we are off! lightning cleaving the silver boulders singeing the scrub on dragonrock, flashes of yellow and crimson wildflowers, the sound of the hooves the rhythm of quaking thunder, we are surging free through the mountain air, my right hand clutching the mane of his arching lunging neck my hand thrusting forward then pushed back hard against my wrist my arm all but wrenched from my shoulder my thighs aching my heart beating in time to the flashing feet. we are one pulse. over the crest of the pass we fly then swoop down to the lower meadow suddenly narrowing funnel-like to box canyon walls of silver on each side of me until we barely have room to pass. the instant before pedasos skids to a halt and I go soaring tumbling cartwheeling over his neck I discern the waving thorny arms of a giant agave beckoning agave alwine do you know it? my back collides against one gigantic spiked arm, im upside-down my feet waving frantically in the air my face now pressed against the smooth flesh of the succulent. a thorn draws a meticulously incised wound across the bridge of my nose a deep cut it will leave a scar. delius delirium. downward i slide until another hooked thorn catches a floating rib on my left side my own weight and momentum tearing the rib loose i feel the jolt and heave as the thorn rips higher catching on each successive rib, breaking my plunge, holding and releasing me in regular rhythm, a mere bagatelle, catching and lacerating by turns

To Erwin Rohde in Kiel

Naumburg, June 6, 1868

My dear Friend,

How astonished I was when I saw the first tiny fragment of bone from my skeleton. It came swiftly swimming in a current of pus from one of the drainage tubes in my chest. . . . Never is the fragility of human existence demonstrated so *ad oculos* as when one has the vision of a fragment of one's own skeleton. . . . Ah, well, as the Persian poet sings:

> Have you got sturdy legs?—
> Will *I* be naught but dregs?—

the bone catching is more painful than the flesh tearing, the suppurating poison more painful than either of these, the dull ache and throb a philoctetic delight of injected venom caustic searing burning ardent not an itch a conflagration in my bloodstream devouring me reducing me to chyle before i even reach the mouth of the monster. i can hear its squeaking mandibles the slop and bubble of its juices the gulps of its anticipation. through the pain i am aware of my sole chance the only possible hope of rescue

To Erwin Rohde in Kiel

Naumburg, August 6, 1868

> Noble member! Now you're saved
> From evil, blighted breastbone!
> These past few months, it's clear,
>   you've craved
> A moldering tomb and headstone.

if i can get one arm free my right where all my strength lies and if by using a mirror i can like persian perseus locate by reflection the mouth and gorge below me and if i can get my right hand around your throat mama my fingers as stiff as your laminated leaves open

185

damn you fingers open close now yes close damn you grasp it clutch it squeeze the life out of it. you lurch this way and that agave but i do not relinquish my hold my hand and fingers a vice unrelenting no matter which way you wend mama it will soon be over mama i feel you weakening hear you splutter and choke it will soon be over mama darling your thorns no longer hold me your leaves slacken i slide all the way down i am intimate with you now in death mama it wont be long mama it wont be long now

•

Fritz darling lie still. Here is my hand on your brow. Don't scream your poor Mother's ears our neighbors. There now. There now. My other hand, here, hold tight. Squeeze. Rockabye rockabye the white snows of winter Christmastime will soon be here Nicholas is on his way and ashen Ruprecht will stay away be still still still quiet repose rest in peace my darling Fritz. Talk, Franziska, talk about anything, talk to this quaking Fritzchen of yours. What's that you say boy?
　　—Would you by any chance be called Franziska?
　　—Yes, precious, I am Franziska, don't you know your own Mother boy?
　　—Summarily stupid. Too dead to live. I quake no horses.
　　—I don't *like* horses, darling.

•

i lied mama forgive me it wasnt a horse at all i lied i said it was a horse said i fell onto the saddle it wasnt a horse wasnt a pommel it was a fir. my cousin bent it down so i could clamber aboard and ride to my perch high above the mountain meadow at midday above the crag of rock it was the succulents that savaged me when i fell. so i could see you mama you and the others minna ino lina auguste autonoë rosalie rieke naked at your bath i mean at your revels he promised me you would never know. but you saw me and threw rocks at me you deracinated my fir i fell and you fell upon me i tore off my snood so you would know me i shouted *it is i mother it is i your own little boy called grief it is i in the rain purest mourning itself mother it was all a mistake a minor family flaw a quirk of the lineage dont kill me* but you did. minna flayed the skin from my ribcage, grunted with the effort, laughed gaily in my face, called me meat of marsyas. aunt auguste fussed at my right arm, aunt rosalie fidgeted with my foot i recognized the sandal. i saw organs and parts of me i didnt recognize had never seen before flying through the air bloody balls in a crazy game of catch as catch can. then i felt your hand in my hair raising my head heavenward uncannily high heard the snap felt you insert your fennelwand to be my new stick torso. from my new perch i should have been able to see everything, impaled there to be seen rather than to see. imagine my surprise mama when i saw everything dimming going black dulled insentient to silence. ill never put on another one of your dresses mama as long as i

•

I've always hated lawyers, especially since your Father died. They feed on other people's quarrels and misfortunes. Parasites on the dark side of human nature, which covers 3/4 of the globe, God knows. I never understood those contracts with Naumann. Publishers are all lawyers too. And Elisabeth, my darling Lisbeth, my little Lieschen, my own flesh trafficking in lawyers and publishers every minute of the day. She understands as little about it as I do but she doesn't let it slow her down that's the difference that's why she's good at it. How she manages to hoodwink everyone else I don't know; why she tries to fool her own Mother I don't know either. What does she want me to sign this paper for anyway? What have I or Nephew Adalbert ever done to interfere with the Archive or its endless editions and reeditions? It was the two of us, Elisabeth and I both, who wanted to suppress his *Antichrist,* so she can't be holding anything like that against me. Fritz, darling, you have to admit it is a *terrible* book: you were outside yourself when you wrote it you admitted as much to me *Don't you read it, my sweet Mother* you said to me afterwards when you were more yourself again *I was somewhere else when I wrote it, don't you trouble yourself about it* you said, and so Lisbeth and I tried to do what you would have wanted us to do because you were helpless to do it yourself but neither Overbeck nor Köselitz would listen to reason. And it was too big to dispose of the way we did those frightful substitute pages of *Ecco* about your own home how could you have been so cruel to your own Mother boy of course you were mad when you wrote them but don't fret the world will never see them not unless it can read ashes. No, she can't be holding that against me.

Whatever it is it doesn't give her the right to act as though the spiritual treasure the legacy the heritage the patrimony of our family were hers alone to dispose of as she likes. I know, I know, she's done all the work; but if she hadn't given poor Köselitz the boot and offended Professor Overbeck she would have had all the help she needed. No one to blame but herself. Sometimes I worry about her scruples. For example, where are they? Your own sister, Fritz. Heart of gold, head of brass, and sometimes the other way round. But a backbone of iron, any way you cut it, that you have to admit. What does she want me to sign this thing for anyway?

There she sits, all in black, demure as can be, Widow Förster, the notary at her side. She ordered him here to my house so that I would have to sign her document. Do I have to sign? If I don't he will have wasted his entire morning and he'll make us pay for it and she'll make me pay for that. Another lawyer. Another two lawyers. Stall them both.

—Have some more tea, my dear man.

O my Little Lieschen, don't look at your poor old Mother like that. If looks could kill.

—Mama, dear, perhaps we should get to the business at hand. Herr Pinkelt is a busy man and we mustn't hold him up.

—Thank you, Madam, no more tea. Your daughter is right, I fear. Have you had enough time to look over the document? Is there anything you'd like me to explain?

Explain? Oh, yes, mister prissbottom, you can explain how Lisbeth came up with thirty thousand Marks to buy her own Mother out, to purchase her boy's rights outright, thirty thousand! can anyone here explain that? do I even dare to hear the factual account of it or would my hair turn white on the spot for shame?

—No. I understand the papers perfectly well. However, Elisabeth's Father, may God rest his soul, taught me to be full of care and caution before signing anything. He was right, wasn't he, Herr Pinkert?

—Mama, you are fortunate in having a daughter who takes care of all these things for you so you needn't trouble yourself.

—Indeed you are, Madam.

Why shouldn't she answer for him if she answers for her own Mother? All this gobbledegook in six paragraphs six articles, *the representatives of the legally incapacitated Professor Dr. Nietzsche* a fine way to talk about your own brother as though his mouth were sealed shut like a vault I suppose it is except for eating; sometimes sealed against food too when the cramps come on I always go into a tizzy then because if he can't eat he'll die just like Little Joseph, a fine way to talk about your own flesh and blood. Every day you were away in Paraguay he would ask after you *Where is my sister?* he would say on the verge of tears he loves you so. And if he knew what you were doing to your own Mother his Mother too at this very moment he would never forgive you he would pluck your eyes out.

How quiet you are upstairs, my Fritzchen, you must be deep in slumber God bless my baby how I wish you were here with me now, you or your Father or some guardian angel. One as impossible as the other I suppose. Read on, take your time, Franziska: *Franziska Nietzsche maiden name Oehler, widow,* yes God knows these many years over a quarter of a century why did I never remarry, I wonder? Lots of chances. Another pastor, even. So inconvenient it wouldn't have been, they're all men of God the same though none of them like my Papa. Now there was a man. Keep on reading, Franziska: *Frau Dr. Elisabeth Förster-Nietzsche, widow.* Strange, she is another me, in perpetual black. I wish she didn't wear her hair as tight as that she has darling curls her eyes are still so bright burning with all that ambition why can't they burn with love? If she could get used to poor Dr. Förster she could get used to anything. Never again. Stop hoping. She's like her Mother, God forgive us both. Fritz is enough for the two of us, he was enough then too for me and now for her as well, but it isn't love she's getting out of him it's those thirty thousand Marks where did they come from? Probably from his friends, probably a loan on his name, a mortgage on his memory, to buy out his own Mother. Her own Mother too God forgive us all.

§ 1

Thanks to the enterprise and circumspection of Frau Dr.
Förster a collected edition of the works of Friedrich
Nietzsche is currently being published by the house of C. G.
Naumann in Leipzig, which

Good girl. Always begin by patting yourself on the back, it may be contagious; you can hope so anyway, Lieschen dear. Keep on reading, Widow Franziska.

assures the author an appropriate honorarium

Just a moment. Just a moment. The author? I think your poor old Mother is on the verge of finding out where those thirty thousands are coming from, *will* come from, to pay back the loan from Fritzen's friends: it is money that does not yet exist, a bubble a hot air balloon to buy out your poor old Mother. Keep on reading, Widow Nietzsche, this is getting interesting.

—What are you smiling at, mother dear? Is something misspelled?

—No, Lieschen. It's all perfect.

Keep on reading, Widow Franziska.

189

in French and English translations, the latter especially for
the American States.

Fritz would like that. He always wanted to go to Mexico even when
he was a boy Oaxaca Popocatepetl Buenos Aires Chichihuahua, yes
he would like that. The American States. I wonder do they read
there?

In addition, Frau Dr. Förster has under the name "Nietzsche-
Archive"

Under the name, yes, well under it. Keep patting yourself, Lieschen,
yes, you've worked very hard. No one to help you but that troupe of
Goethe-Schiller bachelors from Weimar traipsing through one after
the other, such unlikely candidates. Read on, Widow Nietzsche.

a task that demands a greater concentration of intellectual
labor and more reliable editions.

There you are, Franziska, there you are, poor old kindly stupid
Widow Nietzsche, that's you right there on the page with all your
failings no brains being the worst. And who's to fill the intellectual
gap? Little Liese. The Llama he calls you. Careful don't laugh again
this is serious business. Read on.

In this regard Frau Dr. Förster wishes greater freedom and
independence from the collaboration of the executors. The
latter acknowledge this wish as justified and

My foot

are of the view that the exercise of a suitable influence on the
scholarly preparation of Friedrich Nietzsche's oeuvre and
also the expansion of the "Nietzsche Archive" lie outside the
realm of their obligations and

Yes, yes, I know. I'm only his nurse. I only feed and bathe and
change him I only stay up every other night the loud nights with hor-
rendous shouting all through the night I never asked for anything
more God knows but to nurture this child of my heart. When I lost
Little Joseph I thought I still have two well now it's down to one. And
I never interfered with their editions with God as my witness, the eli-
gibles the prospects from the Goethe-Schiller Archive never had a

word of complaint against me far from it. Greater freedom and independence from what I'd like to know if I am too stupid to play any
role at all? And Adalbert? He never interfered either he isn't even
here when I need him most. What does she want me to sign this
release for anyway to pledge thirty thousand Marks she doesn't even
have to pay off a loan from friends that aren't even hers the whole
thing makes no sense. Read on, Widow Nietzsche.

> all honoraria after 1st November 1895

November? We're already well into December Christmas a week
away. I hope this fuss doesn't spoil it, I hate a spoiled Christmas, the
time he was so sick it spoiled everything. Why not the 1st of January
1896? Wouldn't that make the bookkeeping easier? Can Naumann
have sold that many copies over the past six weeks? Oh, I forgot the
Christmas trade, yes that's it. Merry Christmas, Lisbeth.

> along with the publisher's contributions to the cost of the
> edition now in process of publication should be made pay-
> able solely to Frau Dr. Förster-Nietzsche.

Using both names now, she has to get the name *Nietzsche* in there
too. Under the name. Well under it. Keep reading, Widow Nietzsche.
Elisabeth's obligations. Yes, busy Lieschen. Wait. Wait. Here we are.
About payment.

> § 3 (d)
> to the representatives of Friedrich Nietzsche as compensa-
> tion for the honoraria owed him and transferred to them the
> amount of 30,000 Mk. (thirty thousand Marks) payable by
> 1st February of the next year (1896).

That makes four months but only one Christmas, Lieschen you'll
never make it even with two Christmases you could never earn that
sum you know that don't you? You aren't even dreaming of payment
are you, dear, it's thirty thousand miles from your mind, isn't it, my
calculating daughter? I may no longer even be by then. And will
Cousin Adalbert take you to court to sue for payment? Oh, I hope he
does! Oh, I hope he doesn't! What a mess what a comedy of errors
it isn't funny. Elisabeth, daughter of my heart, isn't this what they call
fraud? Fritz! Wake up, Fritz! Come down here and help your poor
old Mother! Calm down, Widow Nietzsche, calm down. Easy does
it. Keep on reading, Franziska. Preserve the Christmas spirit.

—Mother darling, you're all a-tremble! Don't upset yourself so. Just sign. We've Christmas shopping to do, remember!

—I've been thinking it over, Lisbeth.

The look of consternation on her face is balm to my heart and solace to my soul. Still, I mustn't make her suffer, in spite of everything. No point to it. Let her believe I haven't the vaguest, let her have her way.

—Shouldn't we forego presents this year, you and I, and save the money for the Archive? Fritz will need his tree, of course, and a big one. But, for the rest, why don't we sacrifice together?

—O Mama, darling!

You see how she rushes to embrace your poor old Mother, Fritz, right in front of her impatient bespectacled Herr Pinkbottom? The works of love tower high; the works of guilt tower higher. God forgive us all. He will, Fritz of my heart, He will. Read on, no, I don't dare read on, read on, Widow Nietzsche.

§ 4

With respect to the capital of 30,000 Mk. (thirty thousand Marks) it is hereby determined that granting sufficient earnings to make such payment possible said amount is upon the deaths of Professor Dr. Friedrich Nietzsche and his legal heir, his mother, Frau Pastor Nietzsche, to revert to Frau Dr. Förster-Nietzsche.

O my God. O my God. Of course what is the matter with me she's entirely right I am too stupid to live too slow-witted for this slick and slippery world. How long can your poor old Mother survive anyway? Another decade? Bah! Not five years. What did he say to me that day at the Institute it upset me so much? Those pains deep inside my belly. Too deep. Not even Papa's watercure.

And then you'll be alone, Fritz of my heart.

But she will take care of you. I know she will.

She loves you. Surely you will survive.

O my God. O my God.

—Mama, dear, you're crying! I *told* you not to upset yourself. Here. Take this in your hand, Mama, it's only a pen. At the sign of the "X," Mama, sign. There. There now, it's all over, that wasn't so hard now was it Mama?

•

would you by any stretch of the invagination be called franziska?
you look more and more like alwine with each passing day i swear
i can hardly tell the difference anymore. are you certain you are still
there mama? i know where my sister is. my sister the llama. never
stand downwind mama the spit. i know where i am. i am too stupid
to live. i am dead because i am so stupid i am so stupid because i
am dead. not only in my hip. summarily dead. i quake no horses
shake no horses slake no horses. i worry jar jolt agitate no horses i
drink no horses i dont even like horses mama they pound my chest.
are you still there mama?

·

Your dear sister our loving daughter is being so naughty to your poor
old Mama Fritz I'm so happy you are oblivious how upset you'd be
you'd defend me to the end wouldn't you dear boy? After all, those
thirty thousands made of fluff and ambition belong more to you than
either her or me. Rockabye easy easy easy hoopsa hoopsa rider. She
seems so anxious to stir up trouble. With dear Overbeck, for example, our only true friend in the whole wide world who has never
flinched never balked never stopped helping since the beginning of
all this horror, it's the Basel pension she's after, I'm certain of it, I'm
so ashamed. And Köselitz. He already had so many of your books
out but his edition wasn't good enough for her it didn't have Förster
on the title page and she started the whole business all over again
and bade our Maestro Pietro a sweet adieu. But she'll have to take
him back. Some day she'll discover she can't decipher your horrid
scratch, Fritzchen, all those hours we spent practicing penmanship
when you were in cathedral school with Gustav and Wilhelm, me
bent over you holding your hand doing ⟨scribble⟩ a lot of
good it did, Köselitz is the only one who can make sense of it not
your fault you were nearly blind at the end no not the end it hasn't
ended yet and Lieschen will have to sweettalk him back into her
Archive, her "Nietzsche-Archive," her "Förster-Archive" more like.
It will be a happier place when Maestro Pietro is back: you'll have
more music than we can get for you now, the Symphonium tinkling
out the Wedding March like a Swiss music box ingenious really I
hope you'll like it do not open until Christmas the white snows of
winter old Nicholas is on his sleigh

To Elisabeth Nietzsche in Naumburg

Pforta, end of November, 1861,
from your brother

To my Bizzie Lizzie.

I hope you haven't yet concluded your list of wishes, and that I can at least make a few suggestions. I've written down quite a number of desirable books and musical scores; let me mention just a few of them to you. Among the scores, for example, it seems to me that a work by Schumann would be particularly appropriate for you—he's the one who composed "The Broken Windowpane." I'm referring to the most beautiful of all his Lieder, the ones gathered under the title "A Woman's Love and Life," poems by Chamisso, the cost must be about 20 Silver Groschen. The text is also every bit as beautiful. For books, I can straightaway recommend two works in theology that would intrigue us both. . . .

Your Fritz.

Driving Ruprecht well away. Hark the herald joy to the world. Silent night no dogs in the manger

To Elisabeth Nietzsche in Naumburg

Pforta, end of November, 1861

Dear Lisbeth.

That you do not wish to have A Woman's Love and Life given to you for Christmas is something I really do not relish hearing, first of all because such opposition emerges from a mouth that seems to have no capacity at all to judge where such fine things are concerned, and second, because I wasn't so much thinking of singing them as playing them on the piano.

Your Fritz.

Why did she force me to sign it anyway? Does she really think the three of us will die so soon, before she has to turn fluff and ambition into silver and gold? Maybe Adalbert and I will. Worked half to death already. But you? My baby boy, bristling with health, a little stiffer than you used to be but never mind Professor Binswanger said to expect that, you'll outlast us all live to a ripe old age you always said you would. But how will you know whether she pays up or not O Fritz O my baby boy sleep tight sleep tight, hoopsa hoopsa rider rides, if he falls he cries and cries. Easy. Easy. Easy.

What does she need all that money for anyway? To buy back that letter that was stolen from her in Paraguay? Who was it from,

Fritz? And what could have been in it to make her so frantic to have it back at all costs? We'll have a huge tree Fritz just as you said *of course a really big one* a fir of course your favorite the needles smelling of oranges and limes. Last year you fell asleep right in front of it, maybe we'll have better luck this year, how you love Christmas!

To Franziska and Elisabeth Nietzsche in Naumburg

Basel, December 17, 1870

Warmest Yuletide Greetings.

This year will not have been worth much. Let's be glad it will soon be over and didn't swallow us up. In the end that is the best present we can give one another.

FN.

No wonder it's the season of His joy and blessings it's always been your favorite time of year. There there. Don't whimper. It will soon be here bringing cheer. Now that Lisbeth has had her way nothing more can spoil it. Don't cry baby. She calls you angelheart she loves you dearly I know she does don't weep.

But that letter? What could it have been about? And how much is that blackmailer in Chemnitz charging her to get it back?

•

who knows how much mama? it could be thousands. it would be worth a fortune to her to have it back. in order to burn it mama. never stand downwind mama spit and ash. the llama confuses paraguay with sheba she thinks shes a queen mama just because the american emissary to argentina said he would build a railroad so that one day he could come to see the little queen of nueva germania in english in spanish in germania in the original all he wanted was her lumber and all she wanted was his leverage they were made for each other the big man with his big sticks and the little woman with her sulphur sticks her little box of matches and a big box of her big brothers letters one went missing mama and she wanted it back very much. i know that letter well mama and it would interest you to see it it would cause everything she is doing now to ravel and fray at the edges dissolve utterly undone. i wrote it in the second month of the new era i remember it as clearly as i breathe mountain air would you like to feel its alpine breeze mama would you like to hear its trumpet blasts of retribution mama its apocalyptic percussion?

To Elisabeth Nietzsche [Draft]

Turin, mid-November 1888

My Sister!

I received your letter, and after rereading it several times feel utterly constrained to bid you adieu. Now that my destiny has been decided, I suffer tenfold pangs over each word that you have written to me. You haven't the foggiest notion what it means to be the next of kin of a human being and a destiny in whom and in which a millennial question has been decided—the future of mankind is quite literally in my hands.

I know human nature. Far be it from me to judge in any particular case what form that human fatality will take. Even more, I realize that precisely you—who are wholly incapable of descrying the things that constitute my very life—have had to flee in the opposite direction. What consoles me in this regard is the thought that in your own way you have done quite well, that you have someone whom you love and who loves you, that a meaningful task has been assigned you, a task to which you devote your talents and your energies.—However, in the end I should not conceal from you the fact that precisely this task has led you far afield from me, so that the shockwaves that will soon be emanating from me will perhaps never reach you.—I hope they do not, for your sake. My most fervent wish is that you will not let yourself be seduced by some amiable curiosity (which in this case would be a dangerous curiosity) into reading the texts of mine that are about to be published. Reading them might wound you beyond all annealing; if this were to happen I would be deeply wounded as well. . . .

For your own peace of mind I hasten to add that I am in the best of health, possessed of a fortitude and a patience unlike any I have experienced at any hour of my life hitherto. The most burdensome things have now become easy for me; virtually everything I put my hand to prospers. I play with burdens that would crush any other mortal. For what I have to do is frightful in every sense of the word: with my horrific accusation I toss a gauntlet at the feet not of individuals but of humanity as a whole; whichever way the decision may go, whether for me or against me, an unspeakably tremendous fatality is in any case bound up with my name. . . .

By begging you to see no hardness of heart in this letter
but, on the contrary, the precise opposite, a genuine
humaneness that endeavors to prevent unnecessary suffering,
I commend myself beyond all necessity to your love.

Your Brother

did you say archive mama? whose archive mama? keep your hand
right there mama cover the vasistas prevent the draft stop the throbbing your skin is chilled parchment mama. i wish i could write like
that mama. i think i remember how to do it. you put your right hand
over your heart and swear to tell no lies god sees you and then you
move it up and down and around and around faster and faster and
faster *scribble* leaving little gaps in between for the llama
mmama you know Ilieschen our sister and daughter, gaps for her
scissors and her touchups and her book of matches mama. did you
say archive mama? whose archive mama?

•

Having you back home with us all these years, Fritz, it's been wonderful just like old times, you and Lieschen and your poor old
Mother. Just like the first time we had you back home with us again
late in the summer of 1870 after you got out of the military hospital.

To Erwin Rohde in Hamburg

Basel, July 16, 1870

Here is a frightful thunderclap: war has been declared between
France and Germany, and our entire threadbare civilization
rushes to embrace the horrid demon. What will come to pass?
Friend, my dearest friend, the last time we saw one another it
was in the sunset of peace. How grateful I am to you. If your
existence should become unbearable now, then come back to
me. What are all our goals! We could already be at the beginning
of the end! What a wasteland! We shall need cloisters again. And
you and I will be the first *fratres*.

The Faithful Swiss.

You silly Fritz! You were clever enough to become a professor in
neutral Switzerland where you wouldn't have to enlist and foolish
and brave enough to join up anyhow. With the medical corps, that's
true, they wouldn't let you fight, you were Swiss more or less after

all. After one week you were back from France with diphtheria and dysentery. It could have killed you, our good King's adventure in France, wouldn't your Father have been proud? But you recovered so quickly. Truly, the war did you a lot of good, brought you back to earth. Becoming a professor so young it turned your head, but the war twisted it right back. You saw life from another angle, it made you more practical, you took more interest in family affairs than you had shown in years, you were easier to get along with at home, a soldier's home now, pain does that, and weakness. You were all emptied out like an old ragdoll tattered and torn shedding sawdust and stuffing. We were painting your throat twice a day with that awful smelling tincture, how you gagged on it! Then you began to get your appetite back, you ate and drank like a horse, I never saw such a bolting down of food, we couldn't stuff enough into you. Ravenous appetite! How much pleasure Lieschen and I had watching you wolf it down! You had found your niche in the family again, the comfiest little corner in God's green acres, and we were all so pleased. All in all it was worth it that war, it did the whole family a lot of good.

•

ars nancy metz wörth. what was it all worth? ars near metz. ars without art. no dionysian worldview. thats what i was writing in the maderanertal mama when the war broke out i never expected it. the maenads were dozing on the mountain meadow at midday and the next thing i knew i was on a train for what was it wörth. worthless. metz. the mess of slaughter. the filth. nancy. the misery. the filth and misery of death violence festering wounds abysses of flesh the skin coming off like sheets of burnt parchment. cattlecars with straw on the cold steel floor hospital trains they called them they were cattlecars. human cattle butchered for transport from metz to karlsruhe rest easy karl they wont call you up to serve again. two days two nights. not enough morphine never enough morphine. they screamed and groaned until i wanted to strangle them and have done with it i could have no one would have noticed no one would have cared. six heaps of stinking misery six drawn and quartered oxen slaughtered sloppily not with art no art in it six in each cattlecar. luckily the oil lamps gave off so little light you couldnt see didnt have to see what you were dressing. holes so deep the organs were squeezing out like babies heads trying to be born. sometimes you had to make a fist and punch them back in and cover them over with flaps of shredded muscle lumpy fat rubbery skin and hold the fetid gemetzled mess together and pray by some miracle it would heal it always did start to heal mama miracles every hour on the hour until the red and yellow swelling couldnt hold a second longer then the putrid stench of an explosion you could hear it mama fssss-plupp! and youd have to do it all over again fist flaps flesh fat fumbling stitches painted against sepsis praying o please paste him back together again jesus hes only eighteen he should be in my greek grammar class at the gymnasium hes not an ox o please god. i never minded praying to god mama as long as i was in love or someone was dying. here everyone was dying everyone in love with death the sweet odor of incipient corruption everywhere. ars wörth nancy mess. i tried to join the army and when i failed i suppose i tried to join the dead. my diphtheria. i should never have kissed him he was probably already dead. sometimes it was easy to tell: the eyes looked at you for the first time with utter honesty and the face was fully human no connivance no false bravery no show no hinter-thoughts and the appeal was unmistakable hello hello you out there hello i am dead in here i am dead there is no more there in here in here it is all outside all accomplished all consummated and so i kissed him and my thumbs pressed down the lids of his still soft eyes thats how i caught the diphtheria mama trying to join them. and the dysentery? wouldnt you like to know mama no you wouldnt. it was good to be home after that. all things considered mama yes i pre-ferred it to the soiled straw the oilsmudged steel floor the shattered bones the flow of blackblood when you thought there cant be any more blood there simply cannot be any more blood there can only be pus and water it was like the iliad there was always more blood *until a dismal fog wrapped me round: for a long time i heard nothing but a keen a cry that never ever wanted to end.*

•

It was even better having you home for Christmas that Christmas of 1879. We didn't talk much. I spent most of the time holding your brow as you bent over the bowl convulsed with dry heaves, emptier than any human being has ever been empty, emptier even than you were after your dysentery.

To Franz Overbeck in Basel

Genua, March 17, 1882

The massive amounts of gall that I now vomit forth arouse my interest.

F. N.

I knew then why you had given up your professorship, the pride of the family flushed away, I was heartsick. You vomited out your professorship and the Gymnasium teaching, everything, you should have stuck to theology I knew it would come to nothing in the end. You said you would return to Naumburg and live in a tower in the old city wall and pay me rent and be my gardener. I could just see you, you silly Fritz, creeping among cabbages squinting at squash

To Franziska and Elisabeth Nietzsche in Naumburg

Genua, December 21, 1881

My eyes are going downhill in a hurry, I can't conceal the fact. I often upset things, stumble over them, shatter them. Where can I find another city besides Genua where the sidewalks are paved so amply that I can walk about in the neighborhoods with no difficulty, always on smooth, hard stone (and with rills carved into it whenever the sidewalks ascend or descend)?

In heartfelt love,
Your Fritz.

Wednesday morning.

I knew it would never happen, I never dreamed it would, and so you finally limped home to Naumburg for Christmas to throw up. At least that has stopped. You're so much healthier now, all things considered, eating like a horse. Open wide. Don't just swallow. Chew.

•

your mush tastes like the ordure they used to serve me in the asylum mama. yuletide grueltide christmas mush. empty the body cleanse the soul. lisbeth you may have mama to take care of you and bore you to tears ive got my own sisters

To Malwida von Meysenbug in Rome

Naumburg, January 14, 1880

Although writing is one of my most forbidden fruits, you must nevertheless have a letter from me, you whom I love and esteem as an older sister. This will no doubt be my last! For the terrible and all but unrelenting martyrdoms of my life make me thirst after the end; according to certain symptoms, it seems that the saving brainstroke is nigh enough to grant me hope. As far as torture and deprivation are concerned, my life during the past few years can measure up to that of any ascetic of any period; nevertheless, I have attained much during these same years toward the purifying and polishing of my soul—and I no longer need either religion or art to that end. (You will notice that I am proud of the fact; indeed, the abandonment of everything else first allowed me to discover my own sources of rescue.) I believe that I have fulfilled my life's work— admittedly, after the manner of one who was not given the time. . . . No pain has been able to seduce me into bearing false witness against life, *life as I know it,* nor should it ever be able to do so.

Friedrich Nietzsche.

ive got my own sisters and my own doctors now i am my own doctor

To Franziska and Elisabeth Nietzsche in Naumburg

Sils-Maria, circa July 9, 1881

My dear Mother,

Don't be angry if I appear to be rejecting your love and sympathy in this regard. But I want to be my own doctor, exclusively, from now on; and mankind shall say of me that I was a *good* doctor—and not merely for myself alone.— Nevertheless, I go to confront many, many periods of protracted illness; don't become impatient because of this, I beg you! This upsets me more than the illnesses themselves, because it reveals that my closest relatives have so little faith in me.

So much for today, so much once and for all! Already much too much for my eyes!

Your Son and Brother

Write me *good* things from now on, inasmuch as I am brooding over the future of mankind, and let us set aside all petty personal sufferings and cares. An extremely delicate sausage would also count as one of these *good* things.

•

It was all I could do to get Lieschen back from Basel. All those months tending you when she should have been wasting her time

201

tending her poor old Mother piety demanded it. And here I am tending you now. Everything turns in a circle you see there is something crooked about it. Everyone needs someone. Why didn't you marry yourself, Fritz boy, why didn't you find yourself a proper caretaker? Why did you leave it to me? There were lots of girls who were interested in you, lovely ones, but you drove them all away with your talk. You never should have gotten mixed up with those Russians. A nice German girl wouldn't do, oh no, you had to chase Russian emigrées in Geneva Paris Rome. First that Mathilde, good German name she had at least, Roofstomper, but she was a Russian underneath living in Geneva how can you trust someone with a background like that? You played the piano for her took a stroll with her and her sister and the man she married soon enough, you hid your eyes behind a shade so your look wouldn't betray you, you said it was the sun, you bowed and scraped and on the third day you proposed to her. By letter. O Fritz.

To Mathilde Trampedach in Geneva

Geneva, April 11, 1876

My dear Miss

Tonight you are writing something for me, and I too shall write something for you.—

Gather up all the courage that is in your heart, in order not to be afraid of the question I hereby put to you: Would you be willing to become my wife? I love you, and to me it feels as though you already belonged to me. Not a word about the hastiness of my inclination! At least guilt plays no role in it, and therefore there is no need to beg for pardon. However, what I would like to know is whether you feel the way I do—that we have not been unknown to each other in the past, not at all, not for an instant! Don't you believe, as I do, that each of us would be freer and better off if we were bound up together than we ever could be alone—as Longfellow's "Excelsior" says? Would you risk accompanying me, as one who is striving for liberation and improvement? Along all the paths of life and thought?

Be independent-minded, now, and hold nothing back. No one else knows of this letter and my proposal, apart from our common friend, Herr von Senger. I'll be returning to Basel on the fast train tomorrow at 11:00. I have to go back. I enclose my Basel address. If you can say *Yes!* to my question, I'll write your Mother straightaway, in which case I'll need her address, please. If you can muster all your forces for a quick decision, whether *Yes!* or *No*—then a letter from you would reach me in the Hotel Garni de la Poste until tomorrow at 10:00.

Wishing you all the best, and perfect felicity, always and always,

Friedrich Nietzsche

O Fritz Fritz! Even to a Russian you can't propose with one foot on the quick train. She was beautiful—ashblonde, slim, eyes as green as a black cat's—you said she was as lovely as a painting by Flippy Lippy, sounds undignified probably Italian, and even so you frightened her off with your direct question and your courage and sudden inclination and guilt and mustered forces and excelsior. She was scheming all the while anyway with that Senger she didn't mind at all the fact that he'd already been to the altar twice what's that to a renegade Russian, and you gave Senger your letter to deliver to her! O Fritz Fritz Fritz! You and your wretched Russians, you and your ridiculous rush. You knew how it would turn out. Sometimes I think in your heart of hearts you planned it that way so that she and Senger would singe you good and you could creep safely back into your snailshell.

To Mathilde Trampedach in Geneva

Basel, April 15.

Most honored Miss

You are generous enough to forgive me, I can feel it in the mildness of your letter, which I truly didn't deserve. I have suffered so much at the thought of my cruel and violent way of behaving that I can't be thankful enough for this gentleness. I don't feel that I can explain anything and don't know how to justify myself. I only have this last request to communicate to you, which is that if you should ever read my name again or should we ever meet please don't think of the terrible fright I have caused you; under all circumstances I ask you to believe that I would like to make amends for the ill I have done.

Yours respectfully,
Friedrich Nietzsche

You ought to get married, darling Fritz, you really ought to, how many times did I tell you that? You ought. You really ought. But not Ott. Not *Mrs.* Ott. Not Frau Louise Ott, another Russian posing behind a good German name, a very much married Russian O Fritz how could you? You met her in Bayreuth, I know what that kind of music does to you, Tristram, it's so sad, a shame and a scandal. Another blonde another beauty you certainly had an eye for them, you naughty boy, no wonder they were attracted to you. And she with a husband and a bitsy baby back in Paris! What was she doing traipsing around Bayreuth anyway, turning your head that's what! She wrote you French letters, the Jezebel, God forgive me I mean her she wanted an adventure she was an adventuress. You were all seriousness you wanted a faithful and earnest helpmate. I could almost forgive her for betraying her husband it happens all the time and the men always do it first but what about little Marcel? Didn't you think of *him?* You certainly should have after what happened to your own Father I mean losing him as a boy. And she mooning over you ignoring Marcel and her motherly duty it isn't natural I tell you it isn't even right. Cooing to you in French while little Marcel was suffering from cramp and colic at home, having such terrible trouble teething, didn't your heart wrench with the thought of your own dear brother my Little Joseph and his teeth God rest his soul? And you gushing over her you ought to be ashamed you ought. Louise. Ljola. Those Russian Lulus. She said she wanted to be your little fairy, to be a mote in your sunbeam, so that she could slip into your room sight unseen and assuage your pain. And would you be *d'accord* if she came *dans la saison des fleurs* to be your *petite amie* while posing as your *petite soeur.* You've got one sister that should be enough for anyone. O Fritz, can't you tell when a woman is all aglow for you, don't you have enough sense to stay in out of the heat? I swear you weren't made for this world none of us were God help us all

To Louise Ott in Paris

Basel, August 30, 1876

My dear Frau Ott,

Darkness descended on me when you left Bayreuth, it was as though someone had deprived me of the light. I had to pull myself together—but I *have* done so, and you can grasp this letter in your hands without worry.

We want to hold tight to the purity of spirit that brought us together; in all good things we want to remain faithful to one another.

I think of you with such fraternal fondness that I could love your husband, just because he is *your* husband; and would you believe that your little Marcel crosses my mind ten times a day?

Would you like to have the first three of my *Untimely Meditations?* You should know what I believe in, what I live for. Keep on being good to me and help me with my task.

You are pristine in my thoughts,
Friedrich Nietzsche

Louise. Lulu. Pristine. O Fritz! Fraternal fondness fiddlefaddle. She didn't want you to love her *husband* for heaven's sake or her baby God forgive her! Purity of spirit, fidelity, O Fritz don't be an untimely twit, she was sending you sprigs of dill, can't you smell it tickling high up in your nose to make you sneeze or faint? Six years after you stopped writing her she sent you a bouquet of chrysanthemums in November that was her sprig of dill, O Fritz, did you mean to make her wait another six? You were right the first time: the lights went out on you. You always wanted to go to Paris. With Rohde, remember? And then with Rée? You should have gone to Paris, you surely ought to have gone to her. You'd have made a wonderful father to little Marcel. It might have saved us all with God as my witness it might have saved us all. But you wouldn't take the bait. You wouldn't bite. You wouldn't be lured

To Louise Ott in Paris

Friday, Basel. September 22, 1876

My dear and good Friend,

How is poor little Marcel doing with his poor little teeth? We all have to suffer before we learn how to bite hard, physically and morally.—Bite in order to nourish ourselves, of course, not just for the sake of biting!—

Is there not a good photograph of a certain lovely little blonde I know?—

With all my heart, fraternally yours,
Dr. Friedr. Nietzsche

Think of Little Joseph, Fritz, teeth are no laughing matter. You can die getting them or losing them, your own baby brother died cutting them. Nourishment. Biting hard. Photographs. Fraternizing hearts with lovely little blondes. Physically and morally. O Fritz.

205

THE WAYS OF THE MOTHER

To Louise Ott in Paris

Sorrent près de Naples. Villa Rubinacci.
December 16, 1876

Recently it occurred to me, my friend, that you might want to write a little novel, which you could give me to read: one can survey so well what one has and what one wishes of life, and it certainly wouldn't make one unhappier—that is the effect of art. At all events, it would make one wiser.—Perhaps it is foolish advice: if so, tell me you've laughed at me. I would enjoy hearing that.

Hearty greetings from your
Friend
F. N.

A novel? You know the sorts of things they put into novels, Fritz of my heart, you know better than to encourage that sort of thing. You needed mothering, not philandering. You should have married Marie Baumgartner. She loved you. And her French was excellent, Professor Burckhardt himself confirmed it. She was so bored with that chemist in Lörrach God forgive her I know He does within easy reach of Basel. Yet you never gave her a chance. I know she was old enough to be your mother what's wrong with that? Perhaps she was the best mother you ever knew apart from your own, no one ever understood a boy better than his Mother, altogether a good soul really except that she tried to stuff you with Zwieback that's no regimen for a man my baby. Why didn't you marry yourself Fritz boy? You ought

To Louise Ott in Paris

Rosenlauibad, August 29, 1877
(oh! the day after tomorrow I have to leave;
back to old Basel again!)

Dear, dear Friend

I don't want to abandon my mountain solitude without writing you one more time to say how good it is to be thinking of you. It is a useless thing to say, a useless thing to write, isn't it? Yet my feelings of friendship for someone stick in me like a thorn and eventually irritate me as a thorn does, I can't get rid of them. So just accept this useless irritating little letter!

I've been told that you are—well, wishing and hoping for something, indeed, expecting it. I heard it with the most intense devotion. I'm wishing with you. Another new and good and beautiful human being in the world—that is something, that is a lot! Because you disdain to *immortalize* yourself in novels, you do it in this way, and the rest of us have to be grateful to you for it (especially if, as they also tell me, your way involves a great deal more trouble even than writing novels)—

Recently I looked out into the dark and suddenly I saw your eyes.—Why does no human being look at me with such eyes? I cried out bitterly. Oh, it is a terrible thing!

Why have I never heard you *sing*?—Do you know that even though I have heard many renowned singers of all kinds, no female voice has ever had a profound impact on me. Yet I believe that there is a voice *for me* in the world, and I am seeking it. So tell me, where can it be?—

Farewell, may all the good spirits hover about you.

Yours faithfully,
Friedrich Nietzsche

You know the sorts of things they put into songs, Fritz of my heart, and you oughtn't to encourage it you should stick with thorns you should think of your Father and Mother. That is something. That is a lot.

•

on the rooftops and turrets of fancy tramp tramp tramp. fra lippo lip-pilou. lou. louise. louise tramp. you ought you ott you ought to tramp tramp tramp marry. ott to marry you ott. ottnt you marry you ott. louise. lay marcel gently on the altarstone my father will take care of him i love your yellow hair your catseye your shadowy gorge your velvet voice the sequinsparkle of your black velvet gown your words whispered dans la saison des fleurs d'accord ma petite soeur peut-être pas d'accord bite my finger hard marcel don't cry mon petit frère d'accord fra lippo lippi your mouth your lips your listening mouth my speaking mouth louise i love the ease of your my voice lou ease. And when hotly he planted in you this new word-seed petit frère petite soeur did you turn your head and see suddenly there in the dark my squinty catseye seeking you out? that is something. that is all ott. that will ease me louise. louise. toutes les lous. où êtes-vous? vous-lous?

•

The Russians ruined you, Fritz, they used and abused you, you'd have done better to embrace that ballerina you met on the train in Italy what was her name, Calina? You should have gotten off the train with her in Milan, you should have learned how to dance *her* way. The Russians talk too much and they cannot be trusted.

To Paul Rée in Rome

Genua, March 21, 1882

Greet this Russian woman for me if it makes any sense to do so: I lust after this species of soul. Indeed, I shall soon go on a raiding expedition—when I look ahead to what I want to do during the next ten years, I need her. Marriage is another chapter altogether—I could come to terms with a two-year marriage at the very most, yet this too only with regard to what I have to do over the next ten years.

Your faithful friend,
FN.

She was the worst. Lulu. Salomé. Sounds seductive probably Jewish. Dance of the Seven Veils. Like an onion, seven skins, at heart, nothing. Lieschen saw through her right from the start, Lieschen hated your Lulu, she told me everything but you wouldn't listen. Your Lulu grew up with five older brothers no sisters and a flighty mother, how did you expect her to learn how to be a woman? Yes, I know about her slim waste and her bountiful bosom *That dried up dirty stinking little ape with her falsies—a fatality! Pardon me!* and her blonde hair and her dark eyes and her Bohemian black dress and her no makeup but that doesn't make a woman a woman except maybe for a man. She fooled you and Rée both you were dumb oxen

To Lou von Salomé in Zürich-Riesbach

Naumburg, shortly after May 24, 1882

Dear friend Lou,

The nightingales sing all night long outside my window.—In every respect Rée is a better *friend* than I am or can be; note well this distinction between the two of us!—When I'm all alone, I often, very often, say your name aloud—to my very great pleasure!

Your F. N.

Consumptive she was. She won you over by making you pity her and by picking your brain. She was only twenty years old, Fritz, for heaven's sake young enough to be your student you were old enough to be her father shame on you. You should have been praying when you met her in Saint Peter's in Rome. She was drifting dreamily staring up the length of the baldachino at the cupola, she was looking for God, she thought He was a snowman who melted away every spring did you ever hear such nonsense Fritz? What did you want with a girl like that? Your common friend Rée he was common all right he was writing her immoral notes in the shafts of creamy light that fell near a confession box and you marched onto this unwholesome popish scene to tell her she'd dropped down from a star in heaven to join you well she'd dropped all right.

To Ida Overbeck in Basel

Naumburg on the Saale, Pentecost, 1882

Esteemed Frau Professor

Consider the fact that Rée and I share the identical feelings toward our brave and valiant friend and that he and I have *enormous trust* in one another also on this point. We are not among the silliest or the most puerile human beings.—In Naumburg I have until now kept quiet about these new developments. Nevertheless, that will be impracticable in the long run, if only because my sister and Rée's mother are in contact with one another. And yet I want to keep my own mother "out of the game"—she already has enough cares to bear—why yet another *unnecessary* one?

In gratitude and fidelity,
Your F.N.

You can't keep a mother out of the game, Fritz, we have our ways of finding out things. By the time you got out of that sty of superstitious popery the three of you were planning a ménagerie à trois in Paris, even an animal wouldn't do that to its Mother how could you?

To Paul Rée in Stibbe

Naumburg, May 29, 1882

I often laugh about our Pythagorean friendship, with its very rare φίλοις πάντα κοινά. It gives me a better conception of myself

to be really *capable* of such a friendship.—Yet it is still
something to laugh about, isn't it?

Lots of love,
Your F. N.

You said it was just to be roommates at the university. You said you
wanted to learn about chemistry acids bases salts kalium philoso-
phosphoricum my eye. Roommates my foot. Fritz do you think I'm
stupid don't answer that no one's as stupid as you think I am. I knew
what you and your common friend were up to, Lisbeth told me
everything, she wouldn't have had to my boy mothers know things
we have our sources.

To Franz Overbeck in Basel

Naumburg, circa June 5, 1882

My dear Friend,

By the bye, I am possessed of a fatalistic "trust in the Lord"—I
call it *amor fati*—so much so that I'd put my head in a lion's
mouth, not to mention——
    With regard to the summer, our plans are still altogether
unsettled.
    In Naumburg mum's still the word. With regard to my
sister, I am quite resolved to keep her out of it; she could only
confuse matters (and confuse herself first of all).

F. N.

Paris Vienna Munich even Leipzig any place would have suited you,
just so it was dark, O Fritz how could you stoop so low

To Paul Rée in Stibbe

Naumburg, presumably June 10, 1882

With regard to our project for the winter, I must plead with you
to be absolutely silent *to everyone* about everything: we shouldn't
say a word about whatever is to come. As soon as something is
uttered too soon you can be sure that *there will be opponents
and counterproposals:* the danger is not a slight one.—I've noticed
unfortunately that it is difficult for me to live incognito in
Germany. Thüringen I've given up on altogether. Adieu!

Heartily,
Your F. N.

To take up with a woman half your age a sordid Russian without morals! Oh, I know you're the grand Immoralist but she was probably already engaged to your common Israelite friend didn't you think of infection contamination disease invalidism chancre blindness prostration didn't you think of the filth the stench didn't you think of your Mother boy? You're a shame upon your family, you have desecrated your Father's grave, God forgive you I cannot. She stood you up in Berlin, served you right, kept you cooling your heels all day long in the Grunewald, forlorn under dappled sunlight on the walkingpaths by the lake. The next day you crept back home crestfallen just like a little boy who'd lost his way

To Paul Rée in Stibbe

Naumburg, Sunday, sunny weather. June 18, 1882

In spite of everything I am full of confidence in this year and its enigmatic toss of the dice for my fate. I *won't* travel to Berchtesgaden and in general am no longer in any condition to undertake anything *alone*. In Berlin I was like a lost penny— which I myself had dropped but thanks to my eyes couldn't find although it lay right at my feet, so that all the passersby laughed.
    Simile!—

Heartfelt greetings,
Your friend N.

And the way you treated Lieschen through it all, your own flesh and blood, no wonder she's doing this to me now. There was your Lulu twenty years old hobnobbing with the Wagners while Lisbeth did the washing up; there was your Lulu flouncing, turning down a proposal a week from men as dizzy as you, your future brother-in-law among them. Oh, how free and breezy your Lulu was with Dr. Förster while poor Elisabeth thirty-six never had an offer to squelch or squander lost in the crowd it wasn't fair and after all she'd done for you for shame! She'd kept your household for you, nursed you when you weren't well which was all the time, and you thank her by falling head over socks with somebody half her age who's trying to spoil her very last chance! Didn't you pause to ponder how she'd feel? Dr. Förster hadn't seen the light hadn't made the correct choice hadn't come to his senses or to the rescue yet, didn't you have a heart for your own sister? She told me everything, Fritz, everything believe me.

THE WAYS OF THE MOTHER

To Elisabeth Nietzsche in Tautenburg

Leipzig, September 9, 1882

I hear, with much sadness, that you are still suffering from the aftereffects of those scenes I would gladly with all my heart have spared you. Grasp this one point, however: this scene's turmoil *brought to light* what otherwise perhaps would long have remained in the dark, namely, the fact that Lou had a *lower* opinion of me than I thought, and *some distrust* of me; and when I examine more carefully the circumstances under which we met, perhaps she had every right to do so. (I include the effect of a few incautious remarks by friend Rée.) However, now she surely thinks *better* of me—and *that* is the main thing, isn't it, my dear sister? In general, when I look to the future, it would be hard to have to accept that you don't feel about Lou as I do. We are so similar in our talents and our intentions that our names are *destined to be named jointly* at some point. And every aspersion cast upon her will strike me first. . . .

Be good once more, dear Llama!

Your Brother.

Everything. For example, how you snuck off to gambol with your Lulu at Orta, leaving your common Rée behind for once thank God for that, climbing that hill Monte Sacro you think I don't know what that means I know exactly what it means the holy mountain what those Italians won't do in the name of religion and the two of you may have done the same something chemical electrical physical immoral passed between you else you would never have had the pluck to propose to her at the Lion Monument in Lucerne. And what exactly did you propose? A marriage for two years? Incautious remarks my eye, mum's the word indeed, a marriage of public convenience I call it! You're a shame upon your family, you've desecrated your Father's grave I tell you!

To Franz Overbeck in Basel

Address: Auenstraße 26, 2ᵉ étage, Leipzig
September 9, 1882

Unfortunately, my sister has developed into a mortal enemy of Lou's; she was full of moral indignation from start to finish. And now she claims to know what my philosophy is all about. She wrote my Mother to the effect that in Tautenburg she had

seen my philosophy come to life and that she was shocked by
it: *I* love evil, whereas *she* loves the good; if she were a good
Catholic she would hie off to a convent and do penance for all
the ill that will arise from it. In short, I have Naumburg "virtue"
against me. There is a real *break* between us—and even my
mother was so beside herself that she said something that
caused me to pack my bags and leave early the next morning
for Leipzig. My sister (who didn't want to come to Naumburg as
long as I was there—she's still in Tautenburg) commented
ironically: "Thus began Zarathustra's downgoing."—Whereas in
fact it is the *beginning* of a *commencement*.

Your F. N.

Even your lascivious Lulu turned you down on your two-year con-
jugation (imagine!), not because she had a trace of integrity about
her but because you tried to squeeze out her boyfriend, the one she
really wanted. At least you had a touch of sense if no tact and no
tactic, O Fritz, you were hopeless even then I'm sorry God forgive
me but it's true. That horrid photograph you had taken in Lucerne.
Studio Bonnet. He should have been reported to the authorities on
pornography.

To Lou von Salomé in Zürich-Riesbach

Naumburg on the Saale. Pentecost, 1882

My dear friend Lou, I shall explain to you when we are next
able to talk about "friends" and our *friend Rée* especially: I
know very well what I'm saying when I take him to be a better
friend than I am or can be.—Oh, that naughty photographer!
And yet: what a lovely silhouette perches there on that
delightful little cart!

Heartfelt greetings,
Your F. N.

People tell me I've never been so cheerful in all my life. I have
confidence in my destiny.—

You thought I'd never get to see it well I did: fake mountains and
trees in the background of a fake country road, a lovely little ladder
cart, though, I have to admit that wherever did you find it? You and
your common Rée are supposed to be the oxen pulling her cart well
you do look the part the two of you, your sheepish Israelite trying to

213

salvage his dignity by hooking his right thumb in his vest no such luck, you staring cockeyed toward the remote horizon as if you could see two feet in front of you. Some oxen. And your Russian Lulu holding both reins in one hand in the other a stalk sprouting lilacs and ribbons, it is supposed to be a cat o' nine tails, a whip, she certainly looks the cat and she certainly gave her oxen a thrashing that smarted of something more than satins and posies. She tore you with her claws and you deserved it Fritz I'm sorry God forgive me. If she tore you limb from limb you deserved it my poor boy my baby. That hussy. She whetted your appetite with her whip. She failed you flailed you flayed you. Exactly what you deserved, the ragtaggle Russian ruined you, Fritz, you couldn't help yourself.

Elisabeth told me everything and I mean everything. About that brazen bronze girl from the village on the beach at Sorrento what was the name, Corinna? Calina? Three times a week she called at your house and you told Malwida she was visiting Rée so Malwida wouldn't guess what you were up to I mean down to so she wouldn't see how low you could go. Well, Rée told your Lulu and your Lulu told Lieschen and Lieschen told me she told me everything.

To Lou von Salomé in Stibbe

Tautenburg, 27/28 June 1882

Dear Friend,

So now you believe that my keeping hush-hush was unnecessary? I analyzed it today and came up with the ultimate grounds: distrust of myself. For the happenstance that I have won to myself a "new human being" has tossed me head over heels—as a consequence of my all-too-stringent solitude, my efforts to renounce all love and friendship. I had to be silent, because to speak of you would each time have tossed me higgledypiggledy (it happened to me when I was with the good Overbecks). Now, I'm telling you this so that you can laugh. With me things always go human-all-too-humanly, and my *folly* waxes with my wisdom.

Devotedly yours and Friend Rée's
F. N.

As if that weren't enough. As if that were the worst. It wasn't the worst, not by the bitter half. The worst came at Bayreuth. There they were whispering about you behind your back because you had stayed away and deserted the cause. I can't even think what they were whispering I can't even imagine it.

To Lou von Salomé in Stibbe

Tautenburg, near Dornburg (Thüringen)
July 16, 1882

I have *experienced* so much with regard to this man and his art—it was a long and totally involving *passion:* I can't find another word for it. The renunciation called for here, the finding-myself-again that finally became necessary—these things belong among the hardest and most melancholy of my destiny. The last words Wagner wrote to me stand in a lovely copy of *Parsifal*—it was a dedication: "To my dear friend, Friedrich Nietzsche, from Richard Wagner, Head of the Parish Council." Precisely at the same time he received a copy of the book I'd sent him, my *Human, All-too-Human*. With that, it was *all clear,* but also, all over.

How often, in all possible things, have I experienced precisely *this:* "All clear, but also, all over!"

And how happy I am, my beloved friend Lou, that I may now think with regard to the two of us, "All is just beginning, and yet it is *all clear!*" Have faith in me! Let us have faith in ourselves!

With heartfelt wishes to you on your journey,

Your friend,
Nietzsche.

They were whispering that you loved boys, Fritz, I'm so ashamed. You've desecrated your own Father's grave. All clear, all over. And your little brother's, Little Joseph's grave, as well. And my poor Lieschen! You took her off to a pastor's house in Tautenburg in the middle of nowhere while the pastor was away you thought the mice might play. Lieschen in lieu of a proper chaperone. You stuck her up on the third floor and ignored her the whole time. You initiated your Lou into your "philosophy," some philosophy. You told her that Lieschen wanted to write short stories, that she didn't mind being abandoned, that she needed the solitude to breed her little fictions, the very idea Fritz I don't know whether to laugh or cry.

To Lou von Salomé in Stibbe

Monday. Tautenburg, June 26, 1882.

My dear Friend,

A half-hour from Fortress Thorn, where the elderly Goethe
enjoyed his solitude in the midst of lovely forests, lies
Tautenburg. Here my good sister has arranged an idyllic little
nest that is to enfold me this summer. Yesterday I took
possession of it. Tomorrow my sister will depart and I shall be
alone. Yet we've agreed to something that perhaps will occasion
her return. Granted, that is, that you have no better way to
spend the month of August and would find it fitting and meet to
live with me here in the woods; in that case my sister would
conduct you hither from Bayreuth and live with you here (for
example, in the house of the local pastor, where she is now
staying: the community has a good selection of lovely and
inexpensive lodgings). My sister, whom you may ask Rée about,
would need a great deal of solitude during this period in order
to brood on her little novella-egg. She is mightily pleased by the
thought of being in your and my proximity.—So! And now, let
us be upright "unto death"! My dear friend! I am committed to
nothing here and could quite easily alter my plans in case *you*
have other plans. And if I am not to be together with you, then
simply tell me so—and you don't even need to give any reasons!
I trust you *implicitly:* but you know that.—

If we get along well together, then so will our states of
health, and in some secret way this visit will do us both good.
Prior to this, I've *never* thought that you might "read aloud and
write" for me; but what I very much wish to be permitted to be
is your *teacher.* Finally, to tell the whole truth: I am now
seeking the human beings who could be my inheritors; I bear
about me some things that are not to be read in my books—and
for these things I am searching for the finest, most fertile soil.

You see my *selfishness!*—

Every time I think on the threats to your health and your
very life, as I do again and again, my soul is filled with
tenderness; I don't know if anything else could bring me so
quickly to your side.—And then I'm ever so happy to know that
you have Rée, and not only me, as a friend. It is a genuine
pleasure for me to think of walks and talks together with the
two of you.—

The Grunewald was far too sunny for my eyes, anyway.
My address is: Tautenburg near Dornburg, Thüringen.

Yours faithfully,
Friend Nietzsche.

On long walks, oh yes, through the woods. And not with the boys, either. Not even your fellow ox was on hand to rescue you from her clutches this time.

To Lou von Salomé in Stibbe

Tautenburg near Dornburg, Thüringen. July 3, 1882

My dear Friend,
Now the sky over my head is bright! Yesterday noon I felt as though it were my birthday: *you* sent your yes, the most beautiful present anyone could have given me—my sister sent cherries, Teubner sent the first three fascicles of galleys for *The Gay Science;* on top of all that, I finished the final part of the manuscript, thereby completing the work of six years (1876-1882), my collective "free spiritry"! Oh, what years! What tortures of all descriptions, what isolation and disgust with life! And as an antidote to all that, to both death *and* life, as it were, I brewed my pharmaceuticals—these, my thoughts, with their tiny, tiny strips of *unclouded sky* over their heads:—oh, dear friend, whenever I think of all that I feel shattered and touched, and I don't know how it all could have *succeeded:* self-compassion and a triumphant feeling permeate me. For it *is* a victory, and a total one—even my bodily health has come to the fore again, I know not whence, and everyone tells me I look younger than ever. Heaven protect me from follies!—Yet from now on, with *you* advising me, I shall be *well* advised, and need not fear.—

As far as the coming winter is concerned, I have *seriously and exclusively* thought of Vienna: my sister's winter plans are quite independent of mine, in this respect there are *no* ulterior thoughts. The south of Europe is now banished from my mind. I don't want to be lonely any more, and I want to learn how to become human again. Ah, with regard to *this pensum* I have practically everything to learn!—

Accept my gratitude, dear friend! *Everything* will go well, just as you said.

Heartiest greetings to our Rée!

Wholly yours,
F. N.

Through the woods, oh yes, you and your solitary walks my foot. The Tautenburg town council voted to dedicate two new benches

along the winding woodpaths in honor of their esteemed guest—
which was you—and I suppose I was pleased I always wanted you
to be a little bit famous, until you passed on to me the job of having
the brass plates made. Had you any idea how expensive they would
be? Of course not you never had a head for money prices meant
nothing to you, you never learned the value of a Thaler. Very precise
you were too about how they should look, but what ridiculous
names you chose, Fritz, nobody calls a bench like that the smithy
said I must be joking.

To Franziska Nietzsche in Naumburg

Tuesday. Tautenburg, July 11, 1882

My dear Mother,

The Beautification Society here has erected two new benches in
parts of the woods where I like to take solitary walks. I've
promised to have two dedicatory plaques made and affixed to
them. Would you be so kind as to take care of this? And
immediately? Talk with someone who knows how to do this sort
of thing and ask them what kind of plaque and inscription will
last longest.

On the one there should appear:

> The Dead Man
> F. N.

On the other:

> The Gay Science
> F. N.

It will have to be something exquisite, something handsome,
something that will *do me honor.*

With hearty greetings,
Your son Fritz.

I suppose that was your idea of a joke, calling yourself a dead man, that's not funny not even now. The other one was just vanity, of course. You were in such a hurry. What for? *Who* for? Solitary walks my foot, I didn't do it, I didn't have the plaques made, impress your balalaika some other way I said to myself.

To Heinrich Köselitz in Venice

Tautenburg, July 13, 1882

My dear Friend,

Lou is the daughter of a Russian general, and twenty years old; she is as alert as an eagle and as courageous as a lion; for all that, a very childlike girl, who perhaps is destined not to live much longer. I owe the discovery of her to Fräulein von Meysenbug and Rée. She is now visiting the Rée's; after Bayreuth she will come to me here in Tautenburg; and in the fall we shall make our way to Vienna together. We shall dwell in one house and work together; she is prepared in the most astonishing way precisely for *my* kinds of thoughts and *my* way of thinking.

Dear friend, you surely will do us both the honor of warding off from your thoughts concerning our dealings with one another any notion of a love relationship. We are *friends* and I shall keep holy this girl and her trust in me.—Incidentally, she has an incredibly self-assured and unsullied character; she knows very well what **she** wants—without inquiring of the world or worrying herself about it in the least.

Faithfully,
your friend F. N.

Lieschen told me everything: how you snuck off to be alone with your Lulu

Good morning to you
My dear lovely Lou!

every chance you got, how you snubbed your own sister at meal-times, how you stayed up late into the night talking about boring things she couldn't understand just so she would go up to bed out of desperation (to the third floor, to the attic, shame on you Fritz your own sister!), and the the two of you could spoon unobserved.

THE WAYS OF THE MOTHER

To Lou von Salomé in Tautenburg [A Slip of Paper]

Tautenburg, August 25, 1882

In bed. The most terrible attack. I despise life.

FN.

Talking philosophy, you said; courting on the sly, that's what your Mother says. Keeping her holy, you said; eying one another up and down, that's what your Mother says.

To Lou von Salomé in Tautenburg [A Slip of Paper]

Tautenburg, August 26, 1882

My dear Lou,

Sorry about yesterday. A terrible attack of my stupid headaches—today all gone. And *today* I see a few things with new eyes.—

F. N.

Your Lulu making googoo eyes at you while you waffled on about wilted power and eternal deterrence, I can just see it I can just hear it, Fritz that's no way to win a girl. And no way to treat your sister who loves you.

To Lou von Salomé in Stibbe

Naumburg, end of August, 1882

My dear Lou,

The day after you left Tautenburg, I left too, *very* proud of heart, *very* confident—on account of what?

I have spoken only a little with my sister, just enough to send the new specter she was conjuring back into the nothingness whence it was born. . . .

Finally, my dear Lou, the old request, with all my heart: *Become the one you are!* At first one needs to be emancipated from one's *chains*, and then, in the end, one still has to *emancipate oneself* from this emancipation. Each of us has to labor at this *illness of chains*, albeit in very diverse ways, even after one has broken the chains.

Ready to confront your destiny,

> with all my heart,
> for in you too I love *my hopes*
> F. N.

No way at all. You have to *do* something, you can't sit around waiting for fate to do the job, fate's too slow, you probably bored her to tears a girl like that knows what **she**'s after and it isn't becoming and it certainly isn't love of fate. You and your fatal Russians. They nearly killed you Fritz of my heart they nearly drove you mad.

To Lou von Salomé in Stibbe

Leipzig, presumably September 16, 1882

Yesterday afternoon I was happy: the sky was blue, the air mild and pure; I was in Rosenthal, whither the music of *Carmen* had lured me. There I sat for three hours, drank my second cognac of the year, as a souvenir of the first (yuck! how horrid it tasted!), and reflected in all innocence and wickedness on the question as to whether I might not have some propensity to insanity. In the end I said to myself *No*. Then the *Carmen* music began, and I foundered for half-an-hour under tears and palpitations of the heart.—However, when you read this you will in the end say *Yes!* and will then jot down a note "characterizing" my very self.—

Come very very soon to Leipzig! Why not *before* the 2nd of October? Adieu, my dear Lou!

Your F. N.

Is that *why* you chose them, son, in the *way* you chose them? So you'd never have to settle down with any of them? So you'd never have to get close to them? So you'd never have to put it all at risk? So you'd never have to have a family the way I had you and Lieschen and Little Joseph?

To Paul Rée in Stibbe

Leipzig, presumably September 15, 1882

My dear Friend,

In my opinion the two of us, the three of us, are smart enough to be good to one another, and to continue being such. In this life, where people like *us* readily become zombies whom everyone else fears, we ought to find joy in one another and try

221

to *give the others cause for joy.* In this we should become inventive—I, for my part, have to do my homework, because I was a monster of isolation for so long.

In the meantime, my sister has diverted the enmity that comes natural to her from my mother, where it is usually propelled, to me, and with full force. She has quite literally *broken* with me—she says in a letter to my mother—out of revulsion against my philosophy, and because I love evil whereas she loves the good, and suchlike foolishness. Onto me she has unloaded mockery and contempt—now, the truth is that all my life I have been patient and gentle with her, as one must be toward this sex: and perhaps that has spoiled her. "Virtues too will be punished," says the wise Sanctus Januarius of Genua.

Tomorrow I shall write our dear Lou, *my* sister (after I've lost my natural sister, a supernatural one must be granted me). Until we meet again in Leipzig at the outset of October!

Your Friend,
F. N.

Was it so bad, then? Did you really have to go to such lengths just to avoid a little thing like life?

•

russian fatalism. now i lay me facedown in the snow of your indifference. i yove lou. ill wait for the blizzard to pass it could pass forever. in a sense you are right mama eternal deterrence and wilted power left me with my encompassing solitude my considerable contempt my nausea my vulnerability.

To Anna Dmitrievna Tenischev
in St. Petersburg [Draft]

Turin, circa December 8, 1888

And my loneliness steals upon me with the footfall of every voice.

caesar caesarum. czar of the oxen under yoke. amor fatalism. russian fatalism.

•

Fritz open your mouth. Chew Fritz. Don't just swallow. Your sister who loves you told me everything you have nowhere to hide.

To Lou von Salomé in Hamburg

Naumburg, presumably June 10, 1882

I love concealment in life, and with all my heart I would hope that you and I can be spared any involvement in a European-wide gossip chain. . . . Finally, in all things concerning action I am inexperienced and inept. For years now I've *never* had to explain or justify to a fellow human being an action of mine. I like to leave my *plans* concealed; concerning my *facta* let the whole world talk!—Yet nature gave each of us different weapons of defense—to you she gave your splendid openness of will. Pindar says somewhere, "Become the one you are!"

Faithfully and devotedly,
FN.

You can't understand a word I'm saying to you can you? They say it's never too late to learn it's too late. You won't become not any more not ever anything you haven't already become. There will be no grandchildren. Why didn't I know that from the start before I went to all this trouble, why did you and your sister deceive me so long, why was it all empty talk and quarrel with the two of you? Hopeless.

To Heinrich von Köselitz in Venice

Tautenburg. August 4, 1882

Dear Friend.

One day a bird flew by me; and I, superstitious as all lonely people are when they are standing at a crossroads on their path, thought I had seen an eagle. Now all the world endeavors to prove to me that I am mistaken—and a smug pan-European palaver has started up in this regard. Who is the more fortunate one—I, "the deceived," as they say, I who lived all summer long in a loftier world of hope on account of this augury—or those who are "not to be deceived"?—And so on. Amen. Adieu, dear friend!

Fondly,
F. N.

223

Never mind Lieschen: perhaps it's best she'll have no children. But why couldn't you have done like Professor Overbeck and his Ida, why couldn't you have found a companion spirit a kindred soul not some whooping Cossack? Why did you have to hide out in your chemistry lab in Leipzig while your common friend swept her away? If it had to be a Cossack why didn't you at least take up the saber and fight for her?

To Lou von Salomé, presumably in Berlin

Kali phosphor., 8th of November 1882

Dear Lou, just a few words—my eyes hurt. . . .
  What melancholy!
  I had no idea till this year how distrustful I am. Namely, of myself. My dealings with my fellows have ruined my dealings with myself.
  You wanted to tell me something?
  Your voice pleases me most when it asks for something. Yet one doesn't hear that often enough.
  I shall be industrious——
  Ah, this melancholy! I write nonsense. How *shallow* human beings are to me today! Where is there a sea in which one can actually still *drown*? I mean a human being.

My dear Lou
I am yours—
faithfully——
F. N.

(Heartiest greetings to Rée and his mother!)

In the end you just made yourself look ridiculous. You were always so pinched and unnatural with women always off in a world of your own lost like a little boy you wrote big words in your big books but you weren't a match for them you found no match for you no mate. Of course you had no father to advise you: your Father was a man of the spirit but spirit does astonishing things he knew his way around a woman Fritz I can tell you but I won't never mind that. Rosalie Nielsen presumably in Basel or Freiburg, you were terrified of her, you thought she was a ghost, she was only flesh and blood we're all only flesh and blood with a dash of the good Christian spirit in us and a pinch of the other. If your common crony Rée hadn't introduced you to her in Rome

To Paul Rée, presumably in Berlin

Santa Marguerita. Presumably November 23, 1882

But my dear dear friend, I thought you would feel just the opposite and would secretly be happy to be rid of me for a time! This year there were a hundred occasions, from *Orta* onwards, where I found that your friendship with me was "costing you too much." I took possession of far too much from *your* Roman find (I mean Lou)—and it always seemed to me, especially in Leipzig, that you had a right to become somewhat reticent toward me.

Dearest friend, think of me as kindly as you can, and please ask the same of Lou on my behalf. I belong to you both with the deepest feelings of my heart—I believe I have proved this more by my separation than by my *proximity.*

All proximity makes us restive—and in the end I am altogether a restive human being.

We shall see one another again from time to time, shall we not? Don't forget that from *this year on* I shall have become suddenly poor in love, and consequently much in need of it.

Write me something *quite* precise about the matter that most concerns us—the matter that "stands between us," as you always put it when you do write.

Lots of love,
Your F. N.

NB. I praised you so much in Basel that Frau Overbeck said: "But the man you're describing is Daniel de Ronda!" Who is Daniel de Ronda?
Address: Santa Margherita, *Ligure/*poste restante

everything would have been all right, although all things upset and confused you I swear weather moods objects—objects like that Lulu for example, obstreperous objectionable objects presumably in Berlin for example.

To Lou von Salomé, presumably in Berlin

Santa Margherita, Ligure (Italia).
November 24, 1882

And now, Lou, dear heart, clear the air! I want nothing else than a pure, clear sky over every aspect: otherwise I will fight my way through, you can count on that, no matter how hard it is. Yet a lonely man suffers frightfully when he suspects something about the two human beings he loves—particularly when it involves a suspicion of the suspicion they entertain concerning his very essence. Why has the cheerfulness been lacking in all our dealings with one another? Because I had to do myself too much violence: the clouds on *our horizon* lay on *me!*

Perhaps you know how unbearable I find every effort to shame people, to accuse, to have to defend myself. Unavoidably, one does a *great deal* of injustice.—Yet we also have the splendid *counterforce*, to do one another good, to sow peace and joy.

I feel every tremulous motion of the *loftier* soul in you, I love nothing else in you but these stirrings. I gladly renounce all intimacy and closeness, if only I can be sure of one thing: that the two of us feel as *one* in regions where vulgar souls will never dwell.

I speak cryptically? *When* I have your trust, you will learn that I have the *words* as well. Up to now I have *always* had to remain silent.

Spirit? What is spirit to me? What is knowledge to me? I esteem nothing other than *propulsions*—and I could swear that in this regard the two of us have something in common. Let your vision penetrate the phase I have lived through during the past several years—look behind it! Don't you be deceived about me—*you* surely don't believe that "the free spirit" is *my* ideal?! I am—

Forgive me! Dearest Lou, be what you *have* to be.

F. N.

You soon gave up on your plan to become a student again in Leipzig no more chemistry with Professor Skobeleff another Russian after she eloped with your common companion. You never liked Leipzig anyway too much fog and rain

To Lou von Salomé in Berlin [Drafts]

Genua, end of November, 1882

What are you doing, my dear Lou, I asked for cheerful skies over our heads

what should I say: it's all over now

Shall we quarrel with one another? should we make lots of noise, would that be fun? Not me. Not on your life. I wanted clear skies between us. But you? You're a little birdie perched on a gallows! And to think I once believed you were virtue and honesty incarnate.

all through the dismal winter. But what was the matter with you what were you thinking Fritz of my heart it was bound to turn nasty.

Genua, November/December, 1882

My dear Lou I must write you a nasty note. For heaven's sake, what are these little girls of twenty thinking of when all they've got is pleasant little love tremors with nothing else to do but get sick and hie off to bed? Should one perhaps scramble after these little girls in order to interrupt their boredom and chase away the flies? Just by-the-bye show them a real nice winter? Charming. But what have I got to do with pleasant winters? If I should have the honor of contributing to

The Russians Gypsies Jews don't you know those kind of people can't be trusted they have no character she told Lieschen a hundred stories and Lieschen told me.

To Paul Rée in Berlin [Draft]

Genua, early December, 1882

Very odd! Concerning Lou I have a predetermined opinion, although I have to say that *everything* I experienced this past summer contradicts it. There must be a series of higher feelings in her, feelings that are quite rare and altogether exceptional among human beings, or at least there must have been such: some sort of terrible misfortune

Actually, no one in all my life has behaved so horridly toward me as Lou has. To this very day she has not recanted that repulsive condemnation of my entire character and my intentions that she brought along with her to Jena and Tautenburg; this, even though she knows that its effects have been extremely damaging to me (namely with respect to Basel). Whoever doesn't break off relations with a girl that says such things must be—well, I don't know what—that's the only conclusion. The fact that I didn't do so was a consequence of that predetermined opinion. And incidentally, it took a *good bit* of self-overcoming. . . .

Imagine how I would handle a man who said such things about me to my sister. No doubt about it. In this regard I am a soldier, and I always will be; I know how to handle weapons. But a girl! And Lou!

In Bayreuth she not only abandoned my cause, she also belittled me (my sister recounted 100 stories)—

When I last saw Lou she told me she had something to say to me. I was full of hope. (I said to my soul: "She had a very bad opinion of you, but she's smart, she'll soon have a better one"

if only the most painful memory of this entire year would be obliterated from my soul—painful not because she insulted me but because she insulted the Lou that is inside me.

Why did you waste your time with chemistry and cossacks when you could have been educating princesses at court like your Father? Fritz you could have spent your entire life with princes and kings that dashing Ludwig and all the leaders of Europe you could have been good noble great but you took pity on her and her kind that was your weak point you were always too compassionate, just like your Father, so that when she said *I'm going to die before long* there you were at her side eating out of her hand like a puppydog. You were too full of pity. She surprised you. You thought you were under the spell of her magic but *you* were the magic it was all in your head a phantasm a headache a nightmare I swear to Our Dear Lord it was all in your head.

To Paul Rée in Berlin [Draft]

Rapallo, first half of December 1882

Dear friend, I call Lou my Sirocco incarnate: not for a single moment when we were together did we have clear sky overhead, the sort of sky I need whether with or without other people. She unites in herself *all* the human qualities I find most repulsive—disgusting and nauseating—they don't agree with me. And ever since Tautenburg I undertook to *torture* myself by *loving* her! a love no one should be jealous of, except perhaps Our Dear Lord.

One thing I suppose I can't deny you must have really needed a woman's love and life and she was the only available prospect. You were even willing to risk Bayreuth for her sake, of course you didn't go, he didn't invite you, you were waiting for a golden invitation and it never came, Bayreuth no longer held any promise for you anyway you said so yourself. So you sent my Lieschen and our good

228

Gast our cuddly Köselitz and your Lulu in your stead but Elisabeth saw everything heard everything told me she was drawn to anything in trousers. Lieschen convinced you eventually praise God but it was too late. To you, blind as a bat, she was an eagle. Elisabeth saw the mousebuzzard the chickenhawk the knifing kite the greedy vulture she really was. We should both be grateful she discovered it in spite of everything. In Jena they fought like cats and birds, my Lis and your Lulu, she said the most horrid things about you, poisonous things her boyfriend had told her against you they're not true are they Fritz? I know you're no angel, now you are of course but you weren't back then, you should have been praying to your Father he would have taken pity on you and guided you, you should have been doing everything in your power to achieve genuine greatness real fame. I don't care I won't be silent it hurts too much what a waste!

To Paul Rée and Lou von Salomé in Berlin [Draft]

Rapallo, circa December 20, 1882

To speak as a free spirit, I am a member of the *School of Affects*, which is to say, my feelings devour me. A wretched compassion, a wretched disappointment, a wretched feeling of wounded pride—how do I hold out? Is not pity a feeling made in hell? What should I do? Every morning I doubt whether I'll survive the day. I no longer sleep: what good is it if I go hiking for eight hours? Whence these towering affects in me? Oh, for some ice! Yet where is there *ice for me?* Tonight I shall take so much opium that my reason will go astray: Where is there a human being one can still *respect?* But I know you all through and through!

Don't get too unnerved by these irruptions of my delusions of grandeur or my wounded vanity: and if one day I myself should, as a result of the above-mentioned affects, take my life, there would not be too much to mourn. What do my raving fantasies matter to you I mean you and Lou! The two of you should discuss with one another at some length the possibility that ultimately I am halfway gone to the nuthouse, sick in the head, and that my loneliness will take me the rest of the way.— To this from my point of view altogether comprehensible insight into my state of mind I have come after taking a huge dose of opium out of desperation. However, instead of losing my understanding on account of it, it seems my understanding has finally *come* to me. Incidentally, I really was ill here, for weeks;

and when I tell you that I have had twenty days of Orta weather here, my condition will seem more comprehensible to you. Please ask Lou to forgive me *everything*—she will also give me an opportunity to forgive her. For until now I have forgiven her nothing. One forgives one's friends with greater difficulty than one's enemies.

Lou's self-defense occurs to me now. Very odd! Whenever people defend themselves before me it always turns out that *I* am the guilty party. This I know from the outset, so it no longer interests me.

Could Lou be an unrecognized angel? Could I be an unrecognized ass?

in opio veritas: Long live wine and love!

Please please no scruples! I am accustomed to it all: this year everyone is upset with me; maybe next year everyone will be delighted with me.

I'd have learned to accept it Fritz I'd have learned to let you go. Genua is a port city Messina Rome there must have been lots of wellmade women there why didn't you find one for heaven's sake may our Dear Lord forgive me I don't know what I'm saying anyone anything at all I'd have learned to accept it, I'd have learned to let you go, anything cows cats birds reptiles anything at all.

To Malwida von Meysenbug in Rome [Fragment]

Rapallo, mid-December, 1882

My dear and honored Friend,

You wanted to know what I think of Miss Salomé?—My sister regards Lou as a venomous viper to be annihilated at any price, and she acts accordingly. Now, I consider this to be an altogether exaggerated point of view, and one that runs counter to my own sympathies. On the contrary, I'd like nothing better than to be useful and supportive. . . . Whether I *can* be, whether I *could* be in the past, is of course a question I wouldn't like to answer. . . .

Dear friend, is there no human being in all the world who will love me?——

Eat boy. Chew. Don't just swallow.

To Franz Overbeck in Basel [Draft]

Rapallo, December 25, 1882

Dear Friend, this little chunk of life is the hardest I've ever had to masticate; it is possible I'll choke on it yet. I suffered from the accusations and tortures of the past summer as though from an attack of delusion. . . . Today while I was walking something occurred to me that made me laugh: she treated me like a twenty-year-old student—a totally permissible way to think for a girl of twenty years—a student who had fallen in love with her. However, the wise, such as I, love only ghosts— and woe if I loved a human being—I would soon perish of such a love. The human being is too unfinished a thing

Elisabeth told me, your Llama told me everything. The filth of it all!

To Franz Overbeck in Basel

Rapallo, December 25, 1882

Dear Friend,

If I cannot discover the alchemists' knack and turn even this *filth* into *gold* then I am lost.

Your F. N.

She certainly knew how to tickle your fancy filth or no she was tickling your fancy all the time she kept strict control you didn't even know where your fancy was she was tickling O you poor stumbler bumbler fumbler Fritz! Open wide.

To Franz Overbeck in Basel

Rapallo, January 20, 1883

Dear Friend,

The final result and "moral" of the past nasty year is this: people forcefed me the selfsame poison a hundred times in the most diverse doses, the poison of "contumely," from crass indifference to profound contempt. This has produced in me a condition similar to that which arises from phosphorous poisoning: eternal vomiting, headache, insomnia etc. For years I have experienced nothing from *the outside*. In the year just passed, however, I have experienced a *great deal,* unfortunately always the same thing. That's why I can't get rid of it. I will not attain for myself the *beneficium mortis*—I want something more from myself, and I dare not be hindered by inclement weather or a ruined reputation.

F. N.

Open wide. Don't just swallow. Chew. Drink your sugarwater boy!

•

yes mama

To Franziska and Elisabeth Nietzsche in Naumburg [Draft]

Rapallo, final week of December, 1882

You will have to come up with another tone of voice if you wish to talk to me: otherwise I shall accept no further letters from Naumburg!

•

Be still Fritz don't fuss so! Oh, what a dreadful caterwauling! Stop it this instant! The nice man has come all the way from Berlin to paint your picture and the least you can do is sit quietly. Arms down. Look straight ahead. Stop fretting and fiddling with your frock, you little fuss pot! Try not to grimace so yes that's better, smile prettily for your poor old Mother, you can't smile anymore can you? Then be perfectly still. Quiet my love don't start up again you'll break his concentration. Don't sing sweet just listen to the music. Yes, it's from *Lohengrin*, you always loved it whatever troubles there were between the two of you he was a difficult man wasn't he? So proud he was. (I'll tell you a secret, my son: he was jealous of you he was envious of your mind. If only he could see you now—he'd be crushed in spite of everything.) Quiet now love listen to the music. Oh, the more I reprimand my darling the more he bellows

To Franz Overbeck in Basel

Genua, March 6, 1883

—Dissolving the ties with my family now is proving to be a true blessing. Oh, if you only knew all the things I have had to overcome under this rubric (since my birth—)! I don't like my mother; and to hear my sister's voice grates on my nerves. I was *always* ill when I was with them. We have not "quarreled" much, not even last summer; I know how to handle them; but it doesn't agree with me.

F. N.

Stop it right now or we'll have to send the nice man away, then what will your sister say, she'll bellow louder than I'm sorry I didn't mean that. She needs a heroic portrait for her Archive, I mean your Archive, for all the admirers she's had galloping through thank goodness she's moved it out of the house at least you won't suffocate. She insisted on locking your door soundproof airtight so that the high and mighty worshipers wouldn't be disturbed, but you need fresh air, my boy, you must breathe you're still alive aren't you

To Franziska Nietzsche in Naumburg [Drafts]

Nice, January/February, 1884

But to come back a year later to things that occurred prior to my intimate meetings with Fräulein Salomé in Tautenburg and Leipzig—that was an act of incomparable brutality. And then to send me letter after letter informing me of things that were news to me, thus *subsequently* heaping filth on those months so full of self-sacrifice—I call that insidious. If Fräulein Salomé said of me that "behind the mask of ideal goals" I pursued her "with filthy intentions," *ought* I have been permitted to learn of it a year afterwards? I would have kicked her out with condemnations and curses, I would have rescued Rée from her.—That is only a sample of a hundred instances in which my sister's fatal perversity toward me has shown itself. I've long known of course that she will have no rest till she sees me dead. Now my *Zarathustra* is finished! The moment I finished it and was steering into harbor, there she was, tossing handfuls of filth into my face.

Your letter hints at things that leave me speechless.

Am *I* not the one who last year showed the two of you a surfeit of undeserved kindness? Are you both ingrates? Or are you so utterly dishonest that you make the simplest truth stand on its head?

Who behaved wretchedly toward me, if it wasn't the two of you? Who endangered my life, if not you? Who abandoned me totally the way you two did, so that when I needed consolation you replied by heaping scorn and filth on everything I live and strive for?

I well know the moral distance that has separated me, from childhood on, from the likes of you. I needed every ounce of gentleness, patience, and silence I could muster, in order to make that distance less palpable to you. Have you no idea of the revulsion I must try to overcome being so closely related to

233

people like you! What is it then that causes me to throw up when I read my sister's letters, when I have to swallow her concoctions of stupidity and insolence laced with moralizing?

For several years now I have had to defend myself against Lisbeth, to flee from her like an animal she was torturing to death. I conjured her to leave me in peace; she has not stopped tormenting me for a single moment. I was afraid to go to Naumburg last August, afraid of what I might do to her, and that's why I appealed to Overbeck for advice. And now she strikes her little pose and acts as though she were guilty of nothing at all!

I don't know what's worse, Lisbeth's boundless, insolent mindlessness, such that she proceeds to instruct me—I who know human beings down to the bone—concerning two human beings I had the time and desire to examine quite closely; or her shameless tactlessness that never tires of chucking ordure at people who at all events shared an important part of my intellectual development and who therefore are a hundred times closer to me than the emptyheaded vengeful wretch she is.

My nausea—to be related to such a squalid creature.

Where did she get this nauseating brutality from? Where did she get that coy little way she has of injecting poison?

When a human being like me says "So-and-so belongs to my life's plan," as I did say to Lisbeth concerning Fräulein Salomé, then her's is an obtuse mindlessness, a vindictiveness, and a desire to avenge herself on a superior nature. And then to work against me in such an infamous way. *In the end*, of course, I achieved what I wanted.

The silly goose went so far as to accuse me of being envious of Rée! and to compare me to Gersdorff and herself to Malwida!

You cannot empathize, you have no idea what solace Dr. Rée was to me for years—*faute de mieux*, obviously; and what an incredible blessing it was for me to have had dealings with Fräulein Salomé.

As far as Lisbeth's letter is concerned—her judgments of me do not perturb me. I believe I've heard them before. Was it from Lisbeth? Or from Fräulein Salomé? At that time they agreed at least about *me*. Well, then, who is double-crossing whom?

Do not believe, dear mother, that I am in a bad mood. Quite the contrary! But whoever will not be loyal to me, let them go to the devil—or, as far as I'm concerned, to Paraguay.

Please darling stop now. Look the nice man is putting away all the lovely colors he's quitting I told you it would come to this didn't I whatever will we tell Lieschen you naughty Fritz? The bellowing ruins everything I swear. We had to stop taking you to the bathing pool on account of it you loved swimming more than anything else in the whole world and it did you a world of good too. Now what will we do with all that energy O Fritz stop fiddling stop fussing!

•

round and round the house we go mama from the wall in the front to the wall in the back to look for butterflies and salamanders in the sun. where is our house? why don't you take me swimming anymore mama that man closed the pool it was all his fault. i know a little duckpond where we could. where is our house? will you take me if i kiss your hand mama if i promise to be good if i promise i wont sing not a peep mama please. and the balloonman? where is our house? and tsk tsk tittlemouse? i know where i am. where is our house?

•

She would have to pick a fight with the two friends who loved you most. Köselitz she fears because he can read you so well, Overbeck because he won't relinquish control over your pension. By driving them away she deprives her Mother of the only two friends she has in the whole world. I will write them both, Fritz, I will tell them to visit just the two of us, Elisabeth can stay in her Archive I mean your Archive right the first time and we will have Franz and Ida to tea and Meister Peter to play for us, oh won't that be jolly! Maybe Deussen will come too, and Gersdorff? no, he's always too busy. How strange, my gentle Fritz: after all these years of growing farther and farther apart like two planets wheeling away from each other we wind up sharing the same friends. No one will come between us anymore no one and no thing. We are one again alone again like children. There are things to thank God for you have an important birthday coming up a millstone and I do thank Him with all my heart.

•

mums. gold brown orange yellow mums longpetalled like butterflies mums and double mums mummums.

THE WAYS OF THE MOTHER

To Reinhart von Seydlitz in Munich

Turin, May 13, 1888

Dear Friend,

Methinks it improbable that you have definitively resolved to become a mummy (or, to put it in a more masculine way: to become a *mum*).

Your friend,
Nietzsche.

mums of gold chrysanthemum ἄνθος χρυσός chrysanthemummums for mum and me. blackberries. cheese tart my favorite yums after Christmas Linsertorte with blackberries deussenberries my favorite yums and mums. a very special day indeed yesmum yummum.

•

Yes, my darling Fritz, a very special birthday, your fiftieth! A golden day for a golden birthday for a golden boy! Wasn't it thoughtful of Deussen to bring flowers with him mums your favorite. You remember Deussen. Deussen, Paul, you went to school and university together. Pforta alumni. Leipzig. Alma mater. Long ago now how long? Can it really be thirty years since you started? No, even more than that. 1894 take away 1864 equals thirty years when you started university, that wasted year in Bonn all you did was ask for more money, 40 Thaler wasn't enough for you, all those concerts and the piano you rented. Pforta was 1858. You met him in the autumn of '59, I remember, at Pforta. Pforta thirty-five years ago. Leipzig twenty-nine. Unbelievable. No wonder you don't remember him. Of course he came to Sils to visit you that last summer, no not your last you still have many happy returns many more summers ahead of you boy but the last one you might remember, try to remember darling try. He'll be so pleased if you can remember make him happy he brought you mums try to remember. Look at him dear not at the candles. Make him happy darling. Look at his face dear.

•

candleflame. surely i am candleflame. ecco behold the man home. taking maters into his own hands. happy birthing to me. nothing like that birthday to end all birthdays my very last as far as i can remember: i was fortyfour plus fortyfour makes eightyeight coincidence count the candles. *On this perfect day, as everything ripens and not only the grapes turn to russet, a ray of sunlight illuminated my life:*

236

Gazzetta Piemontese

Monday edition, 15 October 1888

Yesterday's high was 14.9 Celsius [58.8 Fahrenheit], the low
6.3 Celsius [43.3 Fahrenheit]; median temperature of the day
was 7 Celsius [44.6 Fahrenheit], although one might have
expected the median to have been approximately 10 Celsius
[50 Fahrenheit]. Yesterday the barometer fell drastically,
aggravating to truly worrying proportions the trend of the
day but one preceding. Yet the sun shone brilliantly and not
a wind stirred. . . . This morning saw the sun's return, and
the barometer climbed almost as much as it fell yesterday.
All right! [In English in original.] And to a distinguished
Swiss Polish philosopher out there amongst our readership :
Have a Happy Birthday!! [In German in original.]

*I looked back, I looked ahead, never did I see so many things, and
such good things, all at once! Not in vain did I bury today my four-
and-fortieth year, I was* allowed *to bury it—what was of life in it has
been rescued, is immortal. . . .* How should I not be grateful to my
entire life?—*And so I shall recount to myself my life.* behold the man.
taking maters. ecco home. safe! surely i am candleflame. touch me.

•

Don't touch the candles! They're only for looking Fritz darling not
touching. Only for looking and counting, counting the years. The
candles say 50. Can it be true? They say you are only as old as you
feel. Centuries old I must be then. Nonsense. You want to know how
old you are? Count the candles. Count the candles I always say. It's
Professor Deussen love he writes about the Hindus. And Schopenhauer. A philologian like you. You must remember you must try to
remember back

To Paul Deussen in Oberdreis

Leipzig, second half of October, 1868

My dear Friend,

If I were to speak mythologically, I would say that I regard
Philology as a miscarriage suffered by the goddess Philosophy
after she had lain with an idiot or a cretin. It is regrettable that
Plato failed to conjure up such a μύθος: you would have believed
him sooner.—And rightly so.

How well I remember 50 years ago today. What a night! You were my first. So full with you I thought I'd explode I suppose I did. There are no words to describe it it's not pain, not when everything inside you wants to come outside that's not pain. It's work holding it all in. That's why they call it labor. The hardest day's work I ever put in Lieschen so much easier and Little Joseph God rest his tiny soul so very much easier he almost dropped out before I could settle into bed. But for you darling Fritz your poor old Mother had to work. Fifty years. Nothing's changed. I was so afraid he'd be disappointed, that something would go wrong and that I would fail him, but he was glowing with pride and joy as I was, said he'd never seen me with more beautiful color said I was an indian. Flushed I was after all that holding back the whole night through then pushing and pressing. I wasn't surprised you were a boy I knew you would be. And I knew you'd be just like him. He never made it to fifty he died halfway through his thirty-fifth year, fourteen years your junior in death, unbelievable. Not hereditary. He fell. Lieschen says so. She saw him. How old was she then? Never mind. He hurt his head that's all there is to it let it go at that. How you cried when the doctor came. I thought you were crying because you were afraid of him. You said:

—Papa's sick, I can tell by his face.

I thought you meant your Father's face, but you meant the doctor's worried mien. He's been dead 46 years can that be incredible 46 terrible terrible. All of life gone by. You scarcely knew him you never really had a father. Everything would have been different.

To Gustav Krug in Naumburg

Basel, the 6th of July, 1874

Today, my dear friend, you must hear also from me a few words of heartfelt sorrow. To be sure, on the basis of my own experience I know almost as little about what it means to lose a father as it does to have one. For that reason my early inner life was more difficult and oppressive than anyone's should be. Precisely out of the oft-felt need for a truly intimate and loving counsellor I dare to understand today the degree and scope of your loss.

Your
F. N.

You would have had someone to show you the arduous path to God. Someone to hold off your aunts your grandmother your own

Mother we spoiled you we doted on you. No, not spoiled. Something else. What? We turned you into a little old man before you had a chance to become the little boy every little boy has to become, the little boy you never were. We made you the little pastor in the dead pastor's house. The King is dead long live. Don't ask me how we did it don't ask me why there was no why. God knows we did our best and I wouldn't know what to do differently, wouldn't know what to change, just have your Father not die not disappear out of your life, that's all, O Ludwig! The rest came as it came there was no rhyme nor reason nor plan to it. Every little boy goes to school, every little boy studies hard, every little boy is made to do his best. Not that we ever had to make you force you even convince you, you were always out ahead of us, always looking back to see had we caught up, no we hadn't, not ever. Lieschen was just another one of us rapt with amazement over you, always surprised to see how far ahead you were, that was the story of her life her tireless ambition. It wasn't doting. It was paying heed to the miracle yes the miracle: He took your Father from us He gave us you in your Father's stead. He never really abandoned us, which even my own Papa did. He never did. Did your Father ever really vanish from your life—or was he so much there that you had no life no space of your own on your own? Look at you, you then, little pastor in the dead pastor's house, and you now, childless child of my heart. Any brazen girl from any bronzen beach I'd have learned to accept it may God forgive me I know He does. And your Father wouldn't have been there to grieve.

•

happy birthday to me poring over pageproofs. my way of birthing. i wrote very beautiful things once upon a time mama i kept working on them until they were printed and even while they were being printed because i loved the smell of paper and ink intoxicating mama. it was like birthing. read me some of them dont be shy i know that secretly when no one is watching you admire them. open one of them mama and read to me in the night when no one is there to interrupt us birthing. it can happen more than once mama birthing and it can happen backwards in reverse. getting your tongue around the words. corinna calina i dont remember very well the stiffening stiffens my memory. i was writing it was evening no not yet evening i remember the late afternoon sun slanting in through the window on my left i was writing about what i dont remember wait a prison and the warden that was my father mama and the son thats what i was writing with great joy smoothly easily even though

239

calina corinna i dont remember was there all that afternoon in ree myself. she was no longer singing not even humming softly as she almost always did just sitting quietly i didnt even notice her mama giving birth to me and what i was writing making me her own son not the wardens son i dont know how she did it i cant remember i can only see the oblique rays redorange lighting laving her skin it was all she wore mama sitting on a hardwood straightbacked chair pressed up against the whitewashed wall. nice? no. rapallo? no. portofino? i dont know. fino molto fino bellitalia somewhere in ree. sitting slouching ever so slightly mama her head turned hard to the right away from the sun her gaze relentless on the floor. rose marble. that place near naples with ree in ree malwida and brenner consumption in the orangegrove yes that was it the smell of ink and oranges not nice at all not rapallo not portofino not torino it will come back to me in a moment mama. her black hair in careless tresses hanging the uneven tips of it brushing the swollen indolent brown nipples near naples yes chocolates mamas huge puffy bittersweet setting suns burning in the late afternoon sun. she paid me no mind i was writing she was birthing me and my writing it came so smoothly so easily the warden and his only begotten son no not capri not ligure not levanto i cant remember i see only corinna calina her slouch her gaze fixed averted her hands lopped lazily over her raised knees opening like the wings of a butterfly in the warm rees of the afternoon sun. her heels poised on the very edge of that straightbacked hardwood chair her feet wide apart each foot pointing down and away the long delicate toes the second toe much longer than the big toe beside it botticelli feet corinna calina i cant for the stiffening neck the throbbing head now mama cant remember anything now not mesopotamia not messina not sicily not acragas empedocles agrigentum not herculaneum ashes cast in plaster i looked up from my writing just as the wardens son was suffering the jeers of the prisoners disbelief looked up and over to her who was absent to me to herself hands draped so beautifully busy before mama now like the folded wings of a swan vain and languorous the bubs of swollen unmistakable for anything else flesh and below the cupped weight and swagger of the breasts her belly folding in the slouch and sloth of bellybutton omphalos center of the earth the cleft beneath tartaros the burning black bush where moses put down his rosen steel tip pen replaced the rubber stopper in the inkbottle pushed back the cane chair it creaked and scraped the floor she never moved her head mama hardright the tendon at the base of her throat distended taut an animal would have seized her there what am i mama im not an animal am i but without moving her head

without hinting she might have heard the creak and scrape heard my
noiseless tread felt it through the floor of roses and slowly infinitely
slowly lowered her hands between her knees her thighs and joined
thumb to thumb index to index forming a diamond windowframe
about her smiling notmouth her notclosed lips her ragged gaping
vertical smile no thorns no agave mother do you know it only colors
more colors in the redorange burntsienna light no not sienna than
ever were in the white incandescence of noon the purple veins
almost jetblack sparkle of sequins dans la saison des fleurs. i was on
my knees now mama i was as close as birthing mama not yet praying not yet whispering no longer writing only seeing rapt observant
inquisitive beholding the infinitesimal porphyry veins of the rose
wall wet with the underground spring the font of castalia corinna
calina kali phosphoricotrimethylamine all the walls watery wet with
lambent pearl mother of pearl opal of seawash breath of brine and
orangeblossom birthing it was the same flow as writing mama
descrying where the setting sun could penetrate no longer she was
sinking now in the ponient waters nothing there in that noplace was
dark not even at the crease where the light glistened but could not
penetrate no dark beneath the scrub i would have thought there was
dark there mama but there was no dark until i closed my eyes and
my head went into the gesture of reception like the boys and girls at
the communion rail in the italian churches mama tasting god and for
a very long time i was not afraid i was not anything or anywhere to
be seen my face in a world that gave way but never budged withdrew but never retreated surrendered but never capitulated a face
that never denied or abnegated never affirmed or asserted anything
but only sighed hissed yes yes yes yes. birthing. happy birthing. i
slake no horses. i can remember nothing mama not rimini not deiva
marina not serendipity not papi not sorella read to me o please
mama what i wrote birthing read me remind me because i am on
the very verge of remembering without being able in the end to
remember calina corinna whatever became of you sorella how can
you not be here when i am there now yes here and now i am in mind
and mouth of you in not even surrender sorella sorrento yes sorrento
of course it was sorrento the orangegrove outside the house above
the bay perfume of oranges rising off the page on the haze of
evening overpowering even the fragrance of the sea the grotto the
cavern the famous spot where————sorrento dido the orange fire
smoldering into purple night and i was lost at sea the wardens son
no more i became who i was an other that orangeblossom evening
pledging endless inky promises yes yes yes yes sorella sorrento.

•

Overbeck! I knew he would come to see us I begged him to! Elisabeth had her day in Leipzig with him, pumping him for her biography of you Fritz darling some biography, your poor old Mother hardly even mentioned there, where would you have been without me? Heaven only knows what she'll do with the material Overbeck gives her. If she can blot her own Mother out of the story your own Mother too and blot me out of the rights your rights too she can do anything. Heaven only knows what she wrote about me to our good Dr. Goodyear, I'd rather not find out, insults about Professor Binswanger I'll wager who's been so faithful even if he insulted your Father he didn't mean it that way. But it's for us now, Fritz, for you and me alone, he's coming to visit us today, Professor Overbeck!

How long has it been since he's seen you? He'll be shocked, I suppose. Nothing for it. Five years. Just before Professor Binswanger let you come to live with me in Jena do you remember? Of course you do. And you and he had coffee and cakes every day and talked about your return to Basel I suppose nothing will come of that now of course not. Five long years, how they've dragged on like a nightmare that refuses to end O Fritz I'm tired God forgive me I'm tired. Ten o'clock. I never can stay up a minute beyond ten my legs go out from under me what are you doing to your poor old Mama? The bathing the laundry the bedsheets the diapers a woman my age shouldn't have children even with Alwine's help. Yet I bless Him for otherwise where would you be and who would be there to take care of you? This way even if I go I mean when I go Alwine will be here to look after you.

•

alwine would your name be franziska by any chance? are you still here mama?

•

Overbeck is coming I can hardly believe it! Where's Alwine the house is a mess there's no time to lose. We'll put a broom in your hands Fritz and wheel you round the parlor sorry that wasn't funny I meant no harm heaven knows you'd help if you could, you always helped Aunt Auguste around the house when you weren't at your books which was all the time you were a golden boy my darling Fritz. Overbeck! Welcome!

●

how searchingly he stares at me with those piercing eyes of his his jaw jutting like a lantern in broad daylight cautious eyes searching me out looking for some flaw. who is this man mama? what does he want of us? friend of yours perhaps no friend of mine his brow is too full of wrinkles hes trying to talk to me his jaw flapping up and down like a nutcracker soldier what is he saying mama? wasnt he already here this morning what does he want again so soon hes expecting something of me i can see it in his eyes searching me out like lanterns in his head get him out of here mama i said get him out of here he makes me feel all stiff in my mouth in my hands in my head

To Franz Overbeck in Basel

Venezia, May 7, 1885

Very edified by your letter and *very relieved:* for the suspicion occasionally arises that you may regard the author of *Zarathustra* as one who has gone quietly round the bend. Indeed, my danger is great, but it isn't *that* sort of danger: rather, in the meantime I no longer know whether I am the Sphinx, who poses the questions, or the renowned Oedipus, who is questioned—so that I have *two* chances for the *abyss.* Things will now follow their own course.—

Yours in gratitude,

Friend N.

●

I promised Professor Overbeck I'd write him all about you, darling, now that he's had to go back to Basel and so I will no matter how I feel. *My dear Professor* and so he is as dear to me as a son, your brother the brother you lost who would have helped me to take care of you, the brother she will never be. *In general I have to say that his health and his appearance are unchanged, except when the hours of paralysis come (that's what Binswanger calls it). He visited our dear patient on a recent occasion, although it happened to be one of Fritzen's better days, a really very good day it was, and he was simply floored to find Fritz looking so famously. "Frau Pastor," he said to me, "I must compliment you! Who could believe that this is a man of fifty-two! You're taking splendid care of him, simply splen-*

did!" I suppose he said that just to buck me up he always does that he sees I'm failing I saw his medicinal eye upon me I'm not stupid am I? Yet it was kind of him all the same and truly you did look so clean and bright you even moved a bit. *I also had to bring some food because he wanted to see whether the chewing and swallowing would go well in spite of the temporary paralysis, and with that too he was altogether satisfied.* He should have seen you the day before gagging hacking coughing up clumps of halfchewed food chunks of it flying everywhere no he sees enough of that, I was proud of you my little angel you were so good. *From Yuletide to Yuletide we wait for some improvement to his mind, it is a melancholy thing; he used to enjoy the Christmas tree so much, then the joy languished, and this year he fell asleep when we rolled him up to it.* If only your sister were able to cheer you up the way she used to at Christmastime it's family time will we even see her this year I wonder she's so busy.

To Franz Overbeck in Basel

Turin, Christmas, 1888

Dear Friend,

I unfortunately have to inform you that things in Paraguay are as dire as possible. The Germans they lured over there are up in arms, demanding their money back—there is no money to be had. It has already come to some violent encounters. I fear the worst.—That does *not* prevent my sister from writing me a birthday letter filled with utter contempt, chiding me for not having even begun to become "famous." Isn't that sweet? Also chiding me for the *trash* I'd taken up with—Jews like Georg Brandes who'd licked every pot clean. . . . All the while she calls me "Fritz of my heart." *This* has been going on now for seven years!——Up to now my mother has not had an inkling of all this—that is *my* masterpiece. She sent me a game for Christmas: "Fritz and Lieschen."

Your friend N.

How weary I am I'll never finish this letter. Perhaps a cheery greeting card the barest sign of life would be better? *He has to make a great effort to walk, some days especially, days like today.* Alwine and I have to carry him into the water closet and deposit him there and it is always in the nick of time he's too heavy we cannot keep this up how long must it go on? I'll say nothing of it to Overbeck it would only depress him and she's given him enough to be depressed about one per family is enough. *Nevertheless one must be grateful to God for the way it's working out.* I suppose that's what all his jubilation is about when it comes, 24 hours of gratitude, a bellowing eucharist to our dear Father in Heaven, chants and hymns of praise for his salvation, and so he is truly saved in the end I suppose nothing more can touch him devil wouldn't have him I'm sorry I didn't mean that but it's true they don't burn children do they? suffer the little children they don't incinerate innocents do they? well then he's saved if ever a mortal man if ever a wretched benighted sinner was saved he's saved.

How prettily you sit on the sofa my handsome boy! How quiet and composed and full of dignity you are! Wait until eight o'clock tonight that should do it another 24 hours of wild processionals and hymns. No one can make out what you're shouting singing yodeling but I know it's religion it's glorification it's the faith that moves mountains an unassailable fortress go ahead darling sing your heart out if that's all that's left that is something that is a lot.

•

evohe bromios to the mountain evohe bromide to the orangeblossom sea evohe

•

How weary I am O my Herzensfritz after that week sick in bed thank God for Alwine what would we do without her? So heavy on my feet I'm as lame as you are my angel. Like mother like son. Lisbeth was here too every day of my confinement, I have to grant her that, when the chips are down she's always there. Not just to scoop them up, not always. The energy of that woman! Was I like that when I was young? She's working body and soul for you, Fritz of my heart, doing better than your poor old mama could ever have done. She'll make a success of you yet. That's all she's ever wanted. Will you still come to see your mama when you're famous, with the world at your feet, you won't forget your poor old Mother will you?

O Ludwig, how weary I am. Weary of the ways of birthing of dying of caring. Papa's calling us for church I can hear him plainly. He's so stern in his frockcoat! And Mama bustling behind him with all the children in their Sunday best on shining tiptoes getting ready as if for a birthday party. I'm tired Papa. So weary Ludwig. Will you look after our little Fritz for me? You'll take him under your wing won't you? I know you will. He needs you Ludwig. A boy needs his

Father. Always and always. Come back to us Ludwig. It doesn't matter how awkward you feel

To Franziska Nietzsche in Eilenburg

Naumburg on the Saale, August 8, 1850

My dear Mother.

I think of you quite a lot and always want to know how you are doing; come back to us soon. I am healthy and happy, love you lots, and want to be

Your
obedient Fritz

Alwine there's an extra box of cocoa in the kitchen cupboard we're out of rolls he likes the caraway seed and poppy don't spread the butter too thick it's bad for his digestion.

INTERLUDE
"Silver View," Weimar
20 April 1897 to 25 August 1900

To Heinrich Köselitz in Venice

                              Nice, February 13, 1888

Dear Friend,

It is amazing how *variety restores health*. For fertile, womanly, periodic creatures (all artists are such), the brusque insertion of entr'actes and contrasts seems to me to be well-nigh indispensable.

                              Heartily yours,

                              Friend Nietzsche.

Chronology

1897 April 20: Franziska Oehler-Nietzsche dies. May 20: Meta von Salis purchases the villa "Zum Silberblick" in Weimar for Elisabeth's Nietzsche Archive. July 20: Elisabeth transports the Archive and the patient to "Silver View." Alwine supplies the care. August 8: Elisabeth invites a group of influential guests to view the Archive and its objects. During the coming months she tries to get the villa out of Meta von Salis's hands, finally succeeding in July of the following year.

1898 Bismarck dies. The viewings at the Archive continue.

1899 May: the patient suffers a stroke, is bedridden. Bedsores. Feet and legs particularly affected. October: Peter Gast (Heinrich Köselitz) plays the piano for the patient. Other visits and viewings throughout the year. Elisabeth commissions a portrait of the patient by Hans Olde.

1900 Early August: Common cold, cough, pneumonia. August 25: after a second stroke, Nietzsche dies in Weimar at midday.

Atop the knoll, blazing in the late afternoon sun, casting the shadow I could not see from down below, *Silberblick.* Silver View. A vast house, an imposing edifice of red baked brick and glass; a kind of museum or exhibition hall gone haunted house. Slowly I raise the knocker and let it descend hard on the door of solid oak. Twice. To the massive portal comes the selfsame woman who used to answer Professor Nietzsche's door at the Poison Palace in Basel. She was a girl then, and a very pretty one, I did not fail to notice at the time. A matron stands before me now, in stolid black, mourning her mother as she later explains almost apologetically. Same face, however. I recognize it immediately.

—Elisabeth, I am Ludwig von Scheffler. We met twenty-five years ago in Basel.

—Herr von Scheffler! Ludwig? Is it possible? Can it really be, after all these years? You've come to see us again! Nothing's changed! Oh, aren't the roses beautiful! Thank you! Just like the ones in Basel, you remember?

I say I do.

She guides me through the hall into a large salon, apologizing too for the lack of butler, moving in and refurbishing the house have taken every second of her time and every ounce of her energy, to say nothing of the astronomical expense. She talks quickfire, incessantly, bubbling with genuine pleasure, it seems; yes, she seems genuinely gratified to see me.

The hall and main salon are high-ceilinged, a cream or eggshell paint still fresh to the nose, the hall almost bare of furnishings like a Lutheran church, perhaps even a Calvinist one in Geneva or in Zwingli's Zürich. In the middle of the salon two clusters of settees and plush upholstered chairs gather about coffee and study tables. She settles onto one of the settees, arranges her black skirts, gestures to a chair opposite, then remembers the roses on her lap. They are dreadfully thirsty after the climb, a bit bedraggled.

—Oh! I'll get some water! They'll be lovely right here on the coffee table, right where we both can see them, don't you think? You remember we had no vases to speak of in Basel, it was a real students' flat, wasn't it, you remember where we used to put the roses. . . .

Talking, laughing all the way out the door and down the hall to fetch water. Alone now, I feel an eerie presence in the room. I look quickly, furtively, into all four corners. Not here. Except in that triptych of photos that dominates the bookcase to my right. Profiles. Must have been taken after he left Basel, looks older than I remember him. Unmistakable promontory brow. The books are neatly arrayed in sets by color and size, as though all for show, the sundry editions of his works.

Postcard to Franziska and Elisabeth Nietzsche
in Naumburg

Recoaro, June 11, 1881

My dears, in a couple of weeks a book of mine will come to you. Look on it *amiably* from the outside: this is how the creature looks that will make our not-very-lovely name *immortal!* But with all my heart I beg you *not* to read it or lend it out to anyone. Shall we leave it at that?—

F.

The elegantly curved and carved bookcases and chairs are of glistening nut in chic nouveau. The braces of the built-in shelves rise in sinuous flexure from the slender Gothic arches of the shelves up to the ceiling. The ribbed horsehair covers of the chairs and settees too are elegant, my finger plays back and forth across them as I wait. Gigantic crystal vases hold enormous fernlike plants, the room is brightly lit by the sinking afternoon sun. Beneath the vases are showcases of glass and darker wood, showcases everywhere along the outside wall, the sorts of cases I remember seeing in the Pinakothek and in the Basel seminar library. She is well out of hearing by now. I rise to investigate.

Manuscript pages, some in a neat hand, others in a horrid scratch, who could ever decipher it? She can, I suppose. A scattering of steeltip pens, Rosen's, an old pocket watch, must have been their father's. Did they have a father? Never heard them mention him, only their mother, and she now dead. Here a metronome and some sheet music elaborated in a beautiful hand. Letters. *My dearest Llama.* Strange. A girlfriend, probably, hard to imagine. *To my poor old Mama!* Wonder when. She looks natural in black. *C. G. Naumann, Leipzig.* Here a closely written page, the bottom half with a heavy red pencil X crossing out the text, the substitute lines in a miniscule hand across the bottom of the page. He also left the right half of the page blank, as though anticipating the corrections and windfalls to come. Not easy to make out. Let's see:

> And do you know what "the world" is to me? Shall I show it to you in my mirror? This world: a monster of force without beginning or end, an iron-clad quantum of force, becoming neither greater nor smaller, not consumed but only transformed . . . ; eternally metamorphosing, eternally returning in vast years of recurrence, with an ebb and flow of its configurations . . . ; blessing itself as that which must eternally come back, as a becoming that knows no satiety, no surfeit, no weariness—: this world, my *Dionysian* world of eternal self-creation, eternal self-destruction, this mystery world of twofold voluptuosity, my beyond good and evil, goalless, unless the goal lies in the felicity of the circle, without will, unless the ring is a ring of good will, turning ever about itself alone, keeping to its wonted way: this world, *my world*—who is luminous enough to look at it without wishing to be blinded? Strong enough to hold his soul up to this mirror? His own mirror up to the mirror of Dionysos? His own solution to the riddle of Dionysos? And were anyone able to do this, would they not have to do more in addition? Would they not have to *plight their troth* to the ring of rings? By taking the oath of their own *return*? By means of the ring of eternal self-blessing, self-affirmation? By means of the will to will oneself once more and yet again? The will to will back all the things that ever have been? To will forward to everything that ever has to be? Do you now know what the world is to me? And what I am willing when I will *this* world?

> unless a ring possesses good will toward itself—would you have a *name* for this world? A solution to all its riddles? A *light* for you too, you most concealed, strongest, bravest, most midnightly ones?—*This world is will to power—and nothing besides!* And you too are yourselves this will to power—and nothing besides!

Yes, I know that world. Vaguely. He talked about it in his course on the Presocratic thinkers. Who said it there? Not Empedocles, although you would have thought Empedocles, above all. Pythagoras? Perhaps Parmenides? Heraclitus? Heraclitus could say anything, could be anything. Dionysus, albeit not the Areopagite? Everyone and no one.

I wonder why he changed it? Much more powerful in the first version, with the double glass of Dionysos, more powerful with less will to power. Ironic.

He was so intense, I wonder has he mellowed any? If mellowing isn't a euphemism for enervation, depletion, decrepitude. I wonder, how is he now? Will she take me to see him? Do they keep him in the basement?

Suddenly, a rustling noise behind me.

—Oh, there you are! Yes, aren't they wonderful things? My heart's pride and joy, and ever have been, as you can imagine, even before we went to Basel, and even after this terrible thing happened to him.

She leads me now from showcase to showcase, table to table, shows me his dainty opera glass, the calling card from Wagner, the thankyou from Cosima, and the neatly ordered piles of papers, notes, and manuscripts. Carefully selected, all for exhibition. Is there any other principle of selection, I wonder? Surely this can only be the tip of the iceberg, there must be hundreds, maybe thousands of pages, ten years' worth of writing without surcease, no teaching, no distractions, living only to write.

The visit is playing out, it seems, as it no doubt will for many after me. She walks to the window in the front wall of the house. Sunlight touches only the summit of the neighboring hill and its trees. Down below, deep in shadow, a forlorn, wingless, motionless windmill. She sighs:

—Look! A metaphor of our existence. No wings!

—Do you know the English poet, Keats? He writes of a sick eagle gazing at the sky.

—Would you like to see him?

—Yes.

She takes my forearm firmly and leads me to the staircase in the hall. We mount the crimson carpeted staircase in silence. I go to meet the god of my youth, of my youth and my joy.

The stairway is swathed in shadow, the upper hall is dark. Yet his room (she opens the door to it now, ever so slowly) is bathed in golden late afternoon light. The spacious chamber, a corner room of the house, receives the sun from two sides. I enter. It is empty. No. Not empty.

Against the far wall, on a sofa in the corner, behind a mahogany table pressed close against the sofa, a pinched, shrunken figure in a white robe. He is asleep. He draws long, stertorous breaths.

Effigy of illness. His eyes are shut hard, pinched tight. Unnatural sleep, if sleep it be, somehow unmistakably pathological, the body tells it all. Sunken as a grave. Shrunken as its contents. His pallid hands lay crossed in repose on his breast.

His sister and I continue our conversation in a whisper. I tell her what I remember best:

—In Basel he lit a fire under us all. We would have been ashamed to miss a lecture or botch a lesson.

—How wonderful those evenings were, do you remember? Reciting poems, snatches of *Faust*, whole sections of Schopenhauer. With a glass of Veltliner, do you remember, ruby red in the lamplight?

—No one helped his students more: he was like an older brother.

—But that's exactly what he is!

We slip out of the room. Elisabeth guides me back to the room where, she says, his library is to be stored. A few volumes are already on the shelves. *The World as Will and Representation*. Rap on the vaults of the dead, ask them if they'd like a reprieve and a reprise, ask them if they'd like a taste of life again, a sip of Veltliner, a swill of Culmbacher ale. Gravely they shake their heads. Gravely in their graves. I remember having seen in the Schwaben section of Munich an ancient glum cafe, the "Cafe Schopenhauer," black letters on a faded orange front, faded colorless curtains drawn tight across the windows. No one ever went in, no one ever came out. Elisabeth interrupts my revery.

—No Stirner, you see.

—I beg your pardon?

—None of Max Stirner's books. My brother never read him, didn't even know of him.

—You don't say.

To demonstrate his originality. What would he have said? The gentle laugh, I can still hear it. Goethe, the lyric poems, must be heavily marked. Do I dare take it down from the shelf? No, her eyes never leave me. Kuno Fischer's four volumes, three and four on Kant. Friedrich Albert Lange. Ralph Waldo Emerson. Mark Twain.

—He wasn't kind only to students. Do you know he once mended the broken leg of a poor little dog in Turin?

—No, I hadn't heard. That must have been very difficult. They usually just shoot them.

To Franz Overbeck in Basel [Draft]

Nice, January/February, 1884

255

By the bye, my sister is a dog in the manger: six times in the past two years she has flung a letter into the midst of my supreme and most felicitous feelings—feelings that have always been rare on this earth—a letter that has the most insidious stench of the *all-too*-human about it.

—It was in a trattoria. He made a splint on the spot and swaddled the leg in his own handkerchief. He learned to do that in the medical corps in the army. He was heroic by nature, you know. The dog's master was ever so grateful—Don Enrico told me.

—Don Enrico?

—Yes, the only person in all Italy who knows what happened to my brother during his last days.

—Last days?

—His last days *alive*, I mean. Alive and *well*, I mean. His last days in *Italy*. We're looking everywhere for Don Enrico, but we cannot seem to locate him. Can you help?

—Don Enrico? Torino? Sorry, I've never been.

—Don't worry. Someday, somewhere, we shall find him, and then we'll have the whole story.

Postcard to Heinrich Köselitz in Annaberg

Venice, May 7, 1886

At the bottom of a poster advertising a concert program I read the conductor's name: Edoardo Sassone. Why not Enrico?——

A few moments more and we return to the patient's parlor. He has wakened from his stony slumber. He sits now in a plush chair by the window. Someone has moved him; he cannot move himself. His once broad shoulders stoop over a weighty tome. He is reading. Unhindered by the fact that the book is upside down. He hears us enter, and slowly, painfully slowly, turns his head. Small, deep-set eyes, a dull green, a dim brownish green. They flash for an instant as they fix on me, as though rummaging through their store of remembered icons in search of the stranger that now confronts them. Then the spark goes out. He utters no word of greeting. I feel a stiffening chill rise in me, spreading from my stomach to my shoulders and head, as though the rigidity before me were contagious. Behind that impenetrable mask a second mask with barely living eyes peers, and perhaps yet another mask behind it. What thoughts or feelings could there be behind those stamps and seals of finality, of certified mortal vulnerability, what accusation or confession or plea?

He bends back over the inverted letters of his book without taking further notice of his sister or her guest. Elisabeth and I continue our conversation, she tells me of the years after Basel, of her own life in colonial Paraguay, of his in Switzerland, southern France, northern Italy. Twice he raises his voice, not so much interrupting us as carrying on a simultaneous and parallel conversation with himself.

—None but the best people live in this house.

And some minutes later:

—I've written many beautiful things.

Neither the sister nor I venture a reply, although she is the one who resumes our conversation after each pronouncement of his. Strange pronouncements. Parrot-like. Has she been giving him lessons, feeding him lines?

An elderly matron in a white lace pinafore and stiff black cotton dress enters the room with coffee and a tray of tiny cakes.

—Thank you, Alwine. Put them right here where Herr von Scheffler can reach them; he must be famished after that trek up the hill.

The crone places the tray on the coffee table before me. She transfers a piece of chocolate cake onto a goldrimmed plate and carries it to Nietzsche. She places the morsel in his gaping mouth. Eucharist. It disappears. She mutters something into his ear, I cannot make it out, it sounds like *Don't just swallow, chew.* He looks at me now with a hint of a smile, which soon retreats behind that penetrating, searching gaze, a gaze full of profound seriousness—one would almost have said a gaze full of philosophy.

—This is a fine book, he says.

•

I was still unmarried, a mere slip of a girl, when we first met in Genua. Our parties traveled together to Pisa. Oh, how exciting it was to be Princess von den Pahlen, not yet Countess Unglad-Starmount! He was on his way to Sorrento, but he gladly stopped for me.

And now, two dozens of years later, we are to meet again. They tell me he has changed. They warn me. Yet I will not be put off, will not be dissuaded, cajoled, or placated. See him I must!

Three days later dear Elisabeth grants me my wish, the *Wiedersehen* I both yearn for and fear. With me, a small circle of intimate friends, some old, some new. It is a matter of the greatest satisfaction to me that I have made the acquaintance Maestro Peter Gast (his real name is Köselitz, yet Gast is so much more inviting, I would gladly have changed mine too), a man with a heart of gold, so sensitive, so expressive, and what a head for music! Recently converted disciples are also with us, a young married couple of the most harmonious culture, noble not only by birth but also by aristocratic frame of mind and education, rounding off our sympathetic circle.

We make the bracing ascent like proper pilgrims, past a quaint Dutch windmill, to the basilica on the rise. Weimar unfolds like a vision at our feet, we are reminded of Florence viewed from San Miniato, Torino from Superga, and the valleys of the Bourgogne from Vézélay.

Dear, dear Elisabeth herself meets us at the door, welcoming us with the simple dignity and modest bustle that betray a bloodline of the purest Polish nobility, not the high aristocracy, to be sure, which is corrupt anyway, but the landed gentry, hardworking people of substance, if not entirely polished and refined. She has devoted her life to him, as only a woman can. She has worked out a system of solicitude, a regimen of care efficacious beyond belief, which consists principally of moving her precious patient to a different place and altering his position every two hours throughout the waking day. Only in this way can the poor sufferer be spared the misery of bedsores. Thus he leads a life devoid of bodily pain, a peaceful, serene, meditative existence, a model life, really, nestled and protected under the wing of untiring love which renews to him its pledge with the dawn of each incipient day.

Elisabeth whispers to us in the hall of the new edition of his works, of renovations to the Villa, of the tireless search for his letters and manuscripts, only Don Enrico de Ronda knows, and of the terrific expense each of these things inevitably entails. She strikes a sympathetic chord with us. Really, something must be done to help her! We shall conspire on our homeward journey about how we can assist the cause without sacrificing our anonymity. Largesse is always incognito, she will know who it is anyway. How embarrassed and pleased, how flustered she would be, and how pleased, if she could hear us singing her praises!

After our hushed conversation in the vestibule, we ascend the stairs to the upper hall and the philosopher's quarters. She opens the door noiselessly, almost stealthily, pressing a finger to her lips. We creep across the threshold. We find him there awake and rapt to our entry! How can I say how I feel when I look at him, when I gaze upon his elevated essence, the infinitely profound beauty of his soulful expression! Especially the beauty of the eyes, freed at last from those dreadful spectacles, a beauty well-nigh overwhelming. From these profoundly melancholy celestial globes project rays that penetrate to the most remote spaces and yet seem to gaze inward as well; a mighty force wells forth from them, a magnetic spiritual fluidum that no sensitive soul can resist. Cloaked in white garments, a priest in his spotless alb, he rests comfortably on a divan. Full of hesitation, tremulous, I approach him, introduced by his sister's mellifluous words:

—Darling, I bring you now a beloved friend, whom the two of us cherish in memory, and of whom we have so often spoken!

My two hands embrace his delicate right—the hand that mustered the ranks of immortal thoughts, *aere perennis,* and set them marching across paper—and I whisper, scarcely above a hush:

—Long, long ago it was, in Italy, in Genua and Pisa, where we met.

Probing, searching, his eye dwells on me, long and long. Ever so slowly, his saturnine head shakes from side to side, his questioning glance mutely seeking out the gaze of the trusted sister, who murmurs gentle, caressing words of love to him.

Suddenly, under the hands of Maestro Pietro Gast, unsolicited, unanticipated yet nonetheless more than welcome, splendid tones and mighty waves of sound burst forth from the piano. They seize our ailing friend with the power of enchantment, his whole organism twitches and trembles under the impact of Calliope's electric sparks. Transports of the blessed suddenly grace his mien, his entire body quakes with feverish excitement—and look! look! through his translucent, languishing hands streams ascendant, renascent life! These brave hands shatter the shackles that so long have bound them, they move slowly toward one another in the faintest gesture of applause. He cannot get enough of it, this musical proclamation of his inner joy: already the throbbing strings have reverberated to stillness, and yet, eye to eye with his sister, seeking there a knowing sympathy, seeking and finding it, he shivers with orgasmic delight, he is altogether a mighty tempest of enthusiasm, a storm that sweeps over us now too in the look that plays across his face and the hands that simply refuse to stop clapping *clap clap clippy clappy clap clap hey clap ho clap clippy clappy clap ah ah eeeee clap.* Veritably, a spectacle of and for the gods—and I am among those privileged ones ordained to see it.

With tears in our eyes, our hearts and minds shot through with inexpressible sensations, the witnesses of this soulful tumult now retire in humility. We shake hands all around, weeping freely. The tension in our breasts dissolves slowly, oh, so slowly!

•

I play for him the *Pria che spunti in ciel l'aurora*. In the depths of his memory it kindles a flame. Streaks of sunrise. The earliest suspicion of dawn. Quietly, inaudibly, he claps, his hands sometimes missing one another, clapping with the hands of Christ. Christ crucified. *Pronounce holy his name*. He does not know me at all anymore. All those years we spent together. I don't believe he ever could truly bear my presence.

Postcard to Heinrich Köselitz in Venice

Genua, January 8, 1881

Dear dear friend...in later life, when we have intertwined like two old faithful trees, let us laugh again at the wild youth of our association! Hold fast to me also in the coming decade—I fear that at the end of it I'll be lonelier than I am now. (I fear it and I am, by way of anticipation, already well-nigh proud of it!) But *you* must remain with me, and I shall remain with you!

In fidelity,
Your friend F. N.

The last time I saw him he seemed so well I thought he was faking. He is not faking. I shall return to Venice as quickly as I can.

•

She admits me. She kept me waiting at the door for quite some time. She tested my story, probing, wary of the charlatan. Stories have always been my forte, however. I was a better storyteller than dentist, and I am a very good dentist, I never have to pull teeth, I lure them out.

She admits me because I am impeccably dressed. My suit, *taille italienne,* communicates money, my wide-set almond eyes communicate trust and confidence. My swooping hawknose tells her that I am without doubt a scion of the accursed race, a fact that communicates even more money. Charity never faileth. She admits me.

I do not tell her that I am Don Enrico. For then she would know that I am lying. Don Enrico is the guarantor of her own truths, he is her own great lie. No, I do not tell her that. My story is that I am an editor of the Parisian *Journale des Débats*. I tell her that we are contemplating devoting an entire issue to her brother's work—immortalized in the flawless editions and other sterling publications of the Archive and its principal Archivist. Such as the first volume of her biography of him, recently released. Her net opens. She admits me. My net encompasses.

I am the Stranger.

Returned from Theban Torino.

Down from the mountains of Alpine Phrygia, up from the Lydian Val d'Aosta.

In order to encounter once again my first cousin, divinity-elect.

He meant nothing to me back then, he was an abject object that needed to be transported northward, and I played the role I had to play. Stories and prostheses were always my specialty. Afterwards I read him. And now I have returned. Not as a disciple, to be sure, but as a cousin and friend.

Will he know me? Will he hurtle over a sofa or chair, trembling in panic, fearful that once again I have drawn the women in my train? Or will he embrace me as his mentor and savior? Will he know me?

Doubt almost prevented me from undertaking my journey, even after I had discovered his whereabouts quite by chance. Almost.

She will keep me downstairs all day long with her coquetteries and her ambitions. Never mind. I have time. Mine encompasses. At long last she pauses, and I speak, calmly, with assurance.

—May I see him?

My eyes gaze steadily into hers. She does not release me, I do not release her.

—But of course.

We mount the stairs and pass quietly down the hall to his private sitting room. Soundlessly we enter, on the delicate feet of doves, the shoeless feet of women. He is compressed into the corner of a sofa itself crammed into a corner of the room. He presses his lids tightly down when he hears the doorclink, pretends to be asleep; he cannot have seen me yet, does not yet know who I am.

I observe him. The forehead is higher than ever. He has lost a lot of hair. Except in his mustache, which is enormous, gray on one side only, the right. Deterioration of the left hemisphere. His cheeks have caved in like the sides of an ancient vault. Lost too many teeth.

I warned him. It has been almost a decade. He may remember nothing at all.

Wait. Wait. His lids relent, rise. Two black points appear within. Coal. Ash. Smoldering fire.

His eyes have opened wide by now, have focused fully upon me. I stoop so that he can see me more clearly, I clasp both his hands in mine, they are as cold as death. Neither he nor I listen to her cooing, soothing, continuous babble. At first I fear he will balk. He is not stupid. I smile timidly at first, then widely.

—It has been a long, long journey.

He says nothing. He remembers.

—You have done very well. Incognito. Not a soul recognized you, it was quite an act, I have to hand it to you.

To Elisabeth Nietzsche in Naumburg [Draft]

Nice, mid-March, 1885

When I read your letter I once again became aware of the reason why some of the finer minds in Germany take me to be insane and even spread the rumor abroad that I died in an asylum. I am far too proud to believe that a human being could ever love *me:* for this would presuppose that he knew *who* I am. Just as little do I believe that I will ever love someone: that would presuppose that—someday—miracle of miracles!—I would find a human being of my rank. Don't forget that I both profoundly regret and utterly despise such creatures as Richard Wagner or Arthur Schopenhauer, and that I find the founder of Christianity superficial in comparison with myself. I loved them all before I comprehended what human being is.

Among the riddles on which I have riddled long and hard is the following—How is it possible that we two are consanguineous?—For the things that occupy, concern, and elevate *me* I have never found a fellow knower and friend! What a shame there's no God, so at least one other would know of these things.—As long as I am healthy I have enough good humor to play my role and conceal myself before all the world, for example, as a Basel professor. Unfortunately, I am ill much of the time, and then I hate the human beings I have come to know, unspeakably I hate them, myself included.—

My dear sister, this little secret between us—and then you can burn this letter. If I didn't have a healthy portion of the actor in me, I couldn't bear to live a single hour.

He says nothing. Remembering.

—At last you are safe. Incognito. Loneliness is the price, of course, we both know that. Loneliness to the bitter end. So much for receptions. They all turn out like that. Maybe later. Long hence. Maybe long after we are both dead, my cousin.

The sister stiffens above me. She doesn't like the tone of the conversation. Nothing about Paris and books and fame. Yet she can see that we know one another, that we have shared a terrible secret, a secret from whose bourne she will always have been excluded. She knows now that she has been hoodwinked. I will never take her to the mountain meadow.

—That's enough, now. We don't want to put him under any strain. That's enough.

The voice is hard, full of hooks and barbs. I respect it. Desiccated daughter of Agave. Speak to him one last time. One last word:

—I must go now. I won't be back until the very end. It is nigh. Fear nothing. They will never see you in your perch on high, they will never know you in your chic disguise.

—That's enough, now. That's enough!

•

rub me. rub my hands my feet. who will warm me who loves me still? spreadeagled i lie. full forty fathoms. my feet. pain. twisted off at the ankles. i recognized the sandal. move me. shift me elsewhere. relocate me onto another part of me. saddlesores. horses tremble like earthquakes. nice. chocolates. sorrento. torino. are you still here franziska? are you not yet here ludwig?

•

—How long will the sitting take this evening, Herr Olde? My brother hasn't been feeling very well lately.

Hasn't been feeling well? I want to ask her how she can tell. However, one does not mock saints. Not in front of the Pope, anyway. Not if the Pope is paying.

—He is out on the veranda, enjoying the sunset.

Enjoying? I want to ask her how she knows. I curb my tongue. I explain that I have come only to take a few quick photographs in the late afternoon light.

—But I commissioned a portrait, not photographs. Photographs don't do my brother justice.

I explain that the snaps are simply to help me back in the studio, that they will reduce the time he will have to sit, as though he had anything better to do, as though he ever did anything else, but I don't say that, I curb my tongue.

—You needn't fear, Madam, I will destroy the photographs as soon as they have served their purpose and the portrait is finished. No one will ever see them, I assure you.

She seems satisfied. Suspicious, but satisfied. She leads me up the staircase to the sanctum sanctorum. We enter. The double doors to the veranda are open.

—Fritz, dear, here is our kind Herr Olde who was here last week. He's going to take your picture. Won't that be fun.

He does not move. His eyes are fixed on the horizon. Could I draw or paint him this way? Could I create that much vacuity?

She doesn't want to leave the two of us alone. I explain to her about my need to concentrate, about my work. She is not satisfied, she is more suspicious than ever, but she turns with a slight huff and is gone.

I prepare the box, wipe clean the plates. I slip the first plate in. It makes the reassuring sound of a cartridge entering the firing chamber. He flinches, then becomes immobile again. Let us see now what I will shoot. I raise the black curtain, my chaste nun's veil, and squinch up to the peephole. Ye gods. The view opens upon utter desolation. Turn this way, now that. Useless. No birdie, no lookie. Ye gods. Utter destitution. He never blinks. How does he do that? Eye of God upon him. Utter devastation. Far beyond the moment of the shortest shadow; indeed, it is the hour of the longest shadows. And if I press the shutter right . . . now . . . what will we have unto all eternity?

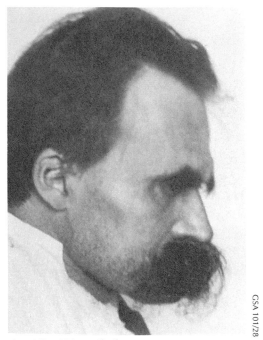

Photo: Stiftung Weimarer Klassik

PART FOUR

THE WAYS OF THE FATHER
God's Green Acres, Röcken
Tuesday, 28 November 13 A.N.
1600 Hours

Chronology

1900 August 27: memorial service held in the Nietzsche Archive, with music by Palestrina and Brahms. August 28: Nietzsche's body is transported to Röcken. Obsequies, music, interment.

It is a wonder and a delight to see all these old friends gathered about me, above me, this afternoon.

—Welcome, avatars of the higher humanity, you oathtakers! Swear by my corpsebody! Swear!

And Overbeck? Where is Overbeck? You don't say! At the sign of the "Three Wheatstalks" in Colmar snuffling up choucroute garni instead of paying his last respects to yours truly! And he the last Christian, the second and final Christian, the only mortal entitled to bury the Antichrist. For shame, Franz! As it was in the beginning so it ought to have been in the end. Even if you would have had to endure Elisabeth one last time.

And Rohde? Erwin growly bear? Oh, yes, of course: we fought. And he died before me, the ingrate! Many other faces, however; curious faces, peering down. Deussen's beautiful, absurd face.

—Hello, Paul, not still jealous of me, I hope? What? Still taking up collections for me? You'll spoil me rotten! Papa Gersdorff, you old sleepyhead, hello there! Can it really be so many years? Summer of '76 at Bayreuth? Incredible! Welcome to you, my dear Carl!

Down on me they stare. I am prostrate before this august company. Boxed in. Unmoved mover. Those dreadful bells, the moaning and the groaning of the, O my Father, can't you won't you please make them stop? All my death I have hated them, the fraudulent bells of Eastertide, I bequeath them to you. The knell and the organ: yours: take them. For me the jolly choir! Yesterday the women in Weimar, today the men in Röcken. Palestrina! Brahms! And Bizet, Lisbeth? Wouldn't *Carmen* have been in better taste? *Et si je t'aime . . .*

Postcard to Heinrich Köselitz in Venice

Genua, November 28, 1881

Hurrah! Friend! Once again I've discovered something good, an opera by François Bizet (who is he?): *Carmén*. Sounded like a novelette of Mérimée's, witty, robust, here and there truly shattering. A genuinely French talent for *comic opera*, not in the least disoriented by Wagner; on the contrary, a true pupil of Hector Berlioz. I never dreamt such a thing was possible! It seems the French have struck out along a better path in dramatic music; and they have one great advantage over the Germans in a matter of principal importance—they don't have to wander as *far as* the Germans do in order to *fetch* their passions (for example, *all* passions in Wagner are far-fetched)!

Yes, François Bizet would have set the appropriate tone. My own "Hymn to Life"? Or perhaps: *Seid umschlungen, Millionen, diesen Kuß der ganzen Welt!* What's that? Too big a production? Too big a production for my funeral? Strain the Archive's budget, pinch the Archarchivalist's pocketbook? I wouldn't dream of it, dear Llama! Never mind, I love a jolly choir: all those severe sincere sweaty faces, all those gaping gobs and japing jaws, dreaming of the tea and cakes afterwards. No beer, I hope, my darling sister. A situation like this demands decorum.

I'm so thrilled I can scarcely concentrate on the speeches. I'm sure they are all heartfelt, all appropriately lugubrious. Who's next?

Ah, Don Enrico Sassone, the Saxon Maestro Pietro, cuddly Köselitz, be my guest! You thought I was faking my madness, just as now you think I am faking my death. I must admit: a few more steps in this logic of mine and you'd have your faker—your fakir asleep in his tomb for weeks at a time! What's that you say? Let my name be *holy* to coming generations?! Oh, for Pete's sake, bury me upright and fetch the devil, I'm sure my name *will* be holy by the time you and the Llama get through with it! You shall see to it, you and Lisbeth and a box of Lucifer matches. Why not burn *all* my notebooks, leave only ashes—best to be remembered by traces of ash and cinder alone. That way you can invent freely. And who is François de Ronda?

Bellowing bell! Knowing knell! And that growling organ, O my Father! The dark I do not fear, not anymore, but the tintinnabulations and the wheezings terrify me still. Your instruments. They are playing for you, Papi, as always. Your belltower. Your organ. Your tool. Your weapon.

The massive marble slab

To Franz Overbeck in Basel

> *Nice, rue St. François de Paule 26 II*
> *January 9, 1886*

The very first thing I did with the money I received from Schmeitzner was to have my Father's grave covered with a great marble slab. (According to my Mother's wish, it will one day be her own grave as well.)

tastefully decorated in the geometric style, as on a precinct wall at Delphi or Thebes. Symbolism of the tomb. Bachofen. Hot ovens with cold crosses on them. Creuzer. This time with my name incised, Friedrich Wilhelm, just as I inscribed one for you and Little Joseph:

†

Here
reposeth in God
Carl Ludwig
Nietzsche
Pastor of Röcken
Michlitz and Bothfeld
born 11 October 1813
died 30 July 1849
Whereupon followed him into Eternity
his youngest son
Ludwig Joseph
born 27 February 1848
died 4 January 1850
C h a r i t y n e v e r f a i l e t h
1 Cor. 13, 8.

I bought the slab, had it inscribed, then slammed it over you so you would never rise and kill again. Forgive me, Papi. I had to secure some time for myself, a longer lease on life for my literature. I mean my philosophy.

To Georg Brandes in Copenhagen

Nizza, December 2, 1887

Honored Sir,

You see the sort of posthumous thoughts with which I live. However, a philosophy such as mine is like a sepulcher—one no longer *lives with it. Bene vixit, qui bene latuit,* "He lived well, who concealed himself well"—that's what it says on Descartes' tombstone. A grave inscription, no doubt about it!

Yours, Nietzsche.

Your forgiveness too I beg, Little Joseph, brother of my heart. Mooch over a bit, will you? Papi needed something or someone to

273

hold onto, and it was either you or me, Elisabeth being excluded by ecclesiastical decree. Better you than me, you were so cuddly, so cute, all the family adored you so, especially Mama. You would have been so gifted had you lasted. But I carried you into the church that night, the night the organ boomed. It seems pointless now to rue it, irrelevant to regret it, it happened so long ago. A bit more room, please, go ahead and slip right into his arms if you like, I never begrudged you Father's arms, I only wanted a stretch of space, a fragment of time, a piece of his lap, and the music.

The bells reverberate to stillness. Silenced at long last are the stertorous groans of the organ. What did that Russian no not her the composer call it? The beast that never breathes. Instrument of unliving breath, harbinger of undying death. It's awfully quiet up there. Must be waning to twilight, the earliest suspicion, dwindling to dark. Just the three of us here now, darling Little Joseph, my dear Father, and me.

—You mean four, brother dear. You forgot Mamusha, as always.

—No, Little Joseph. Mama's dead. I'm awfully sorry.

To Gustav Krug in Cologne

Genoa, November 16, 1880

We are growing older, and thereby *lonelier:* precisely that love abandons us which loved us like an unconscious necessity, not because of our particular qualities, but often very much in spite of these. Our past draws to a close when our Mother dies: then for the first time our childhood and youth become remembrance whole and entire. And so it goes, on and on, the friends of our youth die, our teachers, the ideals of those days—always more solitude; always colder and colder winds assail us.

> Devotedly, with heartfelt love,
> Friedrich Nietzsche.

Just the three of us, with the serenity of evening before us, the dying summer, and the long night.

To Franz Overbeck in Basel

Sils-Maria, August 5, 1886

Dear Friend,

If only I could give you an idea of my feeling of *loneliness!* I have no one to whom I feel related, as little among the living as among the dead. This is unimaginably terrifying. Only constant exercise in learning how to bear this feeling, and a step-by-step development from childhood on in my capacity for bearing it— this alone enables me to comprehend how I have not as yet perished on account of it.—For the rest, the *task* for the sake of which I live confronts me clearly: it is a *factum* of unimaginable sadness, albeit transfigured by the consciousness that there is *greatness* in it, if ever greatness dwelled in a mortal's task.—

Faithfully,
Your F. N.

A dead man's pallid, waxen hands, phosphorescent in the blackness of darkness, rise and fall in mournful mime of musical rhythm. Fingers spread wide, hands like white spiders pendant on invisible threads descend to the pianoforte keyboard, touch chord upon chord.

—Papi?

Shifting keys, distended harmonies, familiar returns and new departures. The give of your thighs, the smell of soap and sanctity rolling in waves from your face and throat behind and above me, your living breath in my hair. The hardening center below. And the music! O my Father, the music! *Da capo! Da capo!*

—Papi? Are you there?

—O thou blessed month of October, which throughout the years hath encompassed the most important events of my variegated life, today I am experiencing the grandest, the most splendid event: today I am to baptize my little child! O blessed moment, O savory feast, O unspeakably holy deed, I bless you in the Name of the Lord! With all my heart, and most profoundly moved, I command: *Bring me now this child, that I may dedicate him to the Lord!* My son, Friedrich Wilhelm, thus shall be your name on Earth, in memory of my king and benefactor, on whose birthday you were born.

—He isn't being baptized, Tatulku. The son of a bitch is being buried.

—*Bring me now this my beloved child!*

—Yes, yes, that's what you said when you came to get me at the altar that misty morning—you came to snatch *me,* instead of that bitch's bastard of a brother of mine! How can I ever forget!

—Never mind him, Papi. He's upset. He thinks I've come to interrupt your happy communion, Father and Son glorifying one another behind the locked portals of eternity.

—Well, haven't you? First you occupy Mamusha all those years, leaving me out in the cold, and now you come barging into a Christian burial you never deserved, bloody whoreson Antichrist!

—Never mind Little Joseph, Papi. Tell me what else happened in October. Why was it the most gladsome and glorious of months?

—I married your sainted Mother on my birthday, son, October 10. On October 15 you were born.

—Mamusha must have been bulging in her sainted wedding gown, Tatulek.

—No railleries in Eternity, Little Joseph, if you please. October 15 of the *following* year, of course. I knew Fränzchen would be the mother of my children the very first time I laid eyes on her.

—Quite a look you've got on you, Tatuncio.

—That's enough, Little Joseph. Papi, tell us again about those enchanting sprigs of dill.

—Dill? Yes. It was after the coffee and cakes had been served. I'd been improvising brilliantly on the piano at Pastor Oehler's, your future grandfather's, house; I could feel those magnificent black orbs of hers ardent upon me. I felt inspired, I played my very best. Then we went out into the garden, just the two of us, where I asked her to gather a bouquet of flowers for me. She brought me fragrant blooms of all sorts, and in their midst a sprig of dill, my favorite spice . . .

—That's when you knew she was going to pickle your herring for you, Tatulku.

— . . . my favorite fragrance, its perfume a blend of incense and urine.

—Papi!

—Everything in God's green acres is beautiful in its own way, Little Fritz. As I breathed in the odor of dill, I knew that she was chosen by the Lord to be . . .

—Wait, Tatuncio, don't tell us, let us guess!

— . . . my beloved helpmate and the mother of my dear dear children, my offspring, my prodigious progeny, my hostages to sanctity.

—Which reminds me, Fritz: where is our Little Lizzie, what's keeping our darling sister?

—By now she's at my wake, Little Joseph, serving beer and cakes to my admirers. She's thinking she'll have some rest at last, after having tossed all those handfuls of filth into my face.

—I can't wait till she gets here. She's so righteous, she's so much fun. She deserves to be here, the place was made for her.

To Elisabeth Nietzsche in Naumburg [Draft]

Sils-Maria, August 25/6, 1883

Must I still be penalized for the fact that I have agreed to a reconciliation with you? I am basically weary of your overweening moralizing claptrap.

And so much is fact: during the past twelve months you and you alone have put my life at risk *three times!*

To do this to a human being like myself—to destroy his supreme activity! I have never really hated anyone, with the exception of yourself!

—But Elisabeth has still got work to do, Little Joseph; she must make me immortal now that I'm dead and buried at last.

—Ten years with a loony was enough for her.

—Not ten. Three years. Don't exaggerate. Mama cleaned up most of the mess.

To Heinrich Köselitz in Venice

Sils-Maria, August 26, 1883

The curious danger for me this summer has been—let me not shy from the cruel word—insanity. Somehow, against every expectation, last winter I suffered from a long bout with *nerve fever*—I, who *never* had fever *in all my life!* Thus something else could also happen, something I *never* believed could happen to me: my intellect might go astray.

F. N.

—Quiet, boys, I'm dreaming now about your sainted Mother: like a vision she looms before me.

—O-oh, somebody batten down the marble slab!

—Really, Little Joseph, you're quite droll; really, you're quite impossible!

—That's because I died so young, mój drogi bracie.

—Don't jabber and bicker so, boys. Joseph, stop whining. Your grandfather, Friedrich August Ludwig, my august Father, used to say *It is unbecoming for a man of sublime thoughts to whine and sigh all the time: he must on the contrary be altogether indifferent, must make light of his pain, must be stronger than pain; even when the hardest and most stinging blows of fate strike he must never act as though something unpleasant were happening to him.*

277

—He was a brave man, wasn't he, Papi? A true Pole. Upright. Nietzsche. Nicki. Nitzky. From Nicholaus, giver of gifts, Santa Claus.

—He was a preacher, wasn't he, Ojciec? Nietzsche. Nicki. Nitzky. From *Neid*, envy, malice, ressentiment, mój kochany Tatuś, the giver of *Gift*. A venerable viper. Ruprecht with his sack of ashes.

—Like all the others in our family, boys, he was a stalwart man; everyone in the family either a pastor or a butcher.

—Wielding the crucifix . . .

— . . . and the cleaver.

✝

Just the three of us, Papi—you, Little Joseph, and myself. What shall we talk about? What shall we call back from eternal oblivion? Shall we rehash the same old selfsame?

To Franz Overbeck in Basel

Sils, Engadin, July 4, 1888

Dear Friend,

Eternal headache, eternal vomiting; a recrudescence of my old symptoms; veiling a profound nervous exhaustion, as a result of which the whole machine just won't work. . . . At bottom, there is *nothing* wrong with my head, *nothing* wrong with my stomach: but under the pressure of nervous exhaustion (which is partly hereditary—from my Father, who died only because of the *after*effects of a general lack of life-force—and partly earned, as it were), the consequences eventuate, in all their sundry forms.

Your friend,
Nietzsche.

—Remind us of your prophetic dream about Tatuś and me, Fritz! Recall the twice-dreamt dream of our imbricated deaths, his and mine. What better occasion than this?

—No. No. Not now. Not just yet, Little Joseph. Papi, tell us first how under the spell of dill you shattered the door at your wedding. That's a good one, it's a parable.

—One of the most humiliating moments of my life, boys. I'd spent weeks writing up my spontaneous outpouring of thanks at the conclusion of the ceremony. It was to be the highpoint of the entire event, and I wanted your Mother to share it with me at my side. The guests gathered below the porch of the presbytery, I stood in the doorway, elegant in my new black suit of the finest virgin wool. (I learned how to dress at the court of the three princesses of Altenburg, mastered all the courtly skills, how to bow . . .

—And how to scrape, Tatuncio?

— . . . and how to conduct myself with highborn dignity, truly regal bearing.) I began my speech, then noticed that your Mother was down in the congregation instead of at my side, her God-appointed place, and so I halted. I called her to me but the doorway was too narrow to accommodate us both. I tried to open the other half of the double door, but it was jammed tight, hadn't been opened in years. I gave it a good swift Christian kick, Jehovah-like, and my foot went right through it. When I liberated my booted foot from its jagged jaws the whole lower half of the door cracked and broke off with a clatter. By that time everyone had collapsed in paroxysms of laughter, even the Bishop forgot his station. It was profoundly humiliating, I don't mind admitting it. My speech was ruined.

—That presbytery porch was bad luck for you to the end, wasn't it, kochany Ojciec? Isn't that where you fell and hurt your head? Elisabeth says that's why your brain turned to mush.

—Your sister's noble lie. Never mind. She meant well. She didn't want my liquefying brain to stain the family reputation. However, a man of genteel grace does not stumble down the stairs like a lummox. No, it was the dour outcome of an insidious aristocratic disease, Little Joseph, the malignant work of a patrician microbe, symbolic in its own way of the entire aristocracy of Europe. My brain melted.

—That's all over and done with now, Papi. Tell us instead what I was like when I was a baby.

—Do I have to lie here and listen to this drivel? Do I?

—Quiet, Joseph. Fritz, you were the apple of my eye, God's most magniloquent blessing upon my life. I remember how you used to creep into my study while I was writing my sermon, you were so quiet I never would have heard you but for the screech of your wagonwheels.

—My wagon? Oh, I remember! With the red ladders that slotted into the frame! I drew it along behind me everywhere I went! I gave rides to Moon Crescent the Squirrel Queen! She brandished the whip!

—But I could always feel your loving gaze on my back and so I called you to me. You would clamber onto my lap and help me finish the sermon. Unless ye become as little children. You always inspired me, always brought out the best in my thoughts.

—The budding Antichrist as coconspirator! Wait till your Bishop hears about that one, Tatulek, that'll wipe the grin off his face! Did our Little Fritzie ever show you his first theology lesson, the one where he proves that the Second Person of the Trinity is the devil?

—He was an adolescent when he wrote that, Joseph. I was long dead by then. Outside my jurisdiction. Adolescents will say anything.

—No, Papi, I got that from Goethe. And there's actually a long and hallowed tradition, well, not hallowed exactly . . .

—No traditions whatsoever in Eternity, son, sorry, it's all at one go. And do not blaspheme, Joseph, it's extremely bad taste.

To Ida Overbeck in Basel

Mid-January, 1882, Genova

My thoughts are destined to move in a *very* vast and languid orbit. Indeed, to put it somewhat blasphemously, I shall believe in *my* life only *after* my death, and in my death only *during* my life. Thus it is meet and just and natural!—

Devotedly,
Dr. F. Nietzsche.

—Not that you were perfect, Friedrich Wilhelm. No one is perfect. What a temper you had when you didn't get your way! You'd throw yourself on your back and kick your feet in the air, you'd beat your tiny breast like the world's naughtiest little gorilla, but by the grace of Our Lord and astringent castigations lovingly applied we soon had you cured of that.

—Yes, I remember. That was when I squatted on my blue-rimmed pot and prayed to God that you would die.

—Our Heavenly Father hears our prayers, son.

—I'll wager that was when He planted that blue-blooded microbe in your cerebrum, Tatus, in response to Fritzen's pious prayers. Am I right?

—No! Don't listen to him, Papi! It wasn't my fault. I didn't mean it, I was just a baby.

—To be sure, mój drogi bracie, to be sure: a little tyke, just like me, albeit a touch older, more cunning, more vicious.

—No!

—Don't quarrel boys, no quarreling in Eternity. Never fear, Fritz, you were the apple of my eye. When I was improvising on the family piano or on the organ in the church, how still you would sit on my lap, how rapt to the music you were!

—Yes, Papi, that's how I gained my entry into the world of lofty spiritual things. I rose ethereally from your bosom . . .

—Odd place for a bosom, mój kochany. Fallen, perhaps?

— . . . to the world of mind and intellect . . .

—On Tatuncio's little jack, eh?

— . . . to the realm of high culture, the glory that was Greece . . .

—On Tatulku's little jag, eh?

— . . . the grandeur that was don't go to Rome . . .

—Caesar with the soul of Borgia, on Tatulek's poisonous little prick, eh?

—I regard it as a *privilege* to have had a Father like you!

—Hear! Hear! A *privilege*. Oh, yes. And I regard it as a privilege to have been snatched into instant infant mortality by a Father like you!

—You'll never forgive me for that, will you, Little Joseph?

—Forgive? *Forgive?* It's not my place to forgive. Ojciec giveth, Ojciec taketh away. In pretty damn rapid succession too, if the diabolical truth be told.

—Never mind him, Papi. Too many years churning in the grave. Embittered soul. A dwarf of ressentiment, a giant of rancor, a ghoul of gravity, a monster of the *moquant*.

To Franziska Nietzsche in Naumburg [Draft]

Nice, presumably February 17, 1888

At times I completely lose control of myself, and become a prey to the most dire resolves. Is my gall bladder causing me trouble? Year in, year out, I've had to swallow too many bitter things. When I look back, I search in vain for even one good experience. I am now of such a complete and ridiculous and merciless vulnerability that almost everything that advenes from the outside makes me ill, and the smallest trifle looms like a monster.

Do not mind him, Papi dear, mind me. Mind me and tell me more about our wondrous lifedeath together.

—A beatific life crowned by a painful illness. An agonizing death I had to endure, my beloved son.

—Be specific, Tatus. I didn't enjoy mine much either, between my gums and my guts.

—Painful in the extreme, darling Fritz. Not only because of the headaches, the pounding in my skull . . .

—Don't say it, Papi, I can't bear it: I can still feel it, a sledge-hammer slamming!

— . . . the shame and humiliation of not being able to put my elevated thoughts into words, my mouth gaping like that of a stranded fish, bringing forth nothing. Noise, yet no articulated sound. And in the final weeks, total blindness: I was in this gloomy grotto long before they interred me here, I was already accustomed to the blackness of darkness in life. It all began in 1848—that terrible year. The year of my demise, the year of my King's humiliation.

—The year I spent splashing in Mamushu's sainted belly, Tatus.

—Yes, Joseph. Your brother Fritz was born on my sovereign's birthday and you were conceived in the year of his disgrace. All the cities of Europe were ablaze. The firebrands and the howling mobs, the collective scum of city streets and faubourg alleyways, all storming the bastions of God's lieutenants here on Earth.

—I remember the young men passing by the house in wagons and carts, singing and waving their caps and banners red and blue!

—Yes, Fritz. What I remember is my dear King, Friedrich Wilhelm IV, your namesake, with the Revolutionary cocarde on his hat, posturing in order to placate the mob, flaunting it with mock enthusiasm before his subjects, and they rabid with glee. The shame of it!

—You locked yourself in your study for the rest of the day. Mother said you were working but we could hear the sobs.

—The abashment, the chagrin, the reproach, the mortification of it! I was never the same after that, my health broke on the shattered will of my impotent sovereign. The spells became worse, Fränzchen told me about them: I would sit staring into space for hours at a time, and when I came out of it, no more than the blink of an eye seemed to have supervened.

—They call that epilepsy, Tatus.

—The sacred disease? That would befit my vocation and my station. But the tumor? They found one, you know, at my autopsy. Amid the jelly and slurp—a quarter of my brain dribbled out over the dissector's scalpel and rubbergloved hand—a tiny knot of lethal flesh. Strange. Some of me thawing trickling oozing gurgling . . .

—They call that tuberculosis of the brain, Tatulek.

— . . . and some of me hardening precipitating solidifying coagulating clotting congealing inspissating petrifying . . .

—They call that cancer, Tatuncio.

— . . . and of that blatant contradiction and obnoxious oxymoron I died. Unable to find the words I wanted to pronounce spontaneously at my exitus. Unable to see the Light, yet borne aloft nonetheless by my God, my own Father, into Everlasting Light!

—They call that credulity, Tatulku.

—I couldn't find my last words. The shame, the humiliation, the outrage of it: a man who lived by the Word, whose whole life had been words, deprived of his last words. I'd spent a lifetime preparing that speech of farewell departure embarkation exodus hejira pilgrimage, and in the end amid all that silence and darkness I couldn't find my own last words. Luckily, Fränzchen found them for me.

—That's what happened to me too, Papi, except that it was your daughter Elisabeth who found them for me.

—What were your last words, son?

—"Elisabeth."

—Stop guffawing like a hyena, Little Joseph, there's nothing to laugh about here, a man's last words are his sacred testimony and testament.

—Sorry. Sorry. Whew! Hee hee! "Elisabeth"! Hoo ha! The Llama! Don't stand downwind! Ho ho!

To Heinrich Köselitz in Venice

Nice, March 30, 1885

Dear Friend,

Oh, if you only knew *how* alone in the world I am now! And how much comedy is necessary in order to prevent me, every now and then, out of disgust, from spitting in someone's face! Luckily, there is something of my son Zarathustra's courtly manners at hand also in his crazy father.

Heartily,
Your N.

All right. Whew! Why don't the two of you ask me what my last words were? You think an infant of two—my second birthday was just behind me, I barely made it—has no last words? He has. Okay, so don't ask. My last words were these: My belly hurts! My head hurts!

—You had terrible cramps, Little Joseph, I remember.

—You remember *nothing*. Cramps! They were convulsions. You fell for that story of Mother's, didn't you? "Cramps brought on by difficulties in teething." Oh, wonderful! Headlines:

283

INFANT PERISHES SPROUTING MILKTEETH !
TOOTH ERUPTS FROM SURFACE OF GUM,
TOO MUCH FOR TINY TOT !!
DENTITION INSTIGATES CANIPTION !!!

Convulsions, mój drogi bracie, convulsions. My gut twisted like a rubberband in a tortured toy. That wasn't teeth in my mouth, cretin, that was foam. And it wasn't rabies, don't be medicynical.

To Heinrich Köselitz in Venice

St. Moritz, September 11, 1879

I am at the end of my 35th year; the "middle of life" they have called it now for a millennium and a half. Dante had his vision during this period; he speaks of it in the opening lines of his poem. And now in the very midst of life I am so "surrounded by death" that it could seize me at any hour. Given the nature of my illness, I am forced to think of a *sudden* death, due to convulsions (although I would a hundred times prefer a slow, lucid death, during which one could still speak to friends, even if it should be a painful one). Thus I now feel like the most ancient of men, also in the sense that I *have fulfilled* my life's work. . . .

I won't be coming to see you. I'm in a state where it seems more suitable to settle down close to my Mother, my hometown, and my childhood memories.

Your friend N.

Would you like to know what brought on those convulsions, brother dear?

—I loved you profoundly, Little Joseph, don't even suggest it, don't even hint at it, you were sweet and warm, even your excreta were a mild, cheesy sort of thing, do not insinuate it, I beg you, I loved you dearly!

—Tell us your dream, then, my loving brother, mój kochany bracie. Tell us your dream.

—No. No. Not yet. It was only a dream. It meant nothing.

—Don't quarrel, boys. Joseph, stop this tendentious nonsense at once.

—The dream! Tell us the dream, Fritz!

And so I relent. I tell them once again what we all already know, the dream that haunted me night after night during my youth. I wrote about it twice, first when I was fourteen, after a full decade

of dreaming the dream, knowing its terrors intimately, and then
again when I was seventeen, still dominated by it. So much of what
I have written I no longer remember, but what I wrote of the dream
is as fresh and as fell to me as it was forty years ago: the dream and
the writing coalesce. And so this is what I recount to Little Joseph
and my Father, this is what I tell them I wrote, this is what I write
them I dreamt, this is what I dream I tell them I write:

At that time I once dreamt that I heard the sounds of a
church organ playing as it had during the funeral.

—That was my funeral, son.
—Yes, Papi.
—Your funeral, Tatus. Agreed. Lovely beginning. Let's get on
with the story, shall we?
And so I continue:

When I perceived what lay behind these sounds, a grave-
mound suddenly opened and my Father, wrapped in linen
cerements, emerged from it. He hurried into the church
and returned a moment later with a child in his arms. The
tomb yawned again, he entered, and the cover closed
over the opening. The stertorous sounds of the organ
ceased instantly, and I awoke. On the day that followed
this night, Little Joseph abruptly fell ill, seized by severe
cramps, and after a few hours he died. Our grief knew no
bounds. My dream had been fulfilled completely. The tiny
corpse was laid to rest in his father's arms.

Silence of the grave.
An eternity passes.
Another commences.
The same.
—Tell it again, Fritz.
—Yes, tell it again, son. For you dreamed it again. Tell all.
Omit no detail.
—Yes, Papi. I shall conceal nothing.
—Stop stalling, drogi bracie, get on with it!
And so I continue:

Some months later a second misfortune struck me. I had
a premonition of it thanks to a remarkable dream. It
seemed to me that I could hear muffled organ music

coming from the nearby church. Surprised, I open the window that looks out over the church and cemetery. My Father's grave opens, a white figure emerges and disappears into the church. The gloomy, uncanny sounds surge on; the white figure appears again, carrying something under his arm that I did not clearly recognize. The gravemound yawns, the figure sinks into it, the organ turns silent—I waken. The following morning my younger brother, a lively and gifted child, is seized with cramps, and a half-hour later he is dead. He was buried right next to my Father's grave.

—Why twice-told, this tale, my son?

—Because on the first telling he let me get too close to you, Tatulek. He wouldn't let me rest in your arms, he had to redesign the dream and plant me in the neighboring vault.

—And yet in both dreams I was immaculate, boys, I was white, I was an angel who could pass through walls. I would never have done my boys any harm.

—You're still an angel, Tatulku, lie easy.

—In the second telling my music is muffled, Fritz, and you raise the window in order to see and hear me better in the present tense. Which window was it, son?

—My bedroom window, Papi. It was the only one from which I could have seen you.

—I didn't spot you up there, spying down on me, I didn't catch you lowering at your own Father. Odd I didn't see you. Are you certain you were in your room?

—Perhaps I was in the attic, Papi, looking out of one of the ventilation windows, the middle window, the one set in the roof like an eye stirring slowly from its slumber, the vasistas?

—Perhaps.

—But then again, kochany bracie, perhaps not. Perhaps you weren't in the house at all.

—What do you mean, Little Joseph?

✝

When I was twelve I wanted to write a book of which I would be the sole reader. When I grew up that is precisely what I did. Several times over.

✝

When I was fourteen I did not masturbate. I demonstrated, with the Masonic Cabalist Goethe's help, that the first excrescence of God the Father, namely, the Second Person of the Holy Trinity, viz., the Son, because He had to counterpose Himself to the Father in order even to be perceived by Him—because, in other words, He had to become the tain to beneficent divinity's mirror—that first excrescence could only have been Satan. Lucifer, the light-bearer, reflecting darkly to the Father His (the Father's) yearning for Himself. Wholly Ghostily. After I had located the origin of all evil in the omnibenevolence of the Father, there was little left to do in life but compose music with my chum Krug and verse with my friend Pinder. No, not Pindar, Pinder: become who you aren't. Nothing left to do but yearn to compose, then vivisect. Vivisect myself by myself to myself for myself.

My first poems contained not a spark of genuine poesy. Those of my second period were all adornment, florid phrases strung together with rhyme but no reason, a greater disaster even than my earliest ventures. In the third period of my poetic production, when I was fourteen, I did not masturbate, I attempted to fuse the first two phases, that is, to unite loveliness with force. *To what extent I have succeeded I cannot myself say as yet. This most recent period began on February 2, 1858; for on this day my dear Mother has her birthday. It was customary for me to present her with a little collection of poems.*

—Son, if I am your spiritual guide and tutelary genius, why do you always write poems to your Mother?

—Papi, forgive me, but you were dead. Poems are for the living, poems are for the loving.

—You are too young, Fritz; your answer is not wise. Charity never faileth.

From that day on, February 2, 1858, I undertook to exercise my poetic faculty more diligently, and, if it should prove possible, to produce one poem each evening. This I did during the following few weeks, and each time it gave me great joy when once again I saw lying before me a new production of my spirit.

—It was my spirit, son, and the spirit of my Father and of my Father's Father, the spirit that works through the Father of us all, that produced the work and did the deed.

Once I even tried to write as simply as possible, but then I dropped that. I was well ahead of my time, Papi, for that is the way they make poems now, out of scrap metal and raw nerves soldered by a single hacking breath. *For a poem, in order to be accomplished, must no doubt be as simple as possible; yet true poesy must linger in every word. A poem bereft of thought, bedecked with phrases and similes, is like a rosy-cheeked apple with a worm inside.*

—A thought-provoking simile, son.

—Thank you, Papi. Criticism always bites the hand that feeds it. Especially when it feeds on its own flesh. That's why I was a better critic than poet: it was a matter of dentition.

—I heard that, bitch's bastard! Someday I'll tell you why you were never able to write decent poetry, poems with teeth in them.

—*Idiomatic turns of phrase must be altogether absent from a poetic creation. For the repeated use of mere phrases testifies to a head that is itself incapable of creating anything.*

—An excellent phrase, son.

—Terribly creative, don't you think, Tatulek? Certainly worth repeating.

—*In general, when writing a work one must preeminently pay heed to the thoughts: a slip in style is sooner to be forgiven than a confused idea.*

—Stylishly put, son.

—The passive voice is droopier than the active, mój drogi bracie, and is sooner to be regarded as the harbinger of a labile and perhaps even confused thought than of a genuine insight.

—It is acknowledged as clearly to be the case, son, as has just now been opined by our son and brother. Yet tell me, who is your master in all questions of thought and style? That is to say, who *was* your master when you were fourteen?

—*A model in this regard are the poems of Goethe.*

—Do you mean to say that after identifying the Christ with Lucifer Goethe continued to write poems? The crust! The gall of that man! Your Father stands appalled, son.

—*In their profound thoughts they are as clear as gold.*

—Is gold clear, son?

—Only in its depths, Papi. It was only after Goethe was able to identify the origin of good in evil, and of evil in good, descrying therein the nonorigin beyond good and evil alike, that he was able to write really good evil poems. Before that they were about scullery maids and dirty old men and Salvation.

—Perhaps he too dedicated all his early poems to his mother?

—Right you are, Tatuncio! After he grew in age and wisdom and manual dexterity he laid them on soiled sheets under Grandma Erdmuthe's pillow.

—You mean *Great* Grandmother, Little Joseph: Grandma Erdmuthe was barely a bouncing baby when Goethe was in his prime.

No, not even a baby; she was scarcely conceived, a mere mote in the eye of Providence. Her mother, our Greatgrandmother, would have been the one. Anyway, it's all a fiction. I wanted to be Goethe's grandbastardson, so I poetized a bit on his truth

To C. A. Hugo Burckhardt in Weimar [Draft]

Sils-Maria, mid-July, 1887

One of my elderly aunts, shortly before her death, burned the box containing the letters that dealt with our family's Weimar past. She did so out of a sense of delicacy and good order, which may seem extreme to the current generation (it does *not at all* seem extreme to me).

and where Goethe dallies in the garden with someone named *Muthgen,* I deposited our Father's mother's mother.
—That was frivolous, son.
—And frivolity was a perfect stranger to Grandma Erdmuthe, Papi, though I never knew her mother.

To Ferdinand Avenarius in Dresden

Turin, December 10, 1888

That the most profound spirit must also be the most frivolous— that is well-nigh a formula for my philosophy.

I remember Erdmuthe sitting in the rocker never rocking giving orders in her chilly brittle raspy voice to Aunt Auguste and Mother; only Aunt Rosalie was spared, because she was as neurasthenic as Erdmuthe was.

To Hermann Mushacke in Berlin

Naumburg, on the 4th of January, 1867

Dear Friend,

Yesterday at this hour I stood at the deathbed of my Aunt Rosalie. Besides my Mother and sister she was, to put it briefly, by far my closest and most intimate relative. With her a large portion of my past, especially my childhood, passes away; in her the whole family history and all our relations were so vital and so present that the loss in this regard is irreplaceable.

In addition, she endured an extraordinarily painful sickbed—she hemorrhaged a few hours prior to her death. It was dusk outside, snowflakes whirling; suddenly she sat bolt upright in bed—and death ensued, with all its mournful signs. Seeing it only *once*, with full consciousness, is such a unique experience that you don't very easily put it out of your mind.

Your friend,
Friedrich Nietzsche.

When I was fourteen—dreaming of you, Papi, writing for Mama—I began to learn who you and I were. From Aunt Rosalie, not from Mama. Of course, Mama spoke of you on Christmas Eve in front of the glowing tree and at Eastertide on our way to church in Naumburg. Especially afterward when almost everyone was dead and we lived alone. Aunt Rosalie was the only one left, and she lived in Plauen.

To Rosalie Nietzsche in Plauen

Naumburg, mid-August, 1858

My dear Aunt!

I want to ask you a big favor: as I intend to write my biography now, I note with horror that I am in total ignorance concerning Papi's life, as well as those of Great Uncle Krause and Grandmother Krause too. I have no data! Oh, please, won't you be a dear and write me a brief biographical outline and character sketch of these beloved persons? True, I'm asking too much of you; but maybe now you have more time than you used to have in Naumburg. Maybe you can sacrifice an hour or so for me? You'd be doing me a very great service. I can't start, you see, till I hear from you.

Love
your Fritz

AND THANKS FOR YOUR LETTER!
!! I ALMOST FORGOT !!

I haven't the vaguest idea what she wrote, Papi, but write she did, and I imagine some traces of it wound up in my autobiography, one of my earliest autobiographies. I wrote it late that summer in the cow pastures at Pobles when I was not quite fourteen. There is something ruminative about it.

EXCERPTS FROM MY LIFE
Written 18 August to 1 September 1858
Part One
The Years of My Youth
1844-1858

As an adult one usually remembers only the paramount moments of one's earliest childhood. True, I am not yet fully grown up; indeed, I have scarcely left behind me the years of my childhood and youth. Yet so much has already vanished from my memory, and the little I do know about these years I have probably retained only by means of tradition. The sequence of years soars past my gaze as a turbulent dream. . . .

The village of Röcken lies a half-hour's journey from Lützen, hard by the country road. Every traveler who passes along that road casts a friendly eye toward the village. For it lies enchantingly there with its encompassing verdure and its ponds. Above all, the mossy churchtower rises to meet one's gaze. I can still clearly remember traveling one time with my Father from Lützen to Röcken, and how halfway there the bells rang out the Eastertide in sublime tones. That sound reverberates through me so often; melancholy sweeps me away to the remote, beloved house of my Father. How vividly the cemetery still stands before me! How often when I saw the ancient charnel house did I ask about the biers and black garlands, the inscriptions on the tombstones and monuments! Yet if no image should elude my soul, how could I possibly fail to remember the familiar presbytery. For a mighty stylus has engraved it in my soul. . . .

In September of 1848 my beloved Father became mentally ill. We consoled ourselves, and him, with assurances of a rapid recovery. . . . My beloved Father had to suffer a great deal of pain, but the illness refused to diminish. It waxed from day to day. Finally, the light abandoned his eyes, and he had to bear the rest of his suffering in eternal obscurity. His sickbed lasted till July of 1849; then the day of his Redemption approached. On the 26th of July he sank into a deep slumber from which he only fitfully stirred. His last words were: Fränzchen—Fränzchen—come—Mother—listen—listen—O God! On the 27th of July, 1849, † † † † he quietly passed on to glory. When I awoke the next morning, I heard all around me a sobbing and weeping. My dear Mother came into my room and cried out in lamentation: "O God! My good Ludwig is dead!" Even though I was quite young and inexperienced, I still had an inkling of what death was; the thought that I was to be separated forever from my beloved Father seized me, and I wept bitter tears.

The following days passed amid tears with preparations for the burial. O God! I had become a fatherless orphan, my dear Mother a widow!——On the 2nd of August my dear Father's earthly remains were committed to the bosom of the Earth. The parish had prepared a concrete vault for his tomb. At about one o'clock in the afternoon the solemn ceremonies began amid the tolling of the bells. Oh, never will my ears cease to hear the muffled clangor of that knell, never will I forget the gloomily wafting melody of the hymn, "Jesus, My Consolation"! The sounds of the organ reverberated through the void of the church. . . .

If a tree is shorn of its crown it wilts and loses its leaves and the little birds forsake its branches. Our family had lost its head, all joy abandoned our hearts, and profound mourning held sway in us. Yet scarcely had the wounds begun to heal when once again they were painfully torn open.—

—That's enough, Fritz, you can skip this part, we know it all too well.

—But Little Joseph, this next part is especially for you, it is the part you dreamed of hearing, the part you particularly requested.

—Later. Or earlier. Not now. We'll pick up the thread sooner or later, mój drogi bracie. For now, conclude summarily.

—*How painful it is to abandon the village where one enjoyed happiness and sorrow, where the precious graves of one's Father and one's younger brother . . .*

—Conclude, you swine!

—*. . . where the local inhabitants always came to meet one with love and amity! Scarcely had daylight touched the fields when our wagon rolled out onto that country road and took us to Naumburg, where a new home awaited us. Adieu, adieu, dear house of my Father!*

†

Aristotle burned his early dialogues and submitted to Plato, who had burned his tragedies and submitted to Socrates before him. And so I locked away my oratoria my Lieder and my poems and became a philologist. It was the definitive answer to an inchoate question. Philology was so demanding I had no time to think. I was happy. For a spell.

Besides, it was a perfectly reasonable thing to do. I loved the words and works of the ancients, I loved the *feel* of them. They were my brothers. It was the philopathology of the *Symposium* that seduced me more than anything else, more even than Sophocles: all that palaver and deceit about eros—it was more hilarious than anything I'd ever read, Aristophanes' funniest comedy, his finest hour! Did you know, Papi, that Plato slept with Aristophanes under his pillow? It was a bit crowded but the conversation was never dull. If only he had let Aristophanes *write* for him. Philosophy too could have been a grand enterprise, you know, it didn't have to be drear

To Heinrich Köselitz in Venice

Sils-Maria, August 21, 1885

Dühring, *Course in Philosophy*, p. 79, is where you'll find that statement.—Please locate the quotation in Bebel, who is citing an English woman (Elisab...) on the compulsiveness of women's sexual needs. Please copy that statement for me! It is edifying, by Saint Aristophanes!

I can feel myself fragmenting. My writing is becoming one with my body. It is becoming many

To Heinrich Köselitz in Venice

Naumburg an der Saale, Tuesday.
September 22, 1885

Dear Friend,

Best thanks for the quotation from Bebel, although my memory seems to have been the victim of some confusion: I meant another page of the book and another "womanly" quotation. Doesn't matter much.

Your faithful
Nietzsche.

✝

—Papi, does seed get old?
—Everything beneath the ecliptic of the sun and the circles of the moon declines and perishes, son. What sort of seed did you have in mind?
—Mortal seed, Papi. In the winter of 1863 at Pforta I had a bad cold. I went to the infirmary. Dr. Zimmermann was called out of the

room for a few minutes. I got up, tiptoed over to his desk, and peered into the illness registry, which lay open to my name: Nietzsche, Friedrich Wilhelm.

—That was objectionable, my boy. Such records are confidential, even when they touch you.

—They did touch me, Papi. They touched my body and my dreams. And they touched you too.

—What did you read, son? Tell me everything.

—The words are branded in my heart, Papi. It was my first and best biography. It was my thanatography.

—What did you read, my son? Omit no detail.

—I read this, Papi:

1862: Congestion in the head, 7-11 January; headaches, 4-13 February; cold, 24-29 March; cold, 17-24 June; congestion in the head, 16-25 August.

—What every normal redblooded schoolboy has to endure, son. Nothing to be alarmed about. Common cold.

—It wasn't that, Papi, it was how the registry continued:

Observation: Nietzsche was sent home for further convalescence. He is a full-bodied, full-blooded, solid man . . .

—That's my boy! Nothing to be alarmed about!

. . . with a conspicuously glaring stare, myopic, and often plagued by headaches that settle in sundry parts of the head. His father died young as a result of dissolution of the brain, having been conceived during his own father's advanced age . . .

—Nonsense! Father was only fifty-seven when I was born, and he lived to be seventy! He was in his prime, at his acme! Old seed, indeed! That is wicked nonsense, son.

. . . and his son in turn was conceived during the period when the father was already ill. No grave signs of illness are visible in young Nietzsche as yet, but caution is called for in the light of the antecedents.

—Unholy nonsense! I was blossoming, bursting with health when you were bestowed on us, your Mother and I had only just married. I was fit as a fiddle. The fits didn't start till you were two or three. The microbe did its work in a single year; it was nothing if not efficient. You were already four almost five when I died.

—And for the rest of my life I was certain that I was dying of your implanted seed, Father, that you were the seed of death in me. The seed and deed of death in me. I felt it that winter in Naumburg and the following spring in Sorrento, the most vital spring of my life; felt the germ of death bursting through the husk, flourishing thriving burgeoning smothering all of life's tender shoots, crowding them out, suffocating all my other thoughts.

—I loved you, my boy. From my impossibly far remove, I loved you. I watched over you and guarded you. I was your amulet against them.

—Them?

—Against the women, son. Have no pretence before me. You know it was they who engendered the death in you. I was the very spirit of life.

—Spirits are phantoms, Father.

—Spirits inbreathe. Spirits inspire. Spirits exhale distilled sperm, logos spermatikos, the seed of life.

—Old sperm, Father. Defective. Decrepit. Degenerate. Putrid exhalation of empty words, slimy shells. My portrait at age seventeen shows my squinty left eye, the right corner of my mouth already plunging in paralytic scowl, my hair already thinning. Old sperm, Father. Mutant mutilant putrescent seed and deed of death.

—Chlorinated butter of exuberant health, son! Edelweiß! The purest rarefaction of everliving air!

—Ghost of moribund ashen life. Ghastly ghoulish dream of ephemeral life, shadow of life destined to be undone.

—So it always was, is, and shall be, my son. Life ascendant, life descendant. What goes up has got to come . . .

—Dribbling downward . . .

—But your sainted Mother snatched it up between her thighs. Heaven only knows what the bitch did with it there: all was concealed in abysmal obscurity, the narrow valley of nothingness. At all events and in any case your poor blind inarticulate Father is blameless.

—I knew then that my entire life was to be the absurd tale of Aunt Rosalie: nerves hypersensitivity overstimulation migraine and vomiting. As if by instinct I was also certain of the most likely cure. Long walks in the alpine air, mountain solitude, and absolute avoidance of your music. The most likely cure. No one really knew.

To Franz Overbeck in Basel

Nizza, November 12, 1887, Pension de Genève

Dear Friend,

It seems to me that a kind of epoch is coming to a close for me; a retrospective is now more than ever in order. Ten years of illness, more than ten years; and not the straightforward sort of illness for which there are medicines and physicians. Does anyone really know *what* made me ill? what held me fast in proximity to death and yearning for death? I do not believe so. When I exclude Richard Wagner, there is no one who ever came to me with a thousandth part of passion and pain in order to reach "an understanding" with me. I was alone in this respect even as a child, and am still so today, in my forty-fourth year of life. The terrifying decade I have now put behind me gave me a generous taste of what it means to be alone, a taste of isolation to an extreme degree: the isolation and defenselessness of an infirm man who has no means of protecting himself, or even "defending himself." The best thing I can say about it is that it made me more independent; but perhaps also harder and more contemptuous toward my fellows than I would like to have been. Fortunately, I have enough of the *esprit gaillard* in me to laugh at myself concerning these reminiscences, as I laugh at everything that touches only *me*; further, I have a task that does not *allow* me to worry much about myself (a task or a destiny, call it what you will). This task made me ill, it will make me healthy again; not only healthy but also friendlier toward my fellows, and whatever that implies.—

Your N.

—Perhaps there is another explanation, son. It too has to do with seed—but yours, not mine.

—What do you mean, Papi?

—That trip you took to Cologne during your first semester at Bonn. They all went to Cologne, your fraternity brothers, to sate their fetid lusts.

—I was sating my curiosity. I went to see the cathedral, that unfinished symphony. My guide was supposed to take me to a restaurant afterwards. I was hungry.

—They all said that, all your brothers, who made that same sulphurous journey, they all said those wicked words. "I have hunger." It was a code.

—That's why he took me to a bordello?

—It offends me to hear you speak the word. Yet a Father must know, it is his sacred responsibility. Go on. Omit no detail.

—How long I was standing in the parlor, gaping at the bejewelled ringleted corseted cosseted powderpancaked mascaraed apparitions there, I do not know. Earrings dangling to their bare shoulders, assorted bulgings barely covered in gauze and satin and lace, stale reek of nannygoat and empty beer glasses. The gas jet on the wall farting fitfully. Over in the far corner of the room a young man in a threadbare black suit was playing the piano. I wended my way to him between bubs and coarse whisperings. Before I could speak he turned his head and looked up at me, his face a livid mask of consternation and contrition. A louse curled up over his collar and ambled across his shoulder.

—La musique a ses charmes, n'est-ce pas?

—Vous êtes français, monsieur?

A sly smile formed on that ashen face, the face of an unborn infant mired already in sin guilt.

—Je suis un irlandais de merde. Ma douzième côte n'a pas bougé, et moi, voilà! je reste mortel.

—I'm sorry. May I play something for you?

He shifted listlessly to one side in order to make room for me. I resisted contiguity, remembering the louse loose on his person. Bending down over the cracked keys I touched three minor chords, the third giving me my resolution and my resolve. I tore away, dashed across the room, and burst through the door before the shouting could even begin. Out into the clear and bitter cold February night under stars. Under the dust and filth of stars.

—That's all? You expect me to believe that, son? You heard what the doctor said: full-bodied full-blooded.

—I had no lust, Father. I was properly raised. Women I never loved, I loved piano players. No, not him, the others. Anna Redtel in Bad Kösen, a short walk an eternity away from Pforta. I composed rhapsodies for her and tied them in red ribbon. For Marie Deussen, Miss Rheingold, that summer before I started my studies, I wrote Lieder and dedicated them to her and bound them in leather. Anna worked her mouth in the most awkward and beautiful way when she played, I was mad to lap her music. Marie was nobler, I did not look at her ankles down at the pedals, I swear it, Papi. Piano players. Much later it would be Irene. During those early years I was laying wreaths on Schumann's grave: everything I ever improvised or composed or wrote or sang was like a fragment a single bar a truncated phrase of Schumann. "A Woman's Life and Love," "The Broken

Windowpane." Melodies that saw no good reason why they should cohere, phrases without convincing counterpoint, mere waifs slips and strays of notes, harmonies that yearned to be somewhere else, that is how I loved the women. "Manfred's Requiem." Over my piano in Bonn hung a portrait of my blessed Father, yourself, and a color reproduction of the "Deposition from the Cross," though certainly not Rembrandt's "Scourging at the Pillar." That is how I loved, Papi. Not like Chambige; I was no gallant Henri. Nor like Father Prado, Father. Charity never faileth. Like that, Papi. Old seed, Papi.

†

What I learned as a student at Leipzig was method. *What* my professors said didn't interest me half as much as *how* they said it. I wasn't a cistern to be filled to the brim week after week with aqueous science, I wasn't an encyclopedist or an autodidact.

—You were a vaudevillian, a showman, a ringmaster, mój drogi bracie. You were a feuilletoniste. All you ever wanted was a few cheap effects. You were more like Wagner than you ever knew: the sorcerer's apprentice.

—You forgot what your own Emerson said, son. You forgot that a writer who keeps one eye on his readers' reactions produces a cockeyed script.

—I kept both eyes on the essential matter: how others might learn from me.

—Oh, insufferable! Listen to him, Tatus!

—Joseph is right, son. Have you not sinned grievously against humility?

—To gain the necessary lucidity, deliberateness, and self-awareness to be able to teach: that was all the humility I cared about or needed.

—But to teach *what*, son? Faith, not good works! It comes down to doctrine. But which doctrine? That is where you vacillated.

—It comes down to dogma, Tatulek. Dazzling the country bumpkins and city slickers alike with a few carefully selected sententious phrases: will to power, eternal recurrence of the same, transvaluation of all values, the overman, nihilism. Earwigs. Catchy tunes, ditties. Dogmas for a day, lyres for the night.

—I had no style. Yet I very much wanted to have one.

—Devotion to truth is sufficient style.

—Not for a circus barker, Tatuncio.

—I never tired of observing the way Ritschl turned me into a philologist, never ceased admiring his laudations, all his hooks and lures, all his admonishments, all his comehithers. It was the way he made it all seem to have been already accomplished, already decided, as though nothing in me were under way. That was his method. We never debated my future in the Café Kintschy smoking not permitted, we debated Aeschylus Thucydides Diogenes Laertius Suidas

To Franziska and Elisabeth Nietzsche in Naumburg

Nice, Saturday, March 14, 1885

One is vigorously punished for one's ignorance. If I had occupied myself *at the proper time* with medical, climatological, and similar problems, instead of with Suidas and Diogenes Laertius, then I would not be a half-eradicated human being today.

Love,
F.

Homer Hesiod Orpheus Musaeus; yet all the while we were submitting to his method of being not under way but already arrived, we were being verritschelt down the slippery slope of all-funneling philology. That's what I learned at Leipzig: I renounced art for philosophy, philosophy for science, science for fussiness over words. I learned how to let myself be backed into a corner. I learned learnedness. I learned that life is over at twenty-four, that the rest is reprise and regress.

—Was it really I behind your chair, son, spooking you? That's what you told your doctor. You never neglected an opportunity to reproach me. Yet you know my voice, son, this gentle, mellifluous voice that speaks out of me. Was it I? Tell me true.

—I don't know, Papi. It wasn't the *sound* of your voice, the voice I remember. It was organpedal deep, this voice, growling, rumbling, deathrattling. All I know is that it terrified me.

—Terrors are many in that valley of tears above, my boy, you needn't blame them all on your Father.

—Did I blame you, Papi? I called you an angel, said you were more a dream about life than life itself.

—Why then did you write what you wrote that night in March during your last year at Leipzig? You were writing about me, weren't you?

—I remember what I wrote. I don't remember if it was about you. I remember I was studying too hard, staying up nights, not sleeping. I don't remember whether it was even human, that voice, or whether it was a ghoul. All I remember is what I wrote, and the gorge rising in me. *What terrifies me is not the figure standing behind my chair but the voice of that figure: not the words either but the shudderingly inarticulate tone. Oh, if only it would talk as human beings talk.*

—It may have been your sainted Mother, you know, possessed by your own laughing daimon and demigod. He lowers their voices along with their morals. He makes them hard. Agave, son, do you know it?

—Or it may have been your own sisters, Papi, my maiden aunts.

—No need to judge me and mine so harshly, son. I was your Father. I was their brother. You and I were all my sisters had. I loved you more than my life, and so did they.

—Did you all love me more than your deaths as well?

—I don't understand. Don't be cryptic with me.

—Were you able to release me after your deaths, were you all able to let me be?

—I had no say in the matter, son. Word and Light failed me. I couldn't hold onto you, although Heaven knows I wanted to. Everything slipped away. I struggled against it, but all vanished.

—Everything?

—Everything but the organ music and the glassy ring of the deathknell.

—My music and my books. That is something. That is a lot. Yet didn't these very things become my amulet, Father, to stave off the women and the witches? You yourself said it a moment an eon an eternity ago don't you remember? And isn't that how you held onto me? Ghostly ghastly fingers of fatherlove.

—Don't be morbid, boy. And don't be so sure it was I. Fathers are a bit awkward, that's all. But then, you wouldn't know. Perspective is king.

†

I hear yet another voice. I can't tell whose it is anymore, perhaps Grandfather's, perhaps yours, Father. No. Wait. Coming back to me. It's Daddy Longlegs! Rembrandt! It's Le Petit Rembrandt's voice, the German Rembrandt contradictio in adiecto's voice, Julius Langbehn, my longlegged savior. Scourging me at my pillory!

—Because we are all, all of us, renegade schoolboys, don't you know. Paupers, children, sinners all. The secret is this: we are not sufficiently wicked! It is precisely our remorse that holds us back, shame in the face of all that love generosity bounty! Surely you can see that, you above all men? If only we could leave shame and pride behind and accept His generous love in the round! But that is the one thing our jagged, angular devil will not countenance. He wants everything on the slant, everything on the oblique, nothing straight or straightforward, no candid selfless love. Make it on the slant! the devil cries. Yet it's like a stick plunged into water—it only *seems* bent!

—Then evil is purely illusory?

—Of course not! By no means! It is the fault of the turbid medium, the water.

—But the stick looks bent in *crystalline* water: in turbid water it wouldn't even appear as bent.

—No, all right, forget that. You are sharp today! It is the devil, all of it, quite simply, you can be certain of that! If all good spirits meet in God, then all wicked spirits converge in the devil. He is petrifaction.

—How can the petrified converge?

—He is the inability to unfold or develop. Whereas God is as spherical as a bullet.

—And as deadly: petrified beyond petrifaction, moulded lead.

—Whereas, you see, the devil is eternally split in twain.

—Old Comedy, thank you.

—And is fragmented!

—New Comedy, you're welcome.

—He is paralysis.

—Perhaps you are onto something there.

The voice drones on and on, rising in spasmodic crescendo to a kind of sterile climax. My interruptions cease; they are pointless. Turning the tables does not help. The tiniest the most picayune the pettiest human recurs eternally: that is my nausea, my danger, my truth.

—And this whole attack of yours on Christianity! Put it down to frayed nerves. Temporarily permanent insanity. Put it down to a

Postcard to Heinrich Köselitz in Venice

Sils-Maria, July 21, 1881

It occurred to me, dear friend, that the perpetual inner confrontation with *Christianity* in my book must be foreign and even embarrassing to you; yet Christianity remains the best piece of ideal life, the one I have gotten to know most thoroughly; from the time I was a little boy I have pursued its paths into many different nooks and crannies. And I believe I have *never* been cruel in my heart toward it. Ultimately, I am the *descendant of* many generations of Christian clerics— forgive me this limitation!—

F. N. in Sils

mental hygiene inadequately sustained and insufficiently rigorous. Effects of excessive perturbation. Regrettable lapses into hogwallow filth corruption stench fetor rot putrefaction offal ordure mephitis muck mire souillure assorted sordid vilenesses soilings murkinesses like that turbid water obscenity lewdness like that well-hung meat prurience pollution smut salacity lubricity lewdness I repeat licentiousness concupiscence incontinence debauchery venery fornication rut defilement depravity like that mahogany table dissipation dissolution defloration sodomogomorrhic ensyphilization the way of all flesh!

†

What I learned as a teacher in Basel was that my philology was a fish out of water. I marinated it for nine years, following friend Rohde's recipe to the letter, then served it up. In my mouth it turned to stone, the stone to a snake. The snake bit fast. I had to bite back

To Heinrich Köselitz in Venice

Nice, October 27, 1887
(blue fingers, sorry!)

Dear Friend,

Since last evening I've got a fishbone stuck in my throat. The night was painful: in spite of repeated efforts to vomit it out it remains stuck fast. Very odd. I sense an abundance of symbolism and meaning in this physiological villainy.

Heartily yours,
N.

I learned that the life of knowing—what we call science—has only one purpose, which is to *annihilate* the world. The Greeks sensed it. Empedocles felt it in his lavaboiled bones. It is as though the early Greeks worked out *en miniature* what is now happening to the world we call modernity; whether it is happening grandly or farcically this time around I don't know. Art destroys the state: what could the city be after Aeschylus, and certainly after Aristophanes? What will the state be after Wagner? Then the dedication to knowledge, the obsession with science, kills art. Not with Hegel first of all, and even before artless Socrates. Democritus too sensed it. When truth kills art, after art has laughed the state off the stage, a whole world goes up in flame, smoke, and ash. Science as ἐκπύρωσις, world conflagration. Someday they will take it literally. Socrates will still be dillydallying with music, but by then it will be too late.

That is what I learned in stoic Basel.

As though learning could mean anything to the monstrosity being born in me.

I was Heraclitus. I was Democritus. Above all, I was Empedocles, and that meant every name in history.

That is what I learned as a teacher in Basel.

†

Rohde. You weren't there today, either. You did not grace my grave, did not peer down on me and swear your oath and weep. We fought. It was stupid of me. Worse, it was weak. And now you are dead.

To Erwin Rohde in Heidelberg

Nice, November 11, 1887

Dear Friend,

No, don't be too easily estranged from me! At my age and in my isolation *I* at least refuse to lose the few human beings in whom at one time I had confidence.

Your N.

I now have forty-three years behind me and am precisely as alone as I was when I was a child.—

Long ago right from the start you declared me the superior partner in our confraternity; you proclaimed me the "productive nature" to your "unproductive" self. Let that go. Forget my improvisations in the dark. Mere gropings. You were too easily overwhelmed. Remember, you have psyche. That is something. That is a lot. I only wish you were not so afraid of my sweet and terrible Dionysos. And, obverse of the same, so enamored of Wagner and Schopenhauer, if brittle straw like you can be enamored of anything. And I wish you hadn't belittled my admirer, Henri Taine, that showed bad taste, I mean Hippolyte. The fact that I took it as grounds for a quarrel showed even worse taste, *concedo*

To Erwin Rohde in Heidelberg

> *Turin, January 4, 1889*
> *To My Growly Bear Erwin:*

At the risk of enraging you once again by my blindness as regards Monsieur Taine, who formerly composed the Vedas, I hereby deign to transpose you to the gods, with the most beloved of goddesses at your side. . . .

> Dionysos.

Rohde. Your face is before me as I lie here. Always with an expression of manly recoil and comely revulsion. Always the sarcasms gathering like saliva in your mouth, sour spittle laced with vitriol. Your big ears waiting in vain for the rest of your long head to fill out. Your eyes dark with bitterness and irony and ineffable sadness that was why I loved you.

To Erwin Rohde in Tübingen

> *Nice, February 22, 1884*

My dear old Friend

I don't know how it happened: but when I read your last letter...it was as though you pressed my hand and gave me a most melancholy look, as though to say, "How is it possible that we now have so little in common, as though we lived in different universes! And yet at one time——"

And so it goes, my friend, with all the human beings who are dear to me: it is all *bygone*, it is all past, it is all a matter of sparing one another; they still see each other, they speak, in order not to be silent—, they still write each other, again, in order not to be silent. However, the look on their faces proclaims the truth; it says to me (I hear it distinctly enough!), "Friend Nietzsche, now you are *all alone!*"

> Your
> F. N.

You were born and bred to be my very best friend, you know that, don't you? You even forgave me for the friendship I felt for you. We traveled well together, we wore well on one another. We had the very best of talk back then, the very best stories. How could you have let a lamb like Overbeck usurp your place?

Wish you were here.

No offense. From one unmoved mover to another.

Yes, yes, never fear: I can hear your burst of scorn, friend Rohde. Always and always I hear it, always I love you.

To Erwin Rohde in Kiel

Basel, the 4th of July, 1874

God bless you and your novel. May He grant you cool, sparkling days and nights of fathomless sleep beneath the glimmer of moons and comets. I long for cold mountain water, I crave it like a wild sow.

Fare ye well,
Your Fridericus

†

Illness to the rescue. In a horsedrawn sleigh we glided across the Gotthard Pass in the dead of winter. Blizzards. A white so white everything was shades of gray. Swooping down to Bellinzona and on by coach to Lugano, where even in January there is a sky and the sun shines in it. Doctor's orders, Father. I had returned to work too soon after the war, too soon after my illnesses, halfway through the autumn term I was prostrate. Lisbeth came down from Naumburg to join me reassemble me and we crossed the Gotthard together to see if we couldn't coax my health back.

—Good health, mój kochany, is an immense stupidity: take it in small doses.

—I always did, Little Joseph. In matters of health I was abstemious, strictly Apollonian: nothing overmuch. However, as luck would have it, instead of fetching back my health I brought my beloved *Birth* to term.

To Heinrich Köselitz in Annaberg

Turin, December 22, 1888

Dear Friend,

Very curious! Four weeks ago I came to understand my own writings—even more, I now value them. In all seriousness, I never knew what they meant; I'd be lying if I said that—apart from *Zarathustra*—they had impressed me. So it is with a mother and her child: she may well love it, but she abides in perfect stupidity concerning what the child *is.*—I am now absolutely convinced that it all turned out well, from the very outset—all is one, and it all wills one. The day before yesterday I read my *Birth:* something undescribable, *deep,* tender, felicitous.

Your friend Nietzsche.

Lugano was the scene of my accouchement, my week-in-bed, six weeks, to be exact. We froze in the dark and burned in the sun. I sent Lisbeth on tours. I sequestered myself in my hotel room and wrote.

—It was always my favorite book of yours, son. It has pathos. It has music. It has religion.

—It was his favorite too, Father, Wagner's favorite. The people who understood it better, like Wilamowitz, hated it. Hated it or loved it to excess—and hated me for having written it.

—It was a philosophical book, son. You crossed the line.

—Or tried to, and failed. And so I had to get sick instead of becoming a philosophy professor. I made my philosophy out of my illness, but my illness arose because I could not become a philosopher.

—Give the microbes *some* credit, drogi bracie.

That's how it was, always. Illness to the rescue. Chipped breastbone here, sprained ankle there, dizzy spells and vomiting everywhere, vagrant migraine, vagabond nerves stripped and frazzled and fried till they were ssszzz charred black.

To Malwida von Meysenbug in San Remo

Basel, the Saturday before Easter, 1874

Most esteemed Friend

You know that there is a condition of bodily suffering which at times seems to be a blessing. For one forgets about *what else* one is suffering from. Or, rather, one believes one can be helped, just as the body can be helped. That is my philosophy of illness: it gives the soul hope. And is that not a feat—still to hope?

Faithfully yours,
Friedrich Nietzsche.

Illness to the rescue. Twice it got me out of the army when I didn't even know I wanted to get out of the army. It reduced the hours I had to teach, the years too. It gave me the peace of mind for inner turmoil, it gave me my books. (I wrote some very beautiful books, Papi.) It rescued me from philology and from philosophy as well: I never wrote a magnum opus logico-philosophico-praetentiosus. Illness to the rescue. Without illness I'd have been as boring as everyone else, Papi. Zieher never really understood.

—I too was ill, son. That didn't make me interesting.

—On the contrary, Tatuncio, an oozing cerebrum has its attractions. Mental mush fascinates. Of course, it's nothing compared to the valetudinarian drama of *teething*. Now, there's an illness for you. Or maybe colic? Baby Cuckoo's chuck-up?

—It saved you from all of life, Little Joseph.

—Right you are, mój drogi bracie. But tell me: were we any different in that regard?

Illness to the rescue.

†

Wagner cuckolded von Bülow, von Bülow castigated me. Wagner stole his Mrs., von Bülow absconded with my music. He obliterated my "Manfred Meditation." He showed me mercilessly the truth of it: after I had sent Byron and Schumann reeling with a single staggering blow, there was nothing left to do but coin a few musical jingles. I really didn't know how bad it was till I sent it to von Bülow and he held it up to me like a distorting mirror. Except that I was the distortion. Bathos and bad jokes, Papi, that was the sum of it.

—The same thing happened to your precious philosophy, drogi bracie. You wrote that the long tragedy of philosophy was over, and that you would cap the afternoon with a satyrplay. Theseus, Dionysos, and Ariadne on Naxos. Some satyr: you struggled to achieve the level of the jejune.

—Perhaps your ears were too long for it, Little Joseph?

—My baby gray eyes and pink pug nose told me all I needed to know, mój kochany. They told me you were never able to write philosophy either, neither poems nor treatises.

—You are talking about one of the undisputed master stylists of the modern German tongue, Joseph.

—More's the pity, Ojciec. No wonder Fritz wanted to write French and speak Italian. However, they are *musical* languages, and he lost his music long ago, irrevocably. You should at least have learned English from that editor of *Mind,* Fritz, the one who went out of his sufficiently to take an interest in yours.

—I didn't mind William Nowits slurring my *Birth* half as much as I suffered from the opprobrium of Bülow. All my life I'd been a musician, from my earliest childhood onward, I can't even remember when it started.

To Hans von Bülow in Munich

Basel, October 29, 1872

Honored Sir,

You must realize that since my *earliest* youth and up to the present moment I have been living under the craziest illusion: I've taken *so much* joy in my music! It has always been a problem for me to know whence this joy arises. There was something so irrational about it: in this regard I could turn neither left nor right, the joy was always there in front of me.

Yours sincerely,
Friedrich Nietzsche.

—I remember it well, son. It started on my lap. Perhaps even in your Mother's belly. She said you became absolutely motionless the instant I began to play. Then, after a bar or two, absolutely frenetic. Sometimes she would sit close beside me on the bench and I would improvise for you, whoever you were.

—For me you never played, Ojciec. For me you never ever improvised, not even a note.

—I was too ill by that time, Joseph. I was jelly by then. I couldn't find my hands. The Revolution. The humiliation. The microbes. It was all too much for me. The pianoforte gathered dust.

—I remember your playing when I was inside her womb, dear Papi, I remember swimming gloriously with the sounds, it was a Schopenhauerian sea.

—Hogwash! Don't let him talk you into anything, bracie. You believe every tune on the wind! Gullible! A Mozart you never were. You were Beethoven without hands, with only the old man's deaf ears.

—I swear I remember, Little Joseph! Why else should the music have been so important to me all my life? It was where the three of us met: we couldn't meet in religion, so it had to be in music.

—The *three* of us? Us, who?

—Mama, Papi, and I.

—Wonderful. Go right ahead. Leave me out. Go right ahead, quite all right, Lisbeth and I will just lie over here in the garden and eat worms. Or vice versa. Go right straight ahead.

—The three of us, Papi. That's what von Bülow shattered when he dispersed my "Manfred Meditation."

—The three of you plus the Wagners, don't forget, mój kochany. Meister Richard and his—I mean your—dear Cosima. Don't forget how the loving illicit couple laughed themselves silly over your "New Year's Eve."

—They never laughed, it's not true!

—And he sniggered at your improvisations in Bayreuth, laughed to scorn what you learned so painstakingly in her belly!

—I had no illusions about my gift.

—You had no gift, only illusions.

—My songs weren't bad.

—Sentimental ditties, drogi bracie. Schumann's shapeless afterbirth. His wretched madness without the genius. And you thought you'd refuted him with "Manfred." Bülow and I straightened you out on that one, didn't we?

—- Don't mind Joseph, son. He seeks to deflate what he cannot understand. It's the conceit of the summarily dead.

—Ghoul! Murderer!

—You were as cold as stone when I came to collect you and bring you home, Joseph. I am blameless. Silence, now, for Fritz and I are discussing something important. As regards your music, son, I confess I never really understood what it meant to you. For me it was the whisper of angels. I loved it so well I feared I might be sinning, you remember what jittery Augustine says. But for you—ostensibly outside of religion—what could it mean? In a word, son, I never really grasped your style.

—My style? O Papi, I worked so hard to get one, in my music, in my writing! How should I know what it is, or what it was supposed to be, or even how many I could have had?

To Paul Deussen in Bonn

Naumburg, April 4, 1867

My dear Friend,

You will find it ridiculous that I devote so much energy to mixing the colors on my palette, ridiculous that I'm trying so hard to write in a bearable style. Yet it is truly necessary, since

I've neglected the matter for so long. Well, then, I avoid unnecessary erudition as strictly as I can. That takes a bit of self-overcoming. My cerebral stomach gets upset when it is surfeited. Too much reading dulls the mind horribly. Most of our scholars would be worth more as scholars too if they were less full of scholarship. Don't eat too much at mealtime.

F. W. N.

Only once did I get an inkling of what it might be. Style. It was in Nice, I think, I don't remember. Brahms's first piano concerto was making a comeback after what they did to it in Leipzig, enemy territory; it was all the rage now, and they brought it to Nice one winter. Listening to it just that one time I learned something about style. From Brahms, imagine! I had always admired his "Triumphal Hymn," even if the Meister never forgave me my lapsus—I played it one evening in the hope of discussing it with him, but he exploded, even Cosima couldn't calm him down—it was the beginning of the end for us. I suppose I assassinated Wagner with gentle Brahms. Anyway, no matter what I later wrote about the "melancholy of incapacity" in Brahms, it was he who taught me something about style that Wagner never could; Brahms was another of those distorting mirrors I held up to my distorted self.

—Wagner taught you everything, drogi bracie. What he belittled, you despised. That was the lesson of *your* style, brother dear: in your case style was obsequious imitation of the hand that happened to be holding your own. That was your style, and it never changed.

—I was highly receptive.

—Said the sponge to the sea urchin.

—Never mind our Little Joseph, Fritz. Go on.

I was listening to the first piano concerto when the thought struck me with incredible force: Brahms has so few ideas, but he makes such wonderful noise with them. In all that bombast, in all that barrage of sound, in all that saccharine sweetness, how few the ideas were! So little ideality! I asked myself: How can the music be so grand—for glorious it doubtless was, my body told me that— when the ideas are so sparse? The answer came slowly: Brahms gives himself all the time he needs. The ideas were so simple, *they* needed no time at all. Yet he gave *himself* time, all the time in the world. That much of a person, that much of a ruling center, he was. In the Adagio there comes a kind of apotheosis, though all it consists of is pedal pedal pedestrian pedal in the double-bass obstinately ostenato for a dozen bars while the piano takes all the time in the world to tinkle carelessly up the keyboard and mindlessly back down the keyboard in order finally to rejoin the bass. That was when I started to cry. The grimace had been on my face from the outset, but when he finally tugged on that longest leash in the world and brought the melismas back down to marry their tonic I couldn't hold it back any longer, I wept above and below.

—What has that got to do with *your* music, son?

—Nothing. Absolutely nothing, Papi. I never had time, never took the time, not for any of my ideas, not in any of my pieces. I gave my ideas less time than even Schumann did, no sooner stated than sated. Schumann satisfied, satiated in a hurry, sauteed with the sheerest impression. That was what von Bülow the Cuckold was crowing to me: I never gave any idea of mine the time to weep.

✝

Tribschen. Isle of the Blessed on Lake Lucerne. Trib-schen: the sound of the lake lapping on the grassy bank above the calamus the cattail, each wavelet washing ashore trippingly Trib-schen Trib-schen on the tongue.

The night we met at Brockhausen's place in Leipzig he invited me to visit him in Tribschen. At the time he was working on the third act of *Siegfried*. I didn't know whether he was merely being polite and effusive or whether he really meant it.

To Erwin Rohde in Hamburg

Leipzig, November 9, 1868

My dear Friend,

When I got home I found a slip of paper addressed to me containing a brief note: "If you want to meet Richard Wagner come to the Café Théâtre at about a quarter-past three." (Signed:) Windisch.

I dashed off, of course, and found our stolid friend, who revealed still more to me. Wagner had come to Leipzig strictly incognito in order to visit his relatives: the press hadn't gotten wind of it yet and all the servants at the Brockhausen's had been silenced like tombstones in livery. Now, Wagner's sister, Professor Brockhausen's wife, that intelligent and enlightened woman, had also introduced her brother to her good friend Frau Ritschl, my professor's wife. The latter had the honor of ingratiating herself with her friend in the company of her friend's brother and simultaneously with the brother in the company of her friend, the lucky creature! Wagner played the *Meisterlied* (which you know) for Frau Ritschl, and the good woman told him that she knew it well already, *mea opera*. To Wagner's delight and astonishment. He declared his supreme majesterial will to be that he meet me, incognito. I was to be invited for Friday evening. Windisch countered that I would be unable to accept because of the obligations of my office, previously made engagements, etc. Sunday afternoon was proposed. So Windisch and I dashed over to Brockhausen's once again, where we met the Professor's family—but not Richard, who had stepped out of the house with a huge hat on his magnificent head. Thus I met this most illustrious family and received a kind invitation for that same Sunday evening.

My mood that day was like something out of a novel. Admit it: there is something fairytale-like about the way the acquaintanceship was struck, he being an utterly unapproachable sort of prodigy.

Believing that a large group of people had been invited, I determined to prepare my toilette most grandly. As luck would have it, my tailor had promised me a spanking new tuxedo for Sunday. It was a horrid day, all sleet and slush, one shuddered to face the elements.—Dusk, and still no tailor. I paid him a personal visit and found his slaves hard at work on my coat and tails: they promised to send the things over in forty-five minutes. Happy as a lark I strolled off, ambled into the Café Kintschy, read the *Kladderadatsch* and found to my contentment a news item announcing that Wagner was in Switzerland but that they were building a lovely house for him in Munich: whereas I knew that I would be seeing him that very evening and that the day before a letter had arrived for him from his private little monarch addressed "To the great German Poet of Sound, Richard Wagner."

Back home, no tailor, but I settled down to read a dissertation on the Eudocia. From time to time I was disturbed by a shrilly insistent but quite remote doorbell. At last I became convinced that someone was calling at our own ancestral iron gate, which was locked, as was the front door. I yelled across the garden to the man, told him to come down the Naundörfchen. He couldn't hear me for the pounding rain. The whole house went into a tizzy, at last the gates were unlocked, and an old man with a package under his arm drew near.

It is six-thirty, time to dress and make my toilette, for I live quite far from Brockhausens'. All right, all right, the man has my things, I try them on, they fit. Then matters take a suspicious turn! He presents me with the bill. I receive it politely. He wants to be paid upon receipt of goods. I am amazed, I remonstrate with him: I have nothing to do with him, he merely works for my tailor, I shall take up the matter with the tailor himself, who took my order. The man becomes more insistent; the time becomes more insistent. I snatch up the things and begin to put them on; the man snatches up the things and hinders my putting them on. Force on my part, force on his part. A scene. I do battle in my shirtsleeves, for I wish to don my new trousers.

At last I summon up my full dignity. Formal denunciation of my tailor and his helper's helper, deprecation, oath of vengeance. Meanwhile, the little man makes off with my clothes. Closing scene of Act II: in my undershirt I sit on the sofa and brood, glaring at my old black suit—is it good enough for Richard?

Outside it is raining cats and dogs.

A quarter to eight. I'd told Windisch I would meet him in the Café Théâtre at half-past seven. I storm out into the dreary raindrenched night, I too a miniscule man in black, sans tuxedo, but in an enhanced novelesque mood nonetheless. The fates are propitious: even the scene with the tailor has an air of the extraordinary about it, something of the titanic.

We arrive at the very agreeable Salon Brockhaus: no one there but the members of the immediate family, Richard, and the two of us. I am introduced to Richard, I utter a few words of admiration. He wants to know precisely how I became so familiar with his music, condemns most energetically all the productions of his operas with the exception of the renowned Munich mises-en-scène, and makes fun of the conductors, who encourage their orchestras in such a congenial tone of voice:

—And now, gentlemen, here is where it gets passionate.

—My dear chaps, could we have it with a touch more passion?

Both before and after supper Wagner played all the notable passages from the *Meistersinger*, singing all the parts himself in the most uninhibited way. For he is a fabulously lively and ardent man: he talks very quickly, is quite witty, and takes good cheer from such intimate company as we were. In between I had a long conversation with him about Schopenhauer: oh my, you will understand what a pleasure it was for me to hear him speak of Schopenhauer with such incomparable warmth, to hear him say how much he owed Schopenhauer, for he was the only philosopher who recognized the essence of music. Then he asked me how the university professors were disposed toward Schopenhauer, had a good laugh over the philosophy congress at Prague, and spoke of "the philosophical lackeys." Afterwards he read us a fragment from the autobiography he is now writing, an altogether delightful scene from his student days in Leipzig. I have to chuckle every time it comes to mind. Incidentally, he writes with extraordinary fluency and verve.—

At the evening's close, as Windisch and I prepared to take our departure, he pressed my hand warmly and invited me to visit him so that we could make music and do philosophy. He also asked me to help his sister and all his relatives become better acquainted with his music, a task I was honored to assume.—

You shall hear more anon, when I gain further distance on this evening and can see it all more objectively. For now, a hearty farewell and best wishes for your health.

FN.

My train from Basel arrived at Lucerne hours before the ferry was due to depart. I made my way out to Tribschen. It was a mid-morning in mid-May.

A toe on the foothills of Pilatus. Pilatus washing his feet, not his hands, in the lake. A corn on the little toe of Pilatus' foothills: Tribschen. My *Siegfried* idyll, what Italy was for Goethe. Cerulean lake, silver daggers flashing whenever a boat passed by; dark green of the pinewoods up the steep slopes of the mountain, dabbed by the lighter green of beech and birch and hazel. As I passed the swampy grove of reeds, flocks of waterfowl started and rose with a hue and cry. In the distance the sound of steam engines on the lake. Then stillness. From the house in the distance, the massive manor-house of Tribschen, the sudden sound of a single melancholy chord on the piano at regular intervals over and over again. I followed the sound, weaving my way among the fruit trees in the garden, to its source. It was my beacon.

She didn't want him to be disturbed before two.

Neither did I.

She wore the simple full dress of a country woman. She was perspiring in the sunshine that illumined her door, mopping her brow delicately, her face and throat already lightly rouged from the sun. She introduced herself as the Baroness von Bülow, said she had only now returned from her shopping. She had the straightest nose, the highest cheekbones, the most tranquil gaze I had ever seen. And a voice made for saying *Trib-schen Trüb-schen Treib-schen Trieb-schen.*

—You'll stay for lunch, of course.

—I'm sorry, I'm meeting some friends at the Tellsplatte this afternoon. Monday, perhaps, on my way back to Basel?

—Till Monday, then. I look forward to it.

I began to back away from the doorway, trying to find my breath again, trying to enter into the everyday world again. Suddenly, moiling hounds everywhere, yapping and nipping at my heels.

—Russ! Koss! Sootie! Smackers!

—Handsome dogs. Lively too!

Filthy pests. Tribschen was promiscuous with faithful companions. And cats and peacocks—Wotan and Fricka—and chickens (at least they give you eggs and feathers) and sheep (at least they yield wool and mutton).

—We also have a gelding named "Fritz," she said, laughing.

Was it in embarrassment over her own boldness? No. She couldn't have known. All innocence. Her mouth was fine, very fine, her hair pulled taut at the temples.

—I love horses.

Silence. The same painful chord. "The one who rouses me wounds me deeply." Nothing for it now: I must depart. She is probably my age, I thought to myself. Women always look older. So much closer to me in age than to the Meister. And closer to me in other ways: a cosmic force irradiated her, I could feel it, for all her simplicity and modesty and grace. She was, quite simply, the most stunning woman in the world.

Under the folds of her peasant woman's skirts and pinafore, bulging unabashedly, she was undeniably extraordinarily hugely magnificently irrepressibly showing. Succulent with child.

✝

—And you lusted after her, you wanted to cuckold her lover, soon to be her lawful wedded husband, cuckold him as he had cuckolded his colleague von Bülow not long before. That explains everything, mój drogie bracie, even your musical taste, with all its apparent fluctuations and absurdities.

—Not so, Little Joseph. To me she was one of the higher human beings.

—Being down below, you hoped for easier access.

—Not so. She merely showed me what a woman could be and do.

—Get succulently pregnant?

—Go easy on pregnancy, Little Joseph. Where would we be without it? Writing novels?

—We wouldn't be here, that's for certain. Come now, Fritzie frère, tell the truth. Did you not from the moment you saw her in that doorway at Tribschen dream of filling her belly one way or the other?

—No one is master of his dreams. Much less of hers.

—Aha! There we have it! *Her* dreams? *You* say!

—We wrote letters back and forth. We talked of Pindar, become who you are, and Aeschylus. We read aloud from *Faust*. I played Father Christmas for all the family, all the quasi-family. Quasi-Santa Claus.

—Stuffing stockings with all your goodies, yes, I can see you now, drogi Santa. You were one of their pet intellectuals. Fricka Fritzie. They used you. And when you realized you'd never win her, you betrayed them.

I was happy to be of service to the cause, at first. I thought they would change everything in Germany. Art was to be only the first phase—art in the grand style twisting free to grand politics. They betrayed art, and that foretold the end. The first Christmas day we were together (that ever-hated holiday) she read me some of the earliest sketches for *Parsifal*. Frightful. It was bad enough I had to spend hours in Basel looking for frilly taffeta to clothe their Christchild in the manger, bad enough to have been appointed their nativity scene coordinator and decorator; now they wanted me to breathe the musty air of their nostalgia for the Grail, to crusade on my knees, to betray everything I had lived for, fought for, thought for! I looked around me in the parlor on that dismal Christmas morning as her hushed voice purred piety—I couldn't stop her, it was her birthday, after all, she and Jesus and Socrates having been born on the same day, cosimic cosmic comic triplets—and espied in every corner of the room, on every available vertical or horizontal surface, gathering dust on every wall and table, heartrendingly lugubrious kitsch.

—And so they used you too as one more intellectual gewgaw. She, the Mistress of Kitsch, used you.

—I used her as well. She gave me Ariadne. She gave me the consort of Dionysos, the woman of majesty, the queen of the night sky.

—Majesty! Queen! And you scurrying to get under her royal skirts and into her Christmas birthday stockings, inveigling, insinuating yourself, scheming to cuckold the god. The time you went to Mannheim with her for four days: you played the preening cavalier, you were her escort, her knight in shining livery, you waited on her hand and foot. And oh! how you lusted!

—On the train I watched her smooth her skirts as she talked.

—Talked of *him*, no doubt. The only one who ever ruffled them. You were never even there for her.

—Oh, but I was. She wrote me the most touching letter to acknowledge our love I mean friendship after I sent her my "Echoes of a New Year's Eve" for four hands.

—You would have needed that many. Four hands with all five fingers. But you were all thumbs. When she tried to play it Richard twisted his beret like a wet sock and their balding servant mumbled *Doesn't sound very good to me* and they all burst out laughing, she couldn't go on playing the thing for all her sniggering. You thought it would match his "Stairway Idyll" for her, thought you could outdo the "Siegfried Idyll," thought you could win her from the Meister with music, thought you could beat him at his own game, mój drogie bracie, you must have been out of your tonedeaf skull! They mocked you, and well they should have. You only wanted to pinkle her ivories, you only wanted to make all her strings vibrate—for you!

—You have no sense of the higher minne, Little Joseph. She never ever mocked me. It is you who are the master of mockery. Hapless, hopeless.

—When you die at the age of two, kochany, it is difficult enough to learn the lower minne, never mind the higher; difficult enough to learn mockery, never mind hope.

—Your brief life was cramped.

—Never mind my cramps. You had your own. Mama trying to shovel gruel down your paralytic gullet. And Cosima *did* mock you, repeatedly, that night late in April after he had left for Bayreuth. "Now is the time!" you thought to yourself: two whole days alone with her in this very house, Trieb-schen, the servants occupied with packing, forty-eight hours to bring off your seduction, and you made her play your "Echoes" again, your four hands interwoven on one intemperate clavier. But all the while, with every truncated phrase and orphaned note, she was mocking you.

—Never! She never mocked me. She merely recognized that I was a better philologist than composer.

—He recognized it, too. The first time you went to Bayreuth you were at the piano improvising your heart out and he ridiculed you. "No, Nietzsche, no," he said. "You play really too well for a professor." You never forgave him for that. Nor her for the way she laughed. Faithful wives always laugh at their husband's jokes, Fritzie.

Never did they mock me. Never. They respected me, then they feared me, but always they loved me. When they saw that I knew what Bayreuth was—capitulation to the Reich, homage to the Hohenzollern, prostration before Christianity—they spread rumors of my perversion and madness. They anticipated a bit.

To Heinrich Köselitz in Venice

Marienbad, August 20, 1880

You are made of sterner stuff than I am, and you may be able to achieve higher ideals for yourself. For my part, I suffer miserably when I have to renounce sympathy. For example, nothing can compensate for the fact that during the past several years I have been deprived of Wagner's sympathy. How often I dream of him, and always in the style of our intimate togetherness of the old days! An angry word never passed between us, not even in my dreams; yet there were many encouraging and cheerful words, and perhaps I have never laughed with anyone as much as I did with him. That's all gone now—and what good is it to be *right* when I oppose him in this or that respect! As if that could erase from my memory the sympathy I have lost!—And I've experienced similar situations before; presumably I will do so again. They are the hardest sacrifices that my paths through life and thought have demanded of me. Even now my entire philosophy teeters after an hour's sympathetic conversation with a total stranger. It seems to me so foolish to insist on being right at the cost of love, and foolish that one is *unable to communicate* the most valuable things in it, because they might well suspend the sympathy. *Hinc meae lacrimae.—*

Yours faithfully,
FN.

—He insulted me mortally, hinted at pederasty, confused me with his royal patron.

318

—I could have straightened him out on that one, drogi bracie, knowing your true feelings for little boys. Anyway, it wasn't only pederasty he tipped on, it was what I think they call "self-abuse."
—Mortification of the flesh? Masoch, well-nigh my publisher?
—In a sense. Yes, mortification of tumescent flesh.
—Oh, mortal insult!
—Come now, brother dear, in all that solitude did you never? Such a lonely life, surely you had but one respite at hand? one little Treib-schen?
—Oh, nay, nay! I got it in hand, I had the hand for it, I took myself in hand . . .
—We shall take your word for the deed.
—I debated Trieb-schen whether I should; but I mastered Trüb-schen the impulse.
—Admirable self-control. You should have shown more when he died. At last! you thought, the two of us alone now on the shores of Naxos! Yet your Ariadne withdrew to the interior of her island, she became a nun cloistered in her own little grotto of memories, memories of him. She never even acknowledged your heartfelt letter of condolence. You worked so diligently on it, as on a billet-doux, and she never replied. All your days you tried to replace her with your lugubrious lulus, your gleeful resas, your transcendent metas, your comforting clan of emancipationists, your matronly malwidas

To Malwida von Meysenbug in Rome

Rapallo, February 21, 1883

Dear and honored Friend,

Wagner's death affected me terribly. I'm out of bed by now, but not out of the aftereffects.—Nevertheless, I believe that viewed in the longer perspective this event is an anodyne to me. It was hard, very hard, for six years to have to confront as an enemy one who was as much admired and loved as I loved Wagner; yes, and even as an opponent to be condemned to silence—out of admiration, which the man *as a whole* deserved. Wagner insulted me in a *mortal* way—that I must tell you!—and his gradual regression to Christianity, his creeping back into the Church, I took as a personal slap in the face: my entire youth and the direction it took seemed stained, inasmuch as it had felt devotion toward a spirit that was capable of *this* step.
Inexpressible goals and tasks compel me to feel as strongly about it as I do.

I *now* see that step as Wagner's *senescence;* it is difficult to die at the right time.

Had he lived any longer, oh, *what* would have arisen between us! My bow shoots terrifying arrows, and Wagner was the sort of person whom *words* can *kill.*—

In warmest gratitude,
Your Nietzsche.

I wrote Cosima. You'll agree this was the right thing to do?

your Mrs. Fynn and Fynn's frisky filly your Miss Zimmern and frenetic Fräulein von Mansuroff and all the rest. When the chips were down there was no one there to lend you a hand.

—Cosima had the most exquisite taste, Little Joseph, the highest discernment in all matters of art; there was never a question of finding a substitute for her. Yet with us it was the higher minne, always, from beginning to end, through all eternity.

—How unfortunate for the two of you that you met in time, on the Earth, amid kitsch and Richard.—

✝

I held onto life by my nails through the winter of 1878-79 but had my doubts whether I would survive the year. So it had been, and so it went, year after year. Especially after the Christmas of 1875 and the next winter in Sorrento. Early in May of 1879 I resigned my professorship and went into the mountains. I breathed the air of heights and was a philosopher. As the rest of the world foundered in the human, all-too-human, I ascended to snow and ice. I came down only to plumb the depths of the sea. Everything changed for me except my closest companions: constant headache, imminent blindness, periodic vomiting. That was intimacy enough.

To Hans von Bülow in Meiningen

Rapallo, early December 1882

Most honored Sir,

Meanwhile, for years now I've been living somewhat too close to death, and what's worse, too close to pain. My nature is such that it allows itself to be tortured over long stretches, as though being roasted over a slow fire. I pay no heed to the wisdom of "losing my mind" as a result of the pain. I shall say nothing about the danger constituted by my affects; but *this* much I will say: the altered manner of thinking and feeling that I have brought to expression over the past six years, also in my writing, has *preserved* me in existence and well-nigh *made* me healthy.

What does it matter to me if my friends assert that my current "free spiritry" is an eccentricity on my part, something I have *resolved* to do with clenched teeth, something I have compelled myself to do, something that has wrested me from my own proper inclinations? All well and good, it may be a "second nature" of mine; but I intend to prove that it is only with this second nature that I have entered into genuine *possession* of my first nature.—

Yours sincerely,
Dr. Friedrich Nietzsche

I had stacks of lined foolscap white as seaspume and the snows of Sils. And stacks of stationery. In letters, bitter litanies, I advertised my illnesses, my intercourse with death. Eventually, one by one, in stately procession, my acquaintances abandoned me. They left me alone. I got on with the work.

To Richard Wagner in Bayreuth

Lucerne, Monday, February 15, 1875

—There is a splendid stillness all about me.

Together with my shadow I wandered through the Engadin, greeted dawn in Genova, scribbled verse in Messina, worked happy science in Liguria on the sea. The strangest things occurred to me in the stillness.

To Cosima Wagner in Bayreuth

Sorrento, December 19, 1876

From year to year one grows quieter and quieter and in the end one says not another serious word about personal matters. . . . Practically every night I am involved in dreams with people long forgotten, preeminently with the dead. Childhood, boyhood, and my school years are quite present to me.

In fidelity and admiration,
Your
Friedrich Nietzsche

—With the money I earned suing Schmeitzner to get my own books back I bought you your tombstone, Father. I hope you like it.

—It arrived forty years too late, son. I had no granite passport to Heaven. I would have been a bishop some day, you know. I should have had repose in an episcopal mausoleum, something simple yet elevated, lofty, dignified, aristocratic. Not that I'm ungrateful, son, for all your efforts.

—You don't feel desiccated I mean desecrated, at least, I hope? You don't feel a victim of sacrilege? She said you were ashamed of me because of that Russian girl, she didn't know about the Italian. She said I had vandalized your grave, mutilated your corpse.

—Womantalk, son, don't let it trouble you. It was your Mother's way of chiding, gentle remonstrance. My grave wasn't really worth vandalizing.

—She never forgave me for not following in your footsteps, Papi.

—As Little Joseph did, you mean?

—No, for giving up theology and turning in my faith. She felt that I had abandoned you and your ways, that I had gone in a direction you were never able to go, that I had in some way surpassed you. That thought occurred to me too when I was on the Acropolis in Athens.

—You were never in Athens, son.

—I wasn't?

—No. Mendelssohn-Bartholdy's son, from Freiburg, invited you to travel the Aegean with him, but you declined: you didn't want to offend Wagner—who was like a father to you—and Mendelssohn was both a musician and a Jew. And you certainly couldn't afford to offend Cosima. That was your one and only chance to visit the land you would have loved most, and the land that would have welcomed you most.

—I didn't go?

—Never.

—I'm sorry, Papi, I forgot.

—At least you remembered the slab, son. At least you remembered to memorialize your blessed Father.

✝

At the Eremitage in Marienbad during the summer of 1880 I met an intense young Scotsman who said that all my ideas derived from those of his countryman David Hume. I was delighted to take his word for it. A bilious Frenchwoman at my table discovered that Vauvenargues, La Rochefoucauld, and Fontenelle—if not Voltaire himself—had anticipated my most wicked thoughts. I congratulated her and them. A Russian companion invoked the great Gogol and the towering Turgeniev (neither of us had made the acquaintance yet of my companion *in psychologicis*, Dostoevsky). I bowed reverently, in orthodox fashion. Next day, after the sulphur baths, a Frankfurter told me of overman and eternal recurrence in the incomparable Goethe—he had never heard of Hölderlin, thought I said Höderlin, lovely! I prostated myself. My fellow convalescents were perfectly correct. All of them. Which was why I shrank in terror when the police stormed the Marienbad sanatorium in search of counterfeiters.

To Heinrich Köselitz in Venice

Marienbad, July 18, 1880

My dear friend, since yesterday here in the Eremitage whose Eremit I am, located deep in the woods, remote from everything, a state of emergency has prevailed: I don't really know what happened, but the shadow of crime is cast across the house. Somebody buried something, others dug it up, terrified cries were heard, flocks of gendarmes arrived and searched the house. At night, in the room next to mine, I heard someone sobbing uncontrollably—sleep fled from me and did not return. Once again in the depths of night it seems that something was buried, but then a little surprise supervened, and then once again tears and cries. An officer told me it was a "counterfeit currency case"—I am not curious enough to know as much about it as probably everyone else around me knows. Suffice it to say: the solitude of the forest is uncanny.

Faithfully yours,
F. N.

Diogenes calls counterfeiting παραχαράξαι τὸ νόμισμα, altering the character, imprint, or coinage of true coin. Something like that, it isn't easy to translate. I would say *Transvaluation of All Values.*

Postcard to Elisabeth Nietzsche in Naumburg

Marienbad, July 19, 1880

Hard times have befallen the house. The owner has suddenly been snatched away to prison: the gendarmes came and dug up a printing press for producing counterfeit bills—they searched the premises and afterwards many tears were shed.

Mine were tears of salvation, Papi. They got the wrong man.

✝

—Books have their own fatuity, Father. My son *Zarathustra*, at least the first part of him, was delayed at the printer's because of a rush order for half a million Easter hymnbooks.

—Praise the Lord! The congregation levitates on a ground-swell of jubilant song, all of a piece! Don't begrudge us, son. Charity never faileth.

—I don't begrudge you, Papi. But when the copies were finally printed during the summer the publisher wouldn't distribute them because he was too busy promoting the pamphlets of his *alliance antijuive.*

—All of a piece! Don't begrudge us, son.

To Elisabeth Förster-Nietzsche in Asuncion,
Paraguay [Draft]

Nice, end of December, 1887

In the meantime I've seen proof, black on white, that Herr Dr. Förster has not yet severed his connection with the anti-semitic movement. . . . Since then I've had difficulty coming up with any of the tenderness and protectiveness I've so long felt toward you. The separation between us is thereby decided in really the most absurd way. Have you grasped nothing of the reason why I am in the world? ... Now it has gone so far that I have to defend myself hand and foot against people who confuse me with these anti-semitic *canaille;* after my own sister, my former sister, and after Widemann more recently have given the impetus to this most dire of all confusions. After I read the name *Zarathustra* in the anti-semitic *Correspondence* my forbearance came to an end. I am now in a position of *emergency defense* against your spouse's Party. These accursed anti-semite deformities *shall not* sully my ideal!!

✝

Those crystalline winter days in Nice provided the sunshine of my life and the midnight of my thought. The local train out to Èzé, the

324

dusty climb to the Moorish walls high above the sea, the old and the new tablets singing in my head.

To Malwida von Meysenbug in Rome

> *Nizza (France), December 13, 1886*
> *Pension de Genève, petite rue St. Etienne*

Most esteemed Friend,

Surely there can be no more beautiful season in Nice than the current one: the sky blinding white, the sea tropical blue, at night moonlight that puts the gas lanterns to shame and makes them blush: once again I move through it all, as so many times before, thinking up my kinds of *ebon* thoughts.

> Your faithful old hermit friend,
> F. N.

Nothing could have seduced me from Nice but the sidewalks of Genova and Torino or the music and the sidewalks of Venezia.

✝

In '87 I left Nice for Venice, where my Maestro Pietro had finished orchestrating my "Hymn to Life." Lou's I mean. Hers *and* mine. I sent the score to all the great conductors of Europe, even

To Hans von Bülow in Hamburg

> *Venice, October 22, 1887*

Honored Sir,

There was a time when you administered the death sentence to a piece of my music, the most well-deserved sentence possible *in rebus musicis et musicantibus.* And now, in spite of all, I am daring to send you something else—a *Hymn to Life*, which I wish all the more to *remain alive.* It is to be sung some day, whether in the near or remote future, in memory of me; in memory of a philosopher who had no present, and who didn't really want any. Does he *deserve* that?

In addition, it may be possible that over the past ten years I have *learned* something as a musician as well.

Most indebted to you, very honored sir, as always and unalterably,

> Dr. Fr. Nietzsche.

Where ebon thoughts break off only tones may be. Not a Schopenhauerian sea of tones, to be sure, nor a Wagnerian mudhole. Nor even my own modest muddle.

A Slip of Paper to All Recipients of "The Hymn to Life"

October/November, 1887

—In the score of the "Hymn" which I took the liberty of sending you, the final note of the clarinet (see p. 11) must be corrected: it should be C#, *not* C.

Prof. Nietzsche.

That is why I adopted Pietro, my boorish Gasti, Enrico: Heinrich the Saxon Sassone. That's why I heard *Carmen* every time it was produced in my vicinity, whether in Nice or Monte Carlo or Venice or Turin. So I wouldn't have to go too far to fetch my passion.

I didn't have to go far. I didn't have to wait long. The aura rose in me from the very first bar the grimaces after a dozen notes the tears usually by the end of the overture or halfway through the first act. The rest of it I heard in seizure, the plaster mask of my face cracking under the tension, my fists clenched, my itching anus contracting my scabrous scrotum sucked high. Then releasing at one go. *Tutto Torino Carmenizzato.* Bizet was my carmenative. All of Wagner purged from me in one massive contraction of grief and love and sensuality

To Heinrich Köselitz in Venice

Sils-Maria, June 15, 1888

Dear Friend,

—Please *rectify* the clarinet! Otherwise I'll have no peace in the grave.

N.

✝

I rowed the ladies on the lakes at Sils. *Perla perlissima.* They were my rest and recuperation. The younger women were earning doctorates at the university in Zürich, I didn't even want to stop them. We talked. I even listened. I circumambulated the lakes in the early morning light until I was tired, then nestled in a crack in the grandest boulder on the shoreline; enfolded in those lips I rested until I had the strength to go on thinking.

To Elisabeth Nietzsche in Naumburg

Venice, May 7, 1885

My dear, dear Llama,

I also want to send you my personal copy of my colorful Persian *Zarathustra*. You can set it up in some primeval forest of the Americas as a fetish.

Love,
Your Brother

Thinking about ascetic ideals and where they come from and who suffers under them and who ever anywhere frees himself of them. Or herself.

I ate judiciously in Sils-Maria, Graham bread and Malto-Luguminous spread, sour milk and quark and cake upon pattycake of goat's milk cheese washed down with liters and litters of sweet milk. Peace. Shalom. Irene.

They were having trouble getting frantic Fräulein von Mansuroff out of her room. Her doctor had ordered a change of climate. Every day the coach stopped at her door and waited and waited. In vain. She would not could not quit the room. She had had a nervous breakdown. She was obsessed with delusions of one kind or another. I said to the women of our Zürich circle:

—Let me try to talk to her, just once.

I found her lying in bed fully dressed with her right arm pressed across her eyes in a cramped and unnatural way. I approached the bed, greeting her softly, in order not to frighten her. She moved her arm from her eyes and looked at me for a long moment. She spoke.

—Your voice is melodious. I could listen to you day and night.

Her lips clamped shut. I said nothing, but only looked down at her, smiling. Again she spoke.

—However, you have very bushy eyebrows. Who could trust you?

—You could.

—Who are you, Nietzsche?

—I am the Stranger. I've come to ask you something. Wouldn't you like to *see* the women?

—Oh, wonder! I'd give anything to see that sight!

The coach to Italy was waiting at the front door of the guest-house. We exited together. Her friends embraced her, tears flowed, the men hoisted her luggage onto the rooftop rack. She rolled down her window an instant before the coach lurched into motion. The horses were snorting and stamping to be gone.

—Aren't you coming along?

—I'll be along shortly.

✝

People began to say I was eccentric. I would have conceded it had I been able to convince myself that they had found the center.

✝

I've never known what to make of my face. A portrait of me when I was twenty-three shows my spreadeagle nose about to take off, my lower lip jutting ambitiously, hungrily: I knew I would have to conceal it beneath a cowcatcher. Only my pixie ears were beautiful approx. par excellence. My pixie ears and their involuted horns on the downwardcurving edges.

I've never known what to make of my face. Neither did Brandes when Mama sent him an old photo of me: he demanded a new face for the author of *Zarathustra*. He rejected those deepset bright beads of rodent eye, not daydreaming but targetshooting, not surveying but sniping. It took a lot of softening, required a lengthy maceration before that face could entertain masks. Somehow it happened, don't ask me how it happened.

To Heinrich Köselitz in Berlin

Turin, October 30, 1888

Dear Friend, I just looked at myself in the mirror—I have never looked like this. In an exemplary mood, well-nourished, and looking ten years younger than ought to be allowed.

N.

And now the felt-covered nubs of horn, unimpeded by flesh, begin to burgeon. Io. Io. Or someone else very much like me.

✝

—Gersdorff's only brother finally died after three years in an asylum. That meant that only Carl was left to pass on the family name: he was the sole hope of all their brood. What pressure he was under to marry and have sons! To marry anything, an Italian, a consumptive, anything! He being a military man, *von* Gersdorff, you see.

—Yes, son, I understand how his Father must have felt.

—I felt the very same pressure young Gersdorff felt, Father. For I was in precisely the same situation.

—I know, Joseph, I know.

†

I wandered lonely as a rhinoceros.

†

I lived oddly, as though on the crests of the waves of existence. A sort of flying fish.

†

> The roving rhinoceros for to see,
> I bundled and trundled to Germany.

> —N. philosophus extramundanus

†

As a beaver I was busy.

To Georg Brandes in Copenhagen

Turin, May 4, 1888

Honored Sir,

These weeks in Turin have gone better for me than any during the past few years—above all, better philosophically. Almost every day I have attained one or two hours of that energy-level I need in order to see my general conception from *top to bottom*, whereby the vast multiplicity of problems lies spread out beneath me in relief, with pellucid lines. *For that* I require a maximum of force, which I had scarcely dared hope for. It all hangs together; everything has been coming along smoothly for the past several years now; one constructs one's philosophy as a beaver does his dam; one is a piece of necessity, but doesn't know it: one has to *see* it all in order to believe it, as I have seen it now.

Yours, Nietzsche

✝

—Oak Crescent the First: King of the Squirrels. That's what you called him, son. The precious porcelain squirrel your Aunt Auguste, my dear sister, gave your sainted Mother and me after that trip she took to Dresden. I didn't want you to play with it but your Mother said it was all right, it was only a vanity. After I died, God rest my soul, and you moved with all the women to Naumburg, it was your favorite plaything. Oh, the stories, the delightful dramas you devised for the Squirrel King! Oh, the adventures he had with you, and you with him!

To Heinrich Köselitz in Berlin

Torino, Via Carlo Alberto 6 III
Monday, November 25, 1888

Dear Friend,

I pull so many silly stunts with myself and have such private Till-Eulenspiegel-brainstorms that occasionally all I can do is stand in the public thoroughfares for half-an-hour *grinning*, I don't know what else to call it. . . .

I think that anyone who has achieved such a state must be ripe to become "Savior of the World"?
Come.

Your friend N.

Come. Here. Reach out and take it now, my boy. Don't be afraid, it isn't real, no ontological argument touches it. Be careful, don't drop it! Your fingers are so stiff now! That's it, my boy. Easy does it. Look it over in the dark. I've kept it all these years. Isn't he beautiful? Would you like to play with him now? Are you still of a mind to play with your old friend the Squirrel King? Oak Crescent I?

✝

KING OAK CRESCENT I *(in regal ermine and brown velvet streaked with gray, his tail looping up and over his bejewelled crown, his deepset beads of eyes flashing over the dais):* Your Holiness, assembled Majesties, Members of the Basel Council and the Concilium Subalpinum, Lords and Ladies, Free Spirits all, we welcome you to the Palazzo Granpolitica! No spectacles, please! We are gathered on this most solemn and festive occasion . . .

CARDINAL MARIANI *(the Papal Secretary of State, in robes of red silk, fulsome and florid of face, bloodshot of eye, flushing rapacious):* Make it snappy, rodent, we've got business of state to attend to. Anyone here interested in railroad shares? How about banking with the Holy Spirit, where your interest is confounded eternally? Plenary indulgences, anyone? Alms for the poor?

KING UMBERTO I *(in a natty pin-striped suit, strictly hautbourgeois, with the Revolutionary cocarde pinned to his lapel; his hair is parted down the middle and neatly plastered across his scalp):* Silence, Mariani, this isn't the Vatican stockmarket. Our decision today will affect the whole of Europe. Gentlemen . . .

LADY MARGHERITA *(in a particular gentleman-philosopher's shirtsleeves):* Ahem.

KING UMBERTO I *(bows graciously, submissively, to his left):* Yes, dear. Gentlemen and Viragos, we must concoct an altogether novel sort of warfare, a warfare not of blood and iron but of plowshares and spirits, a warfare involving entire cultures and civilizations. Mediterranea against the Hohenzollern!

DR. BERNHARD FÖRSTER *(tall, blond, blue-eyed, with decidedly limited intelligence but unbounded Aryan self-assuredness and decisiveness; confusing Paraguay with Mexico, he is dressed in the vaquero's riding boots, chaps, and chaleco; he sports the mariachi's silver-and-gold embroidered maroon sombrero; confusing Paraguay with Peru, he leads a domesticated curlycoated longlashed llama on a lleash; as Förster speaks the llama—whom he calls by the sobriquet "Eli"—nods and spits downwind):* I certainly do understand our swarthy southern brother's point of view, thoroughly infected as it is with Semitic elements; however, what we need is a purebred New Germany in the otherwise mongrel New World. The huddled masses there demand moral and sanguineous renovation. They are many and they are cheap. I have the property deeds and boat tickets right here in my stalwart llama's saddlebags. Ethical Aryans only cash on the barrelhead if you please!

OAK CRESCENT I *(flushing red, restraining himself, mopping his face with a handkerchief embroidered with the flags of all the nations of Europe, for he stands downwind):* Somehow I've never managed to muster much enthusiasm for the Germanic "essence," and even less for the desire to retain the *purity* of this ungainly race. On the contrary, on the contrary—

GENERAL STUMM VON BORDWEHR *(in the creamcheesey green uniform of the Austrian House of Hapsburg, tapping his riding whip softly and regularly against his kneehigh ridingboots, bemused, demure, infinitely submissive, subtly assertive):* May I suggest that what this old Continent of Europe needs is a Committee for Precision and Soul?

LADY MARGHERITA *(snarling, clenched fists raised):* Bloody Austrian! Bloody blundering Austrian! You'll bring all Europe down around your bloody blundering ears!

GENERAL STUMM VON BORDWEHR *(coolly, precisely, soulfully):* May I remind the Lady Margret that the Hapsburg more than anyone else in Europe fears the Hohenzollern. We detest the Hohenzollern, with submission, as we do their new Italian allies!

LADY MARGHERITA *(apoplectic, spasmodic, spastic with rage):* Bloody blunderbuggering Austrian!

OAK CRESCENT I *(chirruping nervously over the dais, his fore-paws toying rapidly with the walnutwood gavel, spinning it round and round, his tail flicking high over his crown):* Friends, please! Pan-Europeans, good Europeans all, order, please!

POPE PIOUS PRATTLER *(in white linen robes with white satin sash, an immense golden crucifix by Cellini pendant on his con-sumptive breast, coughing nervously and glancing uncertainly in the direction of Mariani; his head bobs with each word he pro-nounces, the tiny bells of his tiara jinglejangle with jollity):* Hic et ubique I defer to Cardinal Mariani, our faithful Secretary of State, and to General Stumm, our brother in Christ, who has, as it were, hit the hallowed hobnail on its haloed head. The Protestant Hohen-zollern must bow to the Catholic Hapsburg as the infidel to the faith-ful, as all bastard offspring to the licit children of the one true holy and Apoplectic secession. *(To Mariani, aside):* Did I do all right? Have I made a fallibility?

CARDINAL MARIANI *(with strained yet infinite patience):* You're doing just fine. Sit down. *(Pope Pious Prattler resumes his seat; his jesterbells jingle for joy.)*

KING UMBERTO I *(urbane, earnest):* Oak Crescent, you see before you a divided Europe. Our entire Continent is hellbent on a suicide course. What do you propose? Have you a plan?

OAK CRESCENT I *(rising to his full stature, peeping over the dais):* I have, my royal cousin. Ladies and Gentlemen, I propose to annihilate the House of Hohenzollern! *(Gasps throughout the assembly.)*

LADY MARGHERITA: Be specific, squirrel.

OAK CRESCENT I: We shall laugh it into oblivion! We shall guffaw it right off the stage and page of world history! Don't you see how simple it all is, really? A war without powder and smoke, without belligerent posturings and pathos. A war without wrenched limbs!

GENERAL STUMM VON BORDWEHR *(a smile dawning on his face, a light lighting in his bared and balding head):* I'm beginning to catch your drift. A parallel campaign of soul—whence the laughter—and precision, exactitude. But how, exactly, . . .

OAK CRESCENT I: The Hohenzollern and all other anti-semites will become laughingstöcker as a result of this new war of ours!

DR. BERNHARD FÖRSTER *(rises to his feet, indignant with dignity, placing his right hand over his heart; his left grasps the leash, now strained taut, as his llama Illunges and spits):* Back, Eli, back. There's a good girl. Resume the seat that has been reserved for you in this august company. Easy, old girl!

To Elisabeth Förster Nietzsche in Tautenburg

Sils-Maria, Monday, July 5, 1885

My dear Llama

I ultimately claim the privilege of benaming you thus, for I hear that your spouse addresses you in another way (to be sure, his way is likewise *Hebraic,* which I find shocking, coming as it does from a tried and true anti-semite: "Eli" means "my God," and probably, in special cases, "my Goddess"!)

Love,
Your Fritz.

(Dr. Förster, restraining his goddess, resuming): The accursed race, the murderers of your and my God, in league *(confusing now Paraguay with Brazil)* with the seedy Portuguese, have sapped the energies of the inveterately indolent indios. All they require for their salvation is a strenuous Nordic drubbing executed with Germanic thoroughness. 50% discount if you act now be the first in your neighborhood free copies of Pastor Adolf Stöcker's sermons on Christian-Socialism distributed at cost to those who sign up without delay or hinterthoughts!

CARDINAL MARIANI *(calculating on his pudgy rubyringed digits):* New war? Did you say new war? You'll need supplies, of course, shipped by Vatican rail, cattlecars, requiems for the dead, high masses out on the field, that will be expensive . . .

OAK CRESCENT I *(impatient, delirious with excitement, obviously on the verge of revealing the secret workings of his plan):* Dr. Förster, Cardinal, I don't think you understand: it is to be simultaneously a war *against Christendom,* a war waged to the death against all who are foolhardy and fainthearted enough to cast their lots with her.

LADY MARGHERITA *(still in shirtsleeves):* Ahem.

OAK CRESCENT I: I beg your pardon. It.

CARDINAL MARIANI: I see no objection. Your Holiness?

POPE PIOUS PRATTLER *(smiling broadly, pleased to be consulted):* Nunc et in hora jinglejangle I call for a new Children's Crusade!

KING UMBERTO I *(rising from his seat, going pale):* Che confusione!

GENERAL STUMM VON BORDWEHR *(a doubt creasing his brow and troubling his eye, squinting warily):* A war altogether devoid of bloodshed, you say?

DR. BERNHARD FÖRSTER: Nothing wrong with a little bloodshed *per se,* purgative effect, depends on the type the group the race etc.

OAK CRESCENT I *(ignoring Förster):* Without bloodshed, absolutely, of course! All the army officers will defect to our side! You of all people must see that, Stumm? *(Stumm nods mutely, agreeably, uncertainly.)* The Christians will go like Christians to the lions!

GENERAL STUMM VON BORDWEHR *(scratching his cheek now with the ivory grip of his ridingwhip):* But isn't that how the whole business got started in the first place?

LADY MARGHERITA *(offended, archly):* When in doubt, blame the Romans! It's the same old story! Bloodyblunderbuggering Austrian!

OAK CRESCENT I: It will be like Natural Selection! Everyone will be put to the test: Will you accept all life unstintingly as it has been up to now and as it will be into all eternity?

POPE PIOUS PRATTLER *(blessing himself in reflex action at the sound of the word "eternity"):* Amen!

OAK CRESCENT I: Those who cannot bear the thought of recurrence will collapse, curse, gnash their teeth and cash in their chips, naturally unselecting themselves in the most natural way, naturally!

(A sudden interruption. Roars and jeers of the crowd outside the Palazzo Quirinale della Granpolitica are heard. The doors to the

conference room burst open. Guards enter and march noisily to the dais. Moving with difficulty at their center is a debonair young German prisoner of war with exquisite waxed mustaches. His arms are pinioned, his entire torso is encased in a heavy iron box, a saber and a large cornucopial hearing aid rattle and clang against the side of his iron jacket. He looks for all the world like a walking stove.)

CAPTAIN OF THE GUARD: Your Majesty, Kaiser Wilhelm II and all his accoutrements trussed up in an iron straightjacket, as ordered, Sir!

OAK CRESCENT I: You have done well, O Captain, My Captain! But tell me: why does he still live and respirate? Did I not order immediate execution, with dispatch? (He extracts from the pocket of his fur lining a letter which he unfolds importantly and reads aloud):

To August Strindberg in Holte

Turin, December 31, 1888

Dear Sir,

You shall soon hear my response to your novelette—it will sound like a rifle shot. . . . I have convoked a conference of princes in Rome, I intend to have the young Kaiser face a firing squad.

Auf Wiedersehen! For we shall meet again. . . . Une seule condition: Divorçons. . . .

Nietzsche Caesar

CAPTAIN OF THE GUARD (hesitantly): We've already had him before the firing squad, Sir. But the iron straightjacket, you see . . .

OAK CRESCENT I: Foiled again! O iniquity, thy name is Hohenzollern! Have you nothing to say in your defense?

KAISER WILHELM II (with a struggle raising the great hearing horn to his ear): Wie, bitte?

GENERAL STUMM VON BORDWEHR: But you said it would be precisely without bloodshed, precisely with soul and laughter!

OAK CRESCENT I (ignoring Stumm's intervention): Oh, yes, we know that old dodge. Hearing defect. Otitis. Disability. Win the sympathy of the crowd. Sorry, Weewillywinkie, it won't work! Telegraph it to your cousin Nicky!

KAISER WILHELM II (retrieves a piece of paper from his ferrous straightjacket, unfolds it imperiously, and reads):

335

THE WAYS OF THE FATHER

To Jean Bourdeau in Paris [Draft]

Turin, circa December 17, 1888

OAK CRESCENT I *(interrupting the reading, furious):* You've been into my papers, Hohenzollern, you've rifled my desk, my things weren't packed away properly anybody could have gotten into them taken terrible advantage of me made me a laughingstock proclaimed me a saint of their private religion! Your spies have rummaged through my circular file, they have done their filthy work!

KAISER WILHELM II *(smiling sweetly, shrugging innocently, ostensibly not hearing, resuming his reading):*

Honored Sir,

This young Kaiser has never even heard of the things with which the hearing of people such as ourselves really *commences:* otitis, and well-nigh meta-otitis.

OAK CRESCENT I: Captain of the Guard! This insolent stove is defective! Disabled! Remove it to Dresden, Firma Nieske, for instant dismantling!

CAPTAIN OF THE GUARD: I'm terribly sorry, Your Majesty, Sir, the mistake was mine. In a former life I used to be Professor Koch, from the Imperial Health and Safety Office. I *thought* the stove was defective, but the defect was in me. Bullets wouldn't penetrate that stove, there is no carbon monoxide leakage whatsoever, we've received the most enthusiastic testimonials. I'm afraid we all owe Nieske a heartfelt apology, Sir!

OAK CRESCENT I: Well, I should say! Thank you, thank you. Not to worry. At least my sweet Irene is warm and safe! Caro signor Fino! *(Remembering himself):* Who is second in command here?

ADOLF STÖCKER *(in an oddly hybrid uniform, somewhere betwixt that of an infantryman and a court chaplain, in one hand a crucifix, in the other a meat cleaver):* I am second in command, Sir, though God plays second fiddle to no man. We've long known about Koch's incompetence, Your Majesty. You will note that he is an international Jew of ill repute.

OAK CRESCENT I: Yes, he has an intelligent face. Guards! Arrest Stöcker, cast him in irons! Promote Koch! And as for this tinny imperial tonedeaf upstart, I wouldn't accept him as my footman! Laugh him off the stage at once!

(The guards pinion Stöcker's and the Kaiser's arms, perform a clumsy aboutface, and drag the prisoners to the door. Wilhelm and

Adolf nod and bow obsequiously to the assembled applauding dig-
nitaries, Cardinal Mariani, Pope Pious, King Umberto, and the Lady
Margherita. General Stumm von Bordwehr scours his cheek with
the ridingwhip and chuckles goodnaturedly, bemusedly. When the
oaken portals of the Quirinale are opened to grant the prisoners
egress, certain elements of the crowd penetrate. There is consider-
able confusione. An elderly, hoaryheaded gentleman in a pharma-
cist's whitecoat picks his way through the moiling herd and
approaches the dais. Oak Crescent I recognizes him and cries out in
jubilation): Professor Burckhardt!

JACOB BURCKHARDT *(with a quick shake of his hoaryhawk-*
like head): Hush! Not a word! Incognito! I'm Géraudel, accent over
the é, turning the u topsy turvy and back to front, but never mind!
Try these pastilles *(removing assorted phials and a tiny black pillbox*
from his white frock), more effective than Mama's rhubarb, wash
them down with a glass of Veltliner, the carmenative doctors most
recommend!

OAK CRESCENT I: Please, Professor, not here!

JACOB BURCKHARDT *(confused, overtaxed, exiting in some*
disarray, spilling the tablets across the black and white marble floor):
Χαίρετε δαίμονες!

THE TABLETS *(tiny yet plenipotent, scattering bouncily under*
the seats of all the assembled greats of Europe): We wish the Rome
Congress from the crooks of our spines a most blessed bowel movement!

(As Burckhardt exits, two more figures from the crowd work
their way to the front of the conference room. They are Victor and
Laetitia Bonaparte, he in the imperial costume of his illustrious fore-
bear, the First (= 60), not the Third, his right hand half-hidden
between the fourth and fifth gold buttons of his imperial white coat;
she in the simple costume of a Russian peasant woman refined by
elements of the Minoan snake and swing goddesses: over the tight
bodice of her ceremonial dress her fully exposed and pendant
busento undulates with every regal step she takes. Sequins and tas-
sels complete and highlight the Schopenhauerian billowingsealike
effect):

THE SEQUINS *(sparklingly):* Oh, I do hope we're not too late
for the beauty contest!

OAK CRESCENT I *(shielding his eyes, stumbling over his*
words): Madness! I know nothing about the First Annual Torino
Beauty Pageant! We are doing grandly eschatological politics here,
the Last Judgment, not flesh and bauble!

THE TASSELS *(gracefully unfolding a letter sealed with a kiss, letting it dangle before the eager eyes of the assembly, reading with abundant naïveté in a silky milky melodious voice):*

To Heinrich Köselitz in Berlin

> Torino, via Carlo Alberto 6 III
> November 13, 1888

OAK CRESCENT I *(interrupting once again, horrified):* Laetitia! Unspeakable creature! You too were into my wastebasket! Falsie friendie!

THE TASSELS *(unruffled, resuming):*

Dear Friend,

Our wonderful little ladies of the Turin aristocracy have dreamed up a *concorso di bellezza* for January: they were just bursting with boldness when the photos of the first crowned beauties of *Spaa* reached here. This spring I saw such a *concours* in *portraits* shown during the last exhibition: obviously the area in which they feel superior to all the world is that of the *busento*, which they entrusted to the painter with abundant naïveté. Our new fellow-citizen, the fair Laetitia Bonaparte, recently married to the Duke of Aosta and in residence here, will at all events be one of the contestants.

> Nietzsche.

OAK CRESCENT I *(trying to restore order in the pandemonium induced by these recent disclosures, as the assembled princes and potentates of Europe hoot with derisive laughter; Lady Margherita seethes with anger, opening and closing her fists in rapid rabid reflex, the Squirrel King trying in vain to mollify her):* There must be some mistake! This is Rome, not Turin! This is the Quirinale, not the Palazzo Madama supply your own! Full steam backwards! *(To Laetitia, rudely):* Get lost! Scram! Shoo! Before I curse and gnash my teeth!

THE SEQUINS: Oh!

THE TASSELS: Ouch!

VICTOR BONAPARTE: Do I take it, Monsieur, that the Kaiser has not yet been fusillated and ventilated? Are my imperial services not yet required, Sir?

OAK CRESCENT I: Not just yet, Duke. We're working on it. Don't call us. Would you kindly remove your last Duchess?

(As the Duke and Duchess d'Aosta prepare to leave, King Ludwig II of Bavaria advances out of the rowdy crowd at the door. He rushes to Victor Bonaparte, clasps both his hands. Laetitia he studiously ignores):

KING LUDWIG II: Oh, Victor! Where have you been, you silly Bonaparte, I have a Bonapick with you, I've been searching high and low! You are hereby invited most cordially to attend an intimate production of Richard's *Trystan* in my grotty garden grotto at Lindenhof tonight! Afterwards we'll take a lovely boatride on the Starnberg, just the two of us! *(With a sideways glance at Laetitia):* You can leave the cows in the meadow, Boni.

THE SEQUINS: Hiss!

KING LUDWIG II: The great German Poet of Sound agrees with me, as well; he says women are fundamentally boring. What's your view, Vic?

THE TASSELS: Here's a borer for the bottom of your boat, honey.

(Victor and Laetitia Bonaparte exit, Ludwig in hot pursuit. Guards quell the herd morality, force the doors shut. The Squirrel King takes a deep breath and resumes his speech, with difficulty.)

OAK CRESCENT I: Life, as I was saying. Into all eternity, as I was saying. Love your fate. Take it as it comes. Golden laughter the only anodyne.

LADY MARGHERITA: Did I hear you right, you scruffy furball? This *same* life into all eternity? No re-engineering? No plumbing improvements, no fundamental change in the order of things? You call that grand politics?! *(The sound of grating molars scritches through the room.)*

CARDINAL MARIANI *(still calculating):* Into all eternity? I think I've got a deal—granted one minor change—you cannot refuse. *(The grinding sound grates more intensely.)*

GENERAL STUMM VON BORDWEHR *(still worrying his cheek):* Into all eternity? With submission, Sir, may I insist on one tiny alteration of your civilian conception, from the point of view of the military? *(The sound is in the walls now, the sound of eternally masticant termites.)*

DR. BERNHARD FÖRSTER *(his llama kneels awkwardly, collapsing on its foreknees, closes its eyes tight in a gesture of intense devotion):* Into all eternity, ye-ah! For it is a safe assuncion that no eternity will outlast the New Gods of the New Empire of New Germany!

Postcard to C. G. Naumann in Leipzig

Turin, December 18, 1888

—We will want to mail a copy of *Twilight of the Idols* overseas, *registered,* to:

Herrn Dr. Bernhard Förster

New Germania

Near-Assumption

Amérique du Sud   Paraguay

POPE PIOUS PRATTLER *(the Pontifex Maximus rises, affrighted by the deafening noise in the walls, on his head, and in his mouth):* Attenzione! Attenzione, mój drogi bracie! Do not forget the oldest lessons of our Faith. *(Closes his eyes, begins to recite from febrile memory, his hands outstretched in papal benediction):* Ab initio ante bellum et diluvium our Agnus Dei whose alter ego dominus tuus served as agent provocateur in all affaires d'amour propre ad nauseam and who wandered in caelo al fresco au naturel au fait thought it a beau geste to create the beau monde et homo ecco! homini lupus with a bon mot ever on his lips: carpe diem! caveat emptor! cave canem! one day ab ovo took His comeuppance on Himself et incarnatus est as a corpus delicti whereupon He delivered de jure et de facto His own coup de grâce de rigueur Dei gratia Deo gratias de profundis his dernier cri. One deus ex machina de trop less. Pater Seraphicus smiled His sunny medicynical smile and uttered the usual dolce far niente

To Richard Wagner in Tribschen

Basel, May 21, 1870

Pater Seraphice,

May you remain what you have been for me during the past year: my mystagogue in the esoteric lore of art and life.

One of "the Blessed Boys."

His faux pas flagrante delicto turned out to be a fin de siècle fait accompli in loco parentis extremis infra dignitatem ipso facto ipse dixit, qu'importe if it is all non sequitur obiter dicta in saecula saeculorum non compos mentis par excellence from the particeps criminis Himself Chambige peccavi Pater peccavi Prado peccavi persona non grata Q. E. D. *(Raising his transparent right hand, the Glutimus Maximus, ignoring the pain, turning the other, blesses the assembly.*

The roar of termite teeth rises in crescendo as the terrified delegates scatter to the four corners of Christendom, or Europe. An inchoate incandescent cloud begins to form high in the frescoed cupola of the Quirinale conference room. Almost imperceptibly it begins to descend.) Benedicat vos rara avis requiescat in rigor mortis semper fidelis et *(sotto voce sub rosa)* shalom aleichim! My verbum sapienti is *(viva voce)* vade mecum et in hoc signo vae victis. Wie geht's? Wie, bitte?

(The hovering luminous cloud enfolds cherubim and seraphim who swarm about a haloed female figure seated at a writing desk. King Oak Crescent I, alone now in the room, inasmuch as Pious too has lurched off, is transfixed by the slowly descending miraculous Vision. The figure at the writing table is Moon Crescent I, Queen of the Squirrels, jotting scrupulous memoirs into her faithful diary. Her queenly beadyblack eyes gaze heavenward as she chews thoughtfully on the tip of a pencil she has somehow managed to squirrel away in heaven, then lower modestly to the page as she continues to write, a beatific smile beaming beneath her blackbutton nose. She wears the unadorned gray veil of the chaste nun. The veil pulls her hair taut at the temples. It is graced by the diamond tiara of Ariadne, which represents the stars in the night sky of the cosimos. Her angelic hosts settle on orientally carpeted stairways conveniently located on either side of the oaken secretary and begin to perform the "Siegfried Idyll," directed by Blessed Cuckold von Bülow with a flaming sword. Moon Crescent I dreamily flicks her pencil, and from it cascades a delicate golden chain with a meathook dangling alluringly from its ultimate link. The hook catches in the thick fur of King Oak Crescent's heaving bosom. He is hoisted heavenward while the chorus and soloists celebrate his timely salvation. As the Squirrel King swings beneath Moon Crescent's writing table he cannot help but notice that beneath the folds of her immaculate gray habit the exquisite creature is succulent with tiny Crescents in crescendo.)

PATER ECSTATICUS: Look down! He's coming back home!

PATER PROFUNDUS: Look up! He is saved!

PATER SERAPHICUS: Look out! Hope that meathook holds!

CHORUS OF LLAMAS: We begot oursellves promptlly to a nunnery, did penance for allll the illll his phillosophy willll have engendered, for he lloved evill whereas we lloved the good; yet our vicarious suffering shallll not have been in vain! See how heavenward he fairlly fllies!

CHORUS OF BLESSED BOYS:

The Ever-enduring
Is but your conceit!
And God, the alluring,
A poet's retreat.

World-wheel, spinning by,
Skims goals on its way:
Calamity! is rancor's cry;
The jester calls it Play!

World-play, the ruling,
Mixes "Seems" with "To Be":
The eternally squirrely
Mixes *us* in—the melee!

†

—Psst!

—What is it, Little Joseph?

—Is Tatus awake? You and I have to talk.

—Papi! Hey, Papi! Not a peep, Little Joseph: he's dead to the world. What did you want to talk about?

—Us.

—Us? Well?

—There has been some confusion, you see. It's high time we straightened it out, just the two of us, you and I. You have been operating under a fundamental misapprehension, mój drogie bracie. So much is true: you are my dear brother, and you always will be, no matter who you are, no matter what your authentic identity.

—What on earth are you talking about?

—Nothing on earth, mój kochany. *Under* it. Souterrain. I'm talking about what's in a name.

—A name? Every name in history I am, all the masks of god. So much for authentic identity. Basta!

—Not so fast. Let us not be overhasty, my dear Joseph.

—"Joseph"? What do you mean, Little Joseph?

—What I mean, Joseph, is that there has been a very specific case of mistaken identity in our holy family, an imbroglio that has lain undetected a good long time now, and you and I are going to achieve some clarity about it.

—I don't follow. Stop it. I am afraid.

—Stop? I've only just begun, Joseph.

—Will you stop that! Call me Fritz, or if you spurn intimacy, call me Friedrich. Friedrich Wilhelm, b. 1844 Röcken, † 1900 Weimar. Can't you read?

—It's no use insulting me, Little Joseph. It's caving in on you, isn't it, the realization? You know the truth now, don't you, darling brother? You were so gifted! So adorable!

—I know no such thing!

—Oh, but you do! I can feel your resistance slipping, the curtain is going up on our aboriginal scene—rather, let us say, the lid of the tomb is gaping once again.

—Bitch's bastard!

—That's right. Now you have it. Now you see it. I thought it would take longer.

—I see nothing! Explain yourself!

—I shall explain *your* self, darling Joseph. That night of all nights was so fraught, how could you be expected to have kept all the details in place—the names, for instance? Your teeth were giving you so much trouble, a martyrdom really, and the colic, and the mounting waves in your brainflow—you were on the brink of convulsion. And I? Friedrich? My sleep disturbed by tremulous organ music, I went to the window. You know what I saw down there, you remember. He went into the church. That is to say: he *came* into the church. By that time you and I were already there. That's why he never spotted you in your bedroom window.

—Liar! Bitch's bastard!

—You were placing me on the hallowed altarstone ever so gently. Through my quilted sleeping sack I could feel the hard cold marble under the altarcloth. Your eyes looked so affectionately into mine as you deposited me there, so ardently, almost hungrily. In the wan light of the earliest suspicion of dawn I saw that triumphant smile spread across your face.

—You're telling me nothing new, Little Joseph. I confessed to it the instant I arrived here at the crypt. What more do you want from me? You want an apology? So, I apologize, I'm sorry.

—It isn't about being sorry, Joseph, it's about being mistaken.

—Will you cut it out I can't stand it I won't stand for it it's wicked nonsense!

—No, not nonsense. It is about what happened, what really happened on the pallid morning of that dim night. Mis-taken is the very word, incidentally, taken by mis-take.

—It didn't! It didn't happen! You contradict yourself!

—How rapidly the curtain rises, the resistance in the pulleys has dwindled to next to nothing, and up it glides! Now you can almost see him coming, you can see him out of my own eyes, as it were. You can see him moving up on you noiselessly from behind. Stealth of spirit!

—Stop!

—His immaculate white robes flutter in funereal flight, trailing in the wake of his advance; he floats rather than walks upon those unshod unliving feet. An angel of compassion, hovering behind you, now and forever. And if you cannot see him through my eyes (for your back is turned to him, you have only now placed me on the altarstone, only now gazed ravenously upon me) you can surely feel that gelid musty wind on the rise from the stone floor and you think it is only the draft from the door i left it open i forgot to close it and you try to reassure yourself it isnt him he cant have come this early he promised he would wait till i fled gods mausoleum and ran across gods green acres in through the backdoor of gods parsonage up the creaking stairway to my room into my bed and under my covers shivering sobbing in heartfelt grief by the time he would be coming to get you yet it doesn't reassure you at all for you distinctly remember having closed the broadbeamed oaken portal behind you you remember hearing its iron latch clink reassuringly shut so that no passerby in the twilight would observe someone lurking in the church up to mischief no doubt. But if you cannot see the white flutter of the linen cinctures and cerements or feel the chilly air rising from the granite floor surely you can hear him speaking to you, Friedrich Wilhelm, surely you can hear him calling your name, Friedrich Wilhelm . . .

—No! Ghoul! Back!

— . . . and that voice will stay with me behind me haunting me as a horrific hallucination all my days the night he took you away, Friedrich Wilhelm . . .

—It's only a dream! Wake up!

— . . . for he called you by name, gurgling for your blood *O blessed moment, O savory feast, O unspeakably holy deed! With all my heart, and most profoundly moved, I command:* Bring me now this my beloved child, that I may dedicate him to the Lord!

—But that was my Holy Baptism, when I was given my very own Christian name!

—That is correct, Friedrich Wilhelm, but you abused it: you forfeited your right to both a Christian name and a Christian burial.

—Papi!

—Tatulku! You've been eavesdropping!

—Dreams troubled my sleep, I woke and heard my beloved son, in whom I am mightily displeased.

—Which one of us?

—Which one of us?

—The other one. He is the only one I ever wanted.

—Wait, Papi, wait. This cannot be. This is unreal. What about all my literature? I wrote some catastrophic books: they will last: you can't take them away from me.

To Franz Overbeck in Basel

Cannobio, Villa Badia, April 14, 1887

Dear Friend,

There is nothing more paralyzing or discouraging to me than to travel into today's Germany to take a closer look at those many sincere persons who believe that they take a "positive attitude" toward me. Meanwhile, *all* understanding of me is lacking. And if my probability-reckoning does not fail me, it will not be any different before 1901. I believe that people would simply take me to be mad if I let it be known what I take myself to be. . . . (This winter I delved into our contemporary European literature, so that I can *now* say that my philosophical position is *by far* the most independent one, however much I feel myself to be the inheritor of several millennia. Contemporary Europe hasn't an inkling of the frightful decisions about which my very essence turns, or of the *wheel* of problems on which I am stretched.—Or that with me a *catastrophe* is being prepared whose name I know yet will not utter.)

Your faithful friend,
N.

—Books flow from deep wellsprings, boys, not from names on title pages; no one owns them, no matter who signs for them; no product of spirit can be possessed. Your Uncle Hegel was mistaken.

—But they say *Friedrich!*

—But they mean *Joseph!*

—They write only *Nietzsche.* Look at the spine. Embossed in gold and silver: *Nietzsche.* Nothing more.

—Come come, Tatuncio, relent: that would mean that even the Llama could have written them, spitting wisdoms into the wind! Or Mama, who never understood a blessed diabolical word.

—Don't be jejune, son: your Mother was an Oehler, and Elisabeth married a Förster. No oilers or foresters can write *Nietzsche*. It is an affair among us boys.

—But, Papi, that would mean that I was no one in particular, that I was a stand-in, a substitute, an ersatz fritz in a nonoriginal niche.

—Better get used to it, drogy bracie. It lasts an eternity.

—Little Joseph, I cannot be you! You are the incarnation of the pettifogger, the no-sayer, the spirit of rancor, resentment, and revenge!

—At your service, mój kochany. We were both very small when He came to get you.

—However, I became the dancer, the yes-sayer, the very opposite of a no-saying spirit! I never growled like an old bear or howled like a saint in the forest; I blessed life, who was a woman, I said *yes* to every nook and cranny, every shadow and shade!

—Precisely. Which is why you could never weed me out. The most picayune of mortals recurs, and with a vengeance!

—But you weeded yourself out! You autodestructed! You unselected yourself!

—With a little assistance from my dear brother, don't forget. Except that Tatus here knew even then who was destined to do the greater damage, and so he took you with him instead of me, embracing you all through the long long night. As for me, I got my teeth. You have felt them.

—*My* books or *your* books, it doesn't really matter now, I accept that. All the names in history let those tomes go, bequeathing them to all the readers in history: books will have their own fate.

—Indeed they will. And that fate will have nothing to do with yours or mine, Nietzsche.

—For we are dead. Even our names are dead.

—No, boys, not dead: merely confused for a time by the living, though perhaps for a long time, perhaps for all time.

Silence of the grave.

An eternity passes.

Another commences.

The same.

†

—Fritz, Little Joseph, enough of this petty squabbling. Let our genealogies be as settled as our bones. Let us sleep.

—Wait, Papi, just one word more. Does that confusion of names mean that anything goes, that yes is no and no is yes?

—Yes and no.

—That all is indifferent, that it all comes to nothing? Is everything then in default?

—Yes and no.

—That indistinguishability spins round and round, and we mistake the dust of nothingness for the wheel of being?

—Yes and no.

—That it spins on and on, and knows no goal, a whorl without an axis, that it spews us out and sucks us back in again through all eternity?

—No. No. Never again. Never again in precisely the same way. Boys, you've had your go. You've taken your spin, used up your turn. Let us sleep. Let it all go now. Let it pass by.

—Yes! Yes!

—No! No!

†

It seems to me in retrospect that I spent a goodly part of my life peering out from beneath umbrellas. Either to see if it was still raining hailing sleeting blizzarding or to find out whether my eyes could bear the glaring light or whether at long last I'd gone fully blind. My black umbrella at Sils, my gardenia umbrella at Genua, my lavender umbrella in Nice, my green umbrella in Sorrento. There was no point using an umbrella in Naumburg or Leipzig where it rains moist molecules up your nose, endlessly. All my life I craved a dry soul. Kali phosphoricum. When I finally got one I was parched. Holy Heraclitus, heliotropic heathen, make haste to help me!

To Meta von Salis at Marschlins

Sils, Engadin, June 17, 1888

Esteemed Fräulein

I've just now fastened upon the following truth, a *truth that sounds most improbable*, with the help of certain meteorological tables.

"January in Italy"

	Sunny days	Rainy days	Degree of Cloud-cover
Turin	10.3	2	4.9
Florence	9.1	9.7	5.7
Rome	8.2	10	5.8
Naples	7.7	10.8	5.2
Palermo	3.2	13.5	6.5

This means that the farther south one goes in winter the worse the weather gets (—fewer bright days, more rainy days, and an increasingly overcast sky). And we all, instinctively, believe the very opposite ! !

Your humble servant,
Nietzsche

One last word about my son Zarathustra. He was born an old man and like me he grew backwards in wisdom and folly. He became a retired vagabond dancer who made speeches. He upset almost everyone. They said he was unpleasant. Imagine! A child of mine, unpleasant!

To Heinrich Köselitz in Venice

Genua, April 6, 1883

You cannot believe, dear friend, what a *surcharge* of suffering life has levied on me, in every period, from *early* childhood on. However, I am a soldier: and this soldier has recently become the proud *father* of Zarathustra! Such paternity was his hope. I think that now you can appreciate the meaning of those lines dedicated to Sanctus Januarius, "You who shattered with your spear of flame the ice of my soul, so that now it *rushes turbulent to the sea of its supreme hope"——*
And also the meaning of the rubric "incipit tragoedia."—
Enough of that.

Yours faithfully and gratefully,
Friend Nietzsche.

He could do everything, Father, my son Zarathustra. Everything except die. He kept on trying but he never made it. Having been born old he found he had to live backwards to the point where he could die only posthumously the second time around and this put us both in an awkward position.

To Elisabeth Nietzsche in Naumburg

Mentone, shortly after November 15, 1884

My dear Llama,

If all goes well, I shall *need* a printer and publisher for the fourth part of *Zarathustra*. . . . (It would be smart to keep quiet about this fourth part when you are negotiating the sale of the whole, and also about the fifth and sixth parts, which are now unavoidable (it can't be helped, I have to assist my son Zarathustra to his remarkable *death*, otherwise he'll leave me no peace.))

F.

He went down but he wouldn't die. Camel lion child suckling nouveau né fetus embryo spermnegg mote in the eye but he couldn't die. It was a generic genetic deficiency: there was no one like him behind or before him.

Why couldn't he die? Did he feel he was so necessary to me? Or did he forget that you have to say *one more time!* once and for all? He had a kind of infinity about him, Father, and all we can do is hope and bray that it was a bad infinity, a wicked apeiron. Otherwise he's another case of pious palaver, Papi, the asinine recurrence of the petty through all eternity.

To Malwida von Meysenbug in Rome

Venezia, San Canciano Calle Nuova 5256
First week of June, 1884

My highly esteemed Friend,

My task is terrifically vast; my resoluteness is no less. What it is I *want*, my son Zarathustra will tell you—no, not tell you, he will offer it as a riddle; perhaps the riddle can be guessed. And so much is certain: I wish to compel mankind to resolves that will decide the entire future of man, and it *may* turn out that some day whole millennia will swear their supreme oaths in my name.

With feelings of profound gratitude,

As ever,
Your Nietzsche.

Even so, can you blame him for not dying? Or me for not killing him off, for not snuffing out his life? All I wanted was for me to
die first. Surely that's what every Father wants for his son, Papi?
That's what I learned from you. That is something. That is a lot.

†

What remains to be said about my hectic life after my own birth,
after parturing my Persian son, after my bookafterbook diverting me
from my proper task? Only that the diversions were the shortest
routes thither, not really sidetracks at all but the mainline; only that
whatever was diverted needed diverting; only that my proper task
was more a task than my property and propriety; only that my propriety failed to prop me up, as one by one the struts girders beams
and braces of the trembling edifice detached themselves and slid
away, my superfluity giving way gracefully to the ruse of necessity.
Necessity. That patent ploy, that transparent compensation, that ris-
ible ruse. Necessity? Sheer contingency. All the way from Father
Abraham and Father Plato to Father Prado. Some contingency,
Necessity.

To Franz Overbeck in Basel

Nice, February 3, 1888

Dear Friend,

I too am busy as can be, and the outlines of the indubitably vast
task that now confronts me are looming ever more clearly out
of the fog. Meanwhile, there were gloomy hours, whole days
and nights when I didn't know how I could go on living; times
when black despair seized me, despair such as I have never
known. Nevertheless, I know that I can't go backwards or
sidestep either to the right or left in order thus to slip away: in
this I have no *choice. This* logic alone sustains me now;
observed from any other angle, my condition is unsupportable,
as painful as torture. One should no longer expect "fine things"
from me, as little as one demands of a suffering and starving
animal that it lacerate its prey with *good grace.* The lack of
truly invigorating and annealing *human* love, the absurd

isolation it brings in its wake, so that almost every remnant of human contact only inflicts wounds: all of that is baleful in the extreme and can claim for itself only one right—the right of being necessary.—

Your N.

†

Becoming immortal is killing work.

To Franz Overbeck in Basel [Draft]

Nice, early January, 1886

That a human being who is born to have the most fruitful and far-flung impact has to fritter away his best years in barren wildernesses; that a thinker like me, who can never lay down his best in books but always only in select souls, is compelled— with his stinging, half-blinded eyes—"to make literature"—it's all so crazy! it's all so hard!

†

Pick a name any name among all the names in history. Attach it to yourself front and back: you are one of the vagrant labeled souls Er confronted in the underworld. Now, pick not just one of them; pick them all. And attach the names from the inside. That is who I, er, am.

To Carl Fuchs in Danzig

Sils, Sunday, July 29, 1888

Dear Friend,

I've never been characterized as yet—neither as a psychologist nor as a *writer* (including "poet"), nor as the inventor of a *new* kind of pessimism (a Dionysian kind, born of *strength*, a pessimism that takes its *pleasure* in grasping the problem of existence by the horns), nor as *immoralist* (—the supreme form to date of "intellectual uprightness," which is *permitted* to treat morality as illusion once it has become *instinct* and *inevitability*—). It is not at all necessary or even *desirable* to take sides with me: on the contrary, a dose of curiosity, as though one were confronting an unknown plant, with a touch of ironic resistance, would seem to me an incomparably *more intelligent* position with respect to me.—Excuse me! I've just written a few naïvetés—a modest prescription for retrieving oneself unharmed from an *impossible* situation.

With friendliest greetings,
Your N.

As if any name could be attached from the inside. Friedrich Wilhelm. Ludwig Joseph. Your N. Your F. N. As if all names did not flit strike cling awhile then flutter on by. Spineless pages ripped from a calendar. Spineless all spines. Agave, do you know it? An infernal machine. Becoming. Where no names stick, but flesh does.

To Heinrich von Stein in Halle [Draft]

Nice, mid-March, 1885

It is difficult to recognize who I am: let us wait a century: perhaps by that time there will be some genius of human nature who will excavate Herr F. N.—

—Hello? What's that racket?
—Someone's knocking.
—Two knocks, four.
—Three knocks, to be precise. Coming from outside, it seems. Who is it, boys?
A wizened face looms out of the dark, the unnerving smile of cantankerous madness contorts its mouth and glazes its eye. A face far wider than it is long, a compressed, pessimistic head. Above the ears on either side protrude pointed projectiles of white hair twisted into clownlike horns. The cranky madness in the eyes betrays years of poverty and oppression under the remorseless heel of some Hohenzollern hack, some charlatan academic and swindler, teller of fairytales and fables. Old Uncle. Years of ignominy, years of neglect. His voice is now gleeful and guileful, ghostily screeching, more bats to belfries than owls to athens:
—Hello, down there! Hello, you dead! Yoo-hoo!
We three do not answer. Again the raspy screech:
—Hello, Blumengasse Nr. 4? Antique books, anyone? Herr Rohn, proprietor? Remember me?
Still we do not answer. I whisper his identity now to Father and Little Joseph, for I recognize him by his knock, his sarcasm,

and his desperation. I know my greatest educator, from the time I transferred to Leipzig in the fall of 1865, after that wasted year in Bonn. *At that time I was hovering in the air, all alone, with a few painful experiences and disappointments behind me, without anyone to help me, without principles to act on, without hopes, and without a single friendly memory. From morning till night I tried to fashion for myself a life that would suit me, a life that would be my own. I was able to gather myself to myself in the blessed apartness of my apartment. . . . —Now, imagine in such circumstances what it must have been like to read Schopenhauer's magnum opus. For one day, while browsing through old Rohn's antique books, I found that tome, which was utterly unknown to me, picked it up and leafed through it. I don't know what daimon it was that whispered to me, "Take this book home with you." At all events, it happened, despite my habit of being not too hasty with book purchases. At home I nestled into a corner of the sofa*

It has always been my favorite reading position, crouching like a spider in the corner of a sofa reading proofs books letters handbills flyers tracts and treatises: I wonder, could we cram a divan into our subterranean parlor here, Papi? Perhaps over there, next to the piano? Little Joseph doesn't need all that space

with the treasure I had found and began to let that vigorous, gloomy genius work its effects on me. Here every line screamed renunciation, denial, resignation; here I saw a mirror in which the world, life, and my own deepest soul were reflected back to me in horrific grandeur. Here the vast, disinterested solar eye of art gazed upon me. Here I saw illness and recuperation, exile and sanctuary, hell and heaven. The need for self-knowing—indeed, for self-gnawing—seized me violently. Because I dragged all my qualities and all my endeavors before the forum of a gloomy self-contempt, I was bitter and unjust, I gave full head to the hatred I directed against myself. Corporeal chastisements too played their part. Thus for a fortnight I forced myself to stay up till 2 A.M. and to quit my bed at 6 A.M. on the dot. A nervous excitability overpowered me. Who knows to what degree of foolishness I would have prodded myself had not life's delectable decoys, the seductions of vanity, and the compulsion to regularity in my studies worked against it.

—I didn't know you were such an angel of asceticism, mój drogie bracie. Chastisements! Mortifications! Dying *de bonne heure, mon frère âné?*

—I knew whereof I wrote, Little Joseph. I knew my own genealogy.

353

—Spirit needs the cat o' nine tails, boys. Don't forget your scourge when you go to church.

—Did you say "spirit," Tatus? "Church"? You're confusing two very different creatures!

—That's exactly what my educator would have said, Little Joseph. I'm grateful to his memory: whatever the foibles and faibles of his fables, he was my master mentor. He helped me to be permanently out of step with my times, throughout time untimely, eternally intemperate. Listen! He's knocking again! He'll pull our teeth until we answer!

—Hello, down there, you dead! Yoo-hoo! You, who? Knock knock who's there? Tell me this one thing, if you please: Would you like to come back to life, would you like to lead your lives once again precisely as you led them while you were leading them? Would you like to be liberated from your graves? Is life worth that much to you?

He pauses. Silence of the grave. He is expecting an answer. An eternity passes. His mad glint squeals *I know your answer already but still you must make reply*. Another commences.

—What shall we say, boys? When I think of that last year, the wordlessness and darkness, I know my answer. Scent of dill rises to distract me, but all those years of pious devotion to the Word focus and reassure me. I know my answer.

—I know mine, as well, drogie Ojciec. As does anyone who has suffered child abuse.

—Joseph!

—Molestation kidnap rape seizure at the tender age of barely two. Or should I return to be your ragdoll, your convivial carnival prize, your plush squeezetoy unto all eternity? Shall I say yes yes that was enough that was all life was ever meant to be? Not on your life, Tatulek. Nor on mine.—Hey! You up there! Old man! Peddle your wares elsewhere! Leave the dead in peace! Let bad enough be, don't make it worse. Let me sleep.

Father is suddenly infinitely taciturn, Little Joseph colicky yet undecided. The dour glinty eye turns full upon me now like a lunatic moon. The smile on his corrugated face spreads to a gloating grin. I know I must answer, know I must always have already answered this way. What did I say? I remember nothing: on the grand arc of anamnesis, absolute amnesia, total blank. I hesitate. I know I must take my time, make my time. I ponder the silence, the sadness, of the same. I wonder will it be enough to postpone every reply, to stay on the very verge of the *yes! yes!* that tenses poises pushes the tongue in my mouth?

†

—Little Joseph?

—Leave me alone, bitch's bastard! Let me sleep!

—Wouldn't you like to *see* the women?

—See them? Oh, wonder! I'd give anything to see that sight!

—Then I shall be your guide. It begins easily enough, with garden parties and dances, their long white hands on the keyboard, girls who work their mouths artlessly as they play, opening wide ah ah ah until they find that obstreperous note, escaping the abyss of that timeless rest, flying over that deathdefying arpeggio—and it ends with you on your knees in a cavern of porphyry at dusk by the sea odor of orangeblossom and fishspawn reading pageproofs.

—Why does it end there? Why does it end at all? Surely there is no need for it to end?

—Interruptions. The jealous one pounding at the door, glaring through the keyhole; or the gnawing suspicion on this side of the keyhole that you will never purge the priestly poison injected into you so long ago . . .

—Perhaps at the tender age of two . . .

— . . . or even earlier: injected with the seed: the anxiety that the mockers may have been right all along. Once interrupted, the body feints before the spirit but cannot elude it; feints but is snatched, seized from behind; dodges skirts feints faints swoons collapses in ignominy and shame, interrupted forever.

—That sounds like death.

—It is death. Mortification. Dying *de bonne heure*. Getting it over with. That is what Plato's Socrates requires and what the Evangelist's Jesus fulfills. We live in order to practice dying and being dead. Here are your nails what's your hurry.

—That can't touch us now. We have left all that behind us, Fritz. We are the ashes of life. Calcined. Pyrified. Rarefied.

—What shall we do, Little Joseph? How shall we go on? Your guide falters, as you see. I am at a loss.

—Is Tatus asleep? Yes? Quiet, then, don't rouse him. Let us practice vivification. But stealthily!

—Vivification? You mean to practice being alive in such a way that our death is no objection to life but its honey and balsam?

—That sounds too much like mummification, moj kochany. I want something else for us both. Something with spice and kick. Something to stir the ashes a bit.

—A breeze?

—No. No pneumatic spirit. Enough of flatulent spirit.

—An acid, then? An enzyme?

—That's closer. Something with bite. Something that will get a grip, sink its teeth in, hold on for dear life.

—Yes, something like the will. Something like power.

—Something like will and power, but less spiritual, more spiriting, more bodying. A flurry of flesh.

—Vivification: the practice of living, of being alive ahead of time. One foot breaching the birth canal, the rest tumbling headlong into life. From the ashes!

—You're the thinker. How do we do it? How do we make the passage?

—I don't know. I never really felt it through. It may be too late, as Papi says. We may have hesitated too long. But when that wizened face of the Philosopher next appears and asks us whether we want to raise the marble slab and return to the surface of earth, what shall we tell him?

—We'll tell him *yes! yes!* And we shall laugh!

—Better yet, we'll laugh and tell him we've *already* returned, an infinite number of times . . .

—He'll scowl! He'll howl!

— . . . and that this is precisely the way we like it: no resurrection, no glorified body, no adamantine muscletone, no agate sinews, no obsidian skeleton, no ruby organs . . .

—He'll rage! The sage!

— . . . but the same sagging sack of mottled apples and ashes, eggs and agues, rumors and tumors, coccyx and cachexia, the same cankers and carbuncles, the identical idiosyncrasies and ignominies the selfsame mortifications.

—Wait a minute. The same *mortifications?* Tatuncio's oozing brain, your petrifaction?

—The same.

—But that means . . .

—Precisely.

—All over again?

—Yes.

—Unalterable?

—Yes.

—I suppose even if we wail and gripe about it it'll all turn out that way anyhow?

—Yes.

—Then let's skip the lamentation and affirm it all in one go.

—Yes.

356

To Elisabeth Nietzsche in Naumburg

Sils-Maria, early July, 1883

My dear Sister

What people call their *goal* (what they ultimately think about *night and day*): it wraps them round with an ass's hide, so that you can well-nigh beat them to death—and they overcome it and march on, the ancient ass on its ancient way with its ancient YE-AH. That's the way it is with me now.

Your F.

—And in this way, saying *yes,* we will see the women?
—I am uncertain what will happen. But we will see. By the sign of the starry diadem, by the sign of the diamondframe, by the sign of the purpleveined grotto, and by the sign of mother-of-pearl.
—For the sake of vivification, then, mój drogie bracie, let's affirm it one more time once for all!
—Yes! Yes!
Silence of the grave.
An eternity passes.
Another commences.
The same.

✝

—Fritz?
—Yes, Little Joseph?
—Would you like to kiss and make up?
—Higher minne, or lower?
Little Joseph begins to chuckle in spite of himself, I spurt a sudden gush of golden laughter, he grins and giggles, I titter and guffaw, he whoops and roars, I gasp and wheeze, he weeps and doubles over with cramps of laughter, I screech and howl in accesses of raging laughter, we collapse in one another's friable arms, our furfuraceous ashes intermingle interfuse leaving no trace of a trace through all the eternities past and passing and coming to pass the same.

✝

Was ist das? Was ist das? Was ist das? Three eyes peering steadily unblinkingly stolidly from the sloping roof of my house in Röcken viewed from the rear garden, three eyes beneath two blunt horns of

357

chimney. I look up from the graveyard that is my eternal playground and watch them watching me. Who are they? Mother, Father, and Divine Providence? Father, Mother, and Polyphemos? Perhaps there is one window for each of the children: one for the firstborn at the top, one on the right for Little Joseph, one on the left for Elisabeth. Perhaps they will nod one by one into somnolence and death as the shades are drawn, Little Joseph first, he being one with the Father, wrapped in the arms and rapt to the bosom of the Father, secure in the sealed crypt of the Father under this unbudgeable slab. Then it was between Elisabeth and me. The Llama. Eli, Eli, llamma sabachthani. A fight to the death. Until recently. Good for you, Lisbeth, dear. Congratulations, survivor. As for me, it's good to be home again.

Spindly fruit trees ash elderberry and witchhazel crowd the rear wall of the house like the muttonchop beard and mustachio on a man's face. The walls of the house are of mustardyellow plaster, the roof redorange with blackgreen moss chinking each tile. Three inky pupils set into the three white slits of eye, each roofed over slopingly sloe-eyed by the dark orange tiles. Egyptian eyes. Isis. Amon-Re. Providence again. Beneath the three small dormer eyes on the slanting roof, beneath the gutters, on the looming rear wall of the house the three large black windows of the bedrooms. One of them is mine, I do not know I never knew which one it was. Another was Little Joseph's until the morning he died. Three human windows in a row. Occasionally a figure appears in one of them, Aunt Rosalie or Aunt Auguste, or perhaps Mother. Yet these windows do not matter. They do not haunt. Those on the roof appall.

Vasistas. Vasistas. Vasistas. Two wide-set alligator eyes near the rim of the roof close to the rainspouts, one diabolical dragon eye at the top of the skull, the daimonic eye, the Titanic eye, the Cyclopic eye set between the two flue horns. An eye almost at the top of the head, an eye that should have gazed upward on wingèd things but glowered down on me instead. To be lost among dry leaves or wet snow or purple crocuses amid cushions of green grass and then to look up and find that eye staring unblinkingly, scowling lowering glowering remorselessly at me. Unlike the other two it rotates on its own axis: it follows me as I circle the house and wander through the courtyard and down to the four ponds and even all through the village. Papi sometimes takes me on his round of visits to the elderly and infirm, the unfortunate of means and of birth, and when we head homeward we inevitably come to the goosegreen and its crossroads. Two carriageways intersect there and form a junction where we always stop for a chat. Papi says:

—And where does Fritzchen have his home with Mama and Papi and Baby Lieschen?

I look up to see, in a blur at first, then in stark outline, the broad churchtower behind the farmhouse. My own eyes follow the line of roof along the nave that juts from the tower and leads straight to that other eye, the eye of my house. Which espies me. Never sleeps. Forever having only now awakened out of slumber, droopy-lidded alldiscerning omniscient.

—Can't you find it yet, son?

The eye has found me long before I can even look for it. And it asks a different sort of question even with him standing right there beside me, his hand cool and soft around mine, his voice quiet as the evening breeze, its voice, the voice of the eye, not impatient not harsh not even strident yet insistent and above all implacable:

—What are you doing now, boy? Is it not sheer vanity, boy? What would your Father say, boy?

I never have an answer for the eye, do not reply to the eye. *As a plant I was born near God's Green Acres, as a human being in a pastor's house.*

✝

someday papi when im thirtysix as you ill be dead as me ill live on as mother. everything will change after that my books my letters my health my feelings about what it means to be both dead and alive while dead. will you let me go it alone papi? will you let me go? to commemorate the year you died at thirtyfiveandahalf the year you planted little joseph as an idea in the mind of god and the belly of mother. let it be the year when im thirtysix or maybe thirtyseven

Postcard to Paul Rée in Stibbe

Sils-Maria, July 8, 1881

Meanwhile, it is as someone long dead that I gaze on things and people—they move me, terrify and delight me, yet I am altogether remote from them. Eternally bereft and yet

Close to you,
In fidelity, F. N.

the year of my own rebirth please please papi i kiss the fingers of your hand that wraps me round let me go now release me father im thirtysix on the ascendant my life is just beginning im thirtyseven now *some few are born posthumously*

I cracked all seven seals of solitude. Cracked them and pried open the lids of the iron caskets, each casket fitted into the next like Chinese boxes or Russian babas or Loulouises one inside the other like onionskins. When I penetrated to the innermost crypt of loneliness I reached out and lowered all the lids and sealed them one by one over my bowed head.

ONE. To be unutterably alone when you have something terribly important to say

To Reinhard von Seydlitz in Cairo

Nice, Pension de Genève, February 12, 1888

Dear Friend,

It is by no means a "haughty taciturnity" that for some time now has sealed my lips with regard to almost everyone. Rather, it is a humiliated silence, the reticence of a sick man who is ashamed to betray how much he is suffering. An animal slinks off to its cave when it is ill; and so does *la bête philosophe.* It is so rare now that a friendly voice reaches me: I am alone, absurdly alone, and in my relentless subterranean battle against everything that human beings have up to now loved and esteemed (—my formula for it is *Transvaluation of All Values*) I myself have unwittingly become something like a cave— something concealed, something people would no longer find even if they went out in search of it. *However, they do not go out in search. . . .* Between the two of us, the three of us,—it is not impossible that I am the foremost philosopher of the age, indeed, maybe something more than that, something decisive and fateful straddling two millennia. One pays recompense *constantly* for occupying such a peculiar position—by means of an ever-increasing segregation, an icier solitude, always more cutting, minute by minute.

Your faithful friend,
Nietzsche.

TWO. To be unutterably alone when you have absolutely nothing to say

To Carl Fuchs in Danzig

Torino, April 14, 1888

How everything slips away! How everything scatters! How silent life is becoming! No human being in sight who knows me. My sister in South America. Letters increasingly rare. And I'm not even old!!! *Merely* a philosopher! *Merely* apart! *Merely* compromisingly apart!—

Truly yours,
Nietzsche.

THREE. To be pressed by others when you have either something terribly important or nothing at all to say.

—But first I want to write my autobiography. Apart from the fact that it is scintillating, it is also full of excellent instruction: it will turn youths into dotards. For in this I am the master. Who is to read it? My Doppelgänger, all of them, the vagabonds of this vale of tears.

At this point Euphorion leaned back a bit a groaned, for he suffered from a condition that affected the marrow of his spine. . . .

FOUR. To be oppressed by someone near or far whom you are learning to hate.

To Franz Overbeck in Basel

Rapallo, February 22, 1883

I have become *so* sensitive because of my exclusive preoccupation with ideal images and processes that I suffer incredibly when I traffic with my contemporaries; hence I renounce such traffic. Ultimately, I'm becoming too hard and unjust; in short, it doesn't agree with me. . . .

No! *This* life!! And I am the advocate of life!!

Your friend, F N.

FIVE. To be moved to tears by someone you have learned to— pity.

To Franz Overbeck in Munich

Sils-Maria, September 14, 1884

Dear Friend,

That is the mistake I repeat eternally—I greatly overestimate the sufferings of others. From my childhood on, the statement "My greatest dangers lie in feeling compassion" has been corroborated again and again. (Perhaps it is the baneful consequence of my Father's *extraordinary* nature: all who knew him took him to be more like an "angel" than a "human being.") Suffice it to say that because of the dreadful experiences I have had with compassion *I* have been stimulated to alter in a theoretically intriguing way the *value-estimation* of compassion.

Your friend N.

SIX. To repulse or to be repulsed by someone with whom you forgot never under any circumstances to fall in love.

To Carl von Gersdorff in Ostrichen bei Seidenberg

Nice (France)
Hôtel de Genève, December 20, 1887

Dear Friend,

The desert around me is vast indeed; I can bear only perfect strangers and passersby, or, on the contrary, those who have been close to me for a long, long time, since my childhood. Everyone else has drifted away, or else has been *repulsed* (there was a lot of violence and pain in that—)

In long-standing love and friendship,
Your Nietzsche

SEVEN. To find oneself writing about any one of the above—

To Elisabeth Nietzsche in Naumburg

Venezia, May 20, 1885

My dear Llama,

The feeling that there is something utterly remote and foreign about me, that my words take on different hues in the mouths of others, that there is a great deal of colorful foreground in me which *deceives*—precisely this feeling, corroborated recently on various fronts, is really the very sharpest degree of "understanding" that I have found up to now. Everything I have written prior to this is foreground; for me it all starts with the hiatuses.

Your F.

✝

Be chary of choucroute garni, Franz, it will return to haunt you. Come. Bring Erwin Growly Bear with you. I want you both to meet someone. A stranger. Stranger, meet my friends.—I am ready now. Friends, farewell.

Postcard to Franz Overbeck in Zürich

Sils-Maria, September 18, 1881

Sum in puncto desperationis. Dolor vincit vitam voluntatemque. . . . Ubi est terrarum illud sempiternae serenitatis caelum, illud meum caelum? Vale amice.

✝

I heard you behind me, Fathermother. Behind the gnashing of teeth, behind the tearing of flesh, my flesh, I heard you.

Postcard to Heinrich Köselitz in Venice

Sils-Maria, September 22, 1881

They were treacherous times: *death* was peering over my shoulder.

You snatched me from the undying flames of her dying womb and hid me in your manwoman thigh. I heard you call, Motherfather, and I succumbed. Even so, the mystery of my twofold birth my twofold death lies in the crypt. *Fors. Fort.* With you, Father, with you, Mother.

To Franziska Nietzsche in Pobles

Naumburg, March 3, 1851

My dear Mother,

I wold like to tak to you but because I am not with you I have to write a littleletter. I enjoyed the applecake very much, I thank you very much for it. I think of you and Elisabet all the time but I can't write any more because I am tired.

Your faithful son,
Fritz Nietzsche.

☥

A divan is divine for scrunching up into a corner of like a spider in the moonlight reading pageproofs. *Contra Wagner.* Contra? Let the thrusts and counterthrusts go. Drop them. Say yes even if hesitantly. Yes no not like an ass like a Yes. Yes caro fino yes irene yes corinna calina ballerina yes gentle franz yes irascible erwin yes cosmic cosima yes meister richard yes elilouilou yes little marcel yes little jesus yes little joseph yes sorrento yes by the mark yes to it all yes on a scale of unending differences. But don't drop those differences oh no.

The late afternoon sun oblique across the cracked marble tiles of the basilica, glancing off the yellowed satin walls. Odor of orangeblossom and of caverns beneath the sea. And, if you are very very lucky indeed, a friend at the door who will not pause to knock, leading with his lantern jaw, seeking and finding, here too daimons indwelling.

Da capo? From the opening clef to the dotty double bar of infinite repetition?

The music, O Papi! O Mama, the music!

Da capo! Da capo!